SWIFT'S HOSPITAL

Portrait of Jonathan Swift painted by Francis Bindon in the late 1730s when Swift was planning his hospital.

SWIFT'S

HOSPITAL

A History of
St Patrick's Hospital,
Dublin, 1746-1989

ELIZABETH MALCOLM

GILL AND MACMILLAN

Published in Ireland by
Gill and Macmillan Ltd
Goldenbridge
Dublin 8
with associated companies in
Auckland, Delhi, Gaborone, Hamburg, Harare,
Hong Kong, Johannesburg, Kuala Lumpur, Lagos, London,
Manzini, Melbourne, Mexico City, Nairobi,
New York, Singapore, Tokyo
© The Governors of St Patrick's Hospital, 1989

ISBN 0–7171–1501–1

Print origination by Irish Typesetting and Publishing Co. Ltd, Galway
Printed in Great Britain by The Bath Press, Bath

Jacket illustrations: Photograph of front of hospital and portrait of Swift (*front*).
Endpapers: Detail from John Rocque's 1756 *Exact Survey of the City and Suburbs of Dublin*
showing St Patrick's Hospital in the year before its opening.

Contents

Foreword	vii
Introduction	viii

CHAPTER 1

Dean Swift and Madness	1

CHAPTER 2

Swift's Hospital: The Early Years, 1747-1820	32
The Building and Opening of the Hospital	32
Administration, Staff and Finance	55
Extensions and Maintenance	73
The Patients	83

CHAPTER 3

The Era of Moral Management, 1820-1850	104
Administration, Staff and Finance	105
The Estate	121
The Building	126
The Patients	130

CHAPTER 4

Swift's Hospital: The Years of Decline, 1850-1899	154
Administration, Staff and Finance	154
The Estate	181
The Building	193
The Patients	199

CHAPTER 5

Leeper's Hospital, 1899-1941	216
Transformation: From Asylum to Hospital	216
The Sale of the Estates	234

Wars and Rebellions: The Hospital under Fire   238
In a New State: Growth and Consolidation   245

CHAPTER 6

St Patrick's Opens its Doors, 1942-1977   258

CHAPTER 7

The Era of Community Care, 1978-1989   284

APPENDICES

1. Extracts from Swift's Will and the Charters   292
2. The Governors of St Patrick's Hospital, 1746-1989   307
3. Staff of St Patrick's Hospital, 1746-1989   316
4. The Patients: Statistical Tables, 1841-50, 1874-83, 1869-84   319
5. The Staff: Dr Leeper's List of Daily Duties, October 1899   323
6. St Patrick's Hospital and the 1916 Rising   326

Notes   328
Bibliography   359
Index   373
Abbreviations   384

Foreword

by the Chairman of the Governors of St Patrick's Hospital

The suggestion was first made by one of my colleagues that we of St Patrick's must surely have an interesting story to tell and that, if this were so, it was our duty to ensure that it be told.

Another of my colleagues then introduced us to Professor Gordon Davies of Trinity College, Dublin, to whom we posed two questions: first whether we had in our possession sufficient hitherto unpublished material to justify the writing of a history of the Hospital and, if so, secondly to whom the task of writing it could be entrusted. Having taken a great deal of trouble on our behalf, for which we are most grateful, Professor Davies answered the first question, I believe with some enthusiasm, in the affirmative. Secondly, for which again we are most grateful, he recommended to us Dr Elizabeth Malcolm as our prospective author.

The success of her very considerable endeavours will be judged by her readers. I, for one, am delighted with her book.

Dennis Wardell

Introduction

Dublin, along with London and Edinburgh, has since the eighteenth century been one of the great medical centres of the British Isles. One indication of the city's eminence has been the large number of hospitals that it has boasted. In 1700 there were virtually none, but between 1720 and 1760 seven opened and, by the 1840s, the city had some thirty-five hospitals, dispensaries and asylums. Over the years a number of books have appeared chronicling the histories of many of these hospitals. Initially such books were written to mark centenaries or even bicentenaries, but, in recent years, they have increasingly come to mark closures. For most of Dublin's smaller, older, voluntary hospitals are disappearing and disappearing rapidly. Sir Patrick Dun's, Mercer's, Jervis Street, the Richmond-Whitworth-Hardwicke complex and Dr Steevens have all gone, as medical services are increasingly concentrated in a few large public institutions, like St James's Hospital or the new Beaumont and Tallaght hospitals. Politicians and administrators argue that there were too many small hospitals and that concentration has brought greater efficiency and ultimately higher standards of care. The residents of Dublin, however, seem far from convinced that their hospital services have improved, while historians, and those interested in the city's heritage, can only lament the passing of so many renowned medical institutions.

It should be noted at the outset, however, that this history of St Patrick's Hospital is not written to commemorate anything: not the hospital's opening and certainly not its closure. St Patrick's opened in 1757 and, at the time of writing, shows no sign whatever of closing. On the contrary, this book has been produced in the simple belief that the story of St Patrick's is of historical significance and that it makes a contribution on a number of levels to our appreciation of the development of modern Ireland.

Being a history of a hospital, the book of necessity explores in some detail administrative, financial and medical matters. But, at the same time, it aspires to be more than just an in-house history, chronicling institutional minutiae in isolation from the great events of the day. If nothing else, this study should demonstrate that hospitals—even mental hospitals—are not immune from the currents of political and economic change. St Patrick's has been buffeted, at times almost to the point of submergence, by the wars, rebellions and recessions of the last two and a half centuries. What impact such events have had on the hospital and how it has coped with them are among the main themes of the book. In seeing how this one small institution has weathered the storms of recent Irish history, we may perhaps gain a deeper insight into the processes that have created modern Ireland.

Given this aim, it is hoped that this history of St Patrick's will be of interest, not only to those associated with the hospital, to doctors, to students of Swift, or to lovers of Dublin's past, but to all those, whether professional or amateur, with an interest in modern Irish history. Thus readers will note that a substantial amount of space has been devoted to discussing the hospital's estate and in particular the financial problems associated with estate management. It may at first seem that such complex economic issues are not especially relevant to the history of a medical institution. But, aside from the fact that financial problems have had a profound impact on St Patrick's development, the hospital's estate offers an excellent case study of the difficulties of nineteenth-century Irish landlordism. The St Patrick's estate is therefore of significance, not just in the context of the hospital's history, but also in the wider context of the much debated question of Irish landlord-tenant relations.

In addition to providing insights into aspects of modern Irish history, the story of St Patrick's also tells us a good deal about the development of attitudes towards, and treatments for, mental illness. St Patrick's is the oldest psychiatric hospital in Ireland and one of the oldest in the world and its patient records, though often frustratingly incomplete, afford a rare and valuable insight into changes in psychiatric classification and care. In recent years much attention has been devoted to the history of mental illness, for the subject is a highly controversial one. A good deal of this attention, under the influence of the French structuralist philosopher cum historian, Michel Foucault, and of the anti-psychiatry movement of the 1960s and the 1970s, has been extremely critical. There has, for instance, been a tendency to see psychiatry, not as an altruistic attempt to heal the sick, but as a powerful weapon in the hands of the establishment, used by it to control and silence dissenters. In writing this book I have not followed the tenets of Foucault and his disciples, for I have accepted the reality of psychotic and neurotic illness and the need for psychiatric treatment. Yet, at the same time, I have been influenced by their approach, for, as a historian, I am particularly interested in how familial, social and even political and economic factors have shaped mental illness. Even a cursory perusal of the patient records of St Patrick's shows that events like, for instance, the 1916 rising and the civil war had a significant impact on the mental health of Irish people. In discussing

patients I have thus not dwelt solely on categories of illness, which
are often very vague and unhelpful anyway, but instead I have
attempted to place patients in a family, social and political context.

In the past, historians have been preoccupied with the physical
damage—the deaths and destruction—caused by events like the
1798 rebellion or the Easter rising. But an examination of the history
of St Patrick's is valuable in that it enables us to uncover some of the
psychic damage inflicted by such traumatic events—people did not
have to be killed or lose their homes in order to suffer. Dr W. S.
Hallaran of Cork in his pioneering study of insanity, first published
in 1810, drew attention to the 'terror' caused by the 1798 rebellion
and the records of St Patrick's confirm Hallaran's view that violent
political upheavals took their toll on mental, as much as physical,
health. In light of this fact, it is high time that someone undertook a
systematic study of the patient records of the Irish public asylums
which housed vast numbers of paupers from the 1820s onwards.
For the periods of the Famine or the land war such records could
well prove highly enlightening.

Writing the history of a psychiatric hospital raises certain problems, both ethical and technical. There is for instance the question of
confidentiality. It is important that current, and also future, patients
of St Patrick's should be absolutely sure that their records are
confidential and that their case histories will not be exposed to
public scrutiny. But, at the same time, this need for confidentiality
has to be weighed against the need, in writing the hospital's history,
for as full as possible an examination of the patients, their problems
and their treatments. With the governors' agreement, I have
attempted to balance these two needs by using patients' full names
up to and including 1850, but after that, except in a few special
instances, only the christian name and the initial letter of the
surname have been given. Thus the anonymity of patients admitted
to the hospital since as far back as the 1850s has been preserved.

Another problem which arises in connection with the history of
mental illness is that of terminology. The terms given, both popularly and in medical circles, to patients and their illnesses have
altered drastically over the years, so much so in fact that today some
of the earlier words are liable to give offence. Yet, in the interests of
historical accuracy, though at the risk of offending doctors and
patients, I have felt it necessary to employ the contemporary
terminology. In Swift's day, and for most of the rest of the
eighteenth century, the mentally ill or disabled were referred to as
'lunaticks', 'ideots' or 'fools'. Such words may grate upon the
modern ear, being today terms of abuse, but putting the current
terminology into eighteenth-century mouths would be highly

misleading. It seems to me better that readers should become sensitive to changes in terms, for such changes are important indicators of changes in outlook and attitudes. Thus the eighteenth-century terminology relating to psychiatric hospitals—words like 'cell', 'keeper' or 'physical restraint'—clearly reveals the basically custodial role of such institutions. We know that the custodial role is diminishing when such terms are replaced by others during the course of the nineteenth century.

The founder and still it seems to me the presiding genius of St Patrick's Hospital is Jonathan Swift. For, despite the enormous changes in psychiatric medicine that have occurred since Swift's time, his hospital remains where he instructed that it should be sited; it is governed largely still as he directed; and it offers care to the same sort of people that he first envisaged. One of the main aims of this book has been in fact to lay to rest once and for all the myth of the 'mad dean' who left his money to establish a 'mad-house'. There was nothing irrational in Swift's decision to endow St Patrick's. The real problem, as this study amply demonstrates, is not that he left his money to a 'madhouse', but that he did not leave nearly enough ready cash to enable the institution to be built and operated as a charity.

Swift's epitaph in St Patrick's Cathedral—erected in fact by the governors of the hospital—is justly famous. This book aims to tell the story of his other great legacy to Ireland, Swift's Hospital.

The book could never have been written without the co-operation and support of the present board of governors of St Patrick's Hospital. The governors allowed me unrestricted access to the hospital's archives, though it should be said that the opinions expressed in the work are my own and do not necessarily reflect those of the board. An informal committee was created in the hospital in 1984 to help and advise on the writing of St Patrick's history. The committee was chaired by Mr William Forwood, one of the governors, and consisted of Professor Karl O'Sullivan, the then medical director; Dr Anthony O'Flaherty, a consultant psychiatrist, who replaced Professor O'Sullivan in 1988; Professor J. N. P. Moore, the former medical director; Mr Robert McCullagh, the former secretary, who joined the committee in 1988; and Mr Michael Gill, the managing director of Gill and Macmillan, the publishers. I would like to thank all the committee members for their advice, their criticisms and their always cheerful encouragement. No author could have wished for a more helpful group of advisers. In particular I am grateful to Professor Moore and Mr McCullagh for sharing with me their memories of the hospital over a period of some fifty years. For information on the hospital in more recent times, I would like to thank Dr P. J. Meehan and Professor Anthony Clare. Working in St Patrick's, in Semple's original building and with a vast collection of original documents, has been an exciting experience for a historian more used to the restrictive regimes of libraries. I would like to thank all the staff of the hospital who made my visits such pleasant experiences. In particular my thanks go to Mr Reginald Crampton, secretary/registrar till 1988, and to his successor, Mr Noel Breslin. They both showed great patience in putting up with the niggling queries of a curious historian. My thanks also to their secretary, Miss Frances Behan, who never failed to point me in the right direction.

At Trinity College, Dublin, I particularly want to thank Professor K. Gordon Davies, formerly professor of modern history, who originally recommended to the governors that this book should be written and that I should be the one to undertake the task. I hope that the finished work vindicates his confidence. At Queen's University, Belfast, I am especially grateful to Professor R. H. Buchanan, director of the Institute of Irish Studies, who provided me with the academic facilities that allowed the book to be written.

A number of other people have also helped with specialist advice and information. My thanks go to Dr Robert Mahony, Dr W. E. Vaughan, Dr Edward McParland, the Irish Architectural Archive, Professor Stuart Lewis, Dr Kay Muhr, Professor Aidan Clarke, Mr Basil Clarke, Mr Edward Chandler, Mr Peadar Slattery and Mr Sean Donovan. I am also grateful to the friends who made working in Dublin a real pleasure: Ms Tonie van Marle, Dr Christina Hunt Mahony and most particularly Dr Ruth Sherry and Mr Stephen Lalor.

This book is dedicated to my son, Hartley, who had the good timing to be born just as the last chapter was being completed, and also to his father, Dr Robert Stevens, who did not type the manuscript. That task was ably undertaken by Sue and Frank Ramtohul, to whom go my thanks.

CHAPTER 1

Dean Swift and Madness

Wherever you go in Dublin, whatever books you read, whenever you take part in conversation, Swift will crop up. This has nothing to do with the local patriotism or any exaggerated idea of Swift's importance to Dublin. His scale as a thinker and writer overtops ten generations. . . . In an age given to acute metaphysics and abstract speculation, Swift went straight to the point: his mind had an edge like a razor, but the weight of a sledge. By straightforward thought and cool ability to face facts he reached a position where the rest of humanity are unable to follow.[1]

But Swift? . . . —a vast genius, a magnificent genius, a genius wonderfully bright, and dazzling and strong,—to seize, to know, to see, to flash upon falsehood and scorch it into perdition, to penetrate into the hidden motives, and expose the black thoughts of men,—an awful, an evil spirit . . . this man suffered so; and deserved so to suffer. One hardly reads anywhere of such . . . pain.[2]

At his death in 1745 Jonathan Swift bequeathed his estate to be used to establish a hospital for 'Idiots and Lunaticks'. To many subsequent commentators this has appeared a strange, even an irrational, act and for over two hundred years explanations for it have been offered which have questioned Swift's own sanity. Such speculations are misguided and indeed have been comprehensively refuted, yet they have proved remarkably persistent. In an essay entitled 'Dean Swift's Madness', published in 1834, the humorist Fr Prout (Fr Francis S. Mahony) produced a particularly vivid rendering of the myth of the mad Dean.

Gloomy insanity had taken . . . permanent possession of his mind; and right well did he know that he should die a maniac. For this, a few years before his death, did he build unto himself an asylum, where his own lunacy might dwell protected from the vulgar gaze of mankind. He felt the approach of madness, and like Caesar, when about to fall at the feet of Pompey's statue, he gracefully arranged the folds of his robe, conscious of his own dignity even in that melancholy downfall. The Pharaohs, we are told in Scripture, built unto themselves gorgeous sepulchres: their pyramids still encumber the earth. Sardanapalus erected a pyre of cedar-wood and odoriferous spices when death was inevitable, and perished in a blaze of voluptuousness. The asylum of Swift will remain a more characteristic memorial than the sepulchres of Egypt, and a more honourable funeral pyre than that heaped up by the Assyrian king. He died mad, among fellow-creatures similarly visited, but sheltered by his munificence. . . .[3]

That Swift was mad, and even built a madhouse to be his own last refuge, is not an interpretation restricted to Prout's frivolous essays. As Swift's most distinguished recent biographer, Irvin Ehrenpreis, has written: 'We all have learned that Swift went mad . . . His case was reported at once; and his symptoms have been sketched by no less than four famous writers . . .'[4] On Dr Samuel Johnson's authority we know that Swift 'expires a driv'ler and a show'; Sir Walter Scott, who edited Swift's complete works, found that after 1740 he was stricken by 'violent and furious lunacy'; W. M. Thackeray, on the other hand, regarded Swift's madness as no sudden, unexpected affliction, but merely the culmination and natural outcome of a life of extreme misanthropy. He was, wrote Thackeray in an oft-quoted sentence, a 'monster gibbering shrieks . . . against mankind, — tearing down all shreds of modesty, past all sense of manliness and shame; filthy in thought, furious, raging, obscene'. Aldous Huxley, the fourth writer quoted by Ehrenpreis, drew on modern psychotherapy to discuss Swift's scatology, which he saw as characterised by an 'almost insane violence'. To these four we might add James Joyce, who in *Ulysses* described Swift as a 'hater of his kind [who] ran from them to the wood of madness, his mane foaming in the moon, his eyeballs stars'.[5]

According to such writers then, Swift was not only mad, but harboured a deep and violent hatred of his fellow human beings. This line of thought has continued right up to the present day, with literary critics and commentators of all sorts giving free rein to their amateur medical and psychological opinions. In 1959 in his influential book, *Life Against Death: the Psychoanalytical Meaning of History*, Norman O. Brown included an essay entitled 'The Excremental Vision', which analysed Swift's writings along Freudian lines. This is in fact but one example of a whole school of criticism which attempted, often with rather dubious results, to apply psychoanalytical techniques to Swift's life and work.[6] In the mid-1960s, adopting a rather different approach, Malcolm Muggeridge argued strongly that Swift had contracted syphilis in his youth, when he was 'addicted to what he called low company', and that this in old age had developed into general paralysis of the insane (GPI).[7] More recently still, in his influential *A Short History of Irish Literature*, published in 1986, Seamus Deane tells us that, after the mid-1730s, Swift's life was a 'sad tale of disappointment, frustration, and illness, culminating in three years of insanity . . .'[8] That this view of Swift as a madman, or at the very least as a severely disturbed individual, is not restricted to the critics, but has taken root among the general public as well, is illustrated by an anecdote recounted by Professor J. N. P. Moore, the medical director of St Patrick's Hospital from 1946 to 1977. While conceding that some visitors to the hospital 'glow with reverential pride in the memory of the great man and exclaim with enthusiastic delight when they visit the hospital', Moore nevertheless found an equally typical reaction to be that:

> A visitor to the hospital, on being told the name of its founder, will say, with lowered tone of voice and the pained facial expression one associates with the more awesome experiences of life; 'Of course, Swift was mad, wasn't he?' Or, with the facetious jocularity reserved by so many people for the mentally afflicted; 'He was locked up here himself, I suppose!'[9]

If Swift was mad and, moreover, a 'man-hater', then in the eyes of such writers and commentators his decision to endow an asylum becomes a distinctly sinister act. Perhaps the hospital was not merely a place in which to hide his own madness, but some kind of bizarre joke aimed against the Irish. The oft-quoted lines from Swift's poem 'Verses on the Death of Dr Swift':

> He gave the little wealth he had,
> To build a house for fools and mad:
> And showed by one satiric touch,
> No nation wanted it so much . . . [10]

seem to add substance to this interpretation. Thus, in this view, the hospital was Swift's final and grandest satire: a devastating comment upon the mental capabilities of the Irish nation.

The truth, however, is far less bizarre. Swift was never insane; he did not die a raving madman in his own hospital; nor was his hospital the product of a maniacal joke.

Before examining Swift's real motives, we might ask ourselves why his last years and his last bequest have been so grossly misinterpreted and misunderstood. In considering much the same question, Ehrenpreis pointed to the simple fact that Swift had many enemies, only too ready to circulate exaggerated accounts of his problems. He gives the example of Dr Thomas Birch, a friend of Johnson's, who hated Swift, even though he had never met him. Late in 1744, about a year before Swift's death, Birch wrote to a friend:

> Dr Swift has lately awakened from a mere animal life into a thorough misanthropy and brutality of lust; for he can hardly be restrained from knocking every man on the head, who comes near him, . . . or from attempting every woman that he sees.[11]

These accusations are completely untrue, but such malicious gossip, elaborated upon and spread by his enemies, formed the basis of many later accounts of Swift's last years. Unfortunately, some of his supposed friends, out of ignorance or malice, or perhaps a combination of both, contributed to this picture of Swift as a dangerous lunatic. In a work entitled *Remarks on the Life and Writings of Dr Jonathan Swift* published in 1752, Lord Orrery wrote of Swift's state after 1742:

> His rage increased absolutely to a degree of madness; in this miserable state he seemed to be appointed as the first proper inhabitant of his own hospital, especially as, from an outrageous lunatic, he sank afterwards into a quiet, speechless idiot, and dragged out the remainder of his life in that helpless state.[12]

Here, perhaps, is the source of the story that Swift was the first inmate of his own hospital. Not content, however, with having labelled Swift a madman, Orrery went on to discuss madness at some length, while seeking the cause for Swift's affliction. Conceding that many factors, including strong emotions, poor diet, the consumption of spirits and the weather could contribute to madness, Orrery nevertheless decided that in Swift's case the cause was largely physical. Noting that Swift suffered from increasingly severe deafness, Orrery speculated:

> Possibly some internal pressure upon his brain might first have affected the auditory nerves, and then, by degrees, might have increased, so as entirely to stop up that fountain of ideas, which had before spread itself in the most diffusive and surprising manner.[13]

This seems not an unreasonable diagnosis, suggesting what today would be called a brain tumour. But Orrery combined such plausible speculation with far more fanciful theories. He gave considerable credence to the ancient notion that the moon exerted an influence on lunatics:

> Lunatics are so called from the influence which the moon has over bodies, when its attractive power is greatest, by which means the pressure of the atmosphere being lessened, the humours of the body are more rarefied, and produce a greater plenitude in the vessels of the brain.[14]

The blood was particularly affected, becoming thick, black and sluggish, '. . . from whence, perhaps, [said Orrery] we may in some measure, account for the principal source of Swift's lunacy: his countenance being dark, bilious, and gloomy, and his eyes sometimes fixed, and immovable for a long time.' As apparently a close friend of Swift's, Orrery's tales, whether of brain tumours or moonstruck blood, carried considerable weight. They were quickly refuted by more intimate friends, like Dr Patrick Delany, an executor of Swift's will and a governor of his hospital, but the damage had already been done. Swift's madness seemed to be well-authenticated.

As well as the libels of literary and political enemies and of dubious friends, Swift was also subjected to the mythologising processes of the popular imagination. During his life-time his patriotism and his generosity had made him a hero to the Dublin working class; his birthday for instance was regularly celebrated. An oral tradition grew up around him, just as later happened with other Irish popular heroes, like O'Connell and, to a lesser extent, Parnell. Stories about the 'Dane', particularly his often humorous dealings with servants and tradesmen, circulated in Dublin during his lifetime and for generations after his death. It is not surprising then that myths should attach themselves to his last tangible memorial, his hospital.[15]

Sir William Wilde, a leading Irish ear specialist and father of Oscar, published a book dealing with Swift's health in 1849. In this he said that it was generally believed at the time that 'Swift was the first patient in the hospital.'[16] But this story of a hospital founder being the first inmate of their own institution is not restricted to Swift. We need go no further than Dr Steevens Hospital, next door to St Patrick's, to find a very similar popular myth. In this case it concerns Dr Steevens's sister, Grizel. It was she who administered her brother's will and supervised the construction of his hospital. Dubliners always called it Madam Steevens Hospital and they told how Grizel's mother had been cursed by a beggar woman whom she had refused to aid. As a result Grizel was born with a pig's face and thus always wore a veil in public. She often sat at a window in the hospital; some stories suggested that she hid her pig's face behind a curtain; others that she sat in full public view in order to show that her face was perfectly normal.[17] Grizel Steevens certainly did have a room at the front of the hospital and lived there from its opening in 1733 till her death at the age of ninety-three. A surviving portrait, paid for by the governors of the hospital, suggests that she was no great beauty, but there is no sign of a pig's face.[18] This need to see a hospital as catering to the afflictions of its founder was perhaps a way of reducing grand and rather inhuman institutions to a more human scale. It was also an implicit rejection of charity. In the popular mind Swift's and Steevens's were not the products of the benevolence of the upper classes, but rather monuments reflecting their failings: failings, like madness and physical deformity, which they shared with the lower orders of society. In an age when hospitals without religious affiliations were still a novelty, these stories may also have simply explained new institutions, the motives behind which ordinary people found inexplicable.

There were, however, real events in Swift's life, particularly during the 1740s, which helped give rise to stories of his madness. In 1742, three years before his death, a writ 'de Lunatico Inquirendo' was issued with regard to Swift. After a petition from his friends and the examination of medical evidence, a jury declared Swift to be 'a person of unsound mind and memory, and not capable of taking care of his person or fortune'.[19] This enabled the appointment of a committee of guardians to manage Swift's affairs. A lunacy inquiry was in fact the only legal means by which a person, incapable of looking after him or herself or of conducting business affairs, could be protected. It did not necessarily mean that a person was insane, but it was most commonly used in cases of insanity and was generally considered as tantamount to a legal declaration of insanity. From 1742 till 1745 Swift wrote nothing and was confined to the Deanery, being seen by very few people. During these years stories of 'furious insanity' began to circulate. But, if Swift was not mad, then why was he declared to be 'of unsound mind'? What in fact was wrong with him?

Much ink has been shed by a succession of eminent doctors on the contentious subject of Swift's health, both physical and mental. The truth is that his health was poor: from his twenties he suffered recurrent attacks of giddiness, deafness, loss of memory and nausea, and these became worse as he grew older. Neither Swift nor his doctors really knew what was wrong with him, though he attributed the complaint to having eaten too many apples about the age of twenty-three and sought to remedy it with a variety of pills and potions and also with vigorous physical exercise. In fact Swift suffered from a disease of the inner ear, known as Ménière's Syndrome, which was not fully understood till 1861. Today it can be successfully treated, but in the eighteenth century it was a chronic and disabling disorder. Contrary to Orrery's speculations, the disease did not spread to Swift's brain, but years of ill health undoubtedly influenced his outlook on life. As Dr T. G. Wilson aptly put it:

> A disease in which one can fall out of a chair, in which it may be necessary to lie prostrate to avoid injury through falling, while a world whirling in giddy circles mingles with a background of violent nausea, will leave its mark on any man. Plunged periodically into this violent illness, and immobilized physically and mentally; gradually crawling back to health only to suffer sudden relapse when he felt fully recovered, it is no wonder the Dean became gloomy and morose.[20]

From the mid-1730s, as Swift reached the age of seventy, the illness appears to have become worse. In February 1736 he wrote to his friend, the poet Alexander Pope, 'my giddiness is more or less too constant'; and in December of the same year he told Pope, 'years and infirmities have quite broken me. I mean that odious continual disorder in my head. I neither read, nor write; nor remember, nor converse. All I have left is to walk, and ride.'[21] As Sir William Wilde wrote in his study of Swift's last years, 'up to the year 1742 Swift showed no symptom whatever of mental disease, beyond the ordinary decay of nature'.[22] When he made his final will in May 1740 Swift described himself as 'of sound mind, although weak in body', and this would seem an accurate representation of his health at the time. But, in the year 1742, he underwent a sudden decline which left him virtually unable to speak and apparently unable to understand most of what was said to him. At this stage his friends applied to have him declared of unsound mind so that his financial affairs could be managed for him. A jury of twelve Dublin merchants and tradesmen examined the evidence presented by his friends and concluded that since 20 May 1742 Swift had not been 'capable of taking care of his person or fortune' which was valued at over £10,000.[23]

A committee of guardians consisting of three of Swift's friends, Dr Francis Corbet, a prebendary of St Patrick's Cathedral, Alexander McAulay, a barrister, and John Rochfort, an MP, was appointed to handle financial matters. At the Deanery Swift was looked after by his cousin, Martha Whiteway, and by his housekeeper, Anne

Ridgeway. Visitors were few, consisting mainly of Swift's young cousin, rather confusingly called Deane Swift, and of the Rev. John Lyon, a prebendary of the cathedral, who, though not formally one of the guardians, worked closely with them. Thus for the last three years of his life Swift was almost totally cut off from the outside world and the people familiar with his real condition were few. In such circumstances rumour and gossip thrived. The most authoritative accounts of Swift's last years are contained in letters written by Martha Whiteway and Deane Swift.[24] The picture they paint of the great Dean is certainly distressing: he was largely unable to communicate, but was physically active, often pacing his room for the most of the day; his food had to be cut up for him and, though his appetite was generally good, sometimes he couldn't eat it for hours; while the presence of other people, and particularly his inability to speak to them, disturbed him and made him irritable. Deane Swift, writing, significantly, to Orrery in 1744, complained that: 'A thousand stories have been invented of him within these two years, and imposed upon the world.'[25] He went on to describe several attempts by Swift to speak, which generally ended in failure. The stories of Swift raving were, however, quite untrue: 'he never yet, as far as I could hear, talked nonsense, or said a foolish thing', wrote Deane Swift.[26]

Today Swift's inability to communicate would be termed motor aphasia. It is a common symptom of brain damage, caused by lesions such as tumours or thromboses. But brain damage is not mental illness. The eminent neurologist, Sir Russell Brain, probably provided the definitive account of Swift's last years from a medical point of view in an article published in 1952. Brain was in no doubt that from 1742 Swift was suffering from cerebral arteriosclerosis, with a number of complications, most of which were simply the product of old age. His attempts to speak, described graphically by Deane Swift, were, according to Brain, 'quite characteristic of aphasia'. Swift's case was, in fact, *so* characteristic of aphasia, Brain concluded, that: 'The mystery about Swift is that there ever should have been any mystery about him.'[27] Swift suffered from an accumulation of physical disorders: since his youth he had been afflicted with an inner ear disease which produced periodic deafness and vertigo; by 1737 when he turned seventy he was also suffering from gout and the effects of old age which exacerbated his deafness, poor memory and bad eyesight; then in 1742, when he was seventy-five, he either suffered a stroke or developed a brain tumour which produced aphasia, and thereafter, until his death in 1745, he was unable to communicate with anyone. In the verses he composed in 1731 humorously contemplating reactions to his death, he was not far from the truth when he wrote:

> See, how the Dean begins to break:
> Poor gentleman, he droops apace,
> You plainly find it in his face:
> That old vertigo in his head,
> Will never leave him, till he's dead:
> Besides, his memory decays,
> He recollects not what he says;
> He cannot call his friends to mind;
> Forgets the place where last he dined;
> Plies you with stories o'er and o'er,
> He told them fifty times before.[28]

Sadly for Swift, in the end his illness even deprived him of his great gift of story-telling.

But if Swift was not mad, then we come back to the question of why he left his estate to endow a mental hospital. He himself anticipated this question in 'Verses on the Death of Dr. Swift':

> What has he left? And who's his heir?
> I know no more than what the news is,
> 'Tis all bequeathed to public uses.
> To public use! A perfect whim!
> What had the public done for him? . . .
> And had the Dean, in all the nation,
> No worthy friend, no poor relation?
> So ready to do strangers good,
> Forgetting his own flesh and blood?[29]

The truth is that Swift was deeply interested from a moral and also a philosophical point of view in the issue of madness. Thus it would be quite wrong to ascribe his interest solely to some form of personal neurosis, though, admittedly, modern psychiatry would certainly consider him a neurotic individual.[30] But a number of major literary and philosophical figures in the century from about 1650 to about 1750 including Thomas Hobbes, John Locke, Alexander Pope, Samuel Johnson and Laurence Sterne, all wrote on the subject of madness. The cause and nature of madness and the relationship between madness and reason were widely-debated issues, particularly among the so-called Augustan writers, who included Swift and who have since become noted for their love of well-ordered classicism.[31]

Swift's views on madness need to be seen, not only in the context of this intellectual debate, but also against the background of changes in the way the mentally ill were treated. Up until the seventeenth century the mad were generally looked after by their families or wandered the countryside, often being subjected to abuse and cruelty. There were, however, specialist institutions catering for them, though these were few in number. The most notorious was Bethlem Hospital in London, popularly known as Bedlam. It had been founded in 1247 as the priory of St Mary of Bethlehem and it is first recorded as housing lunatics in the year 1377.[32] But, by Swift's time, the word 'bedlam' had come to be applied to madhouses generally and was synonymous with chaos.[33] In other parts of Europe medieval religious houses caring for the sick and the poor had also housed lunatics and some, like Bethlem, developed into hospitals. But in the seventeenth century governments began to make greater efforts to regulate beggars, vagrants, criminals, lunatics and the poor generally. Particularly after 1650 institutions, called *hôpitaux généraux* in France and *Zuchthäusern* in Germany, were established to confine the poor. Sometimes these had evolved out of earlier monasteries and hospitals; sometimes they were new foundations.[34] In England significant efforts to control vagrants and beggars had begun even earlier, with the basis of a poor law being laid by act passed in 1601 under Elizabeth I. Not till the second half of the century, however, did a system of institutions to house the poor, called houses of industry or workhouses, begin to appear. A workhouse was built in Bristol in 1697 and in 1703 an act was passed to establish a workhouse in Dublin.[35] As we shall see, this particular workhouse, or rather its problems, played an important part in the foundation of Swift's hospital. In considering the growth of institutions to confine the poor and the mad, we need, however, to be careful not to exaggerate the change, as some historians have tended to do. Similar institutions had existed before the seventeenth century and those appearing at this time were often small and were managed by charitable individuals rather than by the state. In Ireland and England at least, it was not till the nineteenth century that huge state asylums began to be built.[36]

In Ireland there are no records of lunatics being housed in monasteries, though this was probably done, even if on a small scale. In Dublin the great medieval hospitals, like that of St John the Baptist at Newgate and St Stephen, which stood on the site later occupied by Mercer's Hospital, almost certainly had some mad patients. But, by the seventeenth century, such institutions had largely vanished and the first places recorded as confining lunatics were houses of correction or prisons, which had been established under an act passed in 1634-5. In 1684 and again in 1701 the keeper of the Dublin house of correction applied to the corporation for money with which to support lunatic inmates and, in the latter year, was granted a specified sum for each.[37] When a workhouse appeared in 1703–4 it was intended to house, not criminals or lunatics, but the able-bodied poor, who were expected to earn their relief through work. But, like the house of correction, the work-house soon found itself having to cater for a vast assortment of needy people, including the young and the old, the crippled and the chronically ill, and also the mad. In fact the demand to accommo-date lunatics was so great that the institution was soon in danger of being overwhelmed.

As well as increasing attempts to regulate the insane, the late seventeenth and early eighteenth centuries also saw important changes in medical option regarding insanity. Ancient beliefs that linked madness with either divine or diabolical possession or with the operations of the four humours were giving way to more mechanistic theories.[38] Yet methods of treatment, like bleeding and purging, originally derived from humoral theory, continued to be used, even into the nineteenth century. New ideas as to the nature of madness did not necessarily mean the discovery of new remedies and thus old methods tended to survive long after the rationale for their use had been superseded. The simple truth was that theories about madness were numerous, but effective treatments were few. The new theories were influenced by the successes of Newtonian physics in unravelling the mechanics of the universe and, as we shall see, they were satirised mercilessly by Swift in *A Tale of a Tub*. To take but one example, Dr Thomas Willis, a pioneer of neurology, advised in 1667: 'Furious madmen are sooner, and more certainly cured by punishments, and hard usage, in a strait room, than by physic and medicines . . . Let the diet be slender and not delicate, their clothing coarse, their beds hard, and their handling severe and rigid.'[39] This may seem an unacceptably harsh attitude to us, but it arose logically out of Willis's theories as to the nature of insanity. He believed that all behaviour was determined by the circulation of vapours, termed 'animal spirits', through the nerves, which were in turn controlled by the brain. Various factors, such as heredity, bad diet and strong emotions, could damage and disorder these spirits. Beatings were a method of driving them back into their proper channels.[40] Roy Porter, in his recent excellent history of English attitudes to madness from 1660 to 1820, has summarised the neurological theory thus:

... the prime model was hydraulic: nerves were seen as hollow pipes, filled under pressure by a fluid composed of the subtlest of bodily particles ... Graphic and easy to visualise, it pictured depression and disorientation as corporeal plumbing failures. If tubes became clogged — if, for instance, 'heavy' diet and low habits were indulged — the fluids grew sluggish, causing 'heaviness' and 'lowness'.[41]

Controversies flourished over the precise manner in which the nerves operated, but the views of Willis and his disciples were extremely influential in medical circles during Swift's lifetime. In intellectual circles there was much debate regarding the relationship between reason and madness. Generally reason was considered the cardinal attribute of humankind and thus, '... in losing his reason, the essence of humanity, the madman had lost his claim to be treated as a human being'.[42] The harshness with which the mad were sometimes treated in the eighteenth century was not therefore the result of wanton cruelty, but reflected contemporary theories, whether neurological or rationalist, as to the nature of their illness.[43]

Swift, like many in the medical profession, was deeply interested in the subject of insanity, but he had little sympathy with the doctors' simplistic theories. He saw madness as a far more insidious influence and many of his greatest satires were devoted to exposing the madness that underlay human life and pervaded human institutions. Perhaps his most sustained portrayals of madness occur in 'A Digression Concerning Madness' in *A Tale of a Tub* (1704), in the account of the academy of Lagado in *Gulliver's Travels* (1726), in *A Modest Proposal* (1729) and in his poem on the Irish parliament, called 'The Legion Club' (1736).

Swift in his approach to madness was influenced by the philosopher, John Locke, who, rejecting all notion of animal spirits, argued that madmen 'do not appear ... to have lost the faculty of reasoning, but having joined together some ideas very wrongly, they mistake them for truths ...'[44] Locke, who was by profession a doctor, rejected the notion of an absolute dichotomy between sanity and insanity; in fact he suggested that any person could fall into madness by the erroneous association of ideas. It was not that madmen lacked reason, but that they reasoned wrongly. This view of madness clearly underlies Swift's famous satire, *A Modest Proposal*, in which the proposer, linking the problems of Irish overpopulation and poverty, puts forward an elaborately argued case for selling Irish babies for food. The proposer is insane, horribly so, but he does not lack reason. On the contrary, he is totally detached and highly rational; what is insane is his association of ideas. Swift thus demolished the simple dichotomy of reason versus madness and demonstrated graphically that reason itself, separated from the emotions, can become a form of insanity. In an age that set so much store by the concept of reason, this was a highly subversive proposition.

As for mechanistic notions of circulating vapours determining human behaviour, Swift lambasted them in his discussion of madness in *A Tale of a Tub*:

> ... I have read somewhere in a very ancient author, of a mighty king [Louis XIV of France], who, for the space of above thirty years, amused himself to take and lose towns, beat armies and be beaten ... burn, lay waste, plunder, dragoon, massacre ... 'Tis recorded, that the philosophers of each country were in grave dispute upon the causes natural, moral, and political, to find out where they should assign an original solution to this phenomenon. At last, the vapour or spirit, which animated the hero's brain, being in perpetual circulation, seized upon that region of the human body, so renowned for furnishing the 'zibeta occidentalis' [i.e. excrement], and, gathering there into a tumour, left the rest of the world for a time in peace ... The same spirits, which, in their superior progress, would conquer a kingdom, descending upon the anus, conclude in a fistula.[45]

Thus did Swift hold up to scorn the influential theories of Thomas Willis, which ascribed madness to bodily 'plumbing failures'.

The most popular metaphor of madness in the seventeenth and eighteenth centuries was Bethlem Hospital or Bedlam in London. In his *Journal to Stella*, Swift records that he toured the hospital in 1710 with a group of friends and, so interested in it was he, that he had himself elected a governor in 1714. Bethlem encouraged the public to visit and exhibited its inmates like animals in a zoo, deriving substantial revenue from the fees charged to visitors.[46] Many writers of the period in treating madness refer to Bedlam, and Swift is no exception. The tour of Bedlam is a motif which crops up in a number of his major satires. In the latter part of 'A Digression Concering Madness', for instance, Swift takes the reader through Bedlam, demonstrating how the inmates could be '... admirable instruments for the several offices in a state, [ecclesiastical] civil and military ...'[47] Among the lunatics he finds suitable candidates for the army, the law, politics, medicine, commerce, the court and even for literature. Through his satire Swift illustrates the thin line that in fact separates the great and successful of this world from the inmates of a madhouse. In later, more savage, satires even this thin

line disappears as, for Swift, Bedlam becomes the world in micro-
cosm. On his tours Swift refuses to allow us to distance ourselves
from the bedlamites, to see them as lacking reason and therefore as
mere animals; his message is that we are all potential bedlamites.

The image of Bedlam is particularly powerful in book three of
Gulliver's Travels and in the poem 'The Legion Club'. In one Swift
satirises scientists and inventors and in the other he attacks Irish
politicians. In book three of *Gulliver's Travels*, Gulliver visits the
academy of Lagado, a centre for scientific research. In his description of the academy, Swift is satirising scientific bodies like the
Royal Society, established in London in 1662, by again using the
motif of a tour through Bedlam. In the many rooms of the academy,
Gulliver finds the inmates attempting to extract sunbeams from
cucumbers and to turn excrement into food; there is an architect
who wants to build houses from the roof downwards; a blind man is
mixing coloured paints by means of smell; and in another room a
professor is demonstrating a machine that can write books automatically, without the operator needing any knowledge of the subject.
These experiments seem quite as mad as the wildest fantasies of any
bedlamite. Yet, Swift, who visited the Royal Society in 1710, actually
drew most of them, without a great deal of exaggeration, from the
society's own published journals.[48] The satire on the Royal Society
is, however, mild compared with the assault Swift launched ten
years later on the Irish House of Commons in his poem 'The Legion
Club'. The poem combines images of a tour of Bedlam with those of
a descent into hell, as Swift pays a keeper to let him see the inmates
of the new Irish parliament house on College Green, which was
under construction in the 1730s. He draws parallels between the
activities of the MPs and those of the bedlamites:

> Let them, when they once get in
> Sell the nation for a pin;
> While they sit a-picking straws
> Let them rave of making laws;
> While they never hold their tongue,
> Let them dabble in their dung; . . .
> Let them 'ere they crack a louse,
> Call for the orders of the House;
> Let them with their gosling quills,
> Scribble senseless heads of bills;
> We may, while they strain their throats,
> Wipe our arses with their votes.[49]

When the keeper brings forward two of his charges, Swift recommends the severe treatment that was common for lunatics at the time:

> Tie them, keeper, in a tether,
> Let them stare and stink together;
> Both are apt to be unruly,
> Lash them daily, lash them duly,
> Though 'tis hopeless to reclaim them,
> Scorpion rods perhaps may tame them.[50]

In 1736 Irish MPs were considering abolishing some of the tithes due to the state church, which they, as landlords, particularly resented. The poem was Swift's bitter response to what he saw as an attack by 'corrupt and slavish . . . misrepresentative brutes' on his church. But he was ill at the time and his rage was doubtless partly a reflection of his own miserable condition.[51]

Throughout his writings, as we have seen, from *A Tale of a Tub* to 'The Legion Club' thirty years later, Swift demonstrated a deep and abiding preoccupation with the issue of madness. Some critics have seen this preoccupation as excessive and as a reflection of Swift's insecurity regarding his own sanity; and indeed, there may be some truth in this interpretation.[52] Yet the issue was much discussed in medical, literary and even political circles during Swift's lifetime. Contemporary writers, like Pope, who showed a similar interest in madness, have not had their personal sanity questioned as a result. But what has really discomforted the critics is not just Swift's interest in madness, it is the ferocity of his satire. It was far too strong for the refined stomachs of the Victorians for instance. Augustine Birrell, later to be chief secretary for Ireland, in reviewing a book on Swift in the 1890s, wrote: 'It is a question not of morality, but of decency, whether it is becoming to sit in the same room with the works of this divine . . . Thackeray's criticism is severe, but is it not just? Are we to stand by and hear our nature libelled, and our purest affections beslimed, without a word of protest?'[53] To Thackeray Swift had been an 'ogre': an obscene and raving madman.[54] Modern critics would not go this far, but some still clearly find parts of his work offensive. Yet to regard Swift as a misanthrope, a hater of his own kind, who through his satires simply portrayed the whole world as a madhouse, is seriously to misunderstand his purpose. He certainly believed that warlike rulers, corrupt politicians, religious enthusiasts, over ambitious scientists and indeed all those with grand schemes to improve or control the world were as mad as the maddest inmate of Bethlem Hospital. But, following Locke, he also believed that any person could succumb to insanity and he desperately wanted his readers to realise the madness that surrounded them and to which they were susceptible. Swift knew, however, that his readers would be loath to listen to such an unpalatable message; they preferred to see madness exhibited safely beind the bars of Bethlem. As Michael DePorte has argued persuasively:

> The audience, hostile to criticism, vigilantly defensive, is, he perceived, the real enemy. In effect the satirist is at war with his readers. They must be outmaneuvered, caught off guard . . . Swift's double view of the reader as both an enemy and a victim needing help is analogous to the prevailing notion of Augustan psychiatry that physician and mental patient are antagonists engaged in a struggle of wills, and that violent means—beating, purgatives, caustic ointments—are required to wrest the sufferer from his delusions. The assumption in each case is that the lunatic perversely cherishes his lunacy and will never willingly succumb to reason.[55]

Swift's satire reaches a level of savagery unequalled in the English language; his writing at times constitutes an assault upon the reader. But he saw this ferocity as necessary to his task and this task was to beat and purge and shock his audience into sanity, into a recognition of their own delusions and of their kinship with the bedlamites. Seen against the background of his writings then, Swift's bequest of his estate to build 'a house for fools and mad' was eminently logical: for most of his life he had wrestled with the underlying madness that he saw all about him; his hospital was to continue the same struggle after his death.

During Swift's lifetime (1667-1745) Dublin, like other major European cities, saw the establishment of a number of major educational, medical and custodial institutions. In 1669 King's Hospital, popularly known as the Blue-coat School, was set up by the corporation at Oxmantown Green for the sons of 'decayed citizens', while in 1684 the Royal Hospital at Kilmainham opened to house military pensioners. In 1711 a 'mad house' was built, attached to the infirmary of the Royal Hospital intended for soldiers, who, 'by unaccountable accidents in the service, sometime happen to become lunatics', and it seems to have remained in continuous use until 1849.[56] In 1699 the corporation received a petition 'setting forth . . . a proposal . . . for erecting a hospital . . . for the reception of aged lunatics and other diseased persons, there being no city in the world so considerable as this city of Dublin where there is not some such'. Dr Thomas Molyneux offered £2,000, 'on the behalf of a gentleman who desires to be nameless', towards the upkeep of such a hospital, while the corporation agreed to grant £200 and land near

St James's Gate.[57] Nothing seems to have come of this interesting proposal, however. It originated in the College of Physicians, which had been constituted by royal charter in 1667 and 1692. Molyneux was active in the College, being elected president in 1701–2. Also active was Dr Richard Steevens, who succeeded Molyneux as president in 1703. It was perhaps the failure of this initiative in 1699 that inspired Steevens to leave his estate, at his death in 1710, to found a hospital.[58]

We know from corporation records that there were 'sick houses' and 'poor houses' in the city during the late sixteenth and seventeenth centuries. Very likely they were survivals from the monasteries that had catered for the poor and sick before their suppression in the 1530s. The hospital and priory of St John without Newgate, for example, which had over 150 beds in the thirteenth century, was suppressed in 1539. But the site was leased by a surgeon and some of the buildings continued to be used as charitable accommodation for the poor and sick during the seventeenth century.[59] But clearly, by the beginning of the eighteenth century, it was felt that the city lacked adequate provision for those in need. The political and economic upheavals of the seventeenth century had helped produce large numbers of vagrants and beggars, who tended to gravitate to Dublin particularly in the spring and summer months before the harvest, adding numerous 'foreign' beggars to the city's own hordes. Swift himself had devoted a good deal of attention to the problem and had devised a scheme whereby parishes would license 'deserving' beggars. But, when tried on a limited scale by the archbishop of Dublin, the scheme proved ineffective in curbing begging.[60] From 1700 onwards, however, the pace of institutionalisation increased strikingly, as private citizens joined the civic authorities in attempts to combat what were perceived as growing problems of poverty, vagrancy and disease. The motives behind the building of institutions to house and treat the poor have been much debated. Some commentators see them as essentially charitable and christian; others, on the contrary, detect a campaign by the rich and powerful to control the have-nots and prevent civil unrest. Doubtless motives were mixed, with self-interest and altruism proceeding hand-in-hand. In 1703–4 a workhouse was built on the site now occupied by St James's Hospital, though by 1730 this had largely been given over to the care of foundling children. About 1708 provision for lunatics had been made at the workhouse by the erection of a number of cells and, even when the institution became a foundling hospital, some lunatics appear to have remained. In 1725, for example, nearly 15 per cent of the inmates of the workhouse were classed as 'madd', 'fooles' or subject to 'fitts'.[61] The mad, as we have already noted, were also housed in the city's prisons. The house of correction, established in the seventeenth century, was rebuilt in 1730 and put under the control of the governors of the workhouse, though the city's main place of confinement remained old Newgate gaol in Cornmarket, which did not move to new premises in Green Street till 1780.[62] The most startling growth in new institutions in the first half of the eighteenth century, however, was not in workhouses or prisons, it was in the provision of hospitals.

In 1718 a house was opened in Cook Street by six surgeons for 'the maimed and wounded poor'; called the Charitable Infirmary in 1728, it eventually became Jervis Street Hospital. After some twenty years of planning and building, Dr Steevens Hospital was finally opened in 1733, to be followed shortly by Mercer's in 1734, by the hospital for incurables in 1744, by the Lying-in Hospital or Rotunda in 1745 and by the Meath in 1753. Thus six hospitals were established in a little over thirty years, followed by a seventh, Swift's own, which opened in 1757.[63] Swift thus lived during Dublin's great age of hospital building and was himself closely involved with a number of these new institutions, both in a personal capacity and by virtue of his position as dean of St Patrick's Cathedral. He was a governor of the workhouse; in 1721 Grizel Steevens invited him to become a trustee of the fund for building Steevens Hospital; in 1725 he was elected to the board of the Blue-coat School; and in 1735 he became a trustee of Mercer's Hospital. But, through friends and doctors he was probably most closely associated with Dr Steevens Hospital. Dr Richard Helsham, Swift's friend and personal physician from at least 1718, was a governor of Steevens's and it was very probably at Swift's suggestion that Stella at her death in 1728 left money to endow a chaplaincy at the hospital.

When Swift came, as he did in the 1720s and 1730s, to consider how he should dispose of his estate, he was faced with a number of possibilities. As we shall see, he was a man who accumulated his wealth slowly and carefully and he devoted similar time and care to deciding exactly what he should do with it. Unfortunately, though, by the time he came to make definite arrangements in the late 1730s his health was so poor that he was not up to the task and was forced to bequeath it to his executors.

In the mid-1720s Swift contemplated endowing a fellowship at Trinity College, Dublin, but in 1727 he rejected this option due to what he saw as the pro-whig sympathies of the provost.[64] By late 1731, however, when 'Verses on the Death of Dr Swift' was composed, he had definitely decided 'to build a house for fools and mad'. In 1732 he discussed his plans with Sir William Fownes. Fownes, a wealthy landowner, was MP for Wicklow Town and a former lord mayor of Dublin, and like Swift, he was a trustee of Steevens Hospital. In September 1732 Fownes wrote at length to Swift, lamenting that Ireland had 'fewer public charitable foundations' than almost any other European country and setting out in detail a scheme of his own for building a 'madhouse'. When he had been lord mayor in 1708, wrote Fownes, he had seen 'some miserable lunaticks exposed to hazard of others, as well as themselves'. Concerned about the problem, he had six 'strong cells' built at the workhouse for the 'most outrageous'. But, within a short time, there were more than forty inmates; 'the door being opened' said Fownes, 'interest soon made way to let in foolish and such like, as mad folks'. Alarmed at the expense and fearful that the workhouse would be swamped by lunatics, the corporation eventually refused to accept any more and returned as many as possible to family or friends. In 1730 the workhouse became a foundling hospital, though it does seem from later records that a small number of lunatics were still housed in Fownes's cells. In the 1750s recalcitrant children were punished by being locked up with the lunatics.[65]

His experience with the workhouse had made Fownes sceptical of the feasibility of a 'bedlam'. 'I own to you' he told Swift, 'I was for some time averse to our having a public bedlam, apprehending we should be overloaded with numbers under the name of mad.' Such appears to have happened in the case of the workhouse and Fownes reminded Swift of the problems being experienced by English asylums, with husbands attempting to be rid of wives or relations to be rid of heirs under the guise of madness. But of late, again moved by the 'dismal circumstances' of real lunatics and by expressions of concern voiced by Archbishop Boulter of Armagh, Fownes had become convinced of the need for action. He envisaged a public, not a private, hospital and one built as inexpensively as possible from public subscriptions to serve the whole country. Swift in conversation with him had apparently mentioned a possible site 'in the heart of the city', but Fownes urged building on the outskirts of Dublin, 'in a good open air, free from neighbourhood of houses' for 'the cries and exclamations of the outrageous would reach a great way, and ought not to disturb neighbours'. Later Fownes suggested a site behind Aungier Street, near Mrs Mercer's house, soon to be Mercer's Hospital. The area would need to be enclosed by a high wall. Fownes saw the hospital as consisting of three sections. There would be six or eight 'strong cells' for 'outrageous lunaticks', like those built in 1711 at the Royal Hospital, and another separate building for 'lunaticks of several kinds as the melancholy etc and some that are unruly by fits [epileptics]'. This latter building would consist of 'lodging cells', measuring 8 or 10 feet, opening onto a gallery. '. . . by intervals' wrote Fownes, 'the objects effected [*sic*] may be permitted to walk at times in the gallerys—this is according to the custom of London'. When St Patrick's Hospital was eventually built twenty years later, it consisted of galleries and cells on the Bethlem pattern, but not separate facilities for unruly or violent patients. This was a major flaw in the hospital's design, which was not rectified for a century. The third section envisaged by Fownes comprised a master's house, a large room for meetings, a kitchen, a storeroom and accommodation for a porter, two attendants, a cook and a maid. All these buildings were to be 'made plain and strong with as little cost as can be'. Fownes was keen to have as inexpensive and simple a scheme as possible. The subscribers were to elect seven from among their number to supervise building, while the College of Physicians was to be asked to choose two or three of its members to advise on matters like appropriate accommodation and food. Fownes feared interference from 'grandees' and 'great folks' seeking to exploit the institution for selfish purposes. Clearly he had the workhouse in mind, but perhaps also Steevens Hospital, which had a large board of eminent members but did not open till more than twenty years after Dr Steevens's death.[66]

Fownes died in 1735, but by then Swift was busy planning the erection of his own hospital. His intentions had become public knowledge and, though some protested, most applauded. When details appeared in the press, they attracted the lines:

> The Dean must die!—our idiots to maintain!
> Perish ye idiots! and long live the Dean.[67]

Friends, however, wrote offering their congratulations. Alexander Pope said he had heard of Swift's plans with 'approbation and pleasure'. Of all charities, he thought, 'this is the most disinterested', for Swift could expect little in the way of thanks from lunatics, who 'most want our compassion, though, generally made the scorn of their fellow-creatures, such as are less innocent than they'. John Barber, another friend and a former lord mayor of London, told Swift that all mankind would applaud his public spirit 'in erecting an hospital for the unhappy. It is truly worthy of your great soul', Barber went on, 'and for which the present and the future age must honour and revere your memory'. Others wrote offering information and advice. Dr John Sican, whose mother was a friend of Swift's, wrote from Paris, describing the 'Bedlam of Paris' as it 'might be a good plan for that you intend to found'.[68]

That Swift's decision to leave his fortune to endow a mental hospital was not considered strange or inexplicable at the time is shown by such letters. Moreover, as we have seen, others had similar plans. The hospital proposed by Molyneaux in 1699 was intended to accommodate lunatics; cells for lunatics were built at the workhouse in 1708 and at the Royal Hospital in 1711. In 1732, after the expulsion of lunatics from the workhouse, Fownes put forward a detailed scheme for a specialist hospital; and in 1734, shortly before Swift's intentions became public knowledge, a group of doctors and clergymen petitioned the Dublin corporation seeking money to turn Mary Mercer's former school and almshouse, on the site of the medieval leper hospital of St Stephen, into a hospital for 'lunatics, or such other poor people whose distempers are of tedious or doubtful cure, such as persons afflicted with cancers, king's evil, leprosy, falling sickness, etc'. They particularly wanted the money to make 'provision for cells for raging lunatics' in the house. Mercer's Hospital opened in the following year with Swift as a governor, though in the event it did not develop a specialist interest in mental illness.[69] In the first half of the eighteenth century Swift, like Grizel Steevens, William Fownes, Mary Mercer and a number of others, was simply trying to replace the poorhouses, almshouses and hospitals, which had flourished in medieval Dublin, but most of which had succumbed during the upheavals of the sixteenth and seventeenth centuries.

Despite much approbation, Swift's plans did not proceed smoothly, however. Problems arose over a number of issues: selecting a board of governors, acquiring a site and putting together enough ready money to purchase an estate, with which to endow the hospital. Matters were not helped by the fact that Swift was seriously ill in the spring of 1736 and again in 1737, when he began to suffer from gout in addition to his other infirmities. His eyesight was failing and after 1735 he does not seem to have been well enough to undertake any more trips outside Dublin.[70] Swift had hoped himself to organise the endowment and erection of his hospital, but the deterioration in his health after 1735 made this a well-nigh impossible task.

In January 1735 he petitioned the Dublin corporation to grant him land at Oxmantown Green, near the Blue-coat School, for his hospital. His choice of a site may partly have been influenced by Fownes, who, in his own plan, had envisaged the secretary of the school acting as agent in the collection of subscriptions for his hospital. Also the area was on the outskirts of the city, largely free from the 'neighbourhood of houses', as Fownes had recommended. A committee of the corporation recommended that the land be granted 'at a pepper corn yearly', as such a hospital 'will be of singular use in this populous city'. The recorder was to advise on the execution of deeds.[71] The recorder, Eaton Stannard, was in fact a friend of Swift's and in April Swift wrote informing him of his intention 'to make the lord mayor, recorder and aldermen my trustees, executors or governors', and it appears that in July he made a will to this effect.[72] The Blue-coat School was also administered by the corporation and this may have been another reason for having the two institutions close together. When in the following year, however, the corporation relaxed some of the restrictions on presbyterians, Swift angrily changed his mind, telling Orrery in March 1737, 'upon the city's favouring fanatics I have altered my will, and not left the mayor, aldermen etc my trustees for building my hospital'.[73] Instead he turned to the governors of Dr Steevens Hospital. In June Swift's friend and physician, Dr Helsham, informed his fellow governors that the Dean intended to vest his fortune in them 'for erecting and supporting a convenient building for the reception of madmen and idiots'. The governors readily accepted the task and appointed a committee to decide on a suitable site.[74] But late in August 1738 Dr Helsham died suddenly. Most authorities consider that this event caused Swift to change his mind once again regarding the board of his proposed hospital.[75] When his final will was signed in May 1740 it did specify that his hospital should be 'near' Dr Steevens's, but it appointed ten of his clerical and legal friends as executors and instructed them to obtain a royal charter incorporating themselves, plus seven ex-officio trustees, as a board of governors for the hospital.[76]

But Helsham's death may not be as important as is usually supposed. In a letter dated 13 July 1738 Swift ordered his Dublin publisher, George Faulkner, to advertise his readiness to lend £2,000 at 5 per cent interest. In the course of this advertisement, Swift said that 'he must leave it [the endowment of his hospital], as he hath done in his will, to the care of his executors, who are very honest, wise and considerable gentlemen, his friends; . . .'[77] This would seem to suggest that as early as July 1738, some six weeks before Helsham's death, Swift had already drafted a will entrusting the establishment of the hospital to a group of his friends. Swift's frequent changes of mind regarding the composition of the board reflect, not simply the indecisiveness of a sick, old man, but the mistrust of committees felt by a man with long experience of institutions of all types. The above quotation referring to his friends, in fact concludes, 'and yet he hath known some of very fair and deserved credit, prove very negligent trustees'. Nor was Swift alone in worrying about the reliability and integrity of charity managers.

Fownes had warned him of the tendency of 'great folks' to interfere
in the running of charitable institutions for selfish ends, and an even
sterner warning had come in 1735 from Benjamin Motte, his
London publisher. While praising Swift's 'noble . . . design', Motte
went on to single out one particular advantage of his proposal:

> . . . you will lay down a scheme, which will be a pattern for
> future founders of public hospitals, to prevent many of the vile
> abuses which, in process of time, do creep into those founda-
> tions, by the indolence, ignorance, or knavery of the trustees. I
> have seen so many scandalous instances of misapplications of
> that kind, as have raised my indignation so, that I can hardly
> think upon it with temper; and I heartily congratulate you that a
> heart to bestow is joined in you with a head to contrive; . . .[78]

Motte was here probably summing up Swift's own attitude. There
are certainly strong indications that he distrusted charitable committees, and the frequent re-drafting of his will which seems to have
occurred during the 1730s indicates his strenuous attempts to 'contrive' a board of governors for his hospital free from 'indo-
lence, ignorance or knavery'.

In relation to private madhouses especially, both Motte and Swift
were probably aware that they were particularly open to abuse.
Complaints of wrongful confinement were frequent in England in
the eighteenth century and, as early as 1728, Daniel Defoe had
called for the suppression of 'pretended madhouses, where many of
the fair sex are unjustly confin'd, while their husbands keep
mistresses, etc., and many widows are lock'd up for the sake of their
jointure'.[79] The cruel treatment of patients was another frequent
source of complaint and indeed Swift's hospital was quite intention-
ally to ally itself with moves towards more humane attitudes and
techniques.[80] Against this background of corrupt and careless
officials, wrongful committals and cruelty to patients, Swift's
anxiety to ensure that his hospital lived up to high standards of
altruism is particularly noteworthy, not to say laudable.

But selecting governors and a site were not the only problems
Swift faced in the years 1735-8. Two other interrelated difficulties
also beset him: he needed to buy an estate, the rents from which
would provide the hospital with an income, and, most important of
all, he needed the money with which to make such a purchase.
Biographies of Swift generally record that he left about £11,000 for
the establishment of St Patrick's Hospital. But the situation was by
no means this simple. In October 1735 he wrote to Lord Orrery
asking if he had 'any middling bit of land worth about £200 a year',

for 'I would desire to be a purchaser, because I design to leave my whole fortune to a public use, for endowing an hospital for lunatics and idiots . . .' Then, however, Swift went on frankly to acknowledge his main problem:

> But how to pay you I am at a loss, all my money being out upon mortgages, some at 5 and some at 6 percent. I believe one of my debtors would be ready to pay me, about or near £3,000, and I could scramble or borrow the other thousand. If this could stand your conveniency, it would remove a great load from my shoulders, and be an ease to my mind, since years and ill health have got possession of me, and I cannot long struggle with either.[81]

One of his debtors did repay him, but, as we have seen, in July 1738 he instructed Faulkner to advertise that he was ready to lend another £2,000. He explained why he did not use this sum to purchase an estate in his advertisement by remarking, 'as to purchasing a real estate in lands, for want of active friends, he finds it impossible'.[82] Obviously Orrery had not been able to help him. Swift seems to have made other attempts too to purchase land, which also fell through: '. . . I find such a difficulty in purchasing land that I resolve not to meddle with it, but leave that trouble to my executors.'[83] In his 1738 advertisement he specified that after his death, the £2,000 lent was to be used by his executors to buy land to endow the hospital. In fact the money was lent to the Denn family, which held land at Saggart, Co. Dublin. As dean of St Patrick's, Swift was entitled to tithes from the parishes of Saggart, Tallaght and Rathcoole and he seems to have known the area well. It was appropriate therefore that, when after Swift's death Philip Denn was unable to repay the mortgage, the governors acquired his Saggart estate in 1750 for the hospital.

Swift may have exaggerated the problems he encountered in trying to purchase an estate, but certainly recovering his fortune from the hands of his debtors was no easy task. When we come to examine the activities of his executors we shall see that this was one of their biggest problems and in fact some of the money was not recovered till more than sixty years after Swift's death. But, despite his doubts regarding the calibre of governors and his inability to purchase an estate, Swift from at least 1731 onwards was determined that his money should go towards the establishment of a mental hospital—'I will never leave anything to any other use', he told a correspondent in February 1735.[84] In this he did not waver, though by 1738 if not earlier, he had realised that the task of setting up the hospital was one he was going to have to leave to his friends.

The provisions of Swift's will relative to the hospital were fairly straightforward, perhaps deceptively so. He named ten executors:

Robert Lindsay, judge of the Court of Common Pleas
Henry Singleton, prime-sergeant at law
Rev. Dr Patrick Delany, chancellor of St Patrick's Cathedral
Rev. Dr Francis Wilson, prebendary of the cathedral
Eaton Stannard, recorder of the City of Dublin
Rev. Robert Grattan, prebendary of the cathedral
Rev. John Grattan, prebendary of the cathedral
Rev. James Stopford, vicar of Finglas
Rev. James King, prebendary of the cathedral
Alexander McAulay, barrister

All were clerical or legal friends, and he instructed them to turn his assets into 'ready money' and to use this to purchase an estate in fee simple, preferably near Dublin, to be rented on leases of no more than thirty-one years (the maximum length of lease allowed Catholics under the penal laws). Rents were to be levied 'reasonably and moderately, without racking tenants'. No person connected with the hospital, or any relative of such, was to be given a lease and no land was to be bought or leased without the approval of a majority of a group of trustees, consisting of the archbishops of Armagh and Dublin, the deans of St Patrick's and Christ Church, the lord chancellor, the state physician and the surgeon general. Perhaps by involving this eminent collection of clerical, legal and medical persons, Swift hoped to keep a check on his executors and particularly prevent any corruption in estate management. As we shall see, this mechanism was not always successful. The income derived from renting the estate was to be used to build and run the hospital. Swift specified that his executors were to acquire land 'near' Dr Steevens Hospital and build a hospital for as many 'lunaticks and ideots' as the income would support. If enough 'lunaticks and ideots' could not be found to fill the institution, then it was to take in 'incurables'. But, on no account was it to accept anyone suffering from an 'infectious disease'. Swift clearly did not want the hospital being turned into a fever or general hospital; he wanted it to treat the most intractable cases. The hospital was to be called St Patrick's Hospital and was to be built in such a manner that it might be enlarged should its income increase. Staff were to be appointed, but salaries were not to exceed one-fifth of the annual income. This clause testifies again to Swift's fear of people exploiting his hospital for personal advantage. Finally, he instructed his executors to apply for a royal charter incorporating them and the seven trustees as a board to manage both the estate and the hospital.[85]

The charter granted by George II on 8 August 1746 rehearsed the provisions of Swift's will and, most importantly, spelt out the structure and functions of the board of governors. Of the executors, seven survived, Lindsay, Wilson and Robert Grattan having died since 1740. These seven and the seven trustees were incorporated as governors of the hospital in perpetuity. The trustees, or charter governors as they came to be called, sat on the board in virtue of the offices that they held. The executors, or elected governors as they were termed, were to be replaced on their deaths or resignations by election. Such elections required a quorum of seven, including either the archbishop of Armagh, the archbishop of Dublin or the lord chancellor, and the only qualification specified for an elected governorship was that the candidate had resided for at least the three previous years in the city or suburbs of Dublin.[86] The full board was to meet at least four times a year, on the first Monday in February, May, August and November. At these charter board meetings, as they were called, leases for renting lands on the estate were to be approved by a majority of the charter governors; the quorum for such meetings being only three governors. Of these charter meetings, that held in November was the most important. At it a secretary, treasurer and any other necessary officers were to be elected for the coming year. Also to be elected was a committee of seven governors to meet on the first Tuesday of every month, with a quorum again being three. This committee was to act as an executive, carrying into effect the decisions of the quarterly charter meetings. It could also make decisions of its own, but these were provisional till confirmed by the next charter board.

The charter also placed some important restrictions on the financial operations of the governors. They were to 'at all time confine their annual expenses and disbursements to their annual income'. Any monies received as gifts or bequests were to be 'lent out at interest, or laid out, from time to time, in purchasing lands, tenements, or hereditaments'. Monies from rents were to be used to feed, clothe and house the hospital's inmates. A limit, however, of £2,000 was placed upon the income that the governors could receive in any one year.[87] Thus the hospital's income was limited and its expenditure prescribed. When we come to discuss the history of St Patrick's we shall see that some provisions of the charter, particularly those relating to income, were disregarded by future boards. But for nearly 150 years, till three supplemental charters were obtained in 1889, 1896 and 1897, the hospital largely operated according to its 1746 charter.

But obtaining a charter was a relatively simple task, compared to that of recovering Swift's money from his mortgages.

When Swift was declared 'of unsound mind' in August 1742, three of his friends, Dr Francis Corbet, Alexander McAulay and John Rochfort, were appointed guardians by the court of chancery to manage his estate and to look after his person. In November the guardians employed Robert King, a Dublin attorney, as their agent. King's job was to receive the income of the estate, mainly consisting of interest on loans and tithe payments, and to pay Swift's expenses. For the next three years King's accounts show that large sums were paid regularly to Anne Ridgeway, who ran the Deanery and cared for Swift, and to the Rev. John Lyon, who handled the affairs of Rebecca Dingley, Stella's former companion. King also paid rent on some of Swift's holdings; he paid for the repair of Swift's churches and for preachers to take his place; and in 1743 he paid Surgeon John Nicholls for treating Swift.[88]

When Swift finally died in October 1745, under his will the estate now passed into the hands of his seven surviving executors, one of whom was Alexander McAulay. Despite McAulay's presence among both the guardians and the executors, a dispute nevertheless quickly arose between the two groups as to the precise value of Swift's legacy. In February 1747 the executors, who in 1746 had been constituted a board of governors by royal charter, complained in the court of chancery that the guardians had not supplied them with any documents, nor did they know how much money King, the guardians' agent, had in his hands. After hearing submissions from the governors, the guardians and from King himself, the court in July 1747 ordered one of its officials to consult with all parties and produce a full account of the estate. Below is a summary of the official's main findings:

Value of Swift's Estate in 1742	£10,562.18.8

Guardians' Accounts 1742-5

Receipts	3,132. 9.8
Expenditure	1,491.16.8
Balance Remaining	1,640.13.0

Executors'/Governors' Accounts 1745-7

Receipts	$2,043.19.11\frac{1}{2}$
Expenditure	$1,019.14. 4\frac{1}{2}$
Balance Remaining	1,024. 5. 7

Debts Still Outstanding in 1747	£10,696.16.5$\frac{1}{2}$[89]

On the basis of this report the court ruled in July 1748 that the balances remaining were to be passed to the governors and that

King was also to surrender to them all relevant documents. Both groups seem to have accepted the court's arbitration amicably: monies and documents were handed over. This reconciliation was doubtless helped by the fact that in 1746 Francis Corbet succeeded G. J. Maturin as dean of St Patrick's Cathedral. Corbet thereby automatically gained a seat on the board and in November 1747 his fellow governors expressed their confidence in him by electing him treasurer.

Sorting out matters with Swift's guardians was, however, probably the least of the governors' problems. Under both the 1740 will and the 1746 charter they were charged with purchasing an estate and building a hospital. In theory they had Swift's legacy, amounting by 1747 to over £13,000 available for these purposes. But, in practice, as the court assessment reveals, the governors in fact had only about £2,700 at their disposal, the remaining £11,000 being still in the hands of Swift's debtors. The calling in of these debts was thus the board's main priority. In October 1747 these debts consisted of:

Mortgages

Deane Swift	3,591. 0.9
Philip Denn	2,787.11.3
Alexander Lynch	2,542.16.5
	£8,921. 8. 5

Loans

Widow Throp	517.15.11
John Cashore	130. 0. 0
James Somervell	115. 6. 1
	£763. 2. 0

Tithes

Dr Francis Wilson	328. 0. 0
Daniel Griffin	$274.14.11\frac{1}{2}$
John Clynch	268.11. 1
Anion Challoner	141. 0. 0
	$£1,012. 6.0\frac{1}{2}$
Total	$£10,696.16.5\frac{1}{2}$[90]

As can be seen, by far the major part of the debt consisted of three mortgages. Between 1726 and 1739 Swift had lent his cousin, Deane Swift, £3,100 under five bonds at 6 per cent interest, the younger

Swift's estate at Castlerickard, Co. Meath, being security for the loan. In 1738-9, under two bonds, Swift lent Philip Denn £2,120 at 5 per cent interest, Denn's estate at Saggart, Co. Dublin, being security. In 1732 an earlier loan of Swift's was transferred to Alexander Lynch. This amounted to £2,000 at 5 per cent and was secured by lands in Co. Roscommon. In 1752, after legal action, the governors were able to recover the money owed them by Lynch, but the other two debts proved much more intractable.

Philip Denn had died about 1740 'in bad circumstances', owing money to a number of creditors beside Swift. In March 1747 the governors decided to foreclose on the mortgage. Other creditors seem to have followed their example for, in July 1750, Denn's estate was sold in chancery to pay his debts. The governors decided to bid for it and to make it the basis of the hospital's estate. By 1750 Denn's debt amounted to some £3,021 and so, when the governors success-fully offered £7,010 to Thomas Denn for his father's land, they were in fact committing themselves to paying about £4,000. Some £3,000 of this sum was paid to Thomas and to his father's creditors in 1751 and 1752. The final payment of £1,000 the governors withheld when the Denn family's ownership of a part of the estate was disputed.

It was Deane Swift's debt, however, which proved in the long run the most difficult to recover. Correspondence between him and the governors reveals that he was exceedingly unreliable in his interest payments, although he did pay some £1,100 between 1748 and 1754. The governors alternately threatened and cajoled him, but it ap-pears that they were reluctant to foreclose as they had done in the case of Denn. Presumably bankrupting their founder's kinsman and friend was considered an unacceptable means of recovering their money. By the mid 1750s, however, the governors were in desper-ate need of ready cash. As we shall see, they were unable to open the hospital because they lacked the money to run it. In these difficult circumstances the governors resorted to the ingenious strategy of selling one of Deane Swift's bonds. In 1726 he had borrowed a little over £1,000 from his famous name-sake to pay debts arising from his father's will. In 1755 the board of the hospital sold this bond, with its accumulated interest, to Thomas Loftus for £1,800. Thereby Thomas Loftus joined the governors in holding a mortgage on Swift's estate and being entitled to regular interest payments. The governors used the cash raised to buy further land at Saggart. This, however, was by no means the end of the story of Deane Swift's debt. Fifty years later, when Deane Swift had been twenty years dead, his estate had finally to be sold in chancery to pay his debts both to the hospital and to the Loftus family.[91]

How much of the remaining smaller debts the governors were

able to recover is not altogether clear from the surviving accounts. Widow Throp repaid her loan in 1749, but Wilson and Challoner both died and legal action had to be taken against their estates. There was, however, another small debt, not recorded in the above list, which is worth taking note of. Swift had since his appointment as dean lent small sums of money, usually £5, to a large number of Dublin tradespeople and shopkeepers. This was called his 'industry money' and it was lent at no interest, repayment not to begin till 14 months after the loan. Swift hoped in this way to help small traders and promote local enterprise. The loans were managed by his housekeeper: first Jane Brent and then, after her death in 1735, by her daughter, Anne Ridgeway. Nearly ninety bonds for such loans survive, covering the period 1718 to 1744.[92] However, having examined these and other documents, the governors in July 1749 reported that they were drawn up in 'an irregular and confused' way, so that they could not find out the exact amount still owing. Anne Ridgeway had handed over £27 and said that the arrears amounted to £208. Being 'a woman of fair good character', the board accepted her word. An account drawn up by William Dryden, the first master of the hospital, shows that he recovered some £22 on fourteen bonds in 1750. Whether any more of this money was forthcoming is not clear. Under Swift's will Anne Ridgeway had been treated generously, being left the rents of two houses, a £100 legacy, a £20 a year annuity and three gold rings. The legacy had been paid to her in 1747, but in 1748 she returned £60 as a donation to the hospital. One wonders if her generosity may perhaps have been partly motivated by concern at the money lost in the industry loan scheme.[93]

Between them Swift's will and the hospital's royal charter provided the governors with an outline of what they had to do. There were many details, however, that they themselves would have to fill in. Lack of money was the most obvious impediment they faced. But, we need to appreciate that the enterprise the governors were embarking on was an unprecedented one. A number of hospitals had certainly been established in Dublin in the preceding thirty years, but purpose-built asylums were unknown in Ireland. In England the only model available was Bethlem Hospital; however, Swift had specifically conceived his hospital in reaction against the abuses prevailing in Bedlam. There were reformers in England too, who wanted to create more humane madhouses. But their first effort, St Luke's Hospital in London, was not planned till 1750 and, when it opened in 1751, it was housed in a renovated foundry rather than in a new building. If anything the founders of St Luke's were probably influenced by the moves to establish a modern asylum in Dublin, rather than the other way round.[94] That the hospital was eventually built and, moreover, that what was built remains in use today is a great tribute to the determination and foresight of the first board of governors.[95]

CHAPTER 2

Swift's Hospital: The Early Years, 1747-1820

Thanks be to God hospitals for lunaticks above all others are most necessary. The friends of people in other disorders can be of some service to them at home and get them cured, but in this most dreadful malady they can get no peace day or night, nor be of any service to them to get them managed or cured. But at the hospital the wit of man cannot contrive better and all is done without any [ill] usage or violence to the patients . . . It is a noble legacy the Dean has left to the public and the governors have improved the plan greatly . . .[1]

He proceeded to the door,—it was fastened. He called aloud,—his voice was echoed in a moment by many others, but in tones so wild and discordant, that he desisted in involuntary terror . . . he tried the window, and then perceived for the first time it was grated. It looked out on the narrow flagged yard, in which no human being was; and if there had from such a being no human feeling could have been extracted.[2]

. . . the building, as directed by Swift, in his will, was erected in the vicinity of Dr Steevens Hospital, adjoining to James's-street, in the city of Dublin. The Dean is said to have observed, that, if it could be made to reach from thence to the Phoenix Park, there would always be a sufficient number of occupants . . . I am informed, that the utmost order and cleanliness prevail throughout this asylum, and that the unfortunate inhabitants are, upon no occasion whatever, subjected to punishment or severity.[3]

THE BUILDING AND OPENING OF THE HOSPITAL

The board of governors of St Patrick's Hospital held its first meeting at Lord Chancellor Newport's house on Friday, 29 August 1746. Of the fourteen members, eleven attended, the absentees being Archbishop Stone of Armagh, Bishop Fletcher of Kildare who was also dean of Christ Church, Surgeon General John Nicholls and Dr Patrick Delany. According to the minutes, little business was conducted, but the charter was read out and seven governors were nominated to form an executive committee. At the next meeting, held on Monday 3 November, in the palace of the archbishop of Dublin, Rev. John Lyon was elected secretary to the board, a position he was to hold for forty years, and William Dryden, a distant relative of Swift's who was later to become steward of Dr Steevens Hospital, was appointed master of the hospital and receiver of its income. Robert King, formerly agent for Swift's guardians, initially acted as legal agent for the governors as well, but in November 1748 he was replaced by Redmond Kane.[4] When Dr G.J. Maturin, Swift's successor as dean of St Patrick's, died suddenly in 1746, he was succeeded by Francis Corbet, who had been one of Swift's guardians. In November 1747 Dean Corbet was elected treasurer to the board, a position he was to occupy for the next ten years.[5] It was these men, the fourteen governors, plus the secretary, the master and the law agent, who were to realise Swift's dream of a Dublin mental hospital, but it was to take them eleven years to do so.

When they first met, late in 1746, the governors faced several pressing tasks: they had to decide on a site for the proposed hospital and acquire the land; they had to ensure that they had sufficient money both to build and to operate the hospital, and they had to agree on a plan for the building and to supervise its construction. Early in 1747 they turned their attention to the first task of acquiring land. Swift had in his will expressed a preference for situating his hospital near Dr Steevens Hospital; the medical facilities of Steevens could thus be availed of in cases of physical illness or injury. Steevens was then in semi-rural surroundings on the western outskirts of the city—just the sort of 'open air' site that Fownes had recommended to Swift back in 1732. This pleasant setting, on a ridge sloping up from the River Liffey, was, in the opinion of the time, calculated to act as a calming influence upon severely troubled minds. At the charter board meeting on 2 February 1747 Archbishop Cobbe of Dublin and John Nicholls, who were both members of the board of Steevens Hospital—Nicholls being in addition visiting surgeon—were asked to apply to their fellow members 'to know whether they can conveniently spare and are willing to set apart and grant to this corporation a piece of ground, part of their possession, for erecting a hospital thereon . . .' The governors of Steevens met on 5 March and agreed to offer $1\frac{1}{4}$ acres of their land—'in front to the lane leading to Bow Bridge 180 feet and from thence to the door of the burial ground 490 feet'—at an annual rent of £10. Meeting two weeks later, the governors of Swift's hospital readily agreed to accept this small plot of land, it being 'a convenient and proper place for building St Patrick's Hospital upon'.[6] They seemed eager to proceed with their task for they decided to lease the land initially, so building work could be expedited. Steevens, under its charter, was only empowered to lease land for a maximum of sixty-one years and thus, in order to acquire the land in perpetuity, the governors had to obtain a special act of parliament, which they did in 1748.[7] Yet, despite this apparent haste, it was to be nearly three years before construction was begun, another three years before it was completed and a further four years before the hospital actually opened to receive patients. A number of factors contributed to this delay, the most important being simple lack of money.

Between 1748 and 1757 Dean Corbet entered his annual accounts in the governors' minute book. The accounts are, unfortunately, not complete, but they do appear to record most of the board's financial transactions. The table below summarises them:

ACCOUNTS OF THE GOVERNORS OF ST PATRICK'S HOSPITAL 1748-1757

Sums rounded off to nearest pound

Year	Income£	Expenditure£	Credit/Deficit£
1748	2,152	153	+1,999
1749	1,854	767	+1,087
1750	342	1,908	−1,566
1751	545	2,081	−1,536
1752	4,230	4,557	− 327
1753	1,518	933	+ 585
1754	392	861	− 469
1755	2,866	2,639	+ 227
1756	1,248	263	+ 985
1757	100	611	− 511
Total	**15,247**	**14,773**	**+ 474**[8]

As regards the receipts side of the ledger, during these ten years the governors had six principal sources of income. Their substantial revenue in the year 1748 was largely made up of money paid over to them by Robert King, the agent for the guardians who had managed Swift's affairs from 1742 to 1745. In 1749, 1752 and 1755 income was boosted by large loan repayments, which, sometimes only after legal action by Redmond Kane, had been extracted from Alexander Lynch, Deane Swift and Mrs Throp. In the years before the opening of the hospital, the governors also received a number of large donations from private individuals or their estates. The main ones were:

John Bolton	£1,000 on condition that he receive a £50 annuity during his lifetime.
Bishop Stearne of Clogher	£600
Sir Richard Levinge	£500
Dr Joshua Pulleine	£500
Rev. John Worrall	£500 plus the leasehold of about 6 acres of land near Kilmainham.
Alderman Benjamin Bowen	£250
Dr Christopher Donnellan	£200
Rev. Robert Grattan	£200[9]

Several of these benefactors had been personal friends of Swift and in recognition of their aid the governors decided to name wards after Levinge, Pulleine, Worrall and Bowen.[10] At various times in fact, up to the beginning of the nineteenth century, the governors were in receipt of bequests—sometimes substantial bequests. But often these proved more trouble than they were worth. A number were successfully contested by relatives, leaving the governors with nothing but legal bills.[11] An odd bequest that the hospital did not benefit from was made by Bishop Richard Pococke of Meath, who died in 1765. He left his estate to endow protestant schools 'while the protestant religion shall continue to be professed in Ireland; but in case the protestant religion be not publicly professed by law, then the said endowment shall go to the Governors of St Patrick's Hospital, founded by Doctor Swift for lunaticks and ideots'.[12] Presumably the good bishop felt that if Protestantism vanished from Ireland, the country would indeed require the services of a madhouse.

The governors, however, did not just passively wait for generous individuals to offer them money, they actively sought donations for the hospital. It was common practice in mid eighteenth-century

Dublin for hospitals and other charitable institutions to solicit funds from the public. Plays and concerts were organised, lotteries run and charity sermons preached, all to raise money. The Lying-in, later Rotunda, Hospital opening in temporary premises in 1745 without any endowment, became especially noted for its pleasure gardens and musical entertainments.[13] But the governors of Swift's hospital did not pursue this particular form of fund-raising. Perhaps they felt that, in light of the abuses prevalent in Bedlam, it was best to keep public entertainment and lunatics well apart. What the board did do, however, was to send out subscription rolls in 1750 to Dublin bankers and 'charitably-inclined' persons who might be prepared to receive donations on behalf of the hospital.

According to accounts drawn up by William Dryden, sixty such rolls were engraved on parchment, sealed with wax and tied with silk ribbon at a total cost of nearly £6.[14] Early in 1751 the board also decided to wait upon the lord mayor to seek funds for a ward to be called the city ward. What, if anything, came of this step is unclear from the surviving records, but no ward appears to have been named after the city. The subscription rolls were clearly circulated well beyond Dublin for, in May 1751, the board, complaining that rolls sent to borough and town magistrates had not been returned except for one from the mayor of Kilkenny, decided to write asking that they be sent back.[15] It would seem then that the call for subscriptions had not been a great success. Corbet's figures are not wholly clear, but they suggest that, while the governors received around £4,200 in voluntary donations up to 1755, they were only able to raise some £450 through subscriptions in 1751 and 1752. Thus fund-raising by means of subscription was not repeated.

The fifth important source of revenue for the governors was the one that Swift himself had envisaged as the hospital's main support: rents from an estate. As mentioned in the previous chapter, the governors bought Philip Denn's estate at Saggart, Co. Dublin, when it was sold in chancery in 1750 and they also set about buying parcels of land that were intermixed with Denn's.[16] By 1756 they had about 900 acres and a significant proportion of the large sums expended in 1751, 1752 and 1755 had gone towards acquiring this. All in all, according to Corbet's accounts, some £6,800 was spent in this way up to 1755. But, while the estate was being bought and organised, income from rents was not substantial, amounting to only £968 during the five years from 1752 to 1756. Through Swift's friend, the Rev. John Worrall, the governors had also acquired nearly six acres at Goldenbridge, near Kilmainham. But the annual rent was only £9.14.0.[17] So, prior to the opening of the hospital, rents were not producing nearly enough to run the institution. As we shall see, this state of affairs was to force the governors to abandon Swift's dream of a charity hospital.

The final source of income for the governors was the Irish parliament. In November 1755 they petitioned the House of Commons for 'some national bounty'. The 'fund of the founder' said the petition, had been exhausted in the building of the hospital and the purchase of the estate. There were not sufficient funds to furnish the hospital, nor would the annual rents cover the costs of running it.[18] When parliament voted a £1,000 grant in the following year, the governors were able to fit up two wards for the reception of patients and, when another petition raised the same sum in 1758, they were able to admit more free patients and to furnish three rooms for paying boarders.[19] But, again in the case of parliamentary grants as with public subscriptions, one has the impression that St Patrick's did not fare nearly as well as other Dublin hospitals. For instance, in 1755-6, just as parliament was granting the governors £1,000, it was giving £6,000 to the Lying-in Hospital to enable it to complete its impressive new building in Great Britain (now Parnell) Street. In 1757, just as St Patrick's was petitioning again, parliament was giving the Rotunda another £6,000, with a further £2,000 for Dr Bartholomew Mosse, its founder. While St Patrick's continued to receive occasional small grants till 1800, in 1785 parliament guaranteed the Rotunda a permanent income by placing a special tax on private sedan chairs, the proceeds of which were to go to the hospital.[20] The lord mayor and corporation also granted money towards a ward at the Lying-in Hospital, something they had apparently rejected doing for Swift's hospital. The contrast between Ireland's first maternity hospital and its first madhouse extended beyond money, however. The Rotunda's new premises were opened by the lord lieutenant amid considerable celebrations in December 1757; in contrast, the opening of St Patrick's Hospital three months previously passed off without any ceremony at all. The truth seems to be that, among Dublin society, few shared Swift's enthusiasm for helping 'lunaticks and ideots'. The Lying-in Hospital, with its splendid gardens and assembly rooms at the top of fashionable Sackville (now O'Connell) Street, was a far more attractive charity than Swift's gloomy madhouse out in Bow Lane.

The fact that the governors had to petition parliament in 1755 and again in 1757 for money with which to open the hospital illustrates the seriousness of their financial difficulties. Dean Corbet's accounts suggest that in five out of the ten years from 1748 to 1757 the board's expenditure exceeded its receipts. As we have seen, nearly half of the money spent went towards purchasing an estate at Saggart. In the mid and late 1750s the governors were preoccupied, not only with opening the hospital, but also with organising their new estate: the land had to be surveyed and accurate maps prepared; existing leases had to be checked and, in some cases, new ones drawn up; and the board had to review the level of rents and decide what to do about tenants in arrears.[21] Much of the work of dealing with the tenants fell to the treasurer—Dean Corbet 1747-55, 1756-7; Benjamin Bowen 1755-6; Anthony Foster 1757-77—but in July 1757 the governors appointed their own land agent for receiving rents in the person of Bernard Kane, a relative of Redmond Kane, their law agent. The earliest surviving rent roll, dating from March 1758, shows 48 holdings, comprising in all nearly 900 acres, with an annual rental of £666 and arrears of £540.[22] It appears that when the governors bought the estate, rents had been lower and arrears higher, Philip Denn clearly not having been a efficient landlord. The board's attempts to clarify boundaries and increase revenue, however, met with resistance from the tenants. Some disputed the accuracy of the new survey; others complained at the level of their rents; while others argued among themselves.[23] It was common practice in the eighteenth century for charitable, educational and professional bodies to own estates, just as today such organisations would probably have money invested in stocks and shares. Land ownership generated income in the form of rents and thus provided financial security—or, at least, it was supposed to do so. As we shall see, however, with regard to St Patrick's estate, the problems of Irish landlordism were such that estates often produced more insecurity than security.

After the purchase of the estate, the construction of the hospital building was the governors' other main task. But, there were also a number of smaller obligations Swift had placed upon his heirs that are worth mentioning briefly. The governors, for instance, were responsible for erecting the famous memorial in St Patrick's Cathedral inscribed with Swift's own epitaph. In December 1747, two years after his death, they ordered that it be made and in October 1749 a Mr Haughton was paid £26.10.0 for the work.[24] The governors, as executors of Swift's will, were also charged with seeing that the bequests made to his friends and relatives were carried out. Sometimes though, they seem to have been rather less than generous in making good Swift's wishes. By November 1748, for instance, John Whiteway's bequest of £100, plus £5 for books to help with his medical studies, had still not been paid and Whiteway issued a 'demand against the executors for his legacy from Doctor Swift'. In response the board instructed Dean Corbet to pay Whiteway £33 and the £5 for books out of the arrears of Swift's tithes that it had recovered. But, as for the rest, the governors urged

Whiteway to sue Mr Cashore of Trim who owed them tithes for Swift's parish of Laracor. This seems a rather niggardly response to Whiteway's just demand, though the board did go on to offer to pay the legal costs of such an action. It is not clear whether Whiteway followed this advice or not, but Cashore did pay the governors £50 in January 1749 and this was passed on to him. Corbet's accounts record that Whiteway received his remaining £17 in August 1749.[25] It is probably a fair reflection of the governors' financial problems that it took John Whiteway four years to recover his modest inheritance. Certainly there seem to have been no hard feelings in the matter for in 1757 Whiteway was appointed the hospital's first visiting surgeon, a post he filled for over forty years.

It was the erection and opening of the hospital, however, that took up most of the governors' attention and much of their income, in the years from 1747 to 1757. In March 1747, as we have seen, Dr Steevens Hospital agreed to provide a small amount of land fronting Bow Lane for the purpose of building St Patrick's. But, in fact, it was nearly three years before construction commenced, as the governors became involved in lengthy discussions over plans and architects. In considering the building of the hospital we need constantly to keep in mind that no such institution had ever been built in Ireland before and, except for Bedlam, there was no comparable building in England either. Thus, the question arises of what or who inspired the building plan? The governors' first step was to build a high wall around the site. This was done in 1747-8 at a cost of £146, the work being supervised by Michael Wills, who had been clerk of works at Steevens Hospital during its construction.[26] Early in 1747 the two medical men on the board, Robert Robinson and John Nicholls, had been asked by their fellow governors to consider 'the size and proportion of the cells for the accommodation of lunatics and idiots' and, at the same time, they and Dean Corbet arranged to inspect the boundaries of the site. Presumably it was felt that, as doctors, Robinson and Nicholls were best qualified to decide on how the inmates of the hospital should be housed. But it was not till a year later, in May 1758, that they finally laid before the board a 'plan for the hospital' and it was decided to advertise for 'proposals' from 'workmen'.[27] In the meantime the governors had been recovering Swift's money from his guardians and had in addition received several large bequests, notably from Bishop Stearne and Sir Richard Levinge.[28] Perhaps it had indeed taken Robinson and Nicholls a whole year to formulate a plan or perhaps the governors were unwilling to proceed to advertise until their finances were in a reasonably healthy state. Whatever the reason, the board quickly accepted proposals for building the hospital put forward by Michael

Wills in July 1748. Wills appears to have drawn up his plan in consultation with Robinson and Nicholls, for the board minutes refer to him working under their 'direction'.[29]

But Michael Wills was not to be the architect of St Patrick's Hospital. At the charter meeting held in November 1748, four months after Wills's plan had been accepted, '. . . George Semple . . . laid before the board a new plan for St Patrick's Hospital with an estimate of the expense and charges of building . . .' Semple's plan was referred to Robinson and Nicholls 'for their inspection in private'. It was also shown to Wills for, by February 1749, he had 'reduced and amended' his own plan as a result of studying Semple's. The governors then ordered Wills's amended plan to be laid before Semple for his comments, and at another meeting in February 1749 they considered both Semple's comments and Wills's response to them.[30] These two architects were obviously competing to design the new hospital, yet the board was cleverly using them to assess each other's proposals. Wills might have seemed the stronger candidate for the job. He was clearly working closely with Robinson and Nicholls—perhaps Nicholls, as a governor and visiting physician at Steevens Hospital, knew him through his work there—and had already supervised the building of the hospital's walls.[31] Semple was a younger, and almost certainly less experienced, man, but he probably had a powerful supporter in the person of Dean Corbet. For, in 1749, just as the governors of St Patrick's Hospital were deciding if Semple or Wills should be their architect, Semple was being employed to add a spire to the tower of St Patrick's Cathedral.[32] Dean Corbet, who was the moving force in efforts to restore the cathedral, must have had a major role in this appointment and, although the evidence is far from conclusive, we can also detect his hand in Semple's selection as hospital architect. Although Robinson and Nicholls had in 1747 been assigned the task of considering plans for the hospital, by 1749 it was Dean Corbet who had taken over this job. All Semple's notes and plans were, for instance, countersigned by him. If Semple did indeed have this man's support, then the board's decision in April 1749 to accept his plan in preference to Wills's is understandable. Wills, however, was clearly unhappy with the outcome and responded by demanding payment from the governors 'for half a year's service'. In December 1749 the board agreed that £39 was a 'reasonable' sum with which to compensate him for his trouble. Ill-feeling between Semple and Wills seems to have persisted though, for in 1751-2 they were engaged in a dispute over plans to re-build Essex Bridge.[33]

Among the papers in the hospital archives is a small, single sheet, undated and unsigned, but headed: 'Offices and Apartments of the following Dimensions in the Plan of George Semple, which are not in Mr Wills's'. Below is a list of seventeen points on which Semple's plan is considered superior, or at least equivalent, to that of Wills: for instance, 'Semple's cells, agree exactly with the cells of Bedlam Hospital'; 'The gallerys in Semple's and Wills's plans 15 feet wide each'; 'The Committee room not in Wills's plan'; 'The surgery in Semple's plan is larger by 6 feet more than the surgery of Bedlam Hospital—Mr Wills has a surgery'; '5 Privy Houses, not one in Mr Wills's Plan'; 'Two yards for burning foul straw—none in Mr Wills's Plan'. These notes must have been made, possibly by the board's secretary the Rev. John Lyon, during the five months from November 1748, when Semple first submitted his plan, to April 1749, when the governors accepted it. They tell us something about Wills's proposal which has not survived, but, perhaps more importantly, they make it abundantly clear that the model upon which St Patrick's was based was Bethlem Hospital in London.[34]

Bethlem had been moved in 1676 from its old site in present-day Liverpool Street, to a purpose-built hospital, described by the diarist John Evelyn as 'magnificently built', at Moorfields, near the present Finsbury Circus.[35] This was the hospital that Swift would have been familiar with, for it occupied the site till its move to Southwark in 1815. When we examine descriptions of the Moorfields building, basic similarities to St Patrick's are immediately obvious, though Bethlem was considerably larger and grander than the Dublin institution. Both, however, were two-storied buildings over a basement floor; both had an entrance hall and offices at the ground floor front, with a grand staircase rising to a boardroom above; both had long galleries with cells opening off them on all three floors; and at the entrance to each gallery was a keeper's room. The most striking difference between the two buildings was that at St Patrick's the galleries, or ranges as they were called, were at right angles to the central block; at Bethlem the galleries extended from either side of the central block. The narrowness of St Patrick's frontage on Bow Lane dictated that the ranges housing patients should be behind the main entrance to the hospital, rather than beside it as at Bethlem.[36]

The notes comparing Semple's and Wills's plans make it clear that the governors wanted not only to reproduce the general lay-out of Bethlem, but some of the proportions as well. At the meeting in April 1749 which finally approved Semple's plan, the board decreed that cells should be eight feet by twelve feet in size, this 'being the proportion observed in the Bedlam Hospital in London' and that the walls separating them should be of brick, 'fourteen inches below and nine inches above'. It is possible that Robinson or Nicholls may have visited Bethlem Hospital at some time or that they may have been in correspondence with some of the governors or doctors there. For it is obvious that, among the governors of Swift's hospital, someone had a detailed knowledge of the size and arrangement of the Moorfields hospital. It is even conceivable that Semple himself had advice from someone connected with Bethlem. In March 1751, while building work was in progress, Semple met with the board and, in an intriguing remark, said that he had been advised about the hospital plan by a Mr Jennings, 'a person well recommended for his skill in the care of lunaticks'.[37] Who exactly Mr Jennings was is not clear, but it is hardly surprising that, in undertaking the construction of such an unusual building, the architect should seek guidance from a person experienced in the management of the insane. Unfortunately, we do not know if Mr Jennings's experience was gained at Bethlem or in a smaller private asylum.

In July 1749 Semple was instructed to supply materials for the foundations of the hospital. In November he informed the board that he had 'laid in a great quantity of materials for the building' and in December the governors ordered that, 'Mr Semple do proceed immediately to execute the front part of the building'.[38] In February 1750[39] Semple signed articles of agreement with the governors and delivered to them a book of plans with explanatory notes. We are fortunate that this book, dated 2 February 1749 under the old-style, Julian calendar then in use, has survived, for it provides a detailed account, not only of Semple's plans, but also of the reasoning behind much of them. The book contains six drawings, plus twenty-three pages of 'further description of the foregoing designs: and the methods intended to be taken in the execution thereof'.[40]

Semple's plan envisaged a simple, U-shaped building, extending down the slope from the narrow frontage on Bow Lane towards Steevens Hospital. The arms of the U, described as the east and west ranges, were to contain the patients' cells opening onto long corridors. As we have noted, the building was to be on three levels: basement, ground and first floors, described in the plans as first, second and third floors. On the basement level both ranges would contain a ward of eight cells, plus a room for a keeper; with male patients in the west range and females in the east. The six rooms in the basement of the front of the building and the five rooms facing them under the courtyard were to be used for a kitchen, laundry, storerooms and as accommodation for servants. On the ground floor above, the ranges were to be laid out in the same manner as in the basement, with eight cells in each for male and female lunatics, giving in all on the two floors accommodation for thirty-two inmates. At the ground floor front there was to be an impressive entrance hall, with a staircase leading to the floor above. The three rooms on each side of the entrance were to be used by the hospital's doctors and officers. In these 1750 plans and notes the first floor was nowhere near as completely laid out as the two floors below. In the front block there was a large room, measuring thirty-three by eighteen feet with fireplaces at each end, for the governors to hold their meetings in. But it was, according to Semple, 'not intended to finish this room at the present, but to allow the walls to dry, and to let the governors have it done, as they may hereafter to think convenient'. The governors had apparently not yet decided how the whole of this floor was to be used, for Semple noted that it might 'be fitted up, for the reception of idiots, or for the reception of such of the lunaticks, as are seemingly cured and made sociable'.[41] It is interesting to observe Semple here proposing the separation of patients according to the nature or seriousness of their disorders. Perhaps this was something that Mr Jennings had suggested to him; certainly, in the late 1720s and early 1730s, additional wards were built at Bethlem Hospital to house patients regarded as incurable.[42] But, Semple's own design of long corridors with small individual rooms opening off them was in fact to make any such separation of patients extremely difficult. Finally, in his 1750 plans Semple provided for airing courts and outhouses, containing baths and toilets, on both sides of the building.

Semple's notes contain fascinating incidental details on many aspects of the building. For instance, the sewers which were to run under and around the hospital before emptying into the Camac River to the west of the site, were to 'widen one inch in every fourteen feet' as they were 'to receive the sullage of many conduits'. In addition, the 'seats of the privies' were to be 'directly over the middle of the sewers, because it is intended that all the water of the baths, cisterns etc, will at certain times be discharged – deluge'.[43] In the event the sewers were to prove inadequate for this 'deluge'. For, despite Semple's obvious concern to provide a proper sewerage and drainage system, his decision to run sewers under the building was to prove a serious mistake. When these pipes cracked or became blocked, as in time they inevitably did, their contents seeped into the walls and basement of the hospital, undermining the structure as well as creating a major health hazard. The walls of the building, Semple decided, were to be four feet thick and of 'common rough stone', faced, on the basement level, with 'plain mountain stone' and, on the ground and first stories, with 'Killgobbin stone'. Semple took enormous care over the mortar to be used for the walls, specifying, among other things, that the sand and water content was to be kept low and that the workmen were to 'apply very hard labour to supply the usual place of water'.[44]

It is in regard to the interior of the hospital, however, that Semple's plans are perhaps most interesting and reveal most clearly the special design problems that he faced. He discussed at some length, for instance, the doors, floors and windows of the cells. The doors had, above all, to be strong: those of the cells being two feet six inches wide by six feet high and made of 'very stout whole deal'. In addition:

> Each of these cell doors must have a small wicket door; to hand the patients their provisions etc. And this wicket door must be about $4\frac{1}{2}$ feet high from the floor and about five by ten inches square. And as the poor patients may at sometime be indolent and not ready to receive their provision from their keepers, there must be a solid bracket of red fir, very stoutly nailed, on the outside of these wicket doors, for the keepers to rest their provision on till they please to take it.[45]

Semple's sensitivity to the problems of the building's inhabitants is here evident, both in his reference to the 'poor patients' and in the care taken to ensure that they should be fed. At the entrances to the wards, in addition to strong wooden doors, there were to be 'iron grated doors, hung on the inside'. These were to be three feet six inches wide by seven feet high and made of 'slender half feet bar iron', each with six upright bars, seven cross bars and one diagonal bar and secured with a sturdy bolt. Similar iron gates secured the wards in Bethlem Hospital and they, plus the use of the word 'cell' to describe patients' rooms, underline the prison-like aspect of eighteenth-century asylums. A further, novel method of restraint for St Patrick's was suggested by Semple's adviser, Jennings, who recommended the installation at the end of each ward of a 'chair firmly fixed near the wall in order to secure raging lunaticks during their extreme illness'.[46] Perhaps this was considered a more humane way of restraining violent inmates than chaining them to the walls or to their beds, as was the practice in Bedlam.

In the basement the cells were to be securely floored with two-inch oak planks—though these proved little use against severe rising damp—and in the two floors above with whole deal. The cell walls were to be lined with brick and the partition walls were to be two bricks thick. All walls were to be plastered with 'common plastering'. For two feet above the floor the cell walls were to be further lined with one-inch thick oak planks. But, 'as the patients are at times very outrageous they will be in danger of being torn off'.

So Semple advised that the wood panelling be not only nailed to the walls, but secured with iron plates set into the floors and with bolts through the partition walls. It must have been rare for an architect to have to incorporate into his design methods to prevent his building from being wrecked by its inhabitants. But, with regard to the cells at least, this is exactly what Semple had to do. As for the cell windows, they were to be small, only two feet six inches square, and to be set at least seven feet above the floor. Moreover, all were 'to be built convex, so that the patients may have nothing to take hold of, when they offer to climb up to the windows'. They were to contain two iron bars and to have 'outside shutters of whole deal hedged and barred so that the keepers, by the help of a stepladder, may shut the patients closely up when any extreme cold weather comes on'. The corridors of the wards were to be flagged with 'common Mountmellick flags'. But, as the cells would need to be washed out frequently, a channel would have to be cut in the flagstones beside the cells, with four or five holes between each cell door. The dirty water could then run into the channel and down the holes into conduits leading to the sewers.[47]

Unfortunately, no pictures of the interior of St Patrick's during the eighteenth century appear to exist, but some idea of what the corridors and cells may have been like can be gleaned from an examination of the eighth painting in William Hogarth's series 'A Rake's Progress'. This picture, painted in the early 1730s and entitled 'The Rake in Bedlam', portrays the new, male incurable ward in Bethlem Hospital and, according to the hospital's historian, it is extremely accurate with regard to the physical details of the building.[48] We see the ward corridor with its iron gate and opening off it are the cells, with their stout doors and small high windows. Ignoring the colourful cast of characters who people the picture, we have here a reasonable representation of the main features of the hospital that Semple built in Dublin in the early 1750s, using Bethlem as his model.

Semple's notes show that he thought carefully about the function of the building and how best to accommodate that in his plans. Some aspects of his design were certainly ingenious, but others were much less successful. Swift had specified in his will that the hospital should be constructed so that it could be enlarged if further money later became available. This specification certainly influenced Semple's design, for the ranges could easily be extended and in his notes he pointed out that: 'There is to be toothing left at the north end of the flank walls; because it is directed, that said building may be "enlarged from time to time as occasion may require"'.[49] But, because the yard between the two ranges was only thirty-seven feet six inches wide, the corridors running down the side facing each other were very dark; and this problem became considerably worse when the ranges were extended later in the century. Further building only accentuated the basic problems of the U-shaped design. Semple's original plans of 1750 show that he only envisaged five windows in each of the inward-facing corridors, yet plans drawn up in 1778 to extend the ranges show ten windows in each corridor and that is certainly the number there today. Whether Semple himself had doubled the number during the course of building in order to admit more light or whether this was done subsequently by someone else is not clear. Strangely though, the 1778 plans only envisaged five windows in the range extensions. But, regardless of how many windows were provided, the ranges remained dark and their outlook rather bleak. The windows in the cells were of course small and well above head height which must have made the cells, too, very gloomy. This problem of light was most severe in the basement. Semple in his plans calls it the first floor, but in the front at least it was below ground level with all the problems of dark and damp that that entails.

As well as lack of light, Semple's plans and notes also suggest that cold would have been a problem. The windows of the range corridors were not glazed, nor did they have shutters. The cell windows did have shutters on the basement and first floor and those on the ground floor were glazed. The keepers' rooms and the rooms in the front of the building were all provided with fireplaces, but the cells and corridors were not. So, in winter, the wards in the ranges would have been extremely cold. In December 1757, only three months after the opening of the hospital, the governors decided to provide stoves for the wards—presumably there had been complaints about the cold. But these stoves do not seem to have been adequate, for in August 1762 there is a reference in the minutes to a plan to build fireplaces in the wards to replace the stoves.[50] Certainly, in the plans of 1778 to extend the ranges, a fireplace was provided in each new corridor.

The actual construction of the hospital appears to have taken place between December 1749, when Semple was ordered to 'proceed immediately to execute the front part of the building', and May 1753, when the governors appointed three inspectors to examine the 'whole work done and finished by the said Semple'. The front was put up first, early in 1750. In July the governors were hoping to receive a loan of £1,000 and Semple was instructed to begin the east range as soon as this loan was received; but it was not till February 1751 that Semple was definitely ordered to proceed due to 'many benefactions already paid in and expected to be paid in a short time'. In May 1751 he was working on the top floor of this range, which had been left blank in his original plans, and approached the governors to know how they wanted it fitted up. They directed him to install cells as on the two floors below. In November the range was inspected by a committee which seems to have criticised some of the stone work, for Semple appeared before the board in person in December and promised 'to take out of the eastern range of the building such slabs or bad stones as are liable to decay and to fix good durable stones in the room of them'. The governors were informed that stone from the quarries at Kilmainham was a 'perishable kind' and Semple was told not to use it. In February 1752, at their next quarterly meeting, the governors considered the building of the west range, but decided that 'the same be not proceeded upon by Mr Semple according to his contract with the governors and that the said contract be mutually dissolved'. This abrupt termination of the project was due to lack of money. Only nineteen days later, however, the governors met again and resolved that, as £1,300 had just been received in benefactions from the Rev. Dr Pulleine and the Rev. John Worrall, Semple should proceed with the west range according to his original plan. In appreciation of these very timely donations two plaques were to be fixed to the outside of the building 'with these words deeply cut and gilt Pulleine ward for 12 patients and Worrall's ward for 12 patients'. By April 1752 the basement of this range was finished and in July Semple was consulting with the board over the front courtyard and the laying of water pipes. In August a committee of the governors was instructed to inspect the materials remaining after the completion of the west range and recommend what should be done with them. Presumably the building was externally complete by this time, though a final inspection was not ordered till May 1753, which suggests that further internal work may have been required. Only in November was this final report received. It must have satisfied the governors, however, for Semple was paid his outstanding money and allowed to take away the leftover building materials from the site.[51]

What is perhaps most striking about this account is the slowness of the construction work and the fact that it was halted on several occasions due to the board's lack of money. The minutes of meetings held between 1750 and 1753 reveal that the governors struggled to raise money to pay for the hospital as building was actually in progress. Sometimes payments to Semple fell considerably behind schedule and, as noted, on at least one occasion Semple's contract was terminated because the board did not have the money with which to proceed. In the contract, signed in

February 1750, Semple had estimated the cost of the whole building at £4,560 and this is what he was paid over the next three and a half years; plus an additional £500 for work not covered in the contract. This sum may have related to the work involved in fitting up the first floor, which had been left uncompleted in Semple's original plans. Thus St Patrick's Hospital took a little over three years to build and cost a little over £5,000. Both the design and some of the construction work were to cause problems in the future, yet, compared to similar institutions, it would seem that the governors got good value for the limited funds invested. The 'magnificent' Bethlem Hospital at Moorfields, for instance, cost £17,000 and took only fifteen months to build in 1675-6. But, within a century, the building was in a dilapidated and dangerous condition due to the poor quality of the brickwork and early in the nineteenth century it had to be abandoned.[52] St Luke's moved from its converted foundry at Windmill Hill in 1787 to a purpose-built hospital in Old Street. This had taken four years to build at a cost somewhere in the vicinity of £46,000. It proved to be a sturdy and enduring building, but at such a huge cost one would have expected it to be.[53] Much closer to home, it is also instructive to compare the erection of Swift's hospital with that of Dr Steevens's. The former opened twelve years after Swift's death, but it was a full twenty-three years after Dr Steevens's death before his hospital accepted its first patients. It took at least thirteen years to build and in fact was not completed when it opened in 1733. Grizel Steevens contributed nearly £15,000 to the project from both her own and her brother's fortunes, while further sums had to be raised by subscription.[54] When viewed in comparison with these other hospitals, the three years and £5,000 it took to build St Patrick's seem very reasonable indeed. Yet the governors' problems were far from over. By 1753 they certainly had a building; what they did not have, however, was the money with which to furnish it, to employ staff and to maintain charity patients. In other words, they were unable to open the hospital and so the building stood empty for another four years.

In the mid 1750s, after the hospital was built, the governors devoted a great deal of attention to organising their Saggart estate. Presumably they planned, following Swift's instructions in his will, that the estate should provide the revenue with which to operate the hospital. The estate occupied a substantial portion of the parish of Saggart, which paid tithes to the dean of St Patrick's and was thus an area with which Swift would have been familiar. Much of the south of the parish was mountainous, taking in the lower slopes of the Wicklow mountains, but most of the governors' estate was in the more prosperous north which supported mixed farming.

Between 1751 and 1755, as we have seen, the governors paid £6,800 to the Denn family and to Edward Butler for about 900 acres of land. The first rent rolls, dating from 1758-9, show that rents averaged about sixteen shillings an acre and that, of the forty-eight holdings listed, nearly a third were over twenty acres.[55] This would suggest that the Saggart tenants were reasonably prosperous farmers. In 1760 the estate even attracted an important industry when eleven acres were leased at £1.7.0 per acre to Thomas Slater who immediately established a paper-mill—thus beginning the well-known Swift-brook Mills.[56] With a larger estate in the Saggart area, the governors could have been reaped a substantial rent—in 1774 a further 300 acres were acquired from Thomas Morgan for a little over £5,000—but their chronic financial problems limited the amount of land they could purchase and this meant that the annual rents produced by the estate were insufficient to support the fifty-four patients for whom the hospital had accommodation.[57]

In their petition to parliament, presented in November 1755, the governors said that they had spent £4,560 building the hospital, but had not been able to admit any patients because there were no funds left to provide furniture and bedding or to maintain them. Swift's legacy was exhausted, except for a few debts which were not likely to be recovered in the near future. Land had been bought and it was hoped that this would yield about £400 a year in rent income. But the governors reckoned that each patient would cost £10 a year to maintain, making in all £540 and that wages for officers and servants would be another £120 a year. Thus they needed at least an extra £260 per annum in order to be able to run the hospital. As we have seen, the Lying-in Hospital, which was in the process of construction, petitioned at exactly the same time and received £6,000, while St Patrick's was awarded a paltry £1,000. Nevertheless, the money was most welcome and, on receipt of it, the board resolved to fit up two wards ready for patients.[58]

Preparing these wards in fact cost £203 and we are fortunate that the tradesmen's accounts for his work have survived among the board minutes. The largest sums were paid to Hugh Wilson, carpenter (£56.6.11½), John Semple, mason and bricklayer (£41.9.10), and Thomas Daly, ironmonger (£40.12.6½). Wilson presumably provided furniture, which would have largely consisted of beds, tables and chairs; money was also paid to Robert Crow, an upholsterer. Daly may have made cooking equipment and grates for fireplaces. Semple, who was a relative of the architect, may have undertaken some structural repairs. Given that the building had been standing empty for so long, maintenance was obviously required. A painter, glazier, slater and plumber were also employed, as was a brazier to provide lamps. One entry in these accounts is particularly intriguing; Daniel Dolan was paid £1.11.10 for 'labour work and watching'. Presumably he acted as a watchman. Vandals were not unknown in the eighteenth century and, even though it was surrounded by a high wall, the empty building would have required protection.[59]

These accounts also contain brief but interesting information on the bedding and other equipment provided for patients and staff. Four lots of blanketing were purchased amounting in all to $192\frac{1}{2}$ yards at a cost of £9.12.0. A Mr Bermingham, who had supplied some of the material, was paid 5s 7d for making up the blankets. Sixty yards of linen were also bought at $9\frac{1}{2}$d per yard for six pairs of servants' sheets. There is no mention of patients' sheets, but twenty-three yards of 'ticking' were bought. This was tough striped linen or cotton, presumably used for patients' sheets. At 13d per yard it was more expensive than the servants' linen and was obviously intended to take a lot more wear and tear. Three rugs at six shillings each were also purchased for the servants, as were sixteen 'caddowes', rough woollen quilts, for the patients. Eating utensils consisted of bowls, 'trenchers' or wooden plates, and 'piggins', which were small pails used for drinking. A cart, a hand barrow and a coal measure were also acquired. The purchase of bedding for patients—'ticking', blankets and 'caddowes'—shows that they slept in beds. This says something about St Patrick's treatment of patients, for in other asylums, like Bedlam for instance, it was not uncommon for patients to sleep on straw laid on the floor because it was found too difficult to prevent them from dirtying or destroying the beds. St Patrick's certainly made use of straw for bedding—in his plans Semple had made provision for the burning of 'foul straw'—but the fact that patients were supplied with wooden beds, sheets, blankets and quilts shows that the governors envisaged them generally sleeping in a normal manner. St Patrick's might have been modelled on Bethlem Hospital in certain respects, but the facilities provided for the comfort of patients were definitely superior.[60]

Having fitted out two wards for sixteen patients, the next task the governors turned to was the employment of staff. In November 1756 John Whiteway was elected surgeon to the hospital, a position he was to fill till his death in 1797. Whiteway, the 'Founder's kinsman' as the board's minutes describe him, was then an assistant surgeon at Steevens Hospital and he went on to pursue a successful medical career, rising to become in 1786 the second president of the Royal Irish College of Surgeons. In July 1757 Robinson and Nicholls were asked by the board to recommend officers and servants 'for the inward business of the hospital' with suggested salaries, while Singleton, Foster and McAulay were asked to do the same for persons to handle the 'outward business of the house'. Before the month was out, Timothy Dyton had been appointed master and Bridget Dryden housekeeper, both at a salary of £10 per annum. Bridget Dryden was the wife of William Dryden, who had been master and receiver of the hospital since 1746. He had, however, resigned this position in 1756 to become steward of Dr Steevens Hospital. Elizabeth Manser was appointed cook and Ann Guy laundry maid, both at £6 per annum. Dyton was empowered to select a male keeper and a porter and Dryden a female keeper, all to be paid £6 per annum. A sum equal to their salaries was also to be paid to each employee as a food allowance. Whiteway's appointment as surgeon was confirmed at a salary of £10 per annum and another £10 for food. Thus salaries and allowances would cost in all £120 per year, as the board had estimated in its 1755 petition. As for the so-called 'outward business' of the hospital, Bernard Kane was appointed agent for receiving rents.[61]

Unfortunately, we know little of the backgrounds of the first employees of the hospital. We can be sure though that they were not trained in the care of the insane. Dyton, for instance, who served as master for twenty-six years, was a printer and publisher and actually ran a printing business in Dame Street while in the employ of the hospital.[62] Another staff member about whom we know a little is the first female keeper. She was Nanny McDaniel and her obituary appeared in the Dublin press when she died in the hospital in 1798 at the extraordinary age of 106. She was a soldier's wife; in fact, she had had two husbands, both of whom had been killed in battle, along with one of her sons. After these harrowing experiences, she was employed by the governors to take charge of the first female patients and, according to her obituary, she was actually the first person to take up residence in St Patrick's. At her death she had been long pensioned off, but the governors had allowed her to continue to live in the hospital.[63]

Having appointed staff in July, in November the governors laid down in detail the duties of each employee. The master had to reside in the hospital. He was to register all patients admitted and to ensure that no one was admitted except on the authority of the board. He was also to see that all fees were paid. He had to provide the necessary supplies for the hospital, such as food, candles and coal, and hand these over to the housekeeper, at the same time furnishing the governors with a weekly account of his purchases. He was also to supervise the porter and keepers and ensure that the orders of the doctors were carried out. The housekeeper, who unlike the master was not specifically required to live in the hospital, was to receive the supplies from the master and to pass these on to the servants or patients as appropriate, providing the master with a weekly account. She was to supervise the cook and laundry maid and to ensure that the hospital was kept clean and that the furnishings were looked after. Obviously the master and housekeeper were envisaged as a team, with equivalent duties and the same salaries, though it was the master who reported to the board. It is therefore not surprising to find at a later date that husbands and wives filled these positions.[64]

The surgeon was simply instructed to attend any visiting governors and to undertake such duties as the physician should direct. The state physician, first Robert Robinson and after his death in 1770 Robert Emmet, was an ex-officio governor, who also acted as a visiting physician to the hospital and Whiteway was primarily responsible to him. It is interesting to note the relative roles of lay and medical personnel at the outset of the hospital. The day-to-day managers, the master and the housekeeper, were not doctors, nor did the keepers have any medical training. But no requirement to certify or attend patients was placed upon the state physician, the surgeon general or even the visiting surgeon. Only with the advent of Dr Emmet in 1770 does it seem that the state physician became actively involved in the admission and treatment of patients and from 1775 he was paid for his trouble. Certainly, though, medicines were used in the hospital, for the apothecary's bills survive, suggesting that Mr Pannell the apothecary was being paid at least £25 per annum for his services, which was a good deal more than the visiting surgeon received.[65] Presumably he, in conjunction with Surgeon Whiteway and with assistance from Dyton, offered such treatments as were available at the time. When we come to discuss the patients, however, we shall see that in the second half of the eighteenth century, asylums were as much custodial as remedial institutions. For the truth was that, beyond bleeding, purging and sedating them, doctors had little to offer the mentally ill in the way of medication.

The cook was to prepare meals and keep the kitchen clean, receiving her directions from the housekeeper, and 'when she can spare time from her kitchen business of which the housekeeper must judge she is to assist in keeping the house clean and helping the woman keeper'. The laundry maid's duties were similarly extended, from washing bedding and clothing, to general cleaning should the housekeeper wish. The keepers, both male and female, were to work under the instructions of the master and were particularly enjoined to keep their wards and cells clean. The

And as to the Residue of my Effects not herein before disposed of, I give and bequeath the Same to A. B. and C. on the Trusts herein after mentioned. That is to say: To the intent that they or the Survivors or Survivor of them may turn it all into ready money, as soon as they can, after my death; and lay out the Same in purchasing lands of Inheritance in Fee Simple, not incumbered with any leases for lives renewable, or with any Terms for years longer than ——, and Situate within thirty miles from the City of Dublin, or in some well-inhabited part of the Province of Ulster. The first three years Income of such lands, to be laid out in buying a piece of Ground Somewhere in the City or Suburbs of Dublin not exceeding half an Acre; and in building an Hospital thereon for Ideots and Lunaticks; which I desire may be called St. Patrick's Hospital; The profits for ever after, to be laid out in providing Victuals, Cloathing, Attendance and all other necessaries for such Ideots and Lunaticks as shall be received into the said Hospital, and in repairing and enlarging the Building, from time to time, as there may be occasion. All which Profits and Income, I desire, may be for ever laid out for the purposes aforesaid, in such manner, and

Original draft, drawn up by Alexander McAulay, of a codicil to Swift's will, embodying his plans for the hospital and endorsed in Swift's own hand, late 1730s.

Accounts of Swift's guardians, 1744-6, particularly showing payments made to Anne Ridgeway, his housekeeper, who cared for him during his final illness.

Pray pay the Bearer Mr Platt Ten Pounds
for Doctor Swifts coffin, being the Sum ordered
by his Executors at our meeting yesterday
9ber: 24 1746 — James King

To
Robt King Esqr ne
Anne Street —

Recd the Contents of the above
from Mr Robt King
Dublin 8 Jany 1746
John Platt
Witness

Bill for ten pounds from John Platt for making Swift's coffin; paid by Robert King, agent for the executors, 8 January 1746/7.

KNOW all Men by thefe Prefents, That I *Philip Den of Sagart in the County of Dublin Gent*

am holden and firmly bound unto *The Rev'd Jonathan Swift Doctor in Divinity Dean of St. Patrick's Dublin* in the Sum of *Two Thousand Pounds*

fterl. *good* and lawful *Money* of Great-Britain, to be paid to the faid *Jonathan Swift* or *his* lawful *Attorney, Executors, Administrators or Affigns*, to the which Payment well and truly to be made, I do bind Me. my Heirs, Executors and Administrators, and every of them firmly by thefe Prefents. Sealed with my Seal, and Dated the *Thirtieth* Day of *December*, Anno Dom. 173*8* and in the *Twelfth* Year of the Reign of our Sovereign *Lord George the 2d* by the Grace of God of Great Britain, France and Ireland *King* Defender of the Faith, &c.

THE Condition of the above Obligation is fuch, That if the above-bounden *Philip Den his* ———

Executors, Administrators or Affigns, they, or either of them, do well and truly Pay, or caufe to be Paid unto the above-named *Jonathan Swift his* Heirs, Executors, Administrators or Affigns, the Sum of *Two Thousand pounds*

fterl. of good and lawful Money of Great-Britain, *on the Thirtieth day of June next together with Interest from the Second day of January next after the Rate of five pounds p Cent p annum*

without Fraud or further Delay. That then this Obligation to be Void and of none Effect, or elfe to ftand and remain in full Force and Vertue in Law.

Signed, Sealed and Delivered in the Prefence of

Philip Den

Bond for loan of £2,000 made by Swift to Philip Denn in December 1738 for which Denn's estate at Saggart, Co. Dublin was security.

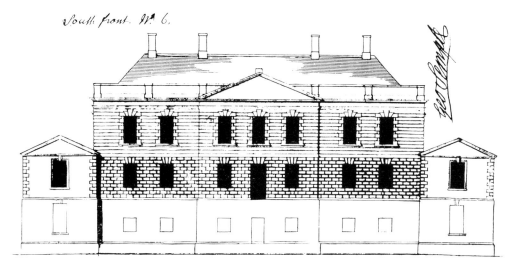

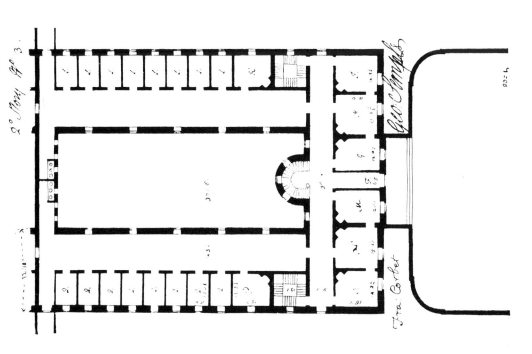

The front and ground floor of St Patrick's Hospital from George Semple's 1750 book of plans: the plan of the front of the hospital shows Thomas Cooley's wings added about 1780.

1755 Slating work Done at Dean Swifts Hospitl
by order of George Simpell
pr John Chesterman

To 1 Slater and 1 Laberor 1 day   0 3 0
To 4 hods of morter ——   0 1 6
To 200 of Slates and a half   0 3 9

Recd from the Govr of St Patricks
Hospl by Wm Dryden eight shills &   0 8 5
five pence being for repairing
the Slating Work at ye John   IC Chesterman
Hospitale 13th Feb 1755   Marke

Bill for 8s 5d from John Chesterman for slating work at 'Dean Swift's Hospital'; paid by William Dryden, the master, 13 December 1755.

A further Description of the foregoing designs. And
the methods intended to be taken in the Execution thereof.

——— That is to Say ———

The Sewers are trac'd out by dotted lines {Of the
of red Ink. In the Geometrical Plan N°. 1. And {Sewers
are to take their rise from the middle of the front part
of the building: And from thence they are to be
dispers'd both ways for the use of the flanks and
offices. And there being no current from
the head, I intend them there (without the house)
not to exceed 9 Inches in the clear. And the head
of those within the house, to be about 5 Inches wide
in the clear: But as these Sewers are to receive
the Scullage of many Conduits. I do intend that
they shou'd widen one Inch in every 14 feet; So
that when the outside Sewer is carry'd from the
middle of the front area, down through the middle
of the Womens Yard, and cross under the Sink & privey
Sheds. I say that this outside Sewer being ab'
300 feet in Length, must be about 2: 6 wide at
the lower end. And both with regard to
the declivity of the ground, and the fall to the
river, these Sewers may be allow'd at the least
about one Inch fall in every seven feet of
their length. So this said outside Sewer will
have about three feet six Inches fall in the
whole, That is, to the North West angle of the
Building. That the seats of the privies are
to be directly over the middle of the Sewer. Because
it is intended that all the water of the Baths, cisterns
&c will at certain times be discharg'd in a deluge.
—— And it is to be observ'd that none of the Conduits
are to come into the Sewers on a right angle. But
on oblique, curv'd lines to prevent Eddys.
⁂ In a Corbel   Note ⁂

Semple's notes regarding the construction of the hospital's sewers: they were to
prove a constant source of problems and a major health hazard for some 150 years.

Friday 29th. August 1746

At the first General Meeting of the Governours of St. Patricks Hospital Dublin founded by the Last Will of Doctor Jonathan Swift at the House of His Excellency the Lord Chancelor —

Governrs. Present

His Excellcy the Lord High Chancellor
His Grace the Lord Arch Bishop of Dublin
The Rt. Revd. the Lord Bishop of Kildare
The Rt. Honble Henry Singleton Esq Lord Chief Justice
Eaton Stannard Esq Record of the City of Dublin
The Revd. Doctor Maturin Dean of St. Patricks
Doctor James Stopford
Doctor James King
The Revnd. Mr. John Grattan
Doctor Robt. Robinson State Physician
Alexander Macaulay Esq. Vicar Genl. of Dublin

On which day, Mr. King Agent for the Governrs. Attended with His Majestys Royal Charter for Erecting & Endowing the said Hospital which was Publickly Read —

Ordered

That the said Charter be Printed and a Sufficient Number of Coppys be sent to Each of the Governours

The

Governrs. Likewise pursuant to the direction of His Majestys Charter did then Nominate & Appt. Seven of the Members Namely —
The Rt. Revnd. the Lord Bp. of Kildare
The Rt. Honble the Lord Chief Justice Singleton
The Revd. Doctor Maturin Dean of St. Patricks
Eaton Stannard Esq Recorder
Alexr. Macaulay Esq.
the Revnd. Doctor James King
the Revnd. Mr. John Grattan

Minutes of the first meeting of the board of governors of St Patrick's Hospital, held at Lord Chancellor Newport's house on 29 August 1746.

emphasis on cleaning arises from the fact that lunatics were known to dirty or destroy their bedding, furnishings and clothing when in violent states. As we have seen, this did not deter the governors from providing them with bedding. Mr Jennings' chairs were located in each ward to restrain particularly violent patients, but, nevertheless, the governors seem to have been resigned to the fact that the staff would be required to do a good deal of cleaning in order to keep the wards habitable.

At the July meeting which appointed staff, Robinson and Nicholls were instructed by the board to draw up regulations for the running of the hospital. It was to approve these rules that the governors met for the first time in the hospital itself on 12 September 1757. The most important dealt with admission procedures. These decreed that the whole board or a committee of at least three governors was to meet every Monday to approve the admission of patients. No one was to be received into the hospital who, at the time of its opening, had been in another institution. Perhaps the governors wanted to ensure that the hospital catered only for those who had previously lacked assistance or perhaps they feared that lunatics who had been confined in prisons or the workhouse would be particularly hard to manage. The admission procedures involved a friend, relative or some person in authority petitioning the governors to receive the patient. This petition had to contain the name and address of the lunatic 'together with an account of all circumstances relative to the disease from the loss of mind to the date of the petition'. These particulars had to be certified by the minister and church wardens of the parish in which the lunatic resided. The petition was to be considered at the Monday meeting and, if granted, was to be 'filed or otherwise carefully preserved'. Unfortunately no such petitions have survived—the surviving admission documentation begins in the 1840s—but admissions were noted in the minutes of board meetings and from this data we can deduce some facts about the early inmates of St Patrick's. The person petitioning for the ad- mission of a patient was obliged to bring that person to the hospital 'in decent clothing' and 'to give security to the governors to receive the patient back when they shall think fit to discharge them'. They also had to pay 6d per week to cover the cost of laundry and to lodge with the master a bond of twenty shillings to pay for funeral expenses should the patient die in the hospital. A register of patients admitted was to be kept. Again, this register has been lost and, of those surviving today, the earliest contains entries dating from the 1790s. The governors then directed that all persons seeking to have patients admitted should attend the following Monday at twelve noon with the necessary petition. The regulations were to be published in the *Dublin Journal* and also inscribed on parchment to be displayed in the hospital itself.[66]

At the next meeting in the hospital on Monday 19 September, ten petitions were approved and the petitioners were instructed to bring the patients to the hospital on the following Monday so that they might be admitted. The minutes record the names of these first patients, six men and four women: Robert Gill, John McEwen, Edward Brabazon, Thomas Wran, William Kelly, Henry McMullin, Margaret Maheney, Anne Murry, Sarah Crofts and Judith McOwen. The patients were referred to as 'pauper lunaticks', even though the funeral bond and laundry fees would presumably have excluded the very poor, unless their parishes were willing to cover these expenses. Unlike the grand opening of the Lying-in Hospital in December, the opening of St Patrick's seems to have occasioned little publicity, though some Dublin newspapers did record that patients were being admitted.[67]

The hospital was now in operation, but only sixteen rooms— probably in fact the two basement wards—had been furnished to receive patients. Two-thirds of the building was still empty and the governors still faced the problem of how, on their limited income, they were to support fifty-four charity patients. In November 1757 they again petitioned parliament and, when another £1,000 was forthcoming in 1758, they were able to accept more patients and to fit up the first floor wards specifically for 'idiots'.[68] But, although public money might enable them to open the institution, the governors clearly could not rely on it to pay their operating costs. Thus, in October 1757, immediately after the first patients had been received, they made a decision which was to shape the whole future character of the hospital. Already Swift's bequest had proved inadequate for the tasks he had laid down in his will; the board had had to seek funds from a number of other sources. Now it turned to a new source: the patients themselves. Swift had wanted his hospital to be a charitable one, accepting patients without charge. But, in October 1757, the governors decided that they did not have the income to operate the institution on this basis and, therefore, that they would accept paying patients, or boarders as they were termed. They ordered two wards for eight males and eight female patients to be opened; these must have been the ground floor wards. But, instead of being furnished by the board, the rooms were to be furnished by the 'friends' of those admitted. In addition, the 'friends' were to pay £22.15.0 on admission, for which sum the patients were to be fed, medically cared for and their laundry done and they were to have 'the constant attendance of a keeper that is one keeper for each ward for the space of one year'. The same sum was to be paid for each year of the patient's residence in the hospital. 'Proper clothing' for boarders had also to be supplied by their 'friends'. In other words, the hospital would house, feed and treat them, but all other necessities and expenses were to be met by those committing them. Boarders were also subject to the standing rules of the hospital, which meant that they had to follow the same admission procedures as pauper patients.[69]

In their 1755 petititon to parliament, the governors, as we have seen, estimated the annual cost of maintaining a patient at £10. By charging boarders more than double this amount, they were persumably hoping to be able to support one free patient for every boarder. When parliament granted the hospital another £1,000 in 1758, the governors ordered three rooms to be fitted up for boarders out of this money.[70] Different classes of boarders in fact quickly emerged, paying different levels of fees and having different facilities.

During the years from 1756 to 1759 the governors had employed staff, furnished the hospital and admitted patients. By 1760 then, 'pauper lunatics' were housed in the basement wards; boarders occupied most if not all of the ground floor; while 'pauper idiots' were confined to the first floor. In 1762 the governors considered erecting a new ward to accommodate convalescent patients. Nothing, however, seems to have come of this interesting idea and, in fact, the design of the building was to make segregating patients, either on the basis of their illnesses or in terms of whether or not they paid fees, far from easy.[71] Income from rents, boarders' fees, bequests and the occasional parliamentary grant made the hospital financially viable, though making ends meet was still a struggle. But, setting aside the compromises that had had to be made and the problems constantly being faced, we can say that, by 1760 Swift's dream of a Dublin-based institution catering for the mentally ill of Ireland had at last been fully realised.

ADMINISTRATION, STAFF AND FINANCE

The management of St Patrick's had been structured in such a way as to give the board of governors sole power in determining the policies, financing and staffing of the hospital. The master was employed at the governors' pleasure to supervise the day-to-day operations. He reported to the board, but was not a member of it and thus had limited say in decision-making. But the fourteen-member board was an unwieldy body: *ex officio* members like the lord chancellor, the archbishop of Armagh and the dean of Christ Church seldom attended, while general meetings had only to be held quarterly, which slowed down decision-making. Power tended in fact to devolve upon the members of the executive committee and officers like the secretary and treasurer, who were elected each year at the November general meeting. The executive was obliged to meet every month, with only three governors constituting a quorum, and in the early years it was this group which effectively ran the hospital.

General meetings were normally held in Marsh's Library, beside St Patrick's Cathedral. Occasionally the archbishop's palace in nearby Kevin Street was used, while especially important gatherings, at which the lord chancellor was present, were held in the parliament house in College Green. Semple had provided a large room on the first floor of the hospital, clearly for the governors, but this was seldom used and in 1781 was divided so as to accommodate chamber boarders, as high fee-paying patients were termed. Why the governors were reluctant to meet in the hospital is not altogether clear. Perhaps it was too far out of town for these busy men— Marsh's Library being more accessible, particularly for the archbishop of Dublin and the dean of St Patrick's—or perhaps the noise and bustle of a busy hospital were not conducive to thoughtful discussion. Whatever the reason, the fact that many of the governors seem seldom to have visited the hospital meant that they were out of touch with its problems. There are references in the minute books to occasional inspections by the board, but these were rare and, moreover, the very fact that the governors had to undertake special inspections before making major decisions suggests that they were not generally familiar with the state of the hospital.

Of the *ex officio* governors the archbishop of Dublin, the dean of St Patrick's Cathedral, the state physician and the surgeon general appear to have been most active. The archbishop generally chaired board meetings. He was thus a frequent attender and would have been very aware of the hospital's problems. He was also very much to the fore in the hospital's lobbying of parliament for government grants to extend and repair the building. Being the successor of Swift, the dean of St Patrick's Cathedral occupied a peculiarly influential position on the board. Francis Corbet enhanced this position by acting as treasurer for most of the busy years from 1747 to 1757 when the hospital was being planned and built. He had worked with Swift as a prebendary of the cathedral and had maintained good, though never intimate, relations with him. It was he, however, who shouldered much of the task of fund-raising during the hospital's construction. And even when he was replaced as treasurer by Anthony Foster he continued to attend board meetings regularly till his death in 1775.

The state physician and the surgeon general, being the only medical men on the board, were also potentially very influential, even though the care of the insane was not at the time considered to be a purely medical matter. From the granting of the charter in 1746 till 1769 the state physician was Robert Robinson, who attended board meetings regularly and obviously took an active interest in the hospital's affairs. The surgeon general for much of the same period was John Nicholls, who had treated Swift in his last years and was both a governor and surgeon at Steevens Hospital. As we have seen, these two men were closely involved in the planning, furnishing and staffing of the hospital. The prominence of medical representation on the board was further enhanced with the appointment in 1770 of Dr Robert Emmet as state physician. We shall treat Emmet's work for the hospital in more detail shortly, but for some thirty years he was a driving force in the hospital's affairs, particularly in financial and medical matters. From 1775 he was in fact paid by his fellow governors for attending patients and this practice continued with his successor, Dr James Cleghorn, who sat on the board from 1803 to 1825. So after 1775, as well as being a governor, the state physician was also the paid consulting physician of the hospital. This dual position put the state physician into close touch with the day-to-day operations of the hospital—something his fellow governors notably lacked—and made him perhaps the most knowledgeable member of the board.

More interesting in many ways than the *ex officio* governors were the seven elected governors, for they chose, or were chosen, to manage the hospital rather than being co-opted into the role by virtue of the position that they held. We need therefore to consider why they sought such a job. The first seven, named in the charter, were the executors of Swift's will: friends he had chosen himself to manage the affairs of his estate. Most of them, in particular the Rev. James King, Bishop James Stopford of Cloyne, Dean Patrick Delany of Down, Chief Justice Henry Singleton and Alexander McAulay, proved assiduous in the fulfilment of their duties. But, by the 1780s, the Rev. John Lyon, the board's secretary and himself a governor from 1773 to 1791, and John Whiteway, the surgeon, were probably the only surviving personal friends of Swift still connected with the hospital. The new generation of governors was perhaps, however, even more interesting than Swift's friends, for it contained some of the most powerful and controversial Irish politicians of the late eighteenth century.

In the last two turbulent decades before 1800 Irish government was largely dominated by three men: John Foster, speaker of the House of Commons from 1785 to 1800, John Beresford, chief commissioner of revenue from 1780 to 1802, and John Fitzgibbon, later earl of Clare, lord chancellor of Ireland from 1789 to 1802. Anthony Malcomson, in his recent, excellent biography of Foster, has characterised the three of them as together forming 'the brains behind reactionary politics in Ireland in the 1790s'.[72] At the same time all three were governors of St Patrick's Hospital. Foster was elected in 1779 in place of his father, Anthony, who had been on the board since 1755; Beresford was elected in 1763; while Fitzgibbon automatically joined the board when he became lord chancellor in 1789. A brief look at each should help elucidate the role of the governors in the eighteenth-century hospital.

Of the three Foster was the one most closely connected with St Patrick's: he and his father together sat on the board for over seventy years. Anthony Foster was a Co. Louth lawyer and MP, who rose to be chief baron of the court of exchequer (1767-77). He was a close friend of the chief justice, Henry Singleton, another Louthman and a governor, and it may well have been Singleton who arranged his election to the board. Two years later, in 1757, Foster was elected treasurer, a position he was to fill for the next twenty years. Malcomson has called him 'the outstanding figure on the Irish bench of his day because of the range of his extra-professional activities', while at the same time acknowledging that Foster 'was an able man whose misfortune it has been to be overshadowed by an even abler son'.[73] Despite his undoubted talents, however, something of a question mark hangs over Foster's treasureship of St Patrick's. The accounts of both his predecessor, Dean Corbet, and his successor, Dr Emmet, appear in the governors' minute book. But, of Foster's accounts, there is no record beyond a note that in May 1780 John Foster delivered his father's accounts for the period 1757 to 1776, plus £222, to the board.[74] This of course does not necessarily prove that Anthony Foster's stewardship was incompetent, but it was during his period in office that the hospital experienced at least one major financial scandal. In 1757 Foster had recommended Bernard Kane for the position of land agent and receiver of rents. In 1771, however, the governors found that Kane owed them over £2,600 in rent arrears; the battle to recover this money from Kane and his associates was to drag on until 1810.[75] In January 1775, while Foster was still treasurer, Dr Emmet was formally thanked by the board for 'inspecting the accounts and bringing them to a precise balance'. Emmet seems in fact to have acted as treasurer from at least 1775, if not earlier, though not formally appointed to the position till December 1777.[76] Admittedly the data is slight, but it does suggest that Anthony Foster in his later years, whether due to ill health or pressure of work, was not fulfilling the role of treasurer as assiduously as required. Nevertheless, John Foster was elected to the board when Anthony died in 1779 and served till his own death in 1828. His political influence, particularly after he became speaker in 1785, was to be of great use to the hospital. When seeking money from parliament to extend the hospital, it was inevitably to Foster that the board turned.

The Fosters were neither an ancient nor a rich family and thus were eager for positions of influence in order to consolidate their political power. Malcomson describes the large array of offices which father and son occupied and the complex network of patronage which they constructed. A governorship of St Patrick's has to be seen in this context. It demonstrated the Fosters' concern for charity, but it also brought them into contact with some of the most influential men in the country, while giving them the opportunity to do favours for their followers by recommending patients for the hospital.

John Beresford was Foster's arch political rival and sat on the board from 1763 till his death in 1805. He came from a prominent landed family, headed by his brother Lord Waterford, with extensive interest in counties Londonderry and Waterford. As chief commissioner of revenue for more than twenty years, Beresford was a powerful figure in Irish political circles. He was less active on the board of governors than Foster; perhaps his more secure political base meant that St Patrick's had less to offer him in the way of political advantages. Of the three, Fitzgibbon seems to have had the least endearing personality. 'Black Jack', as he was known, was ruthless and high-handed and, as a result, far from popular. Ironically he came from a Catholic family, his father having conformed to the Established Church so as to be able to pursue a legal career. Fitzgibbon, however, despised the Irish: a contemporary remarked that he had no other god but British government.[77] He was one of the chief architects of the Act of Union—a measure strongly opposed by Foster. In fact there was intense hostility between Foster and the other two, despite their shared conservative political stance. Foster, for instance, had supported investigations into alleged corruption by Beresford at both the revenue commission and the wide streets board. Fitzgibbon tended to take Beresford's side, partly perhaps because they were brothers-in-law.[78]

In his role as lord chancellor, Fitzgibbon was only expected to attend particularly important meetings of the hospital board of governors. It is probably not without significance, then, that of the five meetings Fitzgibbon appeared at, one was in 1797, two were in 1798 and two in 1799. These of course were years of rebellion, invasion and repression, with the lord chancellor to the fore in rooting out rebels. Archbishop Fowler had ceased chairing meetings early in 1797, presumably because of ill-health—he died in 1801. The primate, Archbishop Newcome, had largely taken over his role, at the same time shifting meetings from Marsh's Library to a committee room of the House of Lords in College Green. This presumably brought the board under the lord chancellor's eye. The active presence at meetings of Dr Emmet, who was known for his radical political views and whose son, Thomas Addis, was a leading rebel, would hardly have pleased him. Interestingly, Emmet did not attend any of the meetings held in 1798-9 at which Fitzgibbon was present. At the June 1798 gathering—the only meeting which Foster, Beresford and Fizgibbon all attended together—the conservative archbishop of Tuam, William Beresford, was elected a governor.[79] Thereafter he and Dean Verschoyle, with some assistance from the primate, chaired meetings till Charles Agar, a political ally of Fitzgibbon, became archbishop of Dublin in 1801. Thus conservative domination of the board was bolstered during the upheavels of the late 1790s. Another possible reason for Fitzgibbon's apparent interest in the board's affairs in 1798-9 is that the hospital held over one thousand acres of land near Ferns in Co. Wexford. This county was one of the principal seats of the rebellion and at least two of the meetings that Fitzgibbon attended discussed the affairs of the Ferns estate. Perhaps the lord chancellor was seeking information from his fellow governors on the political disposition of their tenants. Certainly among the hospital's papers are some brief notes, probably part of a more extensive document, commenting on the political and religious loyalties of some of the Ferns' tenants during the rebellion. For instance, Patrick Macdonnel (or McDonald), who held ninety acres, 'had two sons officers in the rebellion who were killed'; while members of the Byrne (or McByrne) family, who together had over 250 acres, 'were all active rebels—some of them killed in battle'.[80] When exactly these notes were written and by whom is not clear, but they contain just the sort of information which would have greatly interested the lord chancellor.[81] This is speculation of course, but Fitzgibbon's sudden interest in St Patrick's in 1798-9 was almost certainly more than mere coincidence. It would seem fair to assume that an institution, holding land in Wexford and in which Dr Emmet had long played a leading role, would have aroused the suspicions of the rebel-hunting lord chancellor.

Emmet, as state physician, sat on the board from 1770 till his death in 1803 and from 1777 till 1798 he filled the crucial office of treasurer. His contribution to the hospital during these years was immense, as his fellow governors acknowledged on a number of occasions. Perhaps no one else connected with the hospital received as many formal votes of thanks from the board as Emmet.

In January 1775, he petitioned the board for payment for his medical duties and the board agreed to pay him two guineas per quarter out of each boarder's fee for his services. In the course of considering Emmet's claim, the board acknowledged that, since becoming state physician, he had examined and certified all patients admitted to St Patrick's and had attended them without salary, thus providing the governors with far more information on the state of the hospital than had previously been available to them.[82] When the hospital's regulations were drawn up in 1757 it had been intended that the surgeon, in this case John Whiteway, would manage the patients' medical care under the general direction of the state physician and the surgeon general. But Emmet had obviously involved himself far more closely with the patients than had originally been envisaged and thus the board conceded his right to payment for his efforts.

But it wasn't only in the field of medical care that Emmet made his impact upon the hospital. As the board acknowledged in their tribute of January 1775:

> From undoubted proofs of Dr Emmet's great assiduity in the service of this charity, by inspecting the accounts and bringing them to a precise balance, viewing the estate, procuring an accurate map, and forming a judicious scheme for new letting it to advantage: the committee are of opinion that he merits every expression of thanks from the governors, and that this testimony of their approbation ought to be perpetuated by entering it in their books.[83]

Emmet seems virtually to have taken over the jobs of treasurer and land agent, as well as that of physician to the hospital. His personal interest and ability doubtless go a long way towards explaining his activism, but there are suggestions that his intervention may also have been spurred by the incompetence of those already filling these positions. To be fair there is no evidence of incompetence in the case of Whiteway, but as regards Foster and Kane the situation is much less clear. We have already noted the absence of Foster's accounts and the manner in which Emmet was acting as treasurer even before Foster's resignation in 1777. To appreciate, however, the problems created by Kane, we need to look briefly at the affairs of the hospital's estate.

Bernard Kane had been agent and receiver of rents for the Saggart estate since 1757. He had been recommended for the position by

Anthony Foster, and Redmond Kane had put up the £500 security bond that the governors required. Land was being let and leases renewed by the treasurer in the late 1750s, but during the 1760s we hear little or nothing about the estate in the governors' minutes, nor do any rent rolls or accounts survive for this period. In December 1769, however, Kane was ordered to provide the board with up-to-date accounts by the following February.[84] These were then passed on to Foster for examination. Two years later, in May and June 1772, Kane was ordered to lodge all deeds, leases and other estate documents with the secretary, John Lyon, under pain of dismissal, for a discrepancy of somé £2,600 had been discovered in his accounts.[85] Whether or not this discovery was the result of Foster's examination is not clear. Over the next three or four years the governors attempted to recover Kane's debt. He signed several bonds guaranteeing repayment, but these do not appear to have been honoured and, in the meantime, arrears on the estate reached over £1,000. Kane seems in fact to have adopted a rather high-handed attitude. For instance, in accounts he presented in October 1775, he included a bill of over £2,000 for his 'loss of time and trouble' in handling the affairs of the estate during the previous eighteen years.[86] Needless to say, the board was far from impressed by this demand. Some rough notes, made by John Lyon, survive, in which he accuses Kane of understanding 'none of the business belonging to his office as receiver though in possession of the several surveys, which cost the governors a considerable sum of money. He was [Lyon went on] so ignorant of the tenants' holdings in the face of the maps that he did not know by said maps the properties of the tenants.'[87]

In April 1773 Dr Emmet was asked by his fellow governors to negotiate with Kane regarding his debt. This is the first clear indication of Emmet beginning to supersede Foster in the management of the board's financial affairs. Two years later, in 1775, he was given the responsibility, along with Lyon and the new dean of St Patrick's Cathedral, William Cradock, of seeing all the Saggart tenants and ensuring that the arrears were paid.[88] Kane's incompetence and Foster's apparent neglect of his duties, opened the way for Emmet to step in and, during the late 1770s, he was very busy inspecting the boundaries of holdings, negotiating new leases and beginning the enclosure of the commons. As for Bernard Kane, he died insolvent late in 1775 or early in 1776. The governors immediately ordered their law agent to take action against his guarantors for the recovery of his debt and they also decided that their new land agent should provide a huge security bond of £3,000. But, after intermittent legal action over many years, it was not till 1810 that the hospital was able to secure the £2,000 bond that Kane and his friends had signed in 1773.[89]

In February 1779 the board passed another vote of thanks to Emmet for his efforts in reorganising the estate. It followed this up in February 1783 by ordering that 'a piece of plate with a proper inscription be given to Dr Emmet the state physician on account of his unwearied application to the interest of this hospital in all respects as treasurer thereof'. Similarly in August 1792, replying to a query from Dublin Castle, the board went out of its way to mention the 'very diligent, strict and successful attendance of Dr Emmet, the present physician to the hospital, which certainly has been the means of procuring a very considerable increase of boarders therein.'[90] Emmet continued as treasurer till November 1798 when he resigned 'on account of the weak state of his health'. It has been claimed that he resigned as governor, inspired by his own personal nationalist sympathies and by his sons' involvement in the rebellion. The minute books show that this is incorrect and that in fact Emmet continued to attend board meetings till his death in 1803.[91] But it is hard to believe that his resignation as treasurer late in 1798 was not in some way associated with the terrible events of that year. Perhaps he feared that the conservative majority on the board would not have re-elected him to the position, or perhaps his health had indeed suffered as a result of the blows to his family. Whatever the reason, his fellow governors were generous enough to acknowledge, once again, his 'long and faithful services'.

That the board should be highly appreciative of Emmet is understandable, given that a significant number of its other employees proved to be incompetent if not frankly dishonest. The case of Bernard Kane was not in fact an isolated one. The master's duties included the collection of boarders' fees and the purchase of supplies for the patients, which entailed the handling of substantial sums of money. From his appointment in 1757 to his resignation in 1783, the minutes record Timothy Dyton as having received around £11,700 from the treasurer toward hospital expenses. Dyton seems to have fulfilled his functions adequately; the governors did not single him out for special commendation, but in November 1766 they increased his salary by £20, which suggests that they were at least satisfied with his performance. In June 1783, however, Emmet laid before the board detailed financial accounts for the eight years since October 1775; the governors were seeking a parliamentary grant to complete payments on the extension built between 1778 and 1783 and Emmet's accounts were required by parliament. In the course of preparing this submission, irregularities were discovered in the master's accounts and a sub-committee was set up to look more closely into them. The sub-committee was puzzled by the purchase in 1782 of 166 tons of coal, when in the previous four years purchases had never exceeded ninety-five tons per annum. Moreover it was found that Dyton had omitted in his accounts the fees of three boarders amounting to ninety guineas. The minutes record: 'The master hath confessed this error; that it was made through inadvertence and charged himself with the payment since'.[92] Nevertheless, the board was clearly unsatisfied: the housekeeper was ordered to do a full inventory of all the hospital's contents and to purchase nothing further without the consent of the governors. At this point Dyton resigned—'on account of his health', according to the official record. In September the housekeeper, Elizabeth Kinsley, also resigned. Her action is described in the minutes as 'unexpected', but whether or not it had anything to do with Dyton is unclear. Nor is it easy to ascertain exactly how criminal Dyton's failings had been. On stepping down he donated £1,000 in canal bonds to the hospital, for which the governors returned their 'hearty thanks'—though when sold the following year they only raised £600. But in August 1783 they were complaining that he still had £126 of their money. Further light may be thrown on this episode by a much later entry in the minute books. In January 1798 during correspondence with the commissioners of public accounts, the governors mentioned the sum of £3,281, paid to tradesmen, but not properly accounted for by a former master who had died insolvent. They 'were satisfied the greater part of the money had been fairly paid, as appeared by the dispositions of the tradesmen'.[93] Presumably this money was part of the £6,000 parliamentary grant, paid to the hospital between 1778 and 1782 to cover the cost of doubling the size of the building. Emmet, in preparing the accounts to present to parliament in 1783, must have found that Dyton had not kept proper records. The implication, however, is that his actions were careless rather than criminal.

Only a week after Dyton's resignation in July 1783 George Cottingham was chosen to replace him. But Cottingham's tenure as master was a short one and ended even more ingloriously than Dyton's. Cottingham obviously had pressing outside commitments for on several occasions he sought and received permission to make unexplained trips to the country—'for ten days on his private business' said the minutes of the meeting held on 1 August 1785. On 7 May 1787, however, the board adjourned abruptly when it was found that the master's accounts were not 'sufficiently clear'. At the next meeting, held only a week later, it was recorded that 'Mr Timothy Mahony was unanimously elected Master of the Hospital in the room of Mr George Cottingham resigned'. In June Emmet was requested to consult with the law agent to see what steps were necessary to recover the money that Cottingham owed the board; in August Mahony made a deposition before a magistrate stating that Cottingham owed £480; and in November the law agent was instructed to call on Cottingham to get him to sign an agreement, guaranteed by his brother, to pay back the money at £100 per annum. The minutes contain no further mention of this matter, so presumably Cottingham complied with the board's arrangements.[94] In Timothy Mahony, fortunately for them, the governors had at last found a totally reliable master. He held the position till 1812—with the assistance of his son Robert after 1807—and when he resigned due to failing health the board recorded its appreciation of his services by granting him a pension of his full salary which lasted till his death in 1814.

It wasn't only at the top, however, that the board had problems with its employees. The servants also sometimes proved unsatisfactory, though at least their misdemeanours were nowhere near as expensive to the hospital as those of their so-called betters. In March 1784, for instance, Richard Wainhouse, a male keeper, was discharged and Mary Sadler, a female keeper, was 'admonished for her misconduct'. Unfortunately we are not informed as to the nature of this misconduct; the board seems in fact to have been very reluctant to spell out the reasons for an employee's dismissal. In January 1788 a committee had to be appointed to enquire into a complaint of 'improper conduct' among the 'inferior servants'. As a result the porter, Patrick Sullivan, was dismissed, as was Elinor Irwin, a female keeper. We are not informed of Irwin's crime, but in Sullivan's case it was 'drunkenness and extorting fees'; presumably insisting that visitors pay to enter the hospital. But this charge is only recorded in the draft minutes of the meeting; in the final corrected minutes it appears more vaguely as 'various misdemeanours'. In failing to spell out charges against employees, it is unclear as to whether the secretary was seeking to protect the individual's good name, the hospital's reputation or both. The charge of 'extorting fees' in Sullivan's case is an intriguing one, for it was common practice in many asylums, most notably Bedlam, to allow paying visitors to view the inmates. Bedlam in fact derived a substantial income from this practice. But on more than one occasion the governors of St Patrick's made clear that no person was to be 'admitted into the hospital to see the patients, except their own relatives, without an order from a governor'. In order to enforce such a policy it must have been essential to have a porter who was not susceptible to bribery. If some servants misbehaved, others equally proved faithful and reliable and had their devotion recognised by the board. In May 1764 one of Sullivan's predecessors as porter, Pierce Chissel, was 'allowed his provision in the hospital in consideration of his having been suddenly struck with the palsey and incapable of service'. Similarly, in February 1772, Elizabeth Scarlet, the cook, was granted an additional £4 per annum 'to enable her to pay a helper which allowance is given in consideration of her present infirmities and her long and faithful services'. This Elizabeth Scarlet is very possibly the same Elizabeth Manser, appointed cook in 1757 when the hospital opened. The board was also conscious of its employees' comfort: in May 1780 for instance, it ordered that a 'suit of bed curtains' be provided for the housekeeper.[95]

As noted earlier, the staff originally appointed in 1757 consisted of a master, housekeeper, cook, laundry maid, a male and female keeper, a porter and a surgeon to care for approximately fifty patients. In September 1783, with the opening of the first extension to the building which increased accommodation to one hundred, the governors set out a new salary scale. In addition to the master, housekeeper, cook, porter and surgeon, the hospital now employed two laundry women, six ward keepers, a barber, an attendant for each chamber boarder and a physician in the person of Dr Emmet. With the introduction of chamber boarders and the doubling of the numbers of patients, the tasks of the staff were considerably increased and salaries rose accordingly. The master now received forty guineas per annum, plus two guineas for each chamber boarder and one guinea for each ward boarder. The housekeeper received a similar allowance for each boarder, though her annual salary was fixed at thirty guineas. We saw that the master and housekeeper had originally received the same salaries; the ten guinea differential which appeared in 1783 reflected the growing importance of the position of master. It was he who collected patients' fees and this role became increasingly vital as the numbers of boarders rose. The ward keepers, both male and female, the cook and the porter were all paid sixteen guineas; while the chamber attendants received twelve guineas and the barber eight guineas. Dr Emmet's salary, introduced in January 1775 at eight guineas for each boarder, remained unchanged. The surgeon, on the other hand, was paid twenty guineas per annum, plus six guineas for each chamber boarder; in 1803 this was converted to two guineas per boarder. This system of payment per boarder was deliberately introduced by the governors as an incentive to staff:

> The salaries, wages and compensations of the officers and servants will be paid chiefly out of the fund arising from the entertainment of boarders in the hospital and as their pay will

be thereby rendered fluctuating, they will have an additional motive for being more attentive to the boarders, and to act in such a manner as always to have the wards filled if they can.[96]

The staff thus had a financial interest in the boarders; in ensuring that they were well cared for and particularly that their numbers increased.

As mentioned, the hospital was extended in the early 1780s and again in the early 1790s. These constructions, which will be discussed in more detail in the next section, were largely paid for by parliament, but the governors had also been able to increase their income which meant that they were in a position to maintain more patients.

Emmet's management of the Saggart estate had borne fruit in the form of a substantially increased rent roll, though the purchase of additional land in the mid-1770s also helped. When the governors bought the estate they estimated the annual rent income at £400; at the time that Kane's mismanagement was revealed in the early 1770s the rental was £700, though during the 1760s Kane had only been collecting about £500 each year; by 1790, however, the rental had leapt to £1,180. Emmet, with the help of able land agents—first Stuckey Simon and then, from 1783 to 1799, Charles Hamilton—had at the same time succeeded in reducing the arrears substantially, from over £1,000 in 1777 to a mere £20 by 1789.[97]

But, in addition to their lands at Saggart and Kilmainham, the governors had also acquired two further estates during the second half of the eighteenth century; both by means of bequests. In 1767 James Symes, who, according to his will, resided at Hammersmith in Middlesex, bequeathed to the hospital his estate in Co. Wexford. But this legacy proved rather complicated. Symes leased the land, which was just north of the town of Ferns, from the bishop of Ferns and, in his will, he directed that it be held in trust by his nephew, Mitchelburne Symes, with the rents going to St Patrick's Hospital. Out of these a £50 annuity was to be paid to Mitchelburne and his heirs.[98] Thus the governors did not control the estate directly, but had to work through Symes family trustees, as well as dealing with the bishop of Ferns, who was the head landlord. It was the sort of complex arrangement which was almost bound to breed trouble in the future. Nevertheless, for some 120 years successive generations of the Symes family acted as agents for the hospital's Ferns estate. Some land was sold back to the bishop in the early 1780s, but the earliest surviving rent rolls date from the mid 1790s. They show the estate as containing 1,293 acres and producing an annual rent of £426. Out of this sum, however, approximately £170 had to be paid to the bishop, the trustee and the agent.[99] Another, though rather different type of estate, came into the governors' hands in 1788, when the Rev. Dr John Taylor bequeathed them some thirty-eight properties in Francis Street and its adjoining alleys in the heart of the city of Dublin.[100] But again, the governors were in fact only middlemen, for Taylor leased the estate from the Ashbourne Grammar School in Derbyshire. The governors, or rather their Saggart agent, collected the rents, however, which amounted in the mid-1790s to £491 per annum, out of which £228 went to the grammar school.

These new estates in Ferns and Dublin provided a much-needed boost to the hospital's annual income. In 1798, according to a report by a sub-committee of the board, the Saggart and Dublin estates were producing, after all expenses had been paid, £1,052 each year, while Ferns normally yielded about £250, after expenses. This, combined with the boarders' fees, which amounted to £1,945 in 1798, gave the governors a total annual income of over £3,200. Yet, in the same year, the cost of running the hospital amounted to £3,150. There were forty-eight boarders, but only sixty-one pauper patients; nearly forty rooms were thus empty as the board did not have the money to maintain patients in them.[101] The governors were obviously only able to make ends meet in the 1790s by keeping about a quarter of the hospital closed. Yet, the twenty years after 1800 were to prove a far more difficult time financially than the twenty before. Between 1780 and 1800 the governors were able to treble the size of the hospital; between 1800 and 1820 they were to find it increasingly difficult even to maintain the premises.

Up until 1815 the governors had to cope with inflation resulting from the Napoleonic Wars, which raised the prices of provisions and services substantially. But the end of the war brought little relief for, as recession set in, the hospital's tenants found it more and more difficult to make up their rents. On top of these problems the governors also had, since 1801, to face a British government which was becoming more interested in, and at the same time more critical of, asylum management. St Patrick's was particularly vulnerable to criticism over its facilities, for, fifty years after its opening, the building was dilapidated and increasingly out of date.

The price spiral is most obvious with regard to basic food stuffs, particularly meat. Patients appear to have been generally well fed for the governors were at pains to ensure a supply of good quality beef. In 1768 they were paying 2½d per pound to the rather unfortunately named Charles Costly; by 1796 the price had increased to 4½d; but thereafter the cost of the better grades of meat rose rapidly and there were frequent complaints by the board at 'the great dearness of meat'. In 1809 boarders' meat was costing 6½d per pound and paupers' meat 4½d, while in 1814 these prices had reached 8d and 5½d respectively. During that year the master was instructed to find a cheaper butcher and Morgan Brien, who had supplied the hospital since at least 1800, was replaced by Thomas Goodwin, who was prepared to provide beef at 6½d and 4½d per pound. But meat was not the only increasingly expensive commodity. In June 1804 the board had decided that prices were so high it was too expensive to contract for a year's supply of potatoes and oatmeal, as was the normal practice. Instead the master was instructed to buy from week to week at the best available rates. In other instances efforts were made to economise and cut out waste. Thus in February 1800 the board decreed that no coal or candle allowances should be made to officers who did not actually reside in the hospital.[102]

The inflation also affected employees' wages and boarders' fees. In 1796 two guineas was added to the wages of wardkeepers, the cook, the laundress and the porter and one guinea to those of chamber boarders' attendants. In 1801, just five years later, a further two guineas was granted to the wardkeepers and laundry maid and one guinea to the porter, 'on account of the very high price of provisions'. To cover increased expenses the governors put up the boarders' fees. When the hospital was enlarged in the early 1780s the chamber boarders' fee was fixed at sixty guineas per annum and the ward boarders' at thirty-four guineas. These charges remained unchanged till May 1799 when the governors decided that no boarder could be received for less than £40, 'on account of the great rise in every kind of provision'. In 1803 fees were raised again, to eighty, and forty guineas respectively, and ten years later they leapt to one hundred, and sixty guineas respectively. Moreover, in 1803 the master was instructed to be far more vigorous in pursuing relatives of patients defaulting on payment, even to the point of threatening to remove the patients to the workhouse.[103] As we shall see when we come to treat the patients in detail, many obviously had difficulty in meeting these substantial fee rises. In subsequent years, therefore, the numbers of patients transferring from the boarders' side of the hospital to the paupers' side increased markedly.

Despite fee increases, signs of financial strain continued. In February 1802 and again in February 1810, for instance, the treasurer's report showed no money remaining in his hands after the end of the previous year's expenditure. And, as we shall see when discussing the building, the governors could not pay their architect for essential repairs undertaken in 1809-10 and were only able to complete major repairs in 1811-13 with substantial government grants. The economic crisis that Ireland underwent in the first two decades of the nineteenth century is also very evident in the management of the hospital's estates.

Between 1806 and 1808 many of the 31-year leases given during Emmet's reorganisation of the Saggart estate in the mid to late 1770s expired. The contemporary boom in commodity prices was reflected in considerable rent increases. Thus the eleven acres on which Thomas Slator's paper-mill stood, which had been let in 1775 for £1.8.0 per acre, were re-let in 1806 for £3 per acre. Other renewals also point to substantial rent increases. On the Ferns estate, for example, all the leases expired between 1802 and 1810 and rent increases of the order of 100 per cent were the norm.[104] But, with the end of the war in 1815 and a drastic fall in prices, the country quickly slid into a severe depression and the tenants found themselves struggling to pay rents inflated by the wartime boom.[105] This crisis is clearly evident in the figures given below for arrears of rent at Saggart:

SAGGART ESTATE: RENT AND ARREARS, 1812-22

Sums rounded off to nearest pound

YEAR	RENTAL £	ARREARS £
1812	1,701	599
1814	1,701	1,409
1816	1,701	2,342
1818	1,682	3,100
1820	-	2,890
1822	1,510	2,430[106]

The agent for the Saggart and Dublin estates since 1799 had been John Verschoyle, whose older brother, James, was dean of St Patrick's and treasurer of the board of governors of the hospital at the time of his appointment. The Verschoyles, originally seventeenth-century Dutch immigrants, were an influential family, noted as both land agents and clergymen. They acquired land at Saggart and also intermarried with the Fosters and for some 150 years they acted as agents for the governors.[107] Their association with the hospital, however, nearly came to a premature end in 1819 when, at their quarterly meeting in February, the governors dismissed John Verschoyle, giving as their reason that he could not 'by his exertions reduce the arrears within moderate bounds'.[108] But Verschoyle was not prepared to accept this judgment on his management of Saggart without a struggle. In March he replied with a detailed defence of both himself and the tenants. This revealing letter is worth close examination for the light it sheds on the affairs of the estate.

Verschoyle began by assuring the board that the accumulation of arrears was not due to 'any neglect on the part of their agent'; rather he argued that 'the fatality of the times was such that the payment of rents in most instances *could not be enforced*'. He then proceeded to elaborate upon 'the fatality of the times':

> When the great change in public affairs [the end of the Napoleonic Wars in 1815] took place the price of the produce of land became reduced during the first year below one fifth of former rates and cattle nearly in the same proportion—the failure of crops the following year was so fatal that by far the greater part of the tenants had not sufficient from the produce of their farms to support their families; and the succeeding year was not much more favourable: so that many were reduced to actual beggary, which brought about epidemic disease that few of them escaped, and which has not yet entirely subsided; and it was impossible in most instances to enforce payment of rents. Had I resorted to that measure the only mode I could have adopted (for there was nothing to distrain) would be that of throwing the tenants into jail! The consequence of which could not have failed to be a general waste of the farms, as new tenants could not *then* be got to take them even *under half the value of the land.*

Verschoyle, however, was optimistic that the worst was now over. 'The last year's harvest was a productive one and the prices good, consequently the arrear due was diminished, though perhaps not so much as it ought.' Yet he had faith in the Saggart tenants, most of whom he would have known very well. 'They have with few exceptions been industrious and well cropped their farms; so that if it shall please God that the succeeding harvest be favourable there will be abundant means to resort to for payment of a considerable proportion of the arrear as well as the accruing rent.' In the case of one particular tenant, Michael Wogan, whom he had been ordered to evict, Verschoyle stoutly defended his decision not to do so.

> I went immediately after [the November 1818 board meeting] to Wogan's farm to secure any property that might be upon it, but there were not effects to pay keepers, and he being in the act of preparing ground for a crop of wheat which may produce the full amount of his debt, I thought it my duty not to interrupt him, as if I should throw him into jail that stake for the accruing rent as well as the arrear would be destroyed and a considerable

loss must be the consequence, for the ground would remain uncropped and waste till the legal steps to obtain possession could be accomplished, and many small farms are similarly circumstanced.

Verschoyle was adamant that, had he evicted or imprisoned tenants, he would have 'greatly injured the landlords as well as have driven to destruction the greater number of families on the estate'.[109]

Verschoyle's argument obviously swayed the board for at its next meeting in April there was no mention of his sacking, instead he was instructed 'to eject such of the tenants as appear to be insolvent or not disposed to liquidate their respective arrears, and . . . to give further indulgence to those who are poor but industrious and who show a disposition to discharge the whole or part of their debt by instalments'. Given Verschoyle's favourable opinion of the tenants, as expressed in his March 1819 letter, we can presume that he classed most of them as 'poor but industrious'. Certainly in 1820-21 the governors wrote off some forty per cent of the arrears and Verschoyle would have had a hand in this decision. A letter from one tenant seeking a reduction in rent survives from the year 1819, with a strong endorsement on the back from Verschoyle. Rent rolls show that subsequently this tenant's rent fell by a third.[110] Nor, despite the governors' threat, do any tenants appear to have been evicted. Later in the 1820s however, a few evictions did occur as discontent at the level of rents and opposition to enclosure gained momentum.[111]

We saw that in the 1750s the governors had to struggle hard to raise the money both to build and to open the hospital, for Swift's financial legacy had proved insufficient for this task. The first half century of the hospital's operations showed, however, that such money problems were not a temporary phenomenon, but rather amounted to a permanent state of affairs. For, notwithstanding the admission of paying patients and the efforts of eminent governors, like Dr Robert Emmet and John Foster, on the hospital's behalf, St Patrick's struggled to pay its way. In such circumstances it was not able to satisfy the demand for asylum places and, as we shall see, this probably contributed to the government's decision to build its own asylums. By specifying that his hospital should derive its income from the land, Swift had tied St Patrick's to the fate of Irish landlordism. The admission of boarders broadened the hospital's financial base to some extent, but it was still heavily reliant on income from rents. The agricultural depression that hit the country after 1815 thus affected St Patrick's severely, though, in retrospect, it can be seen as merely a foretaste of things to come. For, despite their altruistic intentions, the governors were landlords and as such were destined to share the many trials and tribulations suffered by the Irish landowning class during the course of the nineteenth century.

EXTENSIONS AND MAINTENANCE

Between its opening in 1757 and the end of the century St Patrick's was extended twice, so that by 1800 it could accommodate three times the number of patients it had been able to in the 1750s. But, thereafter, no major enlargement of the building occurred till the twentieth century and in fact, as early as 1808, the governors were having difficulty in finding the money merely to maintain the hospital in sound structural order. The two extensions—one built between 1778 and 1783 and the other between 1789 and 1793—were similar in that each merely added some fifty rooms to Semple's two ranges, thus considerably lengthening the arms of the U in a northerly direction. This accentuated the dark and enclosed atmosphere of the ward corridors and turned the narrow yard between the two ranges into a grim canyon.

But the builder of the first addition to the hospital had in fact suggested an east-west extension. He was Thomas Cooley, a leading Dublin architect, who during the 1760s and 1770s designed the Royal Exchange (now City Hall), built the second Newgate Prison in Green Street and also worked on early parts of what was to become the Four Courts.[112] In 1777-8 he submitted three different plans to the governors of St Patrick's and these were inserted in Semple's 1750 book of plans and notes. The first two would have involved the construction of a cross building terminating the ranges, but the governors rejected these in favour of the third, which simply copied Semple's design and extended the ranges by a little over one hundred feet, giving the hospital fifty-four extra cells.[113] Swift in his will had specified that the hospital should be built in such a way that it could be extended when sufficient money became available and Semple had taken this proviso into account when designing the original building. Simply elongating the arms of the U was the easiest, and presumably the cheapest, way of enlarging the hospital and this doubtless influenced the governors' decision to opt for Cooley's third alternative. There was, however, one novel feature in Cooley's plan: he added small wings to each side of the front of the building. These had the effect of lightening the rather heavy, symmetrical façade, though one wing was later spoilt by the addition of an extra storey.[114] There is no information as to why these wings were built, but they may have resulted from the board's decision to admit what were termed chamber boarders. As we shall see when we come to discuss the patients, chamber boarders, first referred to in 1781, had their own servants and were housed in rooms at the front of the building rather than in cells in the wards. These rooms had originally been intended as offices and accommodation for staff; as already noted, the proposed boardroom on the first floor was divided up for this purpose in 1781.[115] We know that in the late nineteenth century Cooley's wings contained the male and female boarders' drawing rooms and it is possible that they were originally built to accommodate the introduction of chamber boarders by providing facilities for them and perhaps also for the staff whom they had displaced.

Certainly the governors were anxious to encourage the admission of more boarders. In July 1783, after Cooley's extension was finished, they approved a newspaper advertisement that had been drafted by Dr Emmet, soliciting more paying patients and pointing out that

> any profit which may arise therein [from the fee of thirty-four guineas per annum] is to become part of the fund for support of the paupers, the landed property bequested by the ever memorable founder, and other humane benefactors, not being by any means adequate to the support of the institution or its present enlarged scale, and recent admission of forty additional patients. So that sending boarders into this asylum will be not only to make as comfortable provision for them as the nature of their complaints will admit of, but will also be an act of charity, by assisting to provide for a number of poor fellow creatures in the same condition, who may not have friends able to support them.[116]

As we have already seen in our discussion of the staff, in September of the same year the governors introduced what they intended as a further incentive to the admission of boarders by paying staff according to the numbers of boarders in the hospital.

The need for more boarders was dictated by two main factors: the hospital's chronic financial difficulties and the demand for pauper places. We shall see shortly that, from its opening, St Patrick's was a great success, or to put it more accurately, there was a huge demand from all parts of the country for free places in the hospital. So much so that, by the early 1770s, some applicants had to wait years for admission. The decision to double the number of places, taken in the late 1770s, was almost certainly in response to this demand. Emmet's management of the hospital's estate and of its general financial affairs had boosted revenue and in 1776 the governors petitioned parliament for money 'towards carrying on the remainder of building of St Patrick's Hospital not yet completed'. Between 1778 and 1784 some £7,500 was received in three separate grants towards the cost of the extension being built by Cooley.[117] So parliament provided the money to enlarge the hospital, just as it had provided the money with which to furnish and open it in the 1750s, but the governors had to increase their income from rents and boarders' fees in order to pay for the maintenance of additional free patients.

Only six years after the opening of the first extension, building work began on another, similar one. Very little information on this extension survives, however. No plans are extant, for instance, though we know that it added about another fifty-four cells and that it was built by Whitmore Davis, who was architect to the revenue commissioners. John Beresford, the chief commissioner, who was also a long-serving governor of the hospital, may have had a hand in this appointment. The specifications for the building were, however, supplied by Dr Emmet, who seems again simply to have reproduced Semple's design.[118] As both the hospital's physician and treasurer, Emmet was obviously considered to be the governor best qualified to decide upon its building requirements. The board had come into several large sums of money in the 1780s. The bishop of Ferns, for instance, had paid £1,500 for some 250 acres of land at Ferns, formerly held by James Symes, while a legacy of £500 had been forthcoming from Colonel Arthur Gore. And, again, parliament had come up with a grant towards the cost of building, which amounted this time to £2,500.[119]

The money was thus available for a further enlargement of the hospital. Yet, it does seem a little surprising that another major extension should follow so hard upon the heels of the first one, particularly as a report by a sub-committee of the board, dated March 1799, indicated that in 1798 thirty-eight rooms, or a quarter of the hospital, stood empty as the governors did not have the revenue to support any more patients. Although the evidence is far from clear, it appears in fact that the extension built between 1789 and 1793 was erected at the urging of the government and was intended to house the overflow of pauper lunatics from the workhouse.

Workhouses or houses of industry had been built in Dublin, Cork, Waterford and Limerick during the 1770s to house beggars and vagrants, but they quickly attracted large numbers of lunatics. Perhaps partly for this reason there was growing public concern, not to say alarm, at the numbers of lunatics wandering the countryside and this increased during the 1790s and 1800s. Between about 1788 and 1791, just at the time that St Patrick's was being extended, a special building to house lunatics was erected at the Cork workhouse and, by 1816, the Cork asylum had accommodation for 250 inmates. In 1810, in response to complaints that the Dublin workhouse was becoming overcrowded with lunatics, the government employed Francis Johnston to design and build an asylum near the workhouse, again with accommodation for about 250. This institution, the Richmond Asylum, soon became the largest in the whole country and eventually it evolved into the present-day St Brendan's Hospital, Grangegorman. In 1817, at the instigation of Robert Peel, the chief secretary, a parliamentary select committee was appointed to examine the problem of the lunatic poor in Ireland and, as a result of its report, the government began to build a string of public asylums throughout the country in the 1820s.[120] But it would appear that, before it embarked on a large-scale building programme of its own, the government had hoped that extending St Patrick's might help cope with the growing problem of pauper lunacy.

In July 1792 the lord lieutenant wrote to the governors 'relative to the removal of the lunatics from the house of industry'. In reply the governors thanked parliament for its grant of £2,568 towards the cost of building and fitting up 'fifty-four cells for the reception of lunatics and idiots from the house of industry', but, at the same time, they made the point that providing accommodation was really only half the problem. Patients also had to be maintained in the hospital and this was an expensive undertaking. Between June 1790 and June 1791 the governors said that they had an income of £2,584, of which £1,050 came from boarders' fees, but expenses over the same period had amounted to £2,521, leaving them with no scope to admit more pauper patients. In 1787 it had cost £14.7.6 per annum to feed and clothe such a patient and thus for fifty-four the total cost would be £776.5.0 per annum. This figure did not take into account the cost of medical attendance nor the fact that prices had increased significantly in the five years since 1787. The governors declared, however, that they were 'anxious to comply with the desire of the government and contribute to the public good' and thus were willing to maintain fifty-four pauper patients at the 1787 rate. But they could only do this if the government paid £776.5.0. per annum. If not, accepting such a large group of free patients would produce a substantial deficit in their accounts and this was something that they were unwilling to risk.[121] For reasons that are not clear, the government appears not to have taken up this offer and so, during the 1790s at least, the latest extension to the hospital stood largely empty.

We saw in our discussion of St Patrick's finances that, due to the Napoleonic war, costs increased dramatically and income fluctuated unpredictably in the twenty years after 1800. The 1799 sub-committee had reported that it 'found the building in good order' but within ten years, another sub-committee had come up with a rather different assessment.[122] In May 1808 this sub-committee was asked by the board to view the building and decide 'for what number of additional paupers accommodation can be made'. Just ten days later the sub-committee reported that it had 'found the wards in as good order as could be expected considering the description of patients contained in them'. The female wards were full, but there was space for ten extra male paupers. At the same time, the sub-committee noted that the roof was in need of major repair. Nothing appears to have been done about this, but in November the same sub-committee, with the addition of Edward Parke, an architect, was asked to investigate the state of the water closets. In its report, in March 1809, the sub-committee recommended that

> it would conduce much to the safety of the building as well as to the cleanliness and wholesomeness of the hospital if the great conduit for the soil from the water closets was taken down, and a new one erected at a little distance from the north wall of the building which would prevent the injury sustained by the walls from the constant falling of water from the different closets.[123]

Parke estimated the cost of repairs and fees at a little over £300 and he was ordered by the board to proceed with the work. But a year later his bill had still not been paid. This, as the board minutes explained in November 1810, was 'on account of the low state of the funds of the hospital'.[124]

In this very year of 1810, however, the hospital's finances received a most welcome boost, for the governors at last recovered two long-outstanding debts. After attempts extending over more than sixty years, they were awarded £1,780 from the estate of Deane Swift when his lands in Co. Meath, which had passed to his son, were sold on chancery. Theopilius Swift, an eccentric lawyer, had proved as incompetent in money matters as his father. On top of this, the governors also recouped the £2,000 that Bernard Kane's guarantors had owed them for nearly forty years.[125] These windfalls allowed the board to consider undertaking a major programme of repairs and improvements to the hospital. In November 1810 another sub-committee was appointed to examine the state of the building and also to look into the possibility of acquiring more land adjacent to the hospital. Within a week this sub-committee had produced a most revealing report. Firstly, it acknowledged that in the past the governors had devoted the bulk of their income to the maintenance of patients at the expense of repairs to the building. 'In consequence', the hospital was 'now in absolute need of an entire and thorough repair.' Things had deteriorated to such a degree in fact that the building constituted a real threat to those who inhabited it.

> The roof of the hospital [the report went on] is in a state absolutely so ruinous, as well as the several stacks of chimneys, as to threaten the destruction of all who inhabit the premises. There is reason to believe that not only the slating will require to be entirely done anew, but that the woodwork of the roof itself is quite rotten, and will require to be renewed. It will also be necessary to pull down such stacks of chimneys as are now out of order, and to rebuild them. The lower [i.e basement] wards in the hospital are so damp, they will require to be drained, and the nature of the flags with which these wards are floored, being such as is calculated to be always wet, they will require to be new flagged with stones of a better and drier quality . . . the outward walls appear to be much injured by dropping from the eves, and . . . many of the stones are rotten [so that] the latter will require to be picked out and the walls dashed and such measures taken as will prevent future damp.[126]

The report continued by urging the purchase of the land between the hospital and Steevens Lane in order to provide more recreation space for the patients. And it also took up the old question of segregating patients according to the state of their illnesses.

> As soon as the repairs absolutely necessary to the present buildings shall have been accomplished it would be very desirable to have returns erected from the north ends of the wards across the gardens of the master and housekeeper, by which separate accommodation would be obtained for the most maniacal of the patients, constructed for their security, and so far removed from the present wards as to secure the peace and quietness of the convalescent and less turbulent.[127]

The sub-committee of course recognised that the funds of the hospital, even augmented by recent substantial debt repayment, would be 'entirely inadequate' to pay for such major improvements and so it recommended an approach to parliament. Since 1801 the parliament that Ireland looked to was no longer in College Green, but at Westminster in London. Yet, notwithstanding this change, St Patrick's still seems to have been well served by the lobbying efforts of its governors. John Foster, now MP for Co. Louth in the British House of Commons, remained influential in Irish affairs and at the April 1811 board meeting a letter from him was tabled, announcing that parliament had granted the hospital £4,000 towards the cost of repairs. In April 1812 another £4,000 was forthcoming to pay for the completion of the repair work.[128] At about the same time the government requested the governors to accept thirteen pauper lunatics from the Waterford workhouse, which was seriously over-crowded. On this occasion, the board did not quibble, but agreed 'most willingly' and with 'great pleasure'. It would seem, however, that the government paid the maintenance costs this time, for there is a later reference, in the minutes, to some £276 paid from June 1812 to November 1813 'for the maintenance of certain persons kept in the hospital under order of the Irish government'.[129]

But, although parliament was ready to grant large sums to pay for repairs and also to cover the maintenance costs of pauper patients transferred from other institutions, it was not willing to provide money with which to extend the building to accommodate difficult patients separately. Dr James Cleghorn, Emmet's successor as state physician and physician to St Patrick's, later told the 1817 select committee on Irish pauper lunatics that, while 250 cells were being built at the new Richmond Asylum, the government was not prepared to pay for the building of more at another asylum. Although this ruled out extending St Patrick's, Cleghorn was at pains to point out that, despite a shortage of money, the governors had nevertheless moved in 1816 to acquire more land for recreational purposes.[130]

After the repairs to the toilets, roof, walls and basement between 1809 and 1812, the governors' decision to lease more land in 1815-16 was almost certainly a product of growing public concern, both in England and Ireland, regarding facilities for pauper lunatics. We have already seen that a select committee investigated the problem in Ireland in 1817 and it was to this body that Cleghorn reported on the state of St Patrick's Hospital. But, prior to this, between 1814 and 1816 another select committee had examined this situation in England. As part of its evidence, this committee published a letter from Henry Grey Bennet, MP for Shrewsbury and a leading whig advocate of asylum and prison reform, who had inspected St Patrick's in August 1815.[131]

Bennet had many good things to say about the hospital, but he also voiced several important criticisms. He claimed, for instance, that there were 'nearly two hundred persons' living in the building, that some cells were being used to house two patients and that generally the hospital was 'too crowded'. The master, however, informed him that having two patients in one room was 'uncommon'. According to the hospital's own figures, there were 137 patients resident in 1808 and 149 in 1817; to have reached a level of nearly two hundred patients would have required doubling-up in at least a third of the cells and this appears unlikely. What Bennet saw in fact was probably the housing of a large number of staff dependants. With the exception of the master, staff were expected to reside in the hospital without their families, but many seem to have brought spouses and particularly children with them. Certainly at their meeting in August 1815, immediately following Bennet's visit, the governors ordered that 'no person shall be suffered to inhabit the hospital unless he or she shall have been duly admitted as a patient, or be in the employment of the governors'. This order does not seem to have had the desired effect though, for three years later, in 1818, the board was obliged to issue the 'most peremptory' directions to 'servants' to remove their children from the house within two months. Accommodation for staff in the hospital was far from adequate at the best of times, but the addition of large numbers of children would certainly have produced the overcrowding of which Bennet complained. Yet, whether or not children suffered in such an environment is an open question. Bennet referred to one six-year-old, the child of a female keeper, who ran freely among the patients, in and out of their cells, without any harm.[132] Obviously female keepers and domestic staff preferred to have their children with them, even in a madhouse, rather then be obliged to leave them outside.

Bennet found the building itself to be 'clean and in good order'; so presumably the major repairs undertaken between 1809 and 1812 had had the desired effect. He certainly was critical of the basement wards, but for being dark and lacking any view rather than for being water-logged as they appear to have been in 1810. He also singled out the airing courts or yards on each side of the building and criticised them for being far too small. He felt that the patients, though well cared for as regards food, clothing and bedding, lacked occupation of either a productive or a recreational kind. A few, mainly women, helped with cooking and cleaning, but, as for recreation, it consisted of little more than patients walking round the airing yards. Bennet also particularly singled out the hospital's failure to segregate patients according to the nature or seriousness of their illnesses, which he regarded as a major obstacle to recovery.[133]

We shall look further at Bennet's remarks when we come to discuss the patients, but, as regards the hospital's facilities, his criticisms clearly spurred the board into action. In the very same month that he made his visit, a group of governors personally inspected the airing grounds and concluded that they were 'too confined' and should be extended.[134] In 1816 the board leased $2\frac{1}{2}$ acres to the east of the building, 'affording a good view into the Phoenix Park', from Dean Trench of Kildare for ninety-nine years at an annual rent of nearly £46. To the west, they leased part of the old burial ground from Steevens Hospital for sixty-one years at twenty guineas a year and, to the north, part of the steward's garden, also from Steevens. Part of Trench's land was turned into a vegetable garden and Cleghorn reported in 1817 that many patients 'have been employed, with their own consent, in working the ground, and have been much happier and freer from their malady in consequence of it'. A ball court had also been constructed in this field, though Cleghorn, observing that the insane had 'no disposition to co-operation among them', doubted 'if they will ever agree to play a match at ball'. Despite Cleghorn's reservations, the court in fact continued in use for over a century. The ground to the west, acquired from Steevens, was reserved for the recreation of female patients, who were housed in the west range of the hospital. But no special facilities appear to have been provided for them.[135]

Cleghorn in his evidence admitted that 'the reports of the committee of the house of commons' had acted as a spur to the acquisition of more land, but he firmly denied that Bennet's criticism was the sole factor that had motivated this action. He pointed out that in 1810, for instance, the governors had decided to segregate patients, but lack of money, and particularly the government's failure to help, had made this impossible. To understand why Cleghorn should be so insistent in emphasising the governors' own awareness of the hospital's shortcomings and their efforts to overcome them, we need to realise that much of the evidence presented between 1814 and 1817 to both the English and Irish select committees on the insane poor had been extremely critical of existing asylums. The evidence relating to Bethlem Hospital in particular had created a public scandal. It showed that patients were systematically abused: starved, beaten, chained in filthy cells and generally, as the committee itself said, treated worse than animals. Nor was Bethlem wholly exceptional; similar conditions were found to exist in other asylums and also in many of the workhouses accommodating lunatics.[136] Cleghorn was obviously anxious to demonstrate that no such conditions prevailed in St Patrick's, but, at the same time, that the governors were fully aware of the problems that did exist and were seeking to rectify them. He may not have been wholly accurate in denying the impact of Bennet's evidence, but he was on much stronger ground in defending St Patrick's treatment of its patients. By modern standards this of course left much to be desired, but a perusal of the evidence given before the parliamentary select committees concerning the horrendous cond-itions existing in some English asylums and in most Irish work-houses, makes abundantly clear that, by the standards of the time, St Patrick's was a superior institution indeed. Bennet himself, despite his criticisms, had concluded that, if occupation and recrea-tion were improved and classification introduced, 'no establishment could be . . . better'.[137]

That there was a need in Ireland for an institution to house the insane, as Swift had so strongly believed, was amply demonstrated during the first half century of St Patrick's existence. The hospital trebled in size and this growth was largely in response to a demand for places that came from all parts of the country. Although in theory St Patrick's was a privately-run charity, the government showed its awareness of the hospital's important role by providing most of the money needed to pay for extending the building. But, within a relatively short time, it became obvious that St Patrick's was simply not able to cope with the numbers, particularly the numbers of pauper lunatics, wanting accommodation. The work-houses, established from the 1770s onwards, were forced to take in large numbers of the insane, while others continued to be confined in prisons. But, by the early years of the nineteenth century, there was a growing sense of crisis: a widespread belief that insanity was increasing and that the country lacked adequate provision to cope with it. At about the same time, there was also developing, not just in Ireland but in Europe generally, a more optimistic view regarding the treatment of mental illness. The often harsh practices used in eighteenth-century asylums had not proved very effective and by 1800 many of those connected with asylum management were coming round to the idea that a less rigorous regime, in fact a regime that stressed comfort and kindness, might produce more favourable results. It was increasingly felt that if the insane could be committed early in their illness to an asylum and if that asylum could provide proper care and treatment, the chances of recovery were good.[138] This positive attitude towards the role of asylums, plus the growing concern at the numbers of lunatics wandering the countryside, helped persuade the government, firstly to provide money to expand existing institutions like St Patrick's, then to build its own public asylum in Dublin and finally to begin in the 1820s the erection of district asylums throughout the country. The development of this network of government asylums was, however, to alter profoundly both the role and the character to St Patrick's Hospital.

THE PATIENTS

The administration, finances and architecture of St Patrick's all tell us much about the functions of the hospital, but perhaps the most revealing, and certainly the most important, aspect of such an institution is its patients. Yet, particularly in the eighteenth century, it is the patients who are most elusive. Although there is mention of admission documents and registers of patients, none of this material has survived before the 1830s and so, for the first sixty years of the hospital's existence, most of what we know of the patients consists of brief entries and passing references in the governors' minute books. Yet, when collected together and studied carefully, these scraps of information do yield fascinating insights into the three major issues of how the patients lived, how they were treated and who they were.

We have seen already that there were two types of patients admitted right from the opening of the hospital: pauper or free patients and boarders or paying patients. Paupers were classified as either 'lunaticks' or 'ideots'; the former being housed in the basement wards and the latter in the first floor wards. Boarders, who, in addition to paying an annual fee, had to furnish their own cells, were housed in the wards on the ground floor. But, after 1781, the boarders were subdivided into two categories, not on the basis of their illnesses, but in terms of the level of fees they paid and the facilities that were provided to them. Ward boarders, paying a lower fee, were still accommodated in the cells, though they enjoyed a better diet and better furnishings than the paupers. Chamber boarders, paying a higher fee, were provided with their own rooms at the ground and first floor front of the hospital; they also enjoyed a better diet, their own fireplace and the attentions of a personal servant. The table below draws together the scattered statistics that survive on the numbers of patients and the levels of fees charged boarders.

NUMBER OF PATIENTS AND FEES CHARGED AT
ST PATRICK'S 1757-1817

N/K = Not Known.

YEAR	NUMBERS			FEES: GUINEAS P.A.		
	PAUPERS	CHAMBER BOARDERS	WARD BOARDERS	EMPTY ROOMS	CHAMBER BOARDERS	WARD BOARDERS
1757	16	—	N/K	c.32	—	£22.15.0
1762	c.32	—	c.16	None	—	30
1783	N/K	6	34	N/K	60	34
1789-9	61	9	39	38	Not less than £40	
1803	N/K	N/K	N/K	N/K	80	40
1808	86	12	39	10	80	40
1813	N/K	N/K	N/K	N/K	100	60
1815	N/K	15	36	N/K	100	60
1817	96	53		N/K	100	60[139]

It is no easy matter to reconstruct the living conditions of patients in the hospital at this period. No comprehensive account of St Patrick's routines or regulations survives, nor is there even a very adequate description of the hospital. But, drawing on our earlier discussion and with a little informed imagination, we can at least produce a sketch.

All but the chamber boarders, who made up about 10 per cent of patients by 1815, were housed in cells on the three floors of the hospital's long ranges: women in the west range and men in the east. The cells were approximately eight by twelve feet in area, high ceilinged, and with a convex window well above head height. The paupers' cells contained wooden beds and stools, plus bedding supplied by the hospital, but probably little else. The ward boarders' cells, on the other hand, were furnished by their families and friends and so some may have been quite lavish and comfortable. Straw was sometimes used in place of beds, but only, it seems, in cases of particularly violent and destructive patients. Bennet in 1815 saw 'but six straw patients in the whole establishment, two of whom were quite naked, having torn their clothes to pieces'. The cells were not heated, but there were fireplaces burning coal in the corridors outside. The cell doors were fitted with panels enabling food to be passed through to the patients. It was in fact one of the keepers' main tasks to carry food from the basement kitchen to each of the cells, though, after the ranges were trebled in length in the 1780s and 1790s, this must have often entailed a long trip, leaving some of the patients' meals far from hot at the end of it. Not for many years were the patients to have dining rooms, nor till the 1830s were there communal day-rooms. Those patients allowed out of their cells presumably congregated in the corridors and around the fireplaces in winter. Such living conditions may seem somewhat spartan to us and certainly the damp and dilapidated condition the building was in by the first decade of the nineteenth century must have made for considerable discomfort. But, on the other hand, at this time many of St Patrick's patients were drawn from the working and lower middle classes and thus were probably used to far worse. The Rev. James Whitelaw, rector of St Catherine's parish in the Liberties, which supplied a significant number of patients to St Patrick's, in his *Report on the Population of Ireland*, published in 1798, provided a very vivid account of working-class living conditions in his own parish: '. . . I have frequently surprised [Whitelaw wrote,] from ten to sixteen persons, of all ages and sexes, in a room not fifteen feet square, stretched on a wad of filthy straw, swarming with vermin, and without any covering, save the wretched rags that constituted their wearing apparel'.[140]

Certainly with regard to diet, many of the patients in St Patrick's were considerably better off than they would have been outside. Meat was a major item on the menu, along with milk, potatoes, butter, oatmeal, bread and beer. The master and the housekeeper both had gardens—the master's garden is first referred to in 1784—and from these the hospital was supplied with vegetables free of charge. After 1816, as we have already seen, a large garden was laid out in the recently-acquired land between the hospital and Steevens Lane and, by 1818, this garden was producing, in addition to supplies for St Patrick's, over £100 worth of vegetables, including broccoli, and fruit trees for commercial sale.[141] The governors insisted on high-quality food stuffs for the patients, even during times of financial stringency. In June 1810, for instance, when prices were particularly high, they were still ordering 'good cool butter' at 1s 2d per pound, 'unadulterated new milk' at $2\frac{1}{2}$d per quart and the 'very best quality' oatmeal at 18s 6d per hundred weight.[142] Unfortunately, no precise details of meals survive from the period before 1820. But it is reasonable to assume that all patients had three meals a day: breakfast, dinner and supper. The paupers probably had stirabout, or oatmeal porridge, for breakfast; dinner was based on potatoes, with meat three times a week; while supper consisted of bread and milk. Beer was also very likely supplied. Boarders would have had a similar, though rather richer, diet, with better quality meat for dinner every day; beer and perhaps also wine; and tea in addition to milk. As early as 1787 in fact a grocer was contracted by the hospital to supply the boarders with tea and other, unspecified, groceries. Bennet concluded that, considering the 'practice of other well managed establishments', the diet in St Patrick's 'was too generally full'. Certainly the provision of meat, particularly beef, and of tea was far more lavish than most Irish families of the period would have been able to afford. Further information on the boarders' diet is contained in a list of expenses, probably compiled in 1803 to justify the fee rises of that year.

DAILY COST OF MAINTAINING BOARDERS AT ST PATRICK'S c.1803.

	Chamber Boarder	Ward Boarder
	pence per day	
Flesh meat 1¼lb	6¼	6¼
Bread 22 Ounces	3	3
Beer 1 quart	2	2
Milk 2 quarts	4	4
Tea & Sugar	4	3
Coals	6	0½
Candles	1½	0½
Ward Keeper/Servant	10	0¾
Physician	6	6
Total Cost Per Day	3s 6¾d	2s 2d
Total Cost Per Year	£65.03¾	£39.10.10[143]

This table clearly shows the substantial amounts of meat, bread, milk and beer that the boarders were consuming every day. In the case of ward boarders the cost of food made up 70 per cent of the total cost of their maintenance. As for chamber boarders, the higher cost of supporting them was largely a result of the fact that their rooms were individually heated and well-lit and that they were each attended by a servant, whereas the ward boarders had a keeper between eight or nine of them.

Considerable efforts seem to have been made to keep both the building and the patients clean. The interior of the hospital was 'coloured and whitened' in 1768; the exterior woodwork was painted in 1771; while the interior was painted again in 1786 and also in 1801. The practice seems to have been to whitewash the walls of the cells and corridors, while painting the woodwork black.[144] As for the patients, we know that in 1785 each ward was using half a pound of soap every month for washing patients' hands and faces and that a barber was employed to shave the male patients. Baths had been installed when the hospital opened, but, as we shall see, these were probably intended more for the purposes of treatment than of cleanliness. In 1815, however, in seeking a further parliamentary grant to improve facilities, the governors placed baths, for the promotion both of 'health and cleanliness', high on their list of requirements. Semple had built outhouses for baths and toilets, but these must have been damp and cold places, particularly in winter. Indoor water closets appear to have been installed when the building was enlarged in the 1780s and 1790s, though, as we have seen, by 1809 these were leaking so badly as to damage the walls of the building. Heating was provided by coal-burning fires—three on each floor of the ranges and one in each of the rooms at the front of the building used by the staff and chamber boarders. By 1804 the master was buying 150 tons of coal a year at a cost of nearly £30. Lighting was by means of oil lamps and candles. Lamps were probably used in the public areas of the hospital, like the entrance hall, stairs and corridors, while candles were provided to the staff for their rooms and the patients' cells. Bennet noted that the 'galleries' were lighted at night and that the cells were not locked till 8 p.m. in winter and 9 p.m. in summer.[145]

Nothing has been said so far of the medical treatment offered to patients. This is because virtually no information as to treatment is to be found in the surviving documents. Such a matter was left totally in the hands of the medical officers and was never discussed by the governors. Presumably the doctors kept records of their own, but, if so, these were not deposited in the hospital. Eighteenth-century asylums, with their cells and devices of restraint, seem to us more like prisons than hospitals: they aimed essentially to confine and render harmless those regarded as socially disruptive or menacing. In 1800, in a report to the chancellor of the exchequer, the governors appeared to confirm this view when they set out the hospital's basic aims, one of which was:

> the affording of a comfortable asylum to those who may be incurable and exonerating wretched and impoverished families from the expense necessarily attendant upon the support of idiots and maniacs, as well as relieving the public from the disagreeable, and often times dangerous, consequences of such objects being left at large.[146]

Bennet, after his inspection in 1815, certainly complained at the lack of treatment being offered in St Patrick's.

> It appeared to me [he told the parliamentary select committee investigating madhouses], that there was but little medical, and not much mental treatment; it seems to be more a place of confinement that of cure; there is a physician and a surgeon to the establishment [paid out of boarders' fees. But there is] no limitation as to the time for which the patient is kept; he is maintained there as long as his illness requires it; one of the

patients had been there fifty years. There was little or no noise; there were only three persons in manacles and no one in a strait-waistcoat . . . I never witnessed lunatics so quiet and orderly . . .[147]

In his response to these comments in 1817, Cleghorn, the visiting physician, actually argued against medical treatment:

. . . medical treatment in maniacal person, and the insane in general, except in the very early stages of the disease, had ever appeared to me to be of little service towards the cure of it . . . I think, generally speaking, from the experience of fourteen years . . . [the insane] are less subject to bodily disease than other persons; moral treatment, as it is called, is of much more moment than medical . . . The system observed in Swift's Hospital, before I was concerned in it, was of the most humane kind; and it has always been my object to avoid any other coercion or restraint but what was required for the safety of the patients and those around them.[148]

In his rejection of both physical restraint and medical treatment, Cleghorn was here reflecting the growing belief that kindness, comfortable living conditions, healthy recreation and productive occupation were more effective in combating mental illness than pills or potions, chains or straps.

But, in 1817, this was a relatively new view. During the eighteenth century Drs John Whiteway, Robert Robinson, John Nicholls, William Ruxton, Robert Emmet and Clement Archer, practised in St Patrick's and those who were governors, like Robinson, Nicholls and Emmet, had a marked influence upon the hospital's development. For the curing of the insane *was* the governors' main aim—in 1800 they proclaimed the 'most desirable' effect of St Patrick's to be 'the restoration of many patients to their reason and to social life'—and they clearly believed that doctors could achieve this by medical means. They told the chancellor of the exchequer that all governors were 'equally concerned in the regulation of the hospital', but that the 'interior regulation' was 'in a great measure confided to Dr Emmet, who as physician to the state, being officially a governor, and having been appointed by the governors to attend upon the boarders, with a certain allowance of their board money for such attendance, is considered as bound by a governor's trust and by his private interest to be particularly careful and attentive to the interior administration of the hospital'. Although the governors stressed that Emmet's 'conduct therein is under the constant inspection of the board and some of the governors occasionally visit the hospital', it was clear that the physician had sole responsibility for the handling of patients. We also know from apothecaries' bills, which survive from the 1760s and 1770s, that the hospital used drugs in large amounts.[149] But, what these substances were is, unfortunately, nowhere specified. For some notion of the medical treatment employed by doctors like Emmet, we have to turn from St Patrick's to a doctor practising in a Cork asylum.

The most important work by an Irish doctor of the late eighteenth and early nineteenth centuries on the subject of insanity was Dr William Saunders Hallaran's *Practical Observations on the Causes and Cure of Insanity*, published in Cork in 1810 and reissued in a revised form in 1818. From the early 1790s till his death in 1826, Hallaran was physician to the Cork workhouse and asylum, as well as conducting his own private asylum in the city. He had been trained in Edinburgh under Dr William Cullen, one of the most eminent medical teachers of his day and an advocate of Thomas Willis's neurological theories.[150] Hallaran's views are particularly interesting as they illustrate the transition from the physically-based views of doctors like Emmet to the morally-based theories of Cleghorn and his early nineteenth-century contemporaries.

Hallaran, for instance, continued to believe in the use of large doses of purgatives and emetics, given 'at regular intervals [i.e. every hour], in order to maintain a state of nausea, until such a portion of the purgative be taken as might eventually secure a copious discharge from the intestines'. Such a drastic regime was to be employed particularly in cases of recent and severe mania. By such means, after about ten to fourteen days, Hallaran claimed to have reduced 'the most stubborn maniac to a state of relative quiescence'.[151] On the other hand, Hallaran rejected many traditional techniques and remedies, like bleeding, blistering and the use of opium and camphor. Hot baths he thought a helpful stimulant in cases of melancholia, while in severe cases of 'maniacal fever' he recommended three cold showers a day followed by confinement to bed.[152] He also continued to believe in the necessity for physical restraint. Prolonged and severe restraint, like chaining patients to their beds, could certainly be counter-productive, breeding a 'vicious disposition' and a deep sense of injustice in the patient. But moderate methods, like leather straps to restrict the arms and leg irons to impede, but not totally prevent, movement, Hallaran regarded as not merely desirable, but essential. A campaign against all methods of restraint had begun in England during the 1790s at a private, Quaker 'retreat' in York. But Hallaran argued that middle-class quakers, schooled in 'self control' made for very different patients than Irish paupers.'. . . our Irish lunatics are often extremely refractory' he wrote, concluding that the Quaker experience in

York was not applicable to Ireland.[153] Once the lunatic had been quietened, Hallaran strongly recommended the use of the drug, digitalis, which he was convinced could, given in the correct amounts and at the correct times, remove the basic symptoms of insanity.

Hallaran's treatments, however, were not solely medical. He in fact readily acknowledged the 'difficulty of subjecting persons labouring under mental insanity to the influence of means strictly medical'. Moreover, he had found that the patients themselves were often fully alive to the inadequacy of drugs: 'They, as if to escape importunity, will swallow a few portions of medicine the futility of which they appear to anticipate'. In this regard Hallaran was in agreement with the advocates of moral management, for he too felt that the environment in which patients lived, plus their relationship to their doctors, were vital factors in the remedial process. To the doctors he recommended 'tenderness' and 'perseverance, with decision', while, as for the environment, he thought that it needed to be very carefully managed. In the early and acute stages of mania, for instance, it was vital to shield the patient from strong stimuli of any sort. We have already noted how small and high the cell windows were at St Patrick's. But Hallaran argued that such a placing of windows was necessary both 'to guard against glare' and 'to avoid all intercourse from without'. Conversely, the convalescent insane needed to be re-introduced to bright light and to the bustle of the outside world, though in a gradual and controlled manner. Such patients also required exercise and occupation following their long periods of 'tedious confinement'. Here Hallaran was thoroughly in agreement with the moral managers as to the value of the 'business of horticulture'. In the 'easy labour of the garden, in which force is never employed,' he wrote, patients 'never fail to enjoy a happy state of oblivion from their real or imaginary grievances'. In pursuit of this policy, he acquired three acres of land beside the Cork asylum and found that, if patients were forbidden to talk and no unsettling interruptions occurred, 'incredible' amounts of work, four times that undertaken by an ordinary day labourer, could be achieved.[154]

With regard to St Patrick's we know that physical restraint, baths and drugs were used extensively during the early decades of the hospital's existence. When it was being built Semple had installed chairs in each ward to which patients could be strapped, while in his 1816 evidence Bennet mentioned manacles and 'strait-waistcoats'. We have already noted the largeness of the hospital's apothecary's bills, and that only three months after it opened, in December 1757,

Drs Robinson and Nicholls were asked by the governors to arrange for the provision of hot and cold baths. But, after 1800, the tenets of moral management began to have their impact and there was a move away from bodily treatments to more mentally-based ones. Dr James Cleghorn, who served as the hospital's visiting physician from 1803 to 1825, was clearly a vigorous advocate of this new approach. In 1807 and again in 1822 he applied to his fellow governors for leave to go abroad on business. Of the first trip we, unfortunately, know nothing, but in the latter instance the minute book specifies that the object of his trip was 'professional improvement' and the board remarked that it hoped he would, on his return, communicate 'any observations which may occur in the course of his investigations concerning lunatic asylums'.[155] Clearly the governors were keen that St Patrick's should keep abreast of new ideas in the treatment of the mentally ill. In 1815 Bennet had found that Patrick Campbell, who succeeded Mahony as master in 1812, was an 'intelligent man', quite conscious of the need to classify patients and already familiar with the reports of the parliamentary select committee then investigating English madhouses. By the time of Bennet's inspection, then, the governors, the visiting physician and the master were all familiar with and receptive to the new and more optimistic approach of moral management and over the following thirty years this new approach was to have a major impact on St Patrick's. Unfortunately, however, this impact was by no means a wholly positive one.

Aside from how the patients lived and what treatment they received, the other interesting question which arises is, who were they? We have already seen that no patient registers or admission documents survive for the eighteenth century. But in 1769, apparently feeling that they were not being kept sufficiently informed as to the numbers of people admitted to the hospital, the governors ruled that 'for the future, when patients are to be admitted into this hospital, all applications in their favour shall be made to the general board and that no patients be received into the house without their order'.[156] In practice, however, the master and the executive committee, with a quorum of at least three governors, appear to have admitted many patients, though such admissions were considered provisional till confirmed at the next quarterly meeting of the full board. So, after 1769, most admissions were recorded in the governors' minute books.

During the fifty years from the opening of the hospital till the end of 1807, these books mention in all 470 patients received into the institution. This figure certainly does not represent all who passed through the doors of St Patrick's as some admissions were not recorded. Only a relatively small number of boarders are, for instance, listed in the minutes. It seems also that, when more pressing issues like financial problems and questions of estate management preoccupied the board, admissions were neglected or perhaps simply not written down by the busy secretary. So the 470 cases that do appear in the minutes must be regarded as only a sample. Nevertheless, they are a large sample and a fairly random one and thus it seems reasonable, on the basis of these cases, to draw conclusions regarding the whole of the hospital population.

Most admission entries in the minutes are brief, simply giving the name of the patient, if they are a pauper or boarder, a lunatic or an idiot, and possibly also which individuals or parishes had applied for their admission. Sometimes in fact not even this much information is provided, but still, in 94 per cent of the cases we are told the sex of the patient and in 30 per cent what part of the country they come from. With some inmates we can even trace age, occupation, family links, length of residence in the hospital and re-admissions. These cases, however, are all too few. On the whole, reconstructing the backgrounds of patients admitted to St Patrick's during its first half century is not an easy task. The table below, however, represents an attempt to summarise the data that is available.

PATIENTS ADMITTED TO ST PATRICK'S
HOSPITAL, 1757-1807

Overall size of sample: 470

Sex of Patient
(Sample size: 442)
Male   54%
Female   46%

Person Committing Patient
(Sample size: 228)
Parish   36%
Governor   28%
Parent   9%
Husband   7%
Wife   1%
Other   19%

Nature of Disorder
(Sample size: 204)
Lunatic   75%
Idiot   25%

Free or Fee-paying Patient
(Sample size: 328)
Pauper   92%
Boarder   8%
Boarders becoming Paupers 4%

Re-admissions
(Sample size: 470)
Patients re-admitted 3%

Place of Residence
(Sample size: 140)
Dublin City 63%
Leinster   18%
Ulster   11%
Connacht   6%
Munster   2%[157]

The first statistic in the above table indicating the percentages of men and women admitted to St Patrick's is not, on the whole, a very helpful one. The hospital was divided into male and female halves and so one would expect the sexes to be roughly equal. Segregation of male and female patients appears to have been strictly enforced, even down to separate airing yards and gardens. But, in terms of the staff, segregation was more difficult. Bennet, for instance, had been quite indignant over the large number of women in the 'men's galleries', which he claimed was 'greater ... than I ever saw elsewhere'.[158] These women were the so-called 'ward maids', whose main job was to clean the cells and corridors and to remove dirty laundry. The nineteenth century was strongly of the view that the insane should be denied contact with members of the opposite sex as far as possible. Yet, despite Bennet's complaints and others as well, St Patrick's continued to employ female maids in the male wards till the very end of the century.

Much more revealing, however, are the statistics relating to the persons applying for the admission of patients. Originally, according to the admission procedures laid down when the hospital opened, it was intended that relatives or friends should untertake this task and, as can be seen, a significant number of people were admitted by their parents or spouses. It is interesting to note, though, that husbands were far more likely to petition for the committal of their wives that *vice versa*; similarly, brothers committed their siblings more commonly than sisters. In fact, the number of women applying for the admission of patients was extremely small. Aside from a handful of wives committing husbands and sisters committing sisters—but never brothers—there were several cases of mothers committing children. Most of these women seem however, to have been widows. Presumably in a society such as eighteenth-century Ireland, where women lacked the power and status normally accorded to men, the drastic act of having another person, especially a man, committed to an asylum was one they were seldom able to carry out. Only when a male authority figure was lacking were women in a position to act.

Increasingly from the 1770s onwards, petitions for admissions did not come from relatives, or at least not directly so; rather they came from the ministers and church wardens of Protestant parishes, from hospital governors and from other influential individuals. Perhaps this trend partly reflected the growing demand for places, particularly free places, in the hospital. To be sure of securing such a place an applicant needed the endorsement of a clergyman, landlord, or best of all, a governor. Actually governors and clergymen were often the same people, for at different times a number of the elected clerical governors were the ministers of Dublin inner city parishes. For some governors, then, St Patrick's became an important source of patronage. It is almost certainly no coincidence that admission petitions from governors increased markedly after politicians, like John Foster and John Beresford, joined the board. We shall look more closely at the geographical distribution of patients shortly, but, in the present context, it is worth noting that the county producing most patients between 1757 and 1807 was Co. Louth— the home and political base of the Foster family. In the twelve years from 1782 to 1794, when the admission records are unusually detailed, John Foster was the governor making most admission applications: 23 per cent of the total coming from governors, which put him slightly ahead of the archbishop of Dublin. During the same period John Beresford accounted for 8 per cent of applications, while there were others from his brothers, the marquess of Waterford and the bishop of Ossory. As we have already seen, the Fosters in particular derived a great deal of their influence from patronage as they had only arrived in Ireland in the 1660s and appear to have been of lowly origins. They therefore lacked the wealth and traditional power of many of the older Anglo-Irish landed families.[159] For the Fosters a governorship of St Patrick's Hospital obviously offered an opportunity to do favours for supporters in Co. Louth by securing the admission of their mad relatives to the hospital. Asylum accommodation was in extremely short supply in Ireland in the last quarter of the eighteenth century and thus the power to nominate patients to St Patrick's was doubtless a valuable one. The indications are that, during the 1780s and 1790s at least, John Foster used this power to the full.

Dublin clergymen and hospital governors were most successful in getting patients into St Patrick's in the late eighteenth century, but patients were also accepted from certain other institutions. Although plans for the hospital to take large numbers of lunatics from the workhouse fell through in the 1790s, after the building had been enlarged for the first time in the early 1780s some twenty lunatics were accepted from the workhouse and the bridewell, while in 1812, as we have seen, another thirteen were taken from the overcrowded Waterford workhouse. The board did not shrink in certain instances from accepting obviously difficult cases. In 1770, for instance, it admitted two 'dangerous lunatics', both murderers. James Brennan from Co. Westmeath had 'in a fit of lunacy killed his father by a blow from a large wooden candlestick', while Thomas Swinburne, having been acquitted of a charge of murder on the basis of insanity, had gone on to commit 'many acts of violence against different persons'. We do not know who applied for Brennan's admission—friends are referred to though not named—but in Swinburne's case it was Lord Blayney from Co. Monaghan, supported by a 'particular certificate' from the surgeon general, William Ruxton. Presumably the governors would not have admitted such dangerous patients without strong recommendations from influential individuals.[160] Other notable persons petitioning for admissions included the former chief secretary Sir John Blaquiere, the under secretaries Thomas Waite and Charles Saxton, the earls of Roden and Belmore, the duchess of Leinster, Viscount Tullamore, Sir Capel Molyneux, the provost and fellows of Trinity College, Dublin, the banker David LaTouche and the bishops of Cloyne and Ferns.

In some instances the governors gave priority to petitions from persons who had donated money to St Patrick's. In 1764 they decided that, as the Hon. Mrs Jane Bury, sister of Charles Moore, Viscount Tullamore, had given £200 to the hospital, she should be empowered to recommend one patient for admission and a cell should be set aside for the purpose, inscribed with her name and arms. But, as the demand for places intensified in the 1770s, such favoured treatment of donors appears to have lapsed. In 1775, for instance, Mrs Forde, a 'benefactress' of the hospital, applied for the admission of William Carlisle, a 'poor lunatic' tradesman, but it was not till two and a half years later, in 1777, that Carlisle was finally received. And in 1787 the board flatly rejected a request from Sir Kildare Burrowes for the right to recommend a patient for admission. So, while petitions from governors and other influential parties appear to have been given priority, the board became reluctant in the face of a growing demand for places to give anyone an automatic right to nominate patients. Sometimes those recommended even by the most powerful in the land had to wait years for admission. Thus Margery News from Co. Tyrone was not offered a place till February 1776, although her petition, supported by the lord chancellor, had been received in 1774. When she had not appeared by November 1776 her place was offered to the wife of John Frazer, 'long recommended as an unhappy lunatick'.[161]

The table above shows that the majority of patients admitted to St Patrick's were classified as pauper lunatics. The hospital had set aside accommodation on the first floor for so-called 'idiots', but a distinct reluctance to accept obviously incurable cases appears to have developed and thus the numbers of mentally handicapped patients admitted steadily declined. In 1816 the governors also decided not to accept any more epileptic patients, except for those who could pay for their own rooms and servants as chamber boarders. This decision was made, according to the minutes of the meeting, 'in consideration of the impossibility of providing the necessary attendance required for the management of epileptic patients . . . and from the danger accruing to other patients from seeing persons so afflicted in the paroxyms of that disorder'. Essentially the governors were admitting that, with limited staff and without facilities for segregating patients according to their disorders, they could not easily cope with troublesome patients.[162]

As for free patients, or paupers as they were termed at the time, they certainly made up the majority of patients, though 92 per cent rather overstates their numbers. Boarders seem to have accounted for roughly a third of places in the hospital, but their admissions were not recorded in the governors' minutes to the same extent as paupers'. Again, for this same reason, our statistics probably also underestimate the numbers of boarders transferring to the pauper wards. This was increasingly common in the 1790s and 1800s. Undoubtedly the substantial fee increases of these years, combined with the general economic hardship caused by the long war, played a part in this process. The governors were certainly finding it more and more difficult to collect fees. In 1797, 1798 and again in 1799 the hospital's law agent was instructed to take legal action against defaulting relatives, while in 1803, in an unusually severe resolution, the governors declared that, if boarders' fees were not paid quarterly in advance, the master was to give the relatives or friends two weeks to remove the patient from the hospital. If the patient was not removed by the deadline, he or she would be sent to the workhouse. Yet, in many cases, recovering unpaid fees was far from a simple matter. In January 1770, for instance, George Maquay, a Dublin merchant, successfully petitioned to have his aunt, Mary Maquay, admitted as a boarder. In June 1783 Mary Maquay was still a ward boarder, paying thirty guineas per annum. But, in November 1794, close on twenty years after her admission, Mary Maquay was transferred to a pauper ward. Perhaps this move signalled the death of her nephew, or perhaps the state of his business affairs no longer allowed him to find thirty guineas a year with which to support his elderly, insane aunt. Another long-term patient, who suffered the same fate as Mary Maquay through family financial problems, was Katherine Hill. In November 1772 her sister, Elizabeth, petitioned to have her transferred to a pauper ward as a free patient. Nothing seems to have come of this request, perhaps due to the high demand for free places during the 1770s. But, in February 1779, Elizabeth Hill petitioned again, arguing that she had already paid £240 in fees and was now 'unable on account of her years to earn her livelihood as formerly.' This time the board agreed to her request.[163]

We shall see when we come to discuss the occupations of patients and their relatives that some families, who may initially have admitted a member as a boarder in hopes of a cure, found it increasingly difficult to support them over a long period of years. Equally, of course, some families may simply have been unwilling to pay for elderly and incurable relatives, even if the money was available. The governors repeatedly resolved that 'for the future no patient admitted as a boarder shall be received afterwards as a pauper'.[164] Yet, in the face of their own edict, they continued to make such transfers. Moreover, though they threatened in 1803 to remove patients in arrears, there is no evidence that they actually did this at the time. For, despite the admission of paying patients, St Patrick's, under its charter, remained a charitable institution. It was thus more in keeping with the official nature of the hospital for the governors to transfer boarders no longer able, for whatever reason, to pay fees to the pauper wards rather than to expel them.

The above table clearly shows that St Patrick's was by no means a purely Dublin hospital, for at least a third of its patients came from outside the city. The geographical distribution of patients was in fact quite wide. All eighteen of the city's Protestant parishes recommended patients for admission, as did twenty-three out of the thirty-two counties. Within the city, the parishes contributing significant numbers of pauper patients included St Peter's in the Aungier Street area, where the minister was Archdeacon Robert Fowler, a long-serving governor;[165] St James's, which actually included the hospital; and St Michael's and St Catherine's, which took in the nearby High and Thomas Street areas. Others came from more outlying Dublin parishes, like Ringsend, Clontarf, Finglas and Chapelizod. Without the recommendation of their parish officials, many paupers would probably never have been admitted. Yet, the governors also seem at times to have accepted wandering lunatics without parish support. Thus in March 1787, John Cooke Courtney, who had spent several months in the hospital in 1774-5 and been discharged as recovered, was re-admitted, described as a 'wandering lunatick without any place of residence'; and in September 1771 Dr Emmet had been asked to examine and admit immediately 'a male ideot now lying destitute of friends in the market house of Thomas Street'.[166] As for the rest of the country, we have seen that Louth contributed more patients than any other single county, due almost certainly to the political interests of the Foster family in that area. Also striking is how few patients came from Munster. It is unlikely that mere distance was the major deterrent, as counties like Donegal, Londonderry and Mayo sent patients under probably more arduous travelling conditions. But, from the 1770s, accommodation for lunatics was provided in Munster itself. In 1772 an act was passed allowing counties to establish houses of industry for the confinement of vagrants, beggars and the destitute poor generally. Lunatics appear to have been admitted to these institutions, for, under an act of 1787, grand juries were empowered to raise funds to provide accommodation for the insane in asylums attached to workhouses. This apparently was an attempt to remove lunatics from workhouses and prisons where they were proving a disruptive influence. Few counties, however, took advantage of the provisions of this act for they were optional and also had to be paid for out of local taxes. But they were put into effect in Dublin, Cork, Waterford and Limerick, where cells for the insane were built adjacent to the existing workhouses.[167] Presumably, with special facilities available in Cork, Waterford and Limerick, the authorities in Munster were more inclined to send their pauper lunatics to the workhouse asylums than to St Patrick's Hospital in Dublin.

In only nine cases out of our sample of 470 are we told the ages of persons admitted to the hospital. With so few examples it is virtually impossible to generalise regarding the age structure of St Patrick's patients, though it may not be without significance that seven out of the nine were under thirty years of age. With regard to religious denomination there is even less data. The majority of patients were undoubtedly Protestant, given the hospitals' links with the Established Church. But there was certainly no bar against the acceptance of Catholic patients and in 1783, for instance, Anthony Brady, described as a 'popish clergyman', was admitted as a pauper lunatic.[168] If the proportions of Catholics and Protestants were anything like those prevailing in the nineteenth century, then at least a quarter of patients would have been Catholic.

The fact that the families of some of St Patrick's patients were prepared to pay sixty, eighty or even one hundred guineas a year for their accommodation shows that some of the boarders came from quite affluent backgrounds. Often, though, families were not able to sustain this expense indefinitely, which suggests that in many cases the affluence may have been more apparent than real. In twenty-seven cases in our sample we know the occupation of either the patient or the relative petitioning for admittance. Only three out of these twenty-seven can, however, be definitely identified as boarders: one, Mary Maquay, the aunt of a merchant, we have already discussed; the others were Sheppy Green, also a merchant, admitted in 1779 as a lunatic and William Sherlock, a Francis Street clothier, transferred to the pauper wards in 1780.[169] The occupations of merchant and clothier suggest the possibility of prosperous businesses, but hardly substantial wealth. In fact it seems that there was often little to distinguish ward boarders from so-called pauper patients, for many of these latter people were hardly paupers, at least as the word is understood today. Their families may not have been able or prepared to pay out large sums of money in boarders' fees, but they were by no means destitute. Ambrose Cuffe, for instance, who petitioned for the admission of his wife in 1772, was a clerk; Ann Williams, admitted in 1783, was the daughter of a brewer, though admittedly a bankrupt one; Elizabeth Ann Maddock, also admitted in 1783, was a forty year old widow and the daughter of a hatter from Fishamble Street; Castleton Maw, admitted in 1802, was the son of a Co. Wexford surgeon; Thomas Giordani, admitted in 1804, was the son of a music teacher; while James Reilly, also admitted in 1804, was the son of a Co. Meath schoolmaster. But nearly a quarter of these twenty-seven cases were made up of clergymen or their relatives. One should not of course therefore conclude that insanity was particularly prevalent among the Irish clergy. Given that the hospital had been established by a cleric and that clerics were prominent on the board of governors, it is hardly surprising to find the families of clergymen making considerable use of its facilities. Perhaps the most intriguing case, however, among this group of twenty-seven is that of

Catharine Dwyer, who was admitted as a pauper lunatic in 1803, being described as 'an incurable, who was a servant in the hospital and lost her health in it'. This was not to be the last such case and perhaps it was not the first; it is certainly, though, the first recorded one. No further details were given and so we can only wonder at what experiences caused Catharine Dwyer to lose her 'health' in the hospital's service.[170]

There are a few sources, aside from the hospital's own records, which also shed some light on the backgrounds of some of the early patients. John Moore, for instance, was a Carrickfergus merchant, who had returned to Ireland in 1766 with his sister after three years in the American colonies, working for an uncle who was an army sutler. Moore's sister had been unhappy in America and, shortly after their return, he was obliged to have her admitted to St Patrick's. In his journal he recorded her illness thus:

> July 1: my mother and sister fall out and my sister leaves the house; 14: I take her to Larne for some time; August 12: she returns with evident signs of lunacy upon her . . . September 1: we are obliged to confine her close; November 1: her disorder still increasing we have with great difficulty got an order for her admission into Dean Swift's Hospital in Dublin; 17: set off with her; 21: arrive without any accident but much perplexity on the road; 24: leave Dublin and get home on 28.

At first Moore's sister's condition deteriorated, for, in February 1767, he noted that 'the last account from the hospital says my sister is worse to manage than any patient they ever had in the house'. But, by May, St Patrick's was reporting that she was recovering and in July Moore's mother brought her home 'quite well'. Moore was delighted and fulsome in his appreciation of the hospital's work, thanking, first God for its existence and then Swift for his 'noble legacy'. Moore had been able to secure his sister's admission as a free patient, but he thought the thirty guineas a year then charged boarders a reasonable price for 'so well managed' an institution. If he had not been able to get his sister in free, he declared that he still would have wanted to have her admitted, even if it had meant him living 'on bread and water in order to pay'. Moore's business affairs were in fact far from prosperous: his uncle had refused to pay him his wages and was heavily in debt, while a cargo of flour that Moore had had shipped from Philadelphia had been lost at sea and the insurer could not reimburse him as 'he is broke'.[171] Moore was obviously not a 'pauper', as the word is understood today, but, equally, thirty guineas a year was a large sum which he could not easily have afforded. Nevertheless, he would have paid it had it been the only way of securing a place for his sister in St Patrick's. It appears that other families admitting members to the hospital were in rather similar circumstances to John Moore. They sought free admission. But, if the pauper wards were full, as they clearly were in the 1770s, then they either had to accept a long wait or they had to pay to have their relatives admitted as boarders. If the patient did not recover in a relatively short time, however, then a transfer to a pauper ward or discharge became the only options available. No wonder John Moore was so grateful for his sister's free admission.

There is no mention of Moore's sister in the governors' minute book, but, as already noted, patient records for the 1760s are particularly poor. The minute book, however, does record that in January 1787 George Kathrens was admitted as a pauper lunatic on the recommendation of Archdeacon Hastings and St Michael's parish and that he was re-admitted in August 1790. In May 1788 Elizabeth Kathrens, the wife of Murray Kathrens, a boarder, petitioned for his transfer to a pauper ward. The governors judged this a 'compassionate case' and agreed to the request.[172] We know a little more about George and Murray Kathrens, who were in fact cousins, because both had been pupils of the Quaker, Richard Shackleton, at his famous school in Ballitore, Co. Kildare, which educated, among many others, Edmund Burke and Cardinal Cullen. Shackleton's daughter, Mary Leadbeater, was a poet and storyteller, who, in her memoirs, *The Annals of Ballitore*, provided a vivid picture of Kildare life from the 1760s to the 1820s. In *The Annals* she mentions that George and Murray Kathrens returned separately to Ballitore in the late 1780s to visit her father. With Murray, Mary Leadbeater immediately noticed a 'great alteration . . . in his countenance. He who always looked as if he was stifling a laugh . . . now exhibited a picture of deep melancholy.' He had experienced a major financial reverse and 'his mental faculties [had] fallen a sacrifice to his misfortunes'. Although apparently cheered by his visit to his old school: 'Again the clouds gathered, and all was dark. His friends placed him in Swift's hospital for lunatics, where he lived several years, but never recovered his reason.' A few months later, to Mary's surprise, George Kathrens also appeared. Knowing him to be 'a respectable citizen', she was 'shocked to hear him asking pecuniary relief'. It soon emerged, however, that he had just escaped from 'a place of confinement', he too, like his cousin, having been driven mad by economic misfortune. He was returned to Dublin, but escaped again and again returned to Ballitore, impelled by 'the remembrance of his happy childhood'. Unlike his cousin, George's disorder took the form of extreme animation: he claimed to converse with the fairies who taught him songs and verses. But he also complained 'bitterly to his old frineds of the harsh treatment he had met with, he showed them with great indignation the marks which cords had left on his legs'. He was never 'restored to sanity', wrote Mary Leadbeater, though his family 'found means to restrain his wanderings'.[173] George, like Murray, was confined in St Patrick's and his re-admission in August 1790 doubtless took place after one of his escapes to Ballitore. The hospital must have sought to prevent such episodes by tying his legs, though how he was finally prevented from leaving is not made clear. Mary Leadbeater implies that both men were successful and prosperous prior to their encountering financial 'embarrassment', but both ended as pauper patients in St Patrick's. Such 'embarrass-ment' may have made it difficult for their families to afford boarders' fees, or perhaps once the hoplessness of both cases became obvious, their families did not want to be burdened with the payment of large sums for an indefinite period.

In the popular imagination eighteenth-century madhouses, like St Patrick's, are generally portrayed as gothic horrors: gloomy, grim places in which the inmates, often wrongfully incarcerated, were subjected to unspeakable cruelties by sadistic doctors and keepers. In some asylums patients certainly were mistreated, but, even at the time, such places were criticised. Many, however, tried, with the limited knowledge and resources of the period, to cure and comfort severely disturbed people. St Patrick's was such an institution.[174] Living conditions in the hospital may seem very basic to us, but they were probably no worse, and sometimes a good deal better, than many patients were used to outside. By the standards of the time, the diet at least was positively lavish. Unfortunately, our knowledge of the patients and of their medical treatment is rather limited. They came from all over Ireland, though the majority were Dubliners and Protestants. In class terms, most appear to have been working or middle class; few were paupers, despite the use of the term to describe non-paying patients, and equally, except perhaps for a handful of chamber boarders, few seem to have been really affluent. As for their treatment, the hospital's doctors, notably Dr Robert Emmet, who had the prime responsibility for patients from 1770 till his death in 1803, employed many of the accepted methods of the time. The aim largely was to subdue violent or excited patients and to eliminate their most obvious and distressing symptoms. To this end sedatives, emetics, purgatives, bleeding, blistering, hot and cold baths and physical restraint were all employed. Melancholia was often considered a more difficult problem to treat, but again baths, blistering and drugs were used. Towards the end of the century, however, as techinques appeared that were aimed at altering mental rather than physical processes, both maniacs and melancholics were encouraged to work in the laundry or kitchen or in the garden and to take plenty of outdoor exercise. At the same time attempts were made to renovate the building, to brighten it up and generally to create a more comfortable and homely atmosphere.

St Patrick's therefore entered the second quarter of the nineteenth century on a fairly positive note: there was optimism that so-called moral management offered a far more effective way of relieving mental illness than previous harsher, physical methods of treatment and, at the same time, as the country recovered from the long French wars and the economic upheavels of their aftermath, the financial position of the hospital was looking better than perhaps it had ever done previously. Many of these positive signs were, however, to prove in time sadly misleading.

CHAPTER 3

The Era of Moral Management, 1820-1850

Our patients come singly from every part of the country; two of the last that came in were from opposite quarters, one from Larne, another from Connaught, recommended by the Archbishop of Tuam. I hear it rumoured, that it is intended to have either Provincial or County Asylums for Lunatics and Idiots: such a design is founded in wisdom and humanity, and will be a great relief to the pressure on the establishments in the capital. Places of this kind, unless under a strict rule for a limited period of residence, beyond which no person will be allowed to remain in them, must become asylums for mad persons, and not hospitals or places for the cure of insanity.[1]

Upon perusing the Copy of the Charter which recites Dean Swift's Will, I do not observe any Power to admit Patients who pay; but the Foundation is a Charity, and it would be a Breach of Trust to apply its Funds to the Support and Cure of the Rich.[2]

Thomas Larkin 'for many years carried on as a respectable citizen the business of a general and medical bookseller but from losses in trade and other circumstances he has been for some years of unsound mind and totally unable to contribute to the support of memorialist, his four children or himself, but that she has supported his family and herself solely by letting her house in lodgings that her husband until lately has been so comparatively quiet as to admit of his being left in the house, but from the great increase of his disease memorialist finds it impossible to do so any longer as by so doing she would surely be obliged to give up her lodgers which are her sole support.'[3]

It is I assure you a most urgent [case], he is now quite outrageous and was nearly destroying some of the family today in my presence with a large carving knife. I found it necessary to send a keeper provided with a straight waistcoat to remain with him this night. The board will not sit at St Patrick's Hospital for ten or twelve days but if it were possible to provide him immediate admittance it would be most desirable least anything upleasant might occur in the meantime.[4]

ADMINISTRATION, STAFF AND FINANCE

The board of governors of St Patrick's Hospital was an unusual body in several ways. Compared to the governing bodies of many other Irish charitable institutions, it was very active and also relatively small. St Patrick's had fourteen governors, while Steevens had twenty-two and the Rotunda a massive forty-four. Swift, as we have seen, was suspicious of large committees which either did little work or attempted to exploit institutions for their own personal ends. He wanted to 'contrive' a board composed of a small number of committed and hard-working governors. In this aim he was in fact generally successful, although the charter doubled the number of governors by adding a group of *ex officio* members. Swift had envisaged such a group as trustees rather than governors, yet governors like the dean of St Patrick's Cathedral, the state physician and, to a lesser extent, the archbishop of Dublin and the surgeon general, often proved as active as their elected colleagues, if not more so. The early hospital would have suffered a significant loss had it been deprived of the services of Dean Corbet or Dr Emmet. The composition of the elected half of the board and the number of *ex officio* governors changed over the years, as did the balance of power between them. But throughout its history St Patrick's has been managed by a relatively small number of experienced and often influential men — plus, latterly, one woman — many of whom, without any payment, have devoted a good deal of time and energy to the hospital's frequently complex affairs.

In its early years the board was dominated by friends and acquaintances of Swift, many of them clerics. Later in the century, as we have seen, some of the most powerful political leaders of the day occupied seats on it. The state physician, in the persons of Drs Emmet and Cleghorn, was an important figure during the half century from 1775 to 1825 as, in addition to being a governor, he was also the hospital's visiting physician and thus primarily responsible for patient care. During the nineteenth century, however, the composition of the board changed markedly. Put simply, clerics, politicians and doctors were increasingly superseded by businessmen and lawyers. But this was a slow process, not fully realised till towards the end of the century. In 1825, though, the medical influence of the board received a severe check when Dr Cleghorn resigned as visiting physician and was replaced by Dr John Crampton, who was not a governor, but a physician at Steevens Hospital.

In the following year Cleghorn died and his seat on the board was taken by his successor as state physician, Dr Alexander Jackson. Thus the state physician ceased to be the hospital's principal medical officer and an important link between the board and the patients was broken.[5] Jackson, who was physician to the Richmond Asylum, was an active governor, but, despite his considerable experience with lunatics, it was now Crampton who treated the patients at St Patrick's.

Dr Jackson, however, was extremely unhappy at this innovation, feeling that he had been denied his rightful office of visiting physician. In February 1831, in the midst of a serious illness from which he doubted that he would recover, he wrote a dramatic letter to the board, airing his grievances. He claimed that Dr Cleghorn, who was senior state physician, while he served as his junior, hated him. Cleghorn's 'inveterate resentment' resulted from the manner of Jackson's appointment to the junior post in 1803. Cleghorn had regarded the position as in his gift—Dr Emmet had at one stage appointed his son, Thomas Addis, to it—but the chief secretary had rejected this claim and appointed Jackson against Cleghorn's wishes. It was also apparently normal practice for the junior to pay the senior for the privilege of the appointment—Jackson claimed that Cleghorn had paid Emmet—but the chief secretary had forbidden this practice as well. When he found his health declining in 1825, Cleghorn, with the aid of the surgeon general, Philip Crampton, and the dean of St Patrick's, Richard Ponsonby, had arranged the appointment of Crampton's cousin, John, as visiting physician. Jackson interpreted this as a deliberate act of revenge on Cleghorn's part. He maintained in his letter that 'previous to this nomination, the state physician had *always* been the medical attendant [at St Patrick's] . . . Indeed [he continued] it has been uniformly considered by the medical profession in this city as an appendage to the office of state physician'.[6]

Jackson was obviously very bitter over the whole business and went on in his letter to launch a stinging attack on Philip Crampton, who, he alleged, neglected his responsibilities to the hospital by seldom attending board meetings—though he did attend the meeting that appointed his cousin visiting physician. In conclusion, Jackson told the board that, if he died, at least his successor would know from his letter that he had attempted 'to guard my office from encroachment upon the privileges attached to it'. If he lived, however, he assured his fellow governors: 'I shall endeavour religiously to observe the spirit and tenor of Dean Swift's will, and last injunctions, and if he would re-visit this earth I should hope for his sanction in discharging the duties of delegated trust.' Jackson did live and, as we shall see shortly, he was able, by closely observing the provisions of the charter, to obtain a measure of revenge—if not against the deceased Cleghorn, then at least against his allies on the board. Whatever the rights and wrongs of the quarrel between Jackson and Cleghorn, the severing of the link between governors and patients was an undesirable development, though it may have been offset to some degree in 1828 when the board decided to hold its meetings in future at the hospital, rather than in Marsh's Library.[7] This meant that at least now most of the governors were visiting the hospital on a fairly regular basis, which gave them a much better opportunity than previously existed to observe its operations.

Aside from Jackson, the other major medical personality who served as a governor during these years was Sir Philip Crampton, who, as surgeon general, sat on the board from 1813 to 1854. Crampton, as we have seen, was a cousin of Dr Crampton, the visiting physician from 1825 to 1840, and clearly had a hand in his appointment. An elegant dresser, noted wit and great huntsman, Crampton was also very influential in Dublin medical circles during the first half of the century, being elected president of the College of Surgeons on four separate occasions.[8] Along with Dr J. W. Cusack and John Leslie Foster, a nephew of John Foster, Crampton was also one of the commissioners charged with overseeing the building of public asylums in the 1820s and 1830s. Crampton, however, was not responsible for the treatment of patients at St Patrick's. The hospital's visiting surgeon from 1813 to 1861 was James William Cusack, the surgeon at Steevens Hospital. Cusack was one of the most famous surgeons of his day, three times president of the College of Surgeons, and also a noted teacher. One of his sons, Sir Ralph Cusack, was later to be a governor of the hospital, while a niece, Margaret Anna Cusack, achieved notoriety as the 'Nun of Kenmare'.[9] The fact that both the visiting physician and the visiting surgeon, Crampton and Cusack, were based at Steevens Hospital is probably no coincidence. The link with Steevens was obviously convenient for St Patrick's. The visiting physician, who after 1838 was paid £150 per annum for his services, would probably have been expected to attend the hospital several mornings a week, while the surgeon, who was paid £100, may only have been called when required. In cases of particularly serious physical illness, patients could be transferred to Steevens for treatment there.

In retrospect the state physician's loss of the position of visiting physician to the hospital in 1825 can be seen as merely the first step in the swift decline of medical influence on the board. For both the offices of state physician and surgeon general were shortly abolished: the former in 1840 and the latter, after Crampton's death, in 1854. The board was thus reduced by two members, to twelve, and it was not till the late 1880s that another doctor was elected to sit on it. The demise of medical governors opened the way, however, for the visiting medical officers to assume much greater influence within the hospital.

Prominent Anglo–Irish families, which had provided a number of governors in the eighteenth century, continued to do so well into the nineteenth. This was true of both *ex officio* and elected governors. Thus John Beresford, who had sat on the board as an elected governor from 1763 to 1805, was followed by his nephew, Lord John George Beresford, who sat from 1820 to 1862 in virtue of his position as archbishop first of Dublin and then of Armagh. He was succeeded at Armagh by John Beresford's grandson, Marcus Gervais, who served as an *ex officio* governor from 1862 to 1885. Contact with other noted Anglo–Irish families was maintained through the office of dean of St Patrick's Cathedral. The deans in fact tended to be particularly active on the board during the first half of the century, often chairing meetings. Notable in this regard were Deans Verschoyle (1794-1810), Dawson (1828-40) and Pakenham (1843-64). But it was another dean with a famous Anglo-Irish name, who caused the hospital its most serious financial scandal of the period. This was the Hon. and Very Rev. Richard Ponsonby, dean and governor from 1817 to 1828.

The Ponsonbys were earls of Bessborough and had been extremely influential in the Irish parliament during the mid-eighteenth century. Dean Ponsonby's grandfather had been speaker of the Irish House of Commons from 1756 to 1771, while his uncle, George, was a leading whig in the Westminster parliament and had served briefly as Irish lord chancellor in 1806-7. In this capacity he was of course a governor of St Patrick's Hospital. Richard himself pursued a successful career in the Church, rising to be bishop of Derry from 1831 till his death in 1853. But, despite his glittering family background, Richard Ponsonby does not seem to have been a man of great ability or indeed even of great morality. In his lists of Derry clergy, the Rev. James Leslie, while conceding that Ponsonby was affable and good natured, nevertheless says: 'There was nothing very remarkable about him . . . he was a pluralist, and some stories, well vouched, about the administration of his diocese are not to his credit.'[10] This rather harsh judgment would appear to be borne out by some of Ponsonby's dealings with St Patrick's Hospital.

In November 1810 the board of governors agreed to lease the 384 acres of the area known as the mountain commons of Saggart to

Ambrose Moore for thirty-one years at a rent of £200 per annum, the first two years of the lease being rent free due to the 'stony and barren' condition of the land. Moore was the trustee of Lady Mary Ponsonby, wife of George and aunt of Richard Ponsonby. In 1815 George and Richard successfully petitioned the board to allow them to enclose the commons, it having become 'a settlement for lawless and disorderly persons' and being 'quite unsafe' to travel through after dark. Under the hospital's charter governors and their relatives were forbidden to lease land from the board. In 1810 and 1815, however, neither George nor Richard Ponsonby was a governor. But, in 1817 Richard Ponsonby was elected dean of St Patrick's Cathedral and thereby automatically joined the board. No further mention of Moore's lease occurs in the governors' minute book till 1823, when Lady Mary Ponsonby petitioned the board for a new lease on more favourable terms. At a meeting in May 1824, attended by only four governors, but including Dean Ponsonby and Dr Cleghorn, a new lease was granted. This came into operation in March 1825 and was for thirty–one years at a rent of a mere £62 per annum. Apparently the Ponsonbys were in financial difficulties for, when George Ponsonby died in 1817, his friend, Henry Grattan, described his death as 'calamitous' for his family as, with an estate worth £2,900 per annum, he left debts totalling £30,000.[11] As we saw when discussing the estate in the previous chapter, some high rents set during the war-time boom had been reduced by the governors in the early 1820s, but a reduction of three-quarters was unheard of and particularly for land whose value had almost certainly been increased due to enclosure.

Nothing further happened as regards the lease till 1835, when Dr Jackson raised the matter at a meeting and asked for an enquiry. By then Lady Mary was dead, Richard Ponsonby was bishop of Derry and thus no longer a governor and the lease had been sold to other parties. But, in his 1831 letter, Dr Jackson had pledged himself to uphold Swift's will and, moreover, he probably harboured a grudge against Ponsonby, who had been an ally of Dr Cleghorn. Over the next two years the board sought legal advice, first from the solicitor-general and then from a former attorney-general. Both agreed that the 1825 lease amounted to 'an abuse of the charity', for both were convinced that Moore and Lady Mary were acting for Richard Ponsonby and that, when the lease was sold in 1826 after Lady Mary's death, the profit on the transaction had gone to the dean. Thus Richard Ponsonby had traded in hospital land while a governor—a blatant breach of the provisions of the charter. When this opinion was passed on by the governors' legal agent to the then Bishop Ponsonby, he simply replied that the land had been acquired by his family before he joined the board. Therefore, in his view, no breach of the charter had occurred and he defied the governors to take action against him. The board certainly contemplated action in the courts to overturn the lease, but it was advised that its 'long acquiescence' in the existence of the lease, plus the shortness of time it had to run, combined with the money the Ponsonbys had invested in enclosure and improvements, all argued against running 'the risks of an expensive suit for impeaching that lease'. In light of this opinion, the governors resolved to take no further action.[12] This episode of the Ponsonby lease shows how a governor could, with relative impunity and despite the provisions of the charter, abuse his trust over the matter of land. Swift had clearly feared such incidents. Yet, what is striking is how seldom incidents like this occurred. The Ponsonby case is in fact quite exceptional, for, overall, Swift was remarkably successful in contriving an honest board of governors.

Among the elected governors too, at this time, there were a number of clergymen from well–known Anglo–Irish families. The Cradock family, for instance, provided four governors between 1772 and 1851, all of them clerics. The latter two, the Rev. Thomas Cradock and his son, the Rev. Thomas Russell Cradock, between them served as secretary to the board for some fifty years. Another interesting governor in this category was the Hon. and Rev. John Pomeroy, elected to replace John Beresford in 1806; he served as treasurer of the board from 1810 to 1833. He had lost out to Ponsonby in a disputed contest for the deanship of St Patrick's Cathedral in 1817, but he went on to become rector of the fashionable St Ann's Church in Dawson Street. Pomeroy appears to have been a busy and competent treasurer. Certainly, during his tenure of office, the hospital's financial position improved considerably. His interest in St Patrick's was, however, to some extent a family one. The hospital's first housekeeper had been Bridget Dryden (1757-68), who was followed in the post by her daughter, Elizabeth Kinsey (1768-83). This Elizabeth Kinsey had a daughter, also called Elizabeth Kinsey, who in 1800 married Arthur Pomeroy, Viscount Harberton. Arthur was the Rev. John Pomeroy's brother and, when Arthur died in 1832, John succeeded to the title. Thus, by marriage, John Pomeroy was related to both the first master and the housekeeper of the hospital and also, through them, to Swift. The Pomeroy–Dryden–Swift connection is in fact fairly typical of the complex web of family relationships that existed among the Anglo–Irish ascendancy and was reflected among the hospital's governors.

As well as being prominent among clerical *ex officio* and elected governors, the Anglo–Irish were also to the fore among the nonclerical elected governors. Perhaps the most interesting examples of this group at the time were Sir Robert Shaw, who sat on the board from 1814 to 1849, and his son, also called Robert Shaw, who sat from 1828 to 1869. The Shaws had long been connections of the Ponsonby family, a Captain Shaw having carried a wounded General Ponsonby from the field of the Boyne in 1690. But they were not a very wealthy or notable family until Sir Robert's father made a fortune in late eighteenth-century Dublin by dealing in government contracts. They established their own bank and Sir Robert, through an advantageous marriage to an heiress, inherited a fine estate at Bushy Park near Dublin. This recently–acquired wealth enabled Shaw to pursue a political career as MP for Dublin City from 1804 to 1826 and as lord mayor of the city 1815-16. Shaw, assisted by his son, who was a noted amateur photographer, was also active in many of the city's charities.[13] Clearly Sir Robert and his son were just the sort of influential and energetic men that the board needed. They also straddled the worlds of the Anglo–Irish landed gentry and of the Dublin banking and business classes.

Until around 1850 the hospital's governors were mainly drawn from a relatively small group of Anglo–Irish families, notably the Fosters, Beresfords, Ponsonbys, Verschoyles, Pakenhams, Cobbes, Levinges, Fowlers, Cradocks, Cramptons and Shaws. Often, as we have seen, they were related to each other; generally they were political allies, but important rivalries did exist. Most were land-lords; some land agents. A number also had estates in Co. Dublin, sometimes not far removed from the hospital's own. The Ver-schoyles, for instance, acquired land at Saggart, while the Shaws, in the person of Sir Robert's younger brother, Ponsonby, had an estate at Friarstown, only about five miles away. But, beginning before 1850 and increasing rapidly thereafter, we see the appearance of a rather different group of men among the governors: men of urban business and financial backgrounds. The Shaws' banking interests were a sign of things to come, as was the election in 1828 to the board of William Peter Lunel, who served actively till 1843. He was a Huguenot, a connection of the Guinness family, involved in the management of the brewery, and also a director of the Bank of Ireland.[14] Thereafter directors of Guinness's, banks and railway companies were quickly to replace members of the land gentry on the board of governors of the hospital.

Although the governors, or at least some of them, took a close interest in the affairs of St Patrick's, the day-to-day management of the institution was the responsibility of the master. During the first half of the nineteenth century this office was filled by two particu-larly able and reliable men, Patrick Campbell (1812-35) and James

Cuming (1835-58). On his visit in 1815 Bennet had noted Campbell's intelligence and his awareness of current developments in the treatment of the insane. The governors were also appreciative of his efforts and abilities, increasing his salary to £100 per annum in 1814 and £150 in 1816. In the former case they commended Campbell's 'great activity in the duties of his office' and in 1824, noting the marked improvement in the hospital's financial situation, the governors singled out Campbell's 'indefatigable exertions' for special praise.[15] When Campbell retired in 1835, with the board's thanks and a £100 annuity for life, the appointment of his successor proved controversial. Neither James Cuming, nor his wife, Catherine, were members of the Established Church. They had 'distinctly acknowledged themselves to be sectarians in religion calling themselves separatist'. This created opposition among some of the clerical governors and both the dean of Christ Church, Bishop Charles Lindsay, and the archdeacon of Dublin, Dr John Torrens, openly dissented from the decision to appoint Cuming as master and his wife as matron. This decision, however, was to be fully vindicated by the fifty years of service to the hospital given by James and Catherine Cuming and after them by their daughter, Jane Gill. Generally we know very little of the backgrounds of the early masters and housekeepers, particularly what experience, if any, they had of running an asylum. But, in the case of James and Catherine Cuming, we know that they had served previously as steward and assistant steward to the Dublin workhouse. With, in 1828, over 1,200 pauper inmates, including over 400 'idiots and incurable lunatics', and a further 300 patients in the attached hospitals, the workhouse was a vast and unwieldy institution.[16] The Cumings must have found St Patrick's, with its maximum of about 150 patients, a far more manageable institution in comparison.

In the summer of 1842 the board paid nearly £30 for Cuming to visit Hanwell and other asylums in England 'to enable him to form a judgment on the construction and arrangement of lunatic asylums for the reception of patients'.[17] That the Middlesex County Asylum at Hanwell should have been singled out by the board for Cuming to visit is important. The resident physician there between 1839 and 1844 was John Conolly, an Irishman and one of the main advocates of moral management of the insane. Cuming was obviously being sent by the board to observe the system, conducted by one of its chief supporters, at first hand, presumably in order that similar measures might be tried at St Patrick's. As we shall see when we come to discuss the building, steps were taken in the early 1840s to make the hospital more pleasant for patients and these almost certainly grew out of Cuming's visit to Hanwell. The governors' desire to keep up-to-date with the most modern ideas in asylum management is striking, but it is equally striking that they should choose Cuming as their envoy and not one of the medical officers. Dr Cleghorn had gone abroad several times and in 1822 the governors had formally requested him to communicate to them his observations concerning asylums. But, although Cusack took lengthy periods of leave in 1829 and 1837, no requests to him, or to the visiting physician, to inspect other hospitals are recorded. That Cuming was asked to undertake this task testifies to the growing importance of the master, not just in the day-to-day administration of the hospital, but in future plans for patient care and treatment. The logical outcome of this trend was the replacement of Cuming in 1858 by the first medically qualified master. This greatly strengthened the position of the master, but inevitably led to conflicts with the visiting medical officers.

It was also during the tenure of Campbell and Cuming that, for the first time, the office of matron or housekeeper was filled by the master's wife. Bridget Dryden, wife of the first master, William Dryden (1746-57), had served as matron (1757-68), as had her daughter Elizabeth (1768-83), but this was only after William Dryden had left his post. It was not uncommon, however, in the early nineteenth century for husbands and wives jointly to run institutions like hospitals and workhouses. Sexual segregation was usually so strictly enforced that a man was needed to supervise the male side of the institution and a woman the female. Presumably though, it was hoped that the marriage bond would guarantee amicable cooperation. In St Patrick's it seems, however, that Sarah Campbell's formal assumption of the position of housekeeper in 1824 was due more to the incapacity of the previous occupant than to any deliberate change of policy. The sisters, Elizabeth and Dorothy Hankison, had succeeded their mother, Mary, in the job in 1787. There is no mention of Dorothy Hankison in the hospital's records after 1795, but we know that Elizabeth still held the position in 1820 when she suffered a stroke, which left her paralysed. Then, and perhaps even earlier, Sarah Campbell had assumed the duties of housekeeper. Finally, in 1824, the board regularised the situation by agreeing to a pension of £65 per annum, plus continuing free accommodation in the hospital, for Elizabeth Hankison, while deciding to pay the Campbells an extra £100 per annum in recognition of Sarah's services as housekeeper.[18]

Unfortunately, no detailed account of the duties of the master and matron exists for this period, nor are we informed as to those of the rest of the staff. Some clues, however, can be found in the rules issued in 1843 for the regulation of government asylums, as it is likely that the duties of staff in public and private asylums were not dissimilar. The manager of a public asylum had, for instance, to keep all accounts and record books; to ensure that contractors supplied good quality provisions; to hire, fire and supervise all employees; to have 'charge of the instruments of restraint'; to be familiar with the cases of all inmates and to report any problems to the physician; and to inspect the whole of the establishment every morning and evening. The matron was answerable to the manager for the welfare of all female patients, as well as for the operations of the kitchen and laundry.[19] If the master's job at St Patrick's was at all similar to that of the manager of a public asylum, then it obviously was an onerous one. There is no mention at this time, for instance, of the master taking holidays and, indeed, it is hard to imagine how the hospital could have functioned without him. At St Patrick's, in addition, the master had to collect boarders' fees and pursue late– or non-paying relatives. But in 1828, at Campbell's request, a clerk was employed to assist him with the accounts, while in 1840 a part-time accountant and a full-time store clerk were employed to handle both accounts and the supply of provisions.[20] These appointments marked important steps towards freeing the master from some of his more time-consuming administrative responsibilities and allowing him to concentrate more on supervising staff and patients.

In government asylums the keepers were appointed by the manager and were instructed to keep every patient in their charge 'under constant observation'. Yet they were 'never to use any harsh or intemperate language to the patients'; rather, by 'steadiness, kindness and gentleness', were they to 'contribute to that system of moral government upon which the value of the asylum depends'. Keepers had to get patients up in the mornings; help clean and dress them; escort them to the day-rooms; watch them during the course of the day and be on call to handle any problem that might arise during the night. Any change in the patient's condition was to be reported to the manager and entered in a case-book. Public asylums also employed nurses, but these were nurses in the pre–Florence Nightingale sense of the term. They were roughly equivalent to St Patrick's ward-maids: that is, they cleaned the patients' rooms, made their beds, provided clean bedding and linen and helped transport meals from the kitchen.[21]

In 1835 the wages of many of the employees of St Patrick's were increased and an interesting list survives of the staff and their new wage levels.

STAFF OF ST PATRICK'S HOSPITAL AND THEIR WAGES, 1835

Staff	Total Wages
Male Side	£ p.a.
1 Keeper	18
1 Keeper	16
2 Keepers @ £14	28
2 Attendants for Private Patients @ £15	30
1 Head Nurse	12
6 Ward Maids @ £5	30
Female Side	
1 Keeper	12
1 Keeper	10
2 Keepers @ £8	16
2 Attendants for Private Patients @ £6.6.0	12.12.0
6 Ward Maids @ £5	30
Master	150
Matron	100
1 Cook	12
1 Kitchen Maid	5
1 Laundress	15
2 Laundry Maids @ £5	10
1 Gate Porter	12
1 Gardener	21
1 Hall Porter	10
1 Hall Maid	5
1 Store Maid	8

Wages Bill £562.12.0[22]

This bill is not complete, however, as it does not take into account the wages of the clerk nor the fees paid to the two visiting medical officers. Also keepers and attendants were eligible on the basis of good conduct for a one guinea Christmas bonus. What is most striking to the modern eye, though, is the discrepancy between male and female wages. Yet the discrepancy was a good deal less at St Patrick's than in many of the public asylums. In the Richmond Asylum in Dublin, for instance, the manager received £250 per annum and the matron, his wife, only £55; while as for the keepers, males received sixteen guineas per annum, but females only six.[23] Further information on staffing expenses at St Patrick's can be found in the first report made in 1843 by the recently–established lunacy inspectorate. The inspector noted that food for staff, most of whom lived in, cost the hospital £429 per annum, and clothing a further £66.10.0. We know little of the uniforms worn by staff, though in 1850 ten suits were ordered for the male 'servants', consisting of a dark blue coat, blue waistcoat and dark grey trousers and including 'buttons gilt with St Patrick's Hospital'.[24] Staff pensions do not figure in this list of expenses, for they were not automatic but were totally at the governors' discretion. Employees of long standing did petition for them and many received annuities of from £15 to £25; a few were refused, but this was rare and no explanation was ever given.[25]

The above account of staff expenses suggests that, in the 1830s and 1840s, the hospital was spending around £1,000 each year in order to pay and accommodate a staff of about forty, caring for between 130 and 150 patients. Swift in his will had specified that the 'salaries of agents, receivers, officers, servants and attendants, to be employed in the business of the said hospital, shall not in the whole exceed one fifth part of the clear yearly income, or revenue thereof'.[26] In the early 1840s St Patrick's income was around £6,000 a year, so it could not afford to spend much more on the employment of staff.

Financially, the years from about 1820 to 1850 were actually the most successful that the hospital had ever known. When the governors praised Patrick Campbell's management in 1824, they noted particularly that, as a result of his endeavours, they had been able to invest over £4,000 in government stock during the previous few years. By 1830 John Pomeroy, the treasurer, was able to report that, although £1,000 had recently been spent on improvements to the building, the board still had £11,700 invested in $3\frac{1}{2}$% stock. By 1832 the investments were worth £13,700 and, when Pomeroy died the following year, he was not replaced, but instead the hospital opened an account with the Bank of Ireland and directed the bank to handle its investments.[27] Doubtless the fact that directors of the bank, like W. P. Lunel, now sat on the board, played a part in this decision, but clearly also the hospital was operating on a far more substantial financial scale than previously. The decision to employ an accountant, at least part-time, in 1840 is understandable in this context. In the early 1840s income was of the order of £6,000 per annum, half from boarders' fees and the other half from rents. Boarders, most paying either forty, sixty or one hundred guineas a year, made up a third of patients. Expenditure amounted to around £5,500 a year, though at times of falling prices it could be got down to about £5,000. Thus, there were a number of years during this

To the Honourable the KNIGHTS, CITIZENS and BURGESSES, in Parliament affembled,

The HUMBLE PETITION of the

GOVERNORS of St. *Patrick*'s Hofpital, *Dublin,*

Moſt humbly ſheweth,

THAT your Petitioners were incorporated by his Majefty's Charter in the Year 1746, *for erecting an Hofpital near* Dublin, *to receive and maintain Ideots, Lunaticks and Incurables, purfuant to the laſt Will of the Reverend* Dr. Swift, *Dean of St.* Patrick's, who bequeathed his whole Fortune (except fome fmall Legacies) for founding the fame.

THAT your Petitioners have expended the Sum of Four Thoufand Five Hundred and Sixty Pounds in building the faid Hofpital, which is now nearly finifhed, for the Reception of Fifty-four Patients, who cannot be admitted for Want of a Fund fufficient to maintain and to provide Bedding and other Furniture for them.

THAT your Petitioners have agreed for the Purchafe of Lands, which they hope will yield about Four Hundred Pounds a Year.

THAT the faid Purchafe and Building hath almoft exhaufted the whole Fund of the Founder, (and alfo feveral Legacies and Benefactions devifed and given to the faid Hofpital,) except a few Debts, fome of which are defperate, and others not likely to be got in a fhort Time.

THAT the Expence of maintaining Fifty-four Patients, at Ten Pounds each, will amount to about Five Hundred and Forty Pounds a Year, befides feveral annual Sums, neceffary for the Support of proper Officers and Servants to attend them; and therefore that the annual Sum of Two Hundred and Sixty Pounds is ftill wanting to enable your Petititioners to open the Houfe for the Reception of the faid Fifty-Four Patients.

THAT the faid Hofpital is likely to be of great Benefit to the Nation in general, as Applications have been frequently made from different Parts of the Kingdom in Behalf of many unhappy Objects, *both* Ideots and Lunaticks.

Your Petitioners therefore humbly pray for fome national Bounty *to complete this good Work, and that their Cafe will be taken into Confideration by this Honourable Houfe, or that fuch Relief may be granted by your Honours, as to your great Wiſdom ſhall feem meet.*

Given under the Corporation Seal
this Third Day of November,
1755.

Petition by the governors to the Irish parliament for money with which to open the hospital, November 1755.

Plate presented to Dr Robert Emmet, state physician, by his fellow governors in February 1783, in recognition of his services to the hospital.

Portrait of Dr Robert Emmet, governor 1770-1803.

His Grace the Lord Archbishop of Tuam in the Chair   Marsh's Library 5st Novr 1798

Present

The Rev^d the Dean of St Patrick:
The Revd Thomas Cradock.
The Surgeon General,
The State Physician

Ordered –

That the Secretary do order to be printed one hundred Copies of the Charter –

That the Law Agent do enquire of Mr Symes on what terms he will sell the Rent Charge of £50 yearly, affecting the Ferns Estate, & report the same to the Board as expeditiously as possible.

The Dean of St Patricks was unanimously elected Treasurer for the ensuing year, and the Revd Mr Cradock was unanimously elected Secretary – the other Officers were continued in Office for the ensuing year

That the thanks of this Board be given to the Right Honble J^{no} Beresford for his ready attention to the application of this Board, & for having the charge of Insupers against this Board, struck off the Journals of the House of Commons –

That Mary Dowdall be admitted as a Pauper.

Doctor Emmet having, on account of the weak state of his health, declined being re-elected to the Office of Treasurer, – The thanks of the Board were returned to him for his long & faithful services rendered to this Charity in that Office.

Signed   W. Tuam

Minutes of the board meeting held on 5 November 1798 at which Dr Emmet did not seek to be re-elected treasurer, due to the 'weak state of his health'.

Form of Application

FOR

Admission into St. Patrick's Hospital.

Medical Certificate:

I CERTIFY that *Mr Thomas Hobbs* whom I have visited, is now and has been in a state of INSANITY for the last *three weeks* I am of Opinion that *he* is a fit subject for St. PATRICK's HOSPITAL.

Given under my Hand, this *19th* Day of *January* 18*42*

(Name.) *H. Marsh M. D.*
Physician in ordinary to the queen in Ireland

•·• State whether Physician or Surgeon.

(Residence.) *24 Molesworth St*

Application:

HAVING reason to believe, as stated in the accompanying Medical Certificate, that *Captain Thomas Hobbs* resident in the *Frankfort (Kings Co.)* is INSANE, I request *he* may be admitted into your Hospital as a Patient.

Ml Hobbs

Letter of Obligation:

As you have agreed to admit *Thos Hobbs* into your Hospital, as a Patient, I hereby bind *myself* to pay you for said Patient, at the Rate of *one Hundred Guineas* per Annum, payable Quarterly, in Advance; also to provide the necessary Supplies of Clothes, &c. &c., to remove the Patient when required, and to fulfil any other Condition incumbent on *me* as Surety for the Patient, according to your Regulations.

M. Hobbs

To the Governors of St. Patrick's Hospital.

Application for the admission of Captain Thomas Hobbs, 50-year-old, half-pay officer; described as 'irritable' due to 'religion and embarrassment'; admitted January 1842, died in hospital February 1842; G.P.I.?

STATEMENT and ORDER to be annexed to the Medical Certificates authorising the reception of an Insane Person.

The Patient's true Christian and Surname, at full length - - - - - - - *William Henry Singleton*

The Patient's Age - - - - - - - *28 years of age*

Married or Single - - - - - - - *Single*

The Patient's previous occupation (if any) - *Insurance Clerk*

The Patient's previous place of abode - - *46 Cork Street*

The Licensed House, or other Place (if any), in which the Patient was before confined - - - - - - - - - *none*

Whether found Lunatic by Inquisition, and Date of Commission - - - - - *never*

Special circumstances which shall prevent the Patient being separately examined by two Medical Practitioners - - - *none*

Special circumstances which exist to prevent the insertion of any of the above particulars - - - - - - - - *none*

N.B.—If any Query in the Memorial is incorrectly or insufficiently answered, it will be returned.

GENTLEMEN,

Upon the authority of the above statement, and the annexed Medical Certificates, I request you will receive the said *Wm Hy Singleton* as a Patient into your House.

I am,

GENTLEMEN,

Your obedient Servant,

Name - - - - - - - - - - *Robert Singleton*

Occupation (if any) - - - - - *Bank Officer*

Place of Abode - - - - - - *46 Cork St & Sandycove Kingstown*

Degree of Relationship (if any) to the Insane Person - - - - - *Father*

To the Governors of
St. Patrick's Hospital,

It is requested the following QUERIES may be accurately answered.

1.—How long ill? - - - - - - - - *Three Weeks of Illness out of mind*
2.—Probable cause of illness? - - - - *free use of Stimulants*
3.—Species or character of disease? - - *Softening of the Brain*
4.—Religious Persuasion? - - - - - *Protestant*
5.—Whether ill before, and how often? - *Several times ill the past 4 Years*
6.—Whether subject to any other complaint? *no other Complaint*
7.—Whether subject to epilepsy or paralysis? *not at any time*
8.—Whether predisposed to Suicide? - - *no*
9.—Whether any, and what property? - - *none*
10.—From what source or sources derived? - *none*
11.—Reference to two or more respectable }
Persons who can testify to the } *none*
amount of income - - - - - }

A List of Articles of Clothing required on admission will be delivered to the Friends of the Patient, and on default of their supplying Clothing accordingly, or as same become unfit, Articles will be procured, and charged in the account for the Patient.

A Deposit of Five Pounds is required on admission, and to be made up each quarter to meet any incidental expense, or to supply such Articles of Clothing as may be required, any balance remaining to be refunded on the removal of the Patient.

A Letter of Obligation, of which the following is the form, is required, on the proper stamp, at the expense of the Applicant, to be signed by the party sending the Patient to the Hospital, and approved by the Governers, and which signature is to be procured before the admission of the Patient.

LETTER OF OBLIGATION.

In consideration of your having agreed to admit *Wm Henry Singleton* into your Hospital as a Patient, at the rate of £   :   : per annum, payable by quarterly instalments, in advance, that is to say, on the   day of   the   day of   the   day of   and the   day of   in each and every year, I do hereby for myself my Executors and Administrators, undertake so long as the said *W H Singleton* shall remain in said Hospital, to pay and duly discharge the said annual sum or stipend of £   :   : as the same shall become due and payable ; and also to provide the necessary supplies of Clothing for said Patient; and to fulfil all other conditions incumbent on me as Security for the said Patient, according to the Regulations of the said Hospital; and receive and take back the said Patient, from the said Hospital, in case of recovery, or on the first defalcation in payment of said quarterly instalments, or other branch on my part of the regulations of said Hospital.

Dated this   day of   18

To the Governers of St. Patrick's Hospital,
    Dublin.

Application for the admission of William Henry Singleton, 28-year-old insurance clerk; described as suffering from 'softening of the brain' due to 'free use of stimulants'; admitted March 1882, discharged recovered July 1882.

Female nurses at St Patrick's in 1904 with Marie Eynthoven, matron 1901-37, some wearing their R.M.P.A. badges.

period when the hospital was able to make a clear profit of nearly £1,000. Such profits swelled investments.[28]

There were those, however, who were not happy with this very healthy financial situation. Surgeon Cusack certainly was not and in the early 1840s he found powerful allies in the lord chancellor, Sir Edward Sugden, and his advisor, Dr Francis White, surgeon to the Richmond Asylum and the first inspector of lunatics. In 1843 Cusack, as secretary of the College of Surgeons, gave evidence to a Commons select committee investigating medical charities. One of the first issues he was questioned on was the financial situation at St Patrick's Hospital. He told the committee that a 'very considerable' surplus had accumulated since he began attending the hospital in 1813 and he went on to make clear that he regarded this as incompatible with the charitable nature of the institution. He argued that boarders should be received 'at the lowest rate at which they can be maintained at a profit by private institutions', because there were far more people who could pay a little towards their support than there were rich people who could pay a lot. This middling group was largely excluded from the district asylums, which only took paupers, and from the fourteen private asylums, which charged high fees and could only accommodate a few hundred patients. Put simply, Cusack was arguing that St Patrick's should cater more for the middle classes, or at least for those groups which fell between paupers on the one hand and the rich on the other. Cusack also told the committee that he had put his ideas to the lord chancellor who had approved of them.[29]

In July of the same year Dr Francis White testified before a committee investigating the lunatic poor in Ireland. During the course of his evidence White described himself as 'having been myself five years a pupil in Swift's Hospital'. From this remark it would appear that White had been a pupil of Cusack, who was certainly a popular teacher, and that he had studied in St Patrick's as well as at Steevens. This might partly account for White's intense interest in the treatment of the mentally ill, for he was the driving force in efforts to reform the management of asylums in the early 1840s. From 1835 to 1841 he had been surgeon to the Richmond Asylum; in 1841 he was appointed one of the inspectors of prisons, with special responsibility for asylums; in 1843 he had drawn up the new rules governing district asylums; and in 1846, after a long campaign, he succeeded in having a separate lunacy inspectorate established, with himself as first inspector. White, as a medical man, was particularly anxious to see doctors taking a more active role in the management of asylums.[30]

White was rather harsher in his comments on St Patrick's than

Cusack had been. While acknowledging that the hospital was 'very well regulated', he nevertheless declared that, in his opinion, the charter had been 'perverted'. Swift wanted received 'as many idiots and lunatics as the annual income of his lands and effects should be sufficient to maintain', but, during a recent inspection with Lord Chancellor Sugden, White said they had found that 'the rich were always sure to get admission, and that great difficulties in latter years, were thrown in the way of the reception of the poor; and . . . it was often half a year, or even more, before a poor person could get in . . .' Sugden himself wrote a note after the inspection saying that there was a 'danger that accommodation for the rich may exclude from the charity the real objects of the founder's bounty'. He therefore instructed that all boarders in the hospital under chancery orders were to be removed to private asylums. White complained in addition at the high cost of keeping patients in St Patrick's: each pauper cost nearly £30 per annum to maintain, which was double the cost in other asylums. There was little difference, according to him, between the two lower classes of boarders, paying forty guineas and less, and the pauper patients in regard to diet and accommodation. As for the sixty and one hundred guinea boarders, there were 'many very respectable gentlemen and ladies who have their own servants, and who have their dinner in their own apartments, and get that kind of accommodation and that mode of living which it is supposed they would get in their own establishments'. Their diet, in particular, was superior to that of other patients and yet the hospital made a profit on them. White totally disagreed with this practice, arguing that: 'All a patient should be asked to pay should be just what per head is the general cost of each patient'. Sugden also noted after his inspection that no case-books were kept and that there were no proper records of patients under restraint. In addition the apothecary, John Nicholls, did not visit the hospital and thus medicines had to be fetched from his shop in Dawson Street, which caused much trouble and delay in treating patients.

White and Sugden, however, went beyond mere criticism of St Patrick's to advance a novel proposal for its future management. The original idea was White's.

It often occurred to me, when I was president of the College of Surgeons, [he told the committee] . . . that some of the students who were examined after three years probation should be selected to attend the physicians of the Richmond Lunatic Asylum, or Swift's, for six months, and act as clinical clerks. It was my mentioning this circumstance to the lord chancellor that led his lordship to draw up the note I have read.

Sugden's note proposed that:

> Swift's Hospital might be made the foundation of a new system. A school might be established there, and pupils admitted, with great caution. Governors, and keepers, might be trained there, with whom the district and private asylums might be supplied. Moral as well as medical treatment would then have a chance of being followed systematically throughout Ireland. The government might with great advantage advance some small sums to further the object.[31]

Typically White carried Sugden's proposal even further when he told the committee that medical students might also be trained at St Patrick's. If his aim to increase the power of asylum doctors was to be realised, then it was important that they should be properly trained. That doctors and keepers should receive a specialist education may seem obvious to us today, but it was far from obvious in the 1840s, when many people, including many doctors, still believed that little or nothing could be done for the mentally ill. White's proposal reflected his optimism and his faith in moral management, but his optimism was far from universal. No teaching hospital of the sort that White envisaged making St Patrick's existed anywhere in the British Isles and none was to be successfully established for another forty years. His scheme was thus remarkably far-sighted and, had it been implemented, it would almost certainly have made St Patrick's one of the most important mental hospitals in Europe.

But it was not implemented, though it was approved by the board of governors. The medical officers, Cusack and Croker, doubtless in consultation with White, drew up a report in 1845 suggesting how these proposals could be put into effect. The main recommendations were that male patients, curable cases only, should be used for instruction purposes; that these patients should be housed in ward no. 2, adjoining the library; that a clinical clerk should be employed to assist the visiting physician and that he should keep a medical case-book. In April 1846 the board recommended 'the immediate adoption of a system of medical instruction in accordance with the principles explained by the lord chancellor'. The medical officers were to be permitted 'to give clinical lectures in a ward adapted for that purpose', the number of pupils to be determined by the governors. In addition a clinical clerk was to be employed at a salary of £20 per annum. But for reasons that are by no means clear, these resolutions were never put into practice. Perhaps the medical emergency of the Famine diverted attention and resources from the mentally ill. There is also a hint, however, that the governors of St Patrick's may not have been very enthusiastic at the prospect of having their hospital turned into a teaching institution under the direction of the visiting physician. The fact that it took the board two years to agree to Sugden's proposal and that only four governors, including Sugden, attended the April 1846 meeting seems to imply a certain lack of commitment.[32]

In contrast, Sugden's criticism of the boarders' system was acted upon immediately. In April 1843, at a meeting attended by eight governors, the lord chancellor successfully moved that the one hundred guinea and sixty guinea boarders should all be discharged into the care of their relatives by the end of the following quarter. Those paying forty guineas or less were to be continued 'according to the circumstances of the applicant'. This meant the removal of some twenty-five patients and thus St Patrick's, which had begun the year with 155 patients, ended it with only 136. Yet the proportion of boarders in the hospital population did not fall; in fact it rose, from 39 per cent at the beginning of 1843 to 42 per cent in 1845. Most of these boarders, however, were now paying between £30 and £40 per annum and, instead of having their own rooms and servants, they were treated on a par with the pauper patients. In his 1845 report Dr White noted, with approval, the admission to St Patrick's of 'a class of persons who could not afford to pay the usual sum which is charged for admission into any of the private asylums'.[33] It may have seemed a neat arrangement to White, Sugden and Cusack, to slot St Patrick's in between, on the one hand, the public pauper asylums and, on the other, the rich private asylums, but, as we shall see, barring rich patients from the hospital, in the long run, simply resurrected the sort of severe financial problems that the institution had faced continually before 1820.

In his 1845 report, White also praised St Patrick's for being 'very well conducted', but, at the same time, he expressed doubt as to 'whether the asylum, as circumstanced at present, can be rendered an efficient hospital for curable patients'. What he was referring to particularly was the large and indeed growing number of patients classed as incurable. After the removal of the richer boarders in 1843, incurables accounted for 84 per cent of patients; by the end of 1845 their numbers had reached 92 per cent, being 87 per cent of boarders and 95 per cent of paupers. It may well be that the small numbers of patients considered curable was a factor in the collapse of the scheme to turn St Patrick's into a teaching hospital; students could presumably learn little from patients for whom nothing could be done. White certainly singled out the predominance of incurables as a major problem for St Patrick's. But it was a problem that the hospital was coming increasingly to share with the public asylums. For, by the 1840s, the shortcomings of moral management were beginning to become apparent. Asylums built in Ireland amid a wave of optimism in the 1820s were twenty years later full to overflowing with cases regarded as incurable. Yet, further asylums were having to be built, or existing ones enlarged, to cope with the ever-growing demand for places. As asylums were enlarged, however, in a vain attempt to prevent overcrowding, so living standards and the quality of care offered in them declined. The asylum system had not proved the panacea that the moral managers had hoped it would be and, in fact, by the latter part of the nineteenth century, the asylums had become as much part of the problem as of the solution. This applies to St Patrick's Hospital no less than to the public institutions.

THE ESTATE

We saw in the previous chapter that, between 1750 and 1788, the governors had acquired an estate, as they were directed to do under Swift's will. This estate had come to them partly through purchase and partly through bequests and, by the 1820s, had four major components.

THE ESTATE OF ST PATRICK'S HOSPITAL, DUBLIN, 1820

One Irish or Plantation acre equals 1.62 English or Statute acres.

Location	Irish Acres/ Houses	Acquired	Landlord
Saggart	1,870	By Purchase, 1750-75	Governors of St Patrick's
Ferns	1,304	By Bequest, 1767	Bishop of Ferns (to 1839)
Dublin Francis St Area	c.70 Houses	By Bequest 1788	Ashbourne Grammar School, Derbyshire
Goldenbridge	3*	By Bequest, 1752	Petty Canons of St Patrick's Cathedral

* Some of the land originally bequeathed by Swift's friend, the Rev. John Worrall, appears to have been sold to allow the building of the Grand Canal.

By the early 1840s rents from the estate accounted for roughly half of the hospital's annual income.

ESTATE RENTAL, 1840

Location	Rent Roll £
Saggart	1,938
Ferns	1,016
Dublin	372
Goldenbridge	74
Total	3,400[34]

The governors' minute books and estate records are far more informative about the affairs of the Saggart estate than about those of Ferns or Dublin. We know, however, that in 1839 the board purchased the Ferns estate in fee simple for £1,443, plus an annual rental of £221, from the ecclesiastical commissioners. But members of the Symes family remained trustees and agents for the estate and seem to have been allowed a fairly free hand in its management. Admittedly, from time to time, the governors complained at the level of arrears or the failure of the agent to keep them sufficiently well informed, but otherwise, the Symes agency remained unchallenged.[35]

With regard to the affairs of Saggart, there was a good deal of unrest on the estate during the 1820s, with tenants petitioning against the level of their rents and against the enclosure of common land. These protests were by no means always peaceful. In 1822 a corn mill was burnt down, whilst in 1825 the governors' bailiff, Michael Wogan, was murdered, and ditches, which had been dug on the commons, were levelled. The 1820s as a whole were particularly difficult years for Irish agriculture, with almost constantly falling prices, and conflict between the governors and their tenants has to be seen against this background of general economic crisis. In the midst of these troubles, after twenty-seven years as agent, John Verschoyle notified the board that he wished to retire and proposed his son, John James, as his successor. To this the governors readily agreed and, on assuming the position of agent, the younger Verschoyle moved to evict several tenants regarded as particularly troublesome. But, while a handful were evicted, a much larger group of tenants were placated. Between 1829 and 1831, for instance, over £550 in rent arrears, owed by nineteen tenants, was struck off, followed by a further £500, owed by forty tenants, in 1836. In the early 1830s the governors also offered thirty-one year leases to a number of tenants who had previously held their land only on a year-to-year basis, thus affording them a great deal more security. Although a few evictions were carried out in the late 1820s, generally the governors preferred to use the threat of eviction to coerce tenants, for actual evictions often created more problems than they solved.[36]

The 'carrot and stick' policy of giving favourable treatment to some tenants, while acting harshly against others, tended to create friction between tenants. In 1826 Verschoyle senior had attributed discontent with rents to the fact that some tenants had received abatements while others were denied them. But the most serious conflicts occurred when tenants took over holdings from which others had been evicted. One of the tenants most seriously in arrears in 1830 was Catherine Caddell, who had a large family and had inherited her eight-acre holding from her widowed mother. Together mother and daughter had accumulated a rent arrears of £174. In 1830 J. J. Verschoyle reported that he had for a long time wished to re-let the holding, but 'from the disturbed state of the country, bidders would not come forward at auction'. By early 1831, however, Catherine Caddell had finally been evicted. Francis Watters, who had been given a thirty-one year lease of three acres in 1829, offered to take the Caddell holding as well. But when, as a result, he received a threatening letter and had two shots fired at his house, Watters withdrew his offer. In relating the affair to the board Verschoyle said that, 'considering the exertions made by the late tenant to injure any person who might take this land', he had been obliged to organise the harvest himself and 'to keep two men well armed watching it every night till it was disposed of'. Verschoyle obviously knew who was responsible for the attack on Watters, but he had to admit to the board that he had not as yet been able to apprehend them.[37] By evicting Catherine Caddell the governors thus lost any hope of recovering her rent arrears, while at the same time they found themselves unable to re-let the holding. From their point of view it was, therefore, far better if a tenant could be pressured into re-paying some of the arrears, while continuing to pay the current rent. But, it was the Great Famine of the late 1840s which most graphically illustrated the shortcomings of eviction as a policy for dealing with tenants unable to pay their rents.

By 1849 most of the tenants at Saggart were seriously in arrears. This was not due solely, however, to the repeated failure of the potato crop. Most tenants derived money for rents from the cultivation of wheat and grass for hay, but prices were low and, moreover, bad weather had played havoc with the harvest. In August 1850 a petition from sixty-nine Saggart tenants was laid before the board. This appealed 'for a reduction of our present rents in order to meet the depression in the price of all agricultural produce', and went on: 'The awful visitation which it has pleased Providence to inflict on this country in the failure of the potato and wheat crops, the disease among the cattle, together with an increased taxation ... overburdens the land and leaves us your petitioners unable to meet our liabilities.' In his response to the petition, Verschoyle said that he felt rents were 'very reasonable and up to 1846 generally punctually paid', but since then the 'circumstances of the tenantry' had been greatly reduced by the repeated failures of the potato crop, the poor wheat harvests and the fall in grain and hay prices. Moreover, he believed that the 'smaller class of tenants cannot pay any reasonable rent in the absence of the potato', and thus moderate reductions in rent would be to no purpose. Verschoyle urged the governors to use the distress caused by the Famine as an opportunity to consolidate holdings into farms of from twenty to thirty acres, to invest more in their estate and to encourage improvements, in particular better drainage. But he was not in fact advocating widespread evictions; on the contrary, he thought that many insolvent tenants could be removed from the estate 'amicably'. This might be done, he wrote, 'by giving them a small amount of money to take them to America. Then farms might be given to solvent, industrious tenants, already on the estate, and thus the sub-division which took place some thirty years since, might to some extent be remedied.'[38]

The board responded by establishing a sub-committee, which, between September 1850 and May 1851, reviewed every holding on both the Saggart and Ferns estates. But the results of the review were hardly mass evictions: some sixteen tenants at Saggart and ten at Ferns were evicted. Even these evictions seem in a number of instances to have been more apparent than real. Jane Hanlon, for instance, held thirteen acres at £25 per annum at Saggart and was £81 in arrears. But she also held six acres from Verschoyle, where she actually lived. The thirteen acres, on which there was no house, had been subdivided between her son and daughter. The governors considered 'this subdivision of farms amongst surviving children most objectionable and particularly in the case of females'. They thus decided to evict Jane. But, at the same time, they remitted her daughter's arrears and offered the daughter £5 for peaceful possession of her part of the holding. They then offered the whole thirteen acres to Jane's son at a reduced rent and with his arrears up to 1850 remitted. This is clearly an eviction and with a decided prejudice against female tenants, but it is hardly the traditional picture of the poor family being thrown out into a wayside ditch.[39]

The Hanlon case was certainly not an exception. When we look closely at the sixteen Saggart evictions, we find that three of the tenants had died and that five held land elsewhere and were not in fact being thrown out of their homes. In four cases the tenants were offered financial inducements to leave peacefully and in five cases the holding passed into the hands of a close relative. At Ferns there was a similar situation. In four cases the governors decided to offer money, generally between £2 and £4, to encourage tenants to leave peacefully, while in six cases they decided upon ejectment. But, out of these ten, only four seem actually to have lost their land. One, Thady Bulger, with twenty acres and an arrears of £26, had 'cleared out' and taken his family of nine to America. He was in fact evicted *after* he had left. Another two tenants were evicted from only part of their holdings. Mathew Pearson, for instance, was a substantial tenant with two farms of forty-seven acres and seventy-six acres. He was only £6 in arrears in 1851 and was described as of 'very good' character. But he had sub-let his seventy-six acres to five families considered by the governors to be 'paupers'. For this he was evicted from his holding and the 'pauper cabins and gardens' were 'levelled'. Yet he was allowed to retain his other, smaller holding.[40]

The governors followed some of the advice given to them in 1849-50 by their agent, J. J. Verschoyle: in 1851, for instance, they applied to the Board of Works for a loan of over £1,100 in order to drain nearly 10 per cent of the Saggart estate; while the case of Mathew Pearson at Ferns shows that they took a strong stand against sub-division. But their attempts at the consolidation of holdings were, to say the least, desultory: in 1840 50 per cent of the Saggart holdings had been less than five acres; in 1854, after the review, the figure was still 42 per cent. Verschoyle's dream of an estate with most farms ranging in size from twenty to thirty acres remained just that — a dream. During the course of their review the governors had in fact specifically ruled out removing many small tenants. While 'they feel the importance of diminishing the number of small holdings [said the governors] they cannot recommend the forcible removal of old tenants holding even such very small tenements, providing the arrears of rent due be forthwith paid and regularity of payments be undertaken for the future'.[41]

The board of St Patrick's, then, did not engage in the sort of large-scale evictions which characterised some other Irish estates in the wake of the Famine. This may have been commendable on humane grounds, but there was an economic price to be paid for it. The continued existence of a large group of small holders acted as a check upon improvement and also on rent rises. Thus, when the hospital desperately needed to increase its income in the second half of the century, it was unable to boost its rent roll significantly and, in fact, due to the political circumstances of the period, it was forced into granting substantial abatements. In time the governors were to conclude that Irish landholding simply did not offer them an income of sufficient size or flexibility and, like many other Irish landlords, they welcomed the opportunity offered by government, at the beginning of the new century, to sell their estates.

THE BUILDING

Between 1820 and 1850 there were no major extensions to the hospital of the sort built in 1778-83 and 1789-93. During these years nine district asylums were built with accommodation for around a thousand patients and, in these circumstances, the enlargement of St Patrick's was clearly considered unnecessary. But the task of maintaining and, most importantly, of modernising the building went on almost continuously. In fact the erection of new asylums on designs radically different from that of St Patrick's must have highlighted how old fashioned the hospital was as it approached its centenary.

In order to bring St Patrick's into line with the contemporary vogue for moral management, it was necessary to improve the facilities for patient recreation and also to make the building more comfortable. These goals were pursued in a variety of ways. As a result of Bennet's comments in 1815, the governors had sought to acquire more land adjacent to the hospital. In 1816, as we saw, they leased plots to the north, west and east. In the late 1820s a further $1\frac{1}{2}$ acres were leased to the west with the hope that they would be used by female patients for exercise. On his retirement in 1835 the master, Patrick Campbell, recorded that since 1812: 'Nearly five acres of airing and exercise ground has been added and laid out as productive gardens with spacious walks.' As well as supplying the hospital with fresh vegetables, these gardens had yielded an income of £1,313 from the sale of produce. In 1843 half the male patients were working in the gardens. Female patients were, however, denied this exercise, being restricted to indoor, domestic duties. The purchase of six iron garden seats in 1831 suggests that the female role in the gardens was purely sedentary. But, beyond the five acres acquired during Campbell's mastership, the scope for expansion was strictly limited. To the north lay Dr Steevens Hospital; to the east was Steevens Lane; to the south were Bow Lane and James Street, the latter already a busy thoroughfare. Only to the west were there open fields leading eventually to the Royal Hospital at Kilmainham. Through these fields however, ran the Camac River and it is unlikely that the governors would have wished to give their patients access to a river. As Dublin city expanded westwards during the nineteenth century, the chances for the hospital to acquire additional land for building or recreation diminished even further. In this regard St Patrick's differed markedly from the new district asylums, which were increasingly being built outside towns and had substantial amounts of land attached to them.[42]

When the hospital was erected in the 1750s, it was assumed that patients would spend much of their time in their cells, for no special areas were provided for them to socialise or eat in beyond the corridors off which their cells opened. Airing sheds were available for outdoor exercise, but there was no interior equivalent. By the early years of the nineteenth century, however, this was considered a major shortcoming in the hospital's design and in 1829 the governors 'resolved that it appears to be highly expedient to construct day-rooms connected with the several wards, for the comfort and health of the patients'. They decided to consult the eminent architect, Francis Johnston, who was architect to the Board of Works and had designed the district asylums, including the Richmond. He, unfortunately, died within a few days of the governors' decision and so instead they turned to his nephew and assistant, William Murray, who had helped in designing the four district asylums built in the 1820s. Murray provided the plans, while Edward Carolan and Sons of Talbot Street put in the lowest bid for the work. This amounted to £1,480 and the board, in the absence of government aid, decided to sell some of its stock in order to finance the undertaking. During 1830, as well as constructing two day-rooms on each floor, Carolan, under Murray's supervision, also extended the airing sheds by 145 feet and built a new straw house, scullery, drying stove and coach house. Some of the stonework at the front of the building was replaced and extensive new walls were erected.[43]

The governors quickly took advantage of their new day-rooms to deal with another major shortcoming. In 1810 they had petitioned the government to provide them with the money to build day-rooms and to separate convalescent from acute and chronic cases. This money was not forthcoming, however. Finally they paid for day-rooms themselves in 1830, and used them to create the separation of patients that they had long desired. In 1831 they decided to turn the two day-rooms on the top floor into dormitories for nine male and nine female pauper patients, plus two keepers. Thus, for the first time, the hospital could totally separate a small number of patients considered to be close to recovery from the rest of the inmates. When Campbell retired in 1835 it was decided to turn his former kitchen and storeroom into two more day-rooms, these to be used exclusively by boarders. Each was furnished with a carpet, a table and a dozen chairs. In addition the board purchased Campbell's furniture for £48, among which were two card tables and a piano. To what extent the patients were encouraged to play the piano is not clear, but the board obviously did not wish to see the whist games that Campbell had held for the boarders discontinued.[44]

Various other steps were undertaken in the 1830s and early 1840s aimed at creating a brighter and more homely atmosphere in the hospital. For instance, the windows opening on to the corridors were systematically enlarged so as to admit more light. In 1834 the master was ordered to procure dining tables and forms for the wards. This is the first indication of patients eating communally instead of in the solitude of their cells. In the 1830s also iron bedsteads were provided for both staff and patients, to replace the old wooden ones previously used. One interesting, though unexpected, expense at this time was £45 for the repair of the roof and chimneys. This arose out of damage caused by the so-called Big Wind, the storm that devastated the country on the night of 6-7 January 1839. Some of the chimneys appear to have been blown down completely and the board ordered that they be re-erected in brick.[45]

The problem as regards the building that proved most intractable during these years, however, was that of effective heating. Until the 1820s coal-burning fireplaces, situated in the corridors and in some of the rooms, appear to have been the sole source of heat. But, in 1822, Cleghorn, who had recently returned from inspecting hospitals in England, recommended that the board investigate Dr Meyler's hypocaust. This was a system of under-floor heating by hot air from furnaces, somewhat similar to that used by the Romans. A committee, including Cleghorn, Pomeroy, Dean Ponsonby and the archbishop of Dublin inspected the heating system that Meyler had installed in Leinster House, then the headquarters of the (Royal) Dublin Society. The committee was obviously impressed for Meyler was asked to install two hypocausts, one in each of the wings of the hospital. Six months later, in February 1823, Cleghorn, Pomeroy and Ponsonby reported that the hypocausts were in place and functioning. On the top floor of the building a temperature of between fifty-six and fifty-eight degrees had been produced, but, for reasons not explained, the committee considered that the heating of the lower floors had not been adequate. Moreover, the furnaces were consuming three tons of coal a week and part of the apparatus had already been damaged by the heat.

Meyler said that he had never experienced the latter problem before and the committee was sceptical as to his ability to rectify it. In its final report, however, it confessed itself 'at a loss to give at the present moment an ultimate opinion on the absolute success of the plan pursued by Dr Meyler'. The full board proved more decisive though. It decided to pay Meyler £200 for the work already completed, but not to proceed with the installation of any more hypocausts. Clearly the system had not lived up to the governors' expectations.[46]

Nearly ten years later, in 1832, another attempt was made to provide the hospital with a comprehensive heating system. In January Richard Robinson of the Royal Phoenix Iron Works, just across the Liffey in Parkgate Street, advised the board that the 'best and safest mode' of heating the hospital was by means of steam. At a cost of £480 he offered to install a steam boiler in each of the wings of the building, with four-inch steam pipes passing through all the cells at ceiling height. During the summer of 1832 Robinson installed this system in the east wing, housing the male patients, but the governors decided to see how it worked over the coming winter before authorising a similar system for the west wing. Again, however, the heating does not seem to have been a success for there is no mention in the minutes of the west wing being heated and in December 1833 the governors ordered that the steam boiler in the east wing be removed. It was not until the 1880s in fact that a satisfactory heating system was installed.[47]

The first half of the nineteenth century clearly saw a marked improvement in the patients' physical environment, largely resulting from the hospital's adoption of the principles of moral management and their vigorous implementation by Patrick Campbell, master from 1812 to 1835. Parts of the sewerage and drainage systems were overhauled in 1809; the roof and chimneys were extensively repaired in 1811-12; several acres of garden for both recreational and horticultural purposes were purchased in 1816 and 1827; two day-rooms were built on each floor in 1829-30; communal dining facilities were provided in 1834; better beds were purchased in 1836; while the corridor windows were systematically enlarged to admit more light in the late 1830s and early 1840s. Only the governors' attempts in the 1820s and 1830s to provide better heating seem to have been thwarted. Except for the repairs undertaken in 1811-12, for which parliament provided grants totalling a little over £8,000, all these improvements were paid for by the board out of its income from rents and fees—an obvious indication of the hospital's improved financial position. This improved position and the need for better facilities were both partly dictated not just by considerations of treatment, but by changes in the types of patient being admitted to the hospital.

THE PATIENTS

St Patrick's had admitted fee-paying patients from its opening in 1757, though after 1781 these were divided into two groups. By 1820 ward boarders were paying sixty guineas a year for accommodation in a cell, while chamber boarders paid one hundred guineas for their own room and servant. In 1830, however, it was decided to introduce a third class of boarder, to be housed with those 'on the pauper establishment'. This group was to consist of patients whose relatives were unable to pay more than thirty guineas per annum, later raised to forty, and their numbers were not to exceed twenty.[48] Subsequently a fourth class of boarder paying sums less than thirty guineas also appeared. Fees were in fact variable, depending upon the means of the family, but they seldom if ever fell below twenty guineas at this time.

Having dealt with boarders in 1830, a sub-committee was set up in the following year to consider admission procedures for pauper patients, or, as they were coming increasingly to be called, free patients. Owing to 'many changes of circumstances', which probably referred to the opening of four district asylums for pauper patients in the 1820s, the sub-committee recommended that all previous regulations be repealed. In future the admission of free patients was to take place only at the quarterly, full board meetings. The master was to lay before the governors the number of vacancies and all valid applications and they were to determine by ballot, with the chairman having a casting vote, who was to be received. In contrast boarders could be admitted at any time, such an admission having only to be confirmed by a quarterly meeting. One week before each quarterly meeting, the master was to present the medical officers with a list of patients 'for them to record any comment they think fit to make', for the information of the governors. In 1831 also the board ordered the printing of 250 copies of a 'memorial certificate and undertaking' to be filled in by all applicants. These were the first printed admission forms.[49]

In requiring the completion of such forms and, more importantly, in limiting free admissions to quarterly meetings, on top of having established a new class of boarder, the governors were in effect making it more difficult for free patients to gain access to the hospital. The thinking behind this move was made abundantly clear when the sub-committee recommended that in cases of 'equal destitution and affliction' preference should be given to 'those persons who had previously filled the better classes in society — district asylums being now formed at the public expense for the reception of all ranks'.[50] The governors clearly believed that the new pauper asylums had changed the role of St Patrick's. It no longer needed to cater principally for the poor, as Swift had instructed, for the district asylums were intended to do that. Instead it should offer accommodation to those excluded from the district asylums because they were not paupers. With fees of one hundred, sixty and thirty guineas the governors hoped to attract a wide range of patients from the more prosperous classes and, even with regard to free patients, they demonstrated a preference for members of the 'better classes' who had fallen on hard times.

As we have seen, however, there were those, in particular Surgeon Cusack, who strongly opposed this move to re-orient the hospital away from the poor and more towards profit-making boarders. To him, as to his powerful allies, Lord Chancellor Sugden and Dr White, this reinterpretation of the hospital's charter was unacceptable. According to them, the hospital had to follow the dictates of Swift's will, embodied in its charter. From this it was clear that St Patrick's was a charitable institution, not a profitable business catering for the rich. There were private asylums whose *raison d'être* was profit, but Swift's hospital was not one of these. If Cusack, Sugden and White had followed this view to its logical conclusion, they should of course have called for the total abolition of boarders, for Swift never envisaged paying patients of any kind. But, without boarders, St Patrick's would not have been economically viable: the income from the estate was not adequate of itself to support 150 free patients. So, while chastising the governors for not following Swift's dictates, Cusack and his allies themselves condoned the breaching of the charter by advocating the admission of middle-class boarders, paying moderate fees. Thus, the intervention of Cusack, Sugden and White in 1843 did not restore the integrity of the charter, but simply confirmed the expediency of breaching it by admitting paying patients.

Before turning to a consideration of who the patients were during the first half of the nineteenth century, we should look for a moment at changes in their living conditions and forms of treatment. Undoubtedly living conditions became more pleasant and comfortable, particularly for the free patients, at this time. This resulted partly from the governors' adherence to the principles of moral management, but partly also from their decision to take in more boarders. If St Patrick's was to attract more paying patients in greater numbers, then it had to offer good facilities — at least on a par with those offered in some of the private asylums—and the free patients benefited from these as much as the boarders.

An important step towards realising the goals of moral management was taken in 1835 when patients were accommodated according to the seriousness of their illnesses. Prior to 1835, as the diagram opposite illustrates, accommodation depended solely on the fees paid: thus free patients were largely housed in the basement, while first-class boarders occupied the rooms on the ground floor at the front of the building. As we have seen, in 1831 an attempt was made to separate convalescent, free patients, but not until 1835 was a full division, or 'classification' of free patients as it was termed, achieved. The first and second class boarders continued to occupy the best accommodation, but the third class boarders and the free patients were now distributed throughout the three floors of the hospital, according to the stages of their illnesses. Moral management stressed the creation of harmonious surroundings and classification by sex, social class and severity of illness was considered essential. The assumption behind this was that patients needed to be kept with their own kind and protected from the disturbing influences, like the opposite sex, members of different social classses and other patients who were violent or noisy.

Moral management, however, did not only dictate a pleasant environment, good recreational facilities and classification according to the seriousness of the illness, it also dictated that patients should be given productive occupations. Such occupations were intended to benefit the hospital as well as the patient. During Campbell's mastership, five acres of 'productive gardens' had been laid out, with 'spacious walks'. So recreation and commerce went hand-in-hand. This agricultural work was restricted to male patients; females were engaged principally in domestic chores, such as housework, washing, knitting and sewing. In his first report on St Patrick's in 1843, White provided two tables, one summarising the output of the female patients and the other showing how the patients were employed (see pp. 133, 134). If only eighteen of the female patients were engaged in sewing, as the second table shows, then their output, as listed in the first table, was certainly impressive.

As well as physical work and outdoor recreation, the hospital also offered activity of a more intellectual nature to its patients. By 1843 it had acquired its own library. This adjoined ward 2 on the ground floor of the east wing, which housed male boarders and convalescent free patients. In February 1843 the governors decided to employ a librarian at two guineas per annum, to take care of the

DISTRIBUTION OF PATIENTS IN ST PATRICK'S HOSPITAL, PRE-1835 AND POST-1835

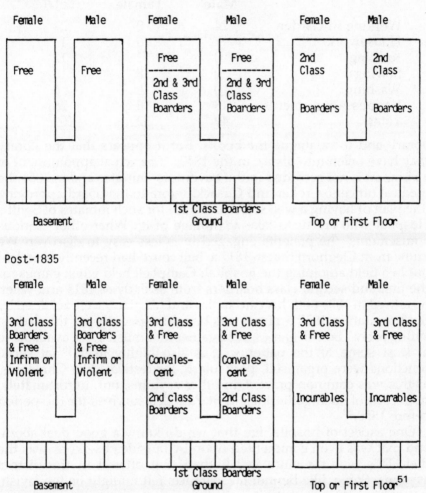

Pre-1835

Post-1835

PRODUCTION OF FEMALE PATIENTS DURING 1843

145 shirts	72 gowns	180 towels
136 shifts	34 quilts	70 bedticks
162 pairs of stockings	160 caps	[mattress or pillow
80 petticoats	114 aprons hemmed	covers]
	206 handkerchiefs hemmed	56 mattress covers

PATIENT EMPLOYMENT DURING 1843

TYPE OF WORK	NUMBERS OF PATIENTS		
	Male	Female	Total
Working in Garden	24	0	24
Housework	7	6	13
Knitting	0	12	12
Sewing	0	18	18
Washing	0	6	6
Various Amusements	18	10	28
Total	49	52	101[52]

library and to catalogue the books. But it appears that the library may have fallen into disuse in the 1840s. The actual appointment of a librarian is not recorded in the governors' minutes and in 1851 the medical officers, Croker and Cusack, wrote to the board approving 'the plan of having a well selected library for such inmates of Swift's Hospital who are fit to take advantage of it'. What other 'various amusements' the patients engaged in is less easy to discover. We know from Cleghorn that in 1817 a 'ball court' had recently been laid out in a field adjoining the hospital; Campbell held whist games for the first and second class boarders from as early as 1815 and when he retired in 1835 both his card tables and his piano were retained by the hospital; in 1855 a piano was bought especially for the 'ladies' sitting room'. So ball games, card games and music were available to at least some of the patients. It is also highly likely that social functions were organised, particularly for festivals like Christmas, as this was common practice in other asylums, but, unfortunately, no record of such gatherings in St Patrick's survives for the period before 1850.[53]

One aspect of hospital life that we do know a good deal about, and that was even commented upon by outside observers, was the diet. This was far more lavish than that offered in the district asylums. Some, like Bennet for instance, felt it might be too lavish, but in his 1843 report White rejected any attempt to economise on food, saying that he believed it should be 'more nourishing' in St Patrick's than in the public institutions. Presumably this was due to the different classes of patients involved. The first detailed account of the hospital diet occurs in the minutes of June 1831 when a new diet proposed by the medical officers was approved by the governors.

What is particularly striking about this diet is that all patients received substantial amounts of meat: the hundred guinea and sixty guinea boarders $1\frac{1}{4}$lb every day and the thirty guinea boarders and free patients 1lb three times a week, in addition to an unspecified

PATIENTS' DIET IN ST PATRICK'S, 1831

Boarders First and Second Class

Breakfast—Bread, butter & tea with stirabout & milk.

Dinner—1¼lb beef, mutton or veal, 6oz bread, 1lb potatoes, 1 quart beer & a pint of soup.

Supper—1 pint milk & 6oz bread.

Boarders Third Class

Breakfast—½lb bread & 1 pint milk.

Dinner—(Sun. Tues. Thurs.) 1lb beef & 2lb potatoes. (Mon. Wed. Fri.) Soup & ½lb bread. (Sat.) ½lb bread & 3 half pints milk.

Free Patients

Breakfast—1 quart stirabout & a pint milk or beer.

Dinner—same as for third class boarders.

Supper—6oz bread & 1 pint milk or beer.

Two ox heads in addition to the usual quantity of beef to be reserved for dinner on Monday, Wednesday and Friday.[54]

amount of meat-based soup on three other days. Pork was available as well for we know that the master was encouraged to keep pigs. The first and second class boarders and the free patients also received significant quantities of beer: the former two pints a day and the latter a possible three pints. From other references in the minute books we know that, as well, the hospital was being supplied with porter and spirits and, from 1850, if not earlier, with larger quantities of sherry and port. Alcohol was clearly readily available—for free patients, even at breakfast. Only the top two classes of boarders were being given tea in 1831, but in 1836 the master was instructed to substitute tea for stirabout at breakfast for all those patients who were 'accustomed' to it and preferred it. Stirabout, an oatmeal-based porridge, had disappeared from the upper class breakfast by the late eighteenth century, but it conti-nued popular among the farming and urban working classes till well after the Famine. Thus, in substituting tea for stirabout in the 1830s, the governors were highlighting the increasing upper and middle-class origins of their patients. It is also notable that this 1831 diet makes no mention of vegetables, except potatoes, though we know that the hospital had its own vegetable gardens. Presumably vegetables such as carrots, turnips or onions, formed part of the soup offered to all patients.[55]

PATIENTS' DIET IN ST PATRICK'S, 1843

Breakfast

1 pint of tea   ½ pint of milk   } to patients
6oz of bread   1 pint of stirabout) } desiring it
1oz of butter

Dinner

Sun. Mon. Tues. Thurs. Sat.

¾lb beef or mutton (about ½lb dressed), with vegetables, 2 lb potatoes, 1 pint soup, with an allowance of beer for the most part.

Wed.

3lb potatoes, 1 quart of soup.

Fri.

3lb of potatoes, 1 pint of milk or 1oz of butter or 1 quart of rice.

Supper

8oz of bread, 1 pint of new or mixed milk, or 6oz of bread and butter and 1 pint of tea.[56]

In the 1843 diet tea figures more prominently than it did in 1831; vegetables were being served separately, rather than only in soup; the amount of potatoes available to the patients had increased substantially, while meat had declined somewhat; and rice was being eaten for the first time.

Aside from vegetables and pork, all food for the hospital had to be bought and in 1843 the cost of provisions was £2,163. Most was supplied by contractors on an annual basis. Meat, beer, bread, soap, candles, milk, butter, coal and straw were all being provided under contract in the 1840s—with the switch from stirabout to tea and bread, the hospital had ceased to contract for oatmeal. In 1850 sugar, tea, rice, barley, port and sherry—all 'of the best description'—were added to the list. Meat, as we have seen, formed a vital part of the diet at St Patrick's. Thomas, and later John, Goodwin were the hospital's butchers from 1814 to 1847. When the contract was renewed each year, the governors were usually at pains to stress that only top quality meat was acceptable, particularly for the boarders: the 'best quality rounds and laps' of mutton and 'prime ribs and sirloins of beef' were insisted upon. The free patients were fed on a somewhat cheaper beef, while soup beef, ox heads and bones were bought to make soup with. Much haggling occurred with the Goodwins, but it was over price rather than quality. The board on a number of occasions threatened to advertise the contract, but only once, in 1841, was a cheaper butcher employed. The Goodwin contract finally lapsed in 1847, when, for unexplained reasons, John Goodwin 'failed to fulfil his contract'. The Goodwins obviously provided good meat, even if the governors at times objected to the prices charged, but with other contractors quality was usually the problem. In 1839, for instance, John Clifford's contract for supplying soap, candles and starch was transferred to Charles Brien, for, 'notwithstanding repeated remonstrances', Clifford continued to offer 'very inferior articles'. In 1847 the contract was again transferred to Brien, this time from William Daniels, who had provided 'quite inferior' candles and 'very bad' soap. In 1837 the milk contract of Mr Caffrey was cancelled due to complaints about quality and the governors resolved to purchase a lactometer so that the master could check the quality himself.[57]

The high standard of St Patrick's diet is highlighted when we compare its cost to the cost of food supplied in the public asylums.

ANNUAL PER CAPITA COST OF FOOD SUPPLIED TO PATIENTS, 1843

St Patrick's Hospital	£11. 7. 3
Richmond Asylum, Dublin	£ 6.19.10$\frac{1}{2}$
Belfast District Asylum	£ 5. 9. 6
North Dublin Workhouse	£ 4. 6. 0 (lunatic inmates only)[58]

In Belfast the cost of food was kept low by supplying meat only to convalescent patients engaged in active work. As regards clothing too, the patients in St Patrick's fared far better than those in the district asylums. In 1843 St Patrick's was spending on average £2.16.2 to clothe each patient; in the Richmond the equivalent figure was £1.0.8$\frac{1}{4}$ while in Armagh District Asylum it was only 16s 7d.[59]

Another striking feature of St Patrick's patients at this time was the large number of those labelled as incurable, amounting in 1843 to 84 per cent. In a medical report submitted to White in that year, Cusack said that: 'Very many of these cases are unmanageable, and require great care and attention.' Yet, in his 1845 report on St Patrick's, White wrote that 'there is no bodily restraint ever used'. One of the cardinal tenets of moral management was that patients should not be subjected to the indignity of physical restraint. In his

1845 report White surveyed the fourteen private asylums, housing in all 276 patients, in operation at the time. Eight of these were in Dublin and two in Cork and more than half of them were operated by doctors. White listed the means of restraint available in them, which included arm and ankle straps, strait waistcoats, leather gloves and muffs. Only two of the private asylums had no means of restraint. But, though most possessed the means, in only one had White actually found patients under restraint. We do not know what methods of restraint St Patrick's possessed at this time — though, in 1815, Bennet had observed three patients in manacles. But if such equipment was still available in 1845, it was clearly not being used. In 1815 the master, Campbell, had stressed to Bennet the 'constant attendance and watchfulness of the keepers' and, in addition, we know from information contained in admission forms that the relatives of violent or suicidal patients could be obliged to pay for a special attendant to supervise them. So St Patrick's seems to have abandoned chains and straps in favour of close and constant supervision.[60]

By 1845 the percentage of patients in St Patrick's considered incurable had reached a staggering 92 per cent. This compared with 70 per cent of patients in the district asylums and 61 per cent of those in the private asylums. When we come to examine the admission forms surviving from the 1840s, we shall find that a third of patients admitted to St Patrick's between 1840 and 1851 had had previous episodes of mental illness; 13 per cent had been suffering from their current illness for more than five years; and 17 per cent of those admitted came directly from another asylum, usually a private one. All this inevitably meant that few patients were discharged as cured and that many spent long periods in the hospital; it also meant that serious attempts at treatment and cure by the medical officers were limited to a very small number of patients indeed.

PATIENTS DISCHARGED IN 1843 AS A PERCENTAGE OF THE NUMBERS IN ASYLUMS ON 1 JANUARY 1844

	District %	Private %	St Patrick's %
Discharged:			
Cured or Relieved	23.0	13.0	7.0
Not Cured	0.4	10.0	4.0
Incurable	2.0	4.0	16.0
Total	25.4	27.0	27.0
Died	7.0	3.0	7.0[61]

If one were to look simply at the total percentage of patients discharged in 1843, it would appear that St Patrick's was doing as well as the private asylums and somewhat better than the district asylums. But, we must remember that 1843 was the year in which the hospital was forced to rid itself of its first and second class boarders. As the above breakdown of the discharge figure shows, the vast majority of those removed in 1843 were not cured or were considered incurable. In 1846, which can perhaps be regarded as a more typical year, still only 7 per cent of all patients were discharged as cured or relieved.

These depressing statistics on the numbers of patients being cured or relieved in St Patrick's in the 1840s raise questions as to the nature of the treatment being practised in the hospital. But, in the absence of case-books or doctors' notes, it is difficult to ascertain exactly what forms of treatment were attempted. There is certainly abundant evidence from at least 1815 onwards that the tenets of moral management were practised. Beyond, however, the creation of a pleasant environment and close supervision, which were intended to calm and control the patients and thus allow rationality to reassert itself, it is difficult to discover what the medical officers were doing. Indeed, it was one of the contradictions inherent in moral management that, while it was championed by doctors like Conolly in England and White in Ireland, who sought a greater role for the medical profession in the running of asylums, it was not in itself a specifically medical remedy. As Andrew Scull has remarked, it was to say the least odd to base claims for professional expertise and autonomy upon a system, the basic ingredient of which was simple kindness.[62] But it would be wrong in fact to conclude that the doctors in St Patrick's were doing little or nothing. We know that both Dr Cleghorn and Surgeon Cusack had definite ideas about how the hospital should be run and were not loath to express these ideas in public before parliamentary committees. Dr Jackson, as both a governor and visiting physician to the Richmond Asylum, was in a strong position to exert influence, while Dr John Crampton, with his cousin, Sir Philip, on the board, was also a powerful individual. If anything, there may have been too many competing medical interests involved.

We know that the medical officers took a hand in determining the patients' diet. When plans were afoot in the 1820s and 1830s to heat the hospital, they were specifically consulted. Accounts survive for the year 1833 which show that in July the visiting physician, Dr Crampton, was paid one guinea each for attending thirty-two boarders and in October he was paid the same sum for attending twenty-nine boarders. At the same time Surgeon Cusack was paid half a guinea each for attending thirty-five and thirty-one boarders.[63] There were some forty-five boarders in the hospital at the time. Obviously most, if not all, the boarders were being seen by the medical officers. Before 1838, however, they were not paid for their attendance on the free patients and so there is no way of knowing how often the free patients received medical attention. But the question still remains: when the doctor did see the patient, what specific treatments, if any, did he prescribe?

Although some of Hallaran's remedies had been thoroughly discredited by the 1830s and 1840s, others continued in use. The 1833 accounts show that hot baths were still common: the keeper, Sylvester Skelly, was paid £4.14.6 in July for supervising such baths. In the same year James Lynam of Townsend Street was paid five shillings for supplying leeches to the hospital. Bleeding was used at the time to relieve a variety of disorders both physical and mental, though Hallaran himself had been sceptical as to its value in cases of mental illness. The 1833 accounts also show that the hospital paid £1.12.6 for trusses and £2.0.0 for coffins. Ironically, one of the deaths recorded in White's first report in 1843 was given as due to a hernia, though the main physical scourge was tuberculosis: it was responsible for a third of the deaths in 1843. A medicine chest, under the medical officers' control, had been procured for the hospital in 1813. But, as we have seen, Lord Chancellor Sugden was critical of the fact that apothecary, John Nicholls, did not visit the hospital. Medicines had to be fetched from his shop in Dawson Street. Campbell had complained at the inconvenience of this arrangement as early as 1833 and the board had agreed with him and appointed a new apothecary with a shop in nearby James Street. But Nicholls immediately petitioned to be reinstated and his influence on the board was such that the master's wishes were over-ruled. The medicines he supplied are nowhere listed, however, though we do know that in 1843 £105 was paid for 'medicines, wine, etc'. It is interesting to see wine being lumped together with medicine. Presumably some of the alcohol being consumed in the hospital was regarded as medicinal. We know also from other sources that emetics and purgatives of the sort that Hallaran recommended were still in use, while opium and other narcotics were frequently resorted to in order to calm violent patients. But, as Andrew Scull has shown, although many different drugs were employed at this time, there was little or no consensus among doctors as to the relative merits of virtually any of them.[64]

During the 1830s and 1840s the hospital, presumably on the advice of the medical officers, began to release patients temporarily and on trial. In 1836, for instance, it was decided that Mary Barton should 'be received as a patient when under excitement and be taken back by her friends when convalescent'. Clearly it was felt that at times patients would benefit from being returned to their families. In 1844 a Miss Fletcher was 'removed on trial and for the benefit of her health'. By these means perhaps it was hoped to counter the effects of institutionalisation. Patients who spent many years continuously in the hospital lost any ability they may have had to cope with the outside world. Allowing convalescent patients out for limited periods or on trial was one way of helping them to readjust to life beyond the walls of St Patrick's. Though, even while resident in the hospital, patients were not totally cut off from outside contact. We know that in 1843, for instance, there were visiting hours of from 10 a.m. to 2 p.m. on Tuesdays and Fridays.[65]

Although under the new regulations introduced in 1831 the medical officers were empowered to report on any patient to the quarterly board meetings, the impression one gains from a close reading of the minutes is that communication was not in fact full and regular. On a number of occasions after 1831 the board was forced to write to the doctors seeking basic information. In 1840, for instance, the medical officers were asked to report any patients they considered unfit for the hospital; subsequently three patients were removed, one of whom had showed no signs of illness since her admission. This, though, was the sort of information that the doctors should have been supplying regularly, without a specific directive from the board. At the same meeting as this request to the doctors was agreed on, the governors also decided to introduce an attendance book to be signed by the medical officers whenever they visited the hospital.[66] These two decisions taken together suggest that the board may have been dissatisfied about the frequency of the doctors' visits and about the information on patients that it was receiving from them. The governors in fact seem to have turned more and more to the master. In Campbell and Cuming and their matron wives, they certainly had able and hard-working employees. We have already commented on the significant fact that it was the master and not one of the medical officers who was despatched in 1842 to inspect Conolly's work at Hanwell. Given that moral management was not a specifically medical treatment and given that the master lived in the hospital and was present at board meetings, while the medical officers did neither, it is perhaps not surprising that the master took an increasingly prominent role in matters relating to the patients.

The simple fact was that by 1850 relations between the governors, the master and the medical officers were becoming more complicated and less satisfactory. The difficulties were as much structural as personal. Once the state physician had ceased to be the visiting physician in 1825 a gap had opened between the board and the doctors working in the hospital and into that gap had stepped the master. He was now the only individual both to be present at board meetings and to be intimately involved with patient care. But his position was hardly satisfactory. He certainly was in close touch with the workings of the board—he arranged meetings and supplied much of the agenda—yet, he was not a member and thus could not formally take part in the decision-making process. The master's position was similarly anomalous vis-à-vis the medical officers. He was in constant contact with the patients and was thus the principal agent of moral management, but he was not a doctor and was not specifically charged with the duty of treating patients. It was a very untidy state of affairs and it is hardly surprising that the doctors, both the visiting doctors and the doctors on the board, were unhappy with it. We know that Surgeon Cusack was critical of the hospital's admission policy, but, not being on the board, it was difficult for him to change it. We also know that Dr Jackson was unhappy: he was on the board, but he was not directly involved in treating patients as his predecessors in the office of state physician had been. Clearly something drastic needed to be done to improve communication between the board and the medical officers and to clarify the role of the master.

Information as to the patients is far more plentiful in the nineteenth century than in the eighteenth, though, as we have just seen, there are still important matters, like methods of treatment, which remain infuriatingly obscure. Nevertheless, we do know a good deal about who the patients were and what was thought to be wrong with them. The main surviving sources of information are the hospital's registry of patients, which was begun in 1835-6 under Cuming, and covers 2,549 patients admitted between 1795 and 1925. In addition there are two lots of admission forms: approximately three hundred forms for the period 1841-53 and two hundred and thirty for the period 1873-87. The registry contains basic data on the patients' backgrounds, illnesses and their stay in hospital. Most of this material appears to have been drawn from the admission forms, which were completed by relatives or friends and also had attached a certificate, signed by two doctors, testifying as to the necessity for admission. These forms, however, were frequently accompanied by letters or petitions from relatives, providing further details of the case. Thus, it is possible to undertake both a statistical analysis of the forms—see Appendix 4—and an examination of specific cases.[67]

By studying the data contained in the first group of admission forms, one can produce a profile of the typical 1840s admission. The patient would be male: an unmarried Protestant, in his twenties or thirties, from Dublin city or one of the surrounding townships. As to occupation, he might still be financially dependent upon his family; if not, then he was likely to be a lawyer, doctor, clergyman, farmer, clerk or either a soldier or sailor. His admission to St Patrick's would have been applied for by his parents or by a brother. He probably had had previous episodes of mental illness and he may have already spent time in a private asylum; in the present instance, he would possibly have been ill for over a year. The nature of his illness was likely to be described as mania or a form of mania. Its cause was probably unknown, but, if it was known, it was most likely given as over-work, financial worries or intemperance. As to the outcome of a typical case admitted in the 1840s, the patient had a good chance of being discharged as recovered or relieved, but there was at least a one in three chance of him eventually dying in the hospital.

The surviving admission forms are, however, a trifle misleading in suggesting that males out-numbered females in the ratio of six to four. This may have applied to admissions, but, when we look at figures for the numbers resident in St Patrick's at any one time, we find that the sexes were roughly equal, though if anything females slightly out-numbered males. This apparent inconsistency arises from the fact that there was a more rapid turnover of male patients: more men were indeed admitted than women, but women tended to stay significantly longer in the hospital. A similar phenomenon occurs as regards boarders and free patients. More boarders were admitted during the 1840s than free patients, but at the same time large numbers of boarders were discharged, compared with very few free patients. Thus, during the 1840s only about 40 per cent of the hospital's resident population were boarders.

Aside from the fact that women tended to stay considerably longer in St Patrick's than men, there were a number of other interesting differences between the sexes. Female patients were far less likely than males to be married and they were also less likely to be discharged as unrelieved. Both these facts almost certainly contributed to the tendency of women to remain longer as patients. Without a spouse prepared to take them from the hospital, even if they were no better, women had less chance of being discharged. Women tended also to be admitted to St Patrick's for rather different reasons than men. Menstrual and birth complications figured largely among the reasons put forward for female breakdowns, as did general ill health; while grief at the death of a loved one was a far more significant factor among women than it was among men.

A statistical survey can certainly tell us a good deal about St

Patrick's patients, but in order to gain a clearer insight into their predicaments, we really need to look at specific cases. In examining individual patients and particularly the reasons for their committal, we should, however, be alive to a number of factors: familial, social, economic and even political.

In a recent article, Mark Finnane, who has written the most important account of Irish public asylums, argues that the reasons for committal should be sought, not in abstract categories of illness, but in the context of the family: '. . . it is the history of familial relations [he writes] which is essential to appreciating the decision to commit'.[68] Why a family decided to take the drastic step of having one of its members admitted to an asylum is for Finnane the crucial question, and he gives less importance to the issue of clinical diagnosis. It is certainly true as regards St Patrick's in the 1840s that admissions were family matters, for, although the majority of patients were single, most appear to have been living with their families prior to commital and most were committed by a close relative. In only about 5 per cent of admissions did the application come from a person not related to the patient. A case that provides an apposite illustration of Finnane's point about the importance of the family context is that of Thomas Larkin. He was a fifty-five year old, former bookseller of Lower Gardiner Street, who had spent some months in St Patrick's in 1827. But, when he showed signs of improvement, his wife, Mary, had removed him, obviously preferring to care for him at home. We know little of his illness, as it was simply described as 'insanity' and was put down to 'losses in trade'. In order to care for her sick husband and four children, Mary Larkin had been forced to let her house in lodgings. But, in April 1843, she again applied for Thomas's admission to the hospital. 'Until lately', her petition said, he had been 'so comparatively quiet as to admit of his being left in the house.' But 'from the great increase of his disease', which seems to have manifested itself in violent behaviour, his wife now found it 'impossible' to continue caring for him 'as by doing so she would surely be obliged to give up her lodgers which are her sole support'. It was obviously a cruel dilemma for Mary Larkin. Initially she placed him in Dr Eustace's private asylum in Glasnevin, but the fee of £5 a week quickly proved to be beyond her means. So in May 1843 Thomas Larkin was admitted to St Patrick's at £20 per annum, though even this sum was too much, for in July 1844 Mary Larkin successfully applied to have him transferred to the free list. Thomas Larkin eventually died in the hospital in May 1865 from an inflammation of the left lung.[69] The immediate cause of Larkin's admission in 1843 was not therefore his illness; he had been ill for at least fifteen years. The immediate cause was the fact that his illness was beginning to threaten his wife's livelihood. This case certainly lends support to Finnane's view that the family context and particularly family problems are often more important in explaining admissions than simple categories of illness. Thomas Larkin was also typical of many St Patrick's patients in having been ill for a long time and having been transferred from a private asylum. Patients seem often to have been admitted to expensive private asylums while there was some hope of a cure, but once such hope was gone, then relatives turned to St Patrick's with its lower fees and possibility of free accommodation. This is undoubtedly one reason why the hospital accumulated so many incurable cases—a long history of illness preceding admission made cure, or even relief, highly unlikely.

Family financial problems, like those experienced by Mary Larkin, seem to have been behind many decisions to commit a relative and this was especially so in cases of dependent women. In the early 1840s Fr Mathew's temperance crusade forced many publicans out of business. Mary Anne Hickey, born in 1819, was the eldest of five daughters of Charles Hickey of New Market, Dublin, a brewer. Both Hickey and his wife were dead by 1837, leaving their daughters, with an income of only £70 a year between them, in the care of their uncle and aunt, Julia and Denis Ford of Castle Street. Mary Anne was first admitted to St Patrick's late in 1837, suffering from grief, presumably caused by the deaths of her parents, and was removed a year later by the Fords, being described as that stage as 'convalescent'. In March 1841, however, according to a medical certificate, she became insane due to 'anxiety about her health'. This diagnosis is rather misleading for, in their petition seeking her re-admission to the hospital in April 1841, her uncle and aunt presented an altogether different picture of the causes of Mary Anne's relapse. According to them, she had been 'perfectly well' from her discharge up until March 1841, but the 'small property . . . belonging to the family had ceased to exist, it being derived out of two public houses, which in consequence of the march of temperance were obliged to be given up to the landlords . . . which leaves the said Mary Anne Hickey without any means of support whatsoever'. Mary Anne was re-admitted as a free patient in June 1841 and died in St Patrick's in February 1863 from tuberculosis.[70] The deaths of her parents, the loss of the family's income and possibly an uncle and aunt not eager to have to support five penniless young women, all obviously played a part in the collapse of Mary Anne Hickey's mental health.

There were in fact a number of young or middle-aged women admitted to St Patrick's in the 1840s whose fathers, previously prosperous, had died unexpectedly, leaving little or no money.

Some of these women were forced to take jobs as governesses or music teachers in order to support themselves. But most seem to have been ill-prepared for this new and insecure style of life. Anne Barter, a fifty year old, unmarried, Protestant governess from Cork, was committed by her sister Matilda, also a governess, in November 1842, suffering from melancholia caused by 'distress of mind'. On the death of their father Perkins Barter, a 'gentleman' of Cork city, both sisters were forced to seek employment as governesses. Anne lived for seventeen years with the Hoare family of Factory Hill who were relatives; Matilda lived for nineteen years with the Morrises of Dunkettle and had by 1842 spent a further seven years with the Newmans of Mallow, who were also relatives. Matilda thought that it was the death of Edward Hoare and the subsequent break-up of his family that had 'laid the foundation of the melancholy disease an all-wise Providence has seen fit to afflict my dear sister with for nearly the last eight years'. With financial help from relatives, Anne had been kept in various private asylums, notably Dr Osborne's. But 'resources [were] daily diminishing' and Matilda's 'own subsistence [was] most precarious and doubtful'. She now wanted her sister to be placed in a 'safe and permanent asylum'. Her memorial was signed by members of some of Cork's leading landed families, including two Newmans, two Longfields, two Bernards, two Lombards, one Becher, plus the bishop of Cork and Lord Carbery, and it was accompanied by a strong recommendation from Dr Thomas Osborne, Hallaran's successor as physician to the Cork asylum. Anne Barter was admitted in November 1842 at £20 per annum and died in the hospital in October 1853.[71] Governesses, forced to leave their own families by death or financial hardships and likely to be ejected abruptly from their employer's family on the maturing of children or the deaths of parents, lived a precarious life, both economically and emotionally. That a significant number ended up in St Patrick's Hospital is not surprising.

Another group of women particularly at risk of admission through family financial problems, were middle-aged and elderly spinsters dependent on their brothers for support. In January 1843, for instance, Robert Story, a solicitor practising in Mountjoy Square, applied for the admission of his sister, Eleanor, who was a forty-one year old, former post-mistress from Swanlinbar, Co. Cavan. She was described rather vaguely as having been of 'unsound mind' for 'some time'. In a letter accompanying the application form Robert Story wrote that his sister was wholly dependent on him and he offered £28 for her yearly upkeep in the hospital. Apparently the governors considered this amount insufficient for, in an obviously ill-tempered letter to the master, probably written in February,

Robert Story regretted 'that the memorial to have Miss Story placed in your asylum on the £28 class had failed' and claimed to be 'at a loss to know the cause, as she has really no means, except depending on me who have a family of my own to support'. I wish now', he went on curtly 'to place her on the class at forty guineas and to try hereafter to have it reduced, and to have her removed as soon as possible, and will thank you to inform me if there is now a vacancy, as if so, I shall call on you this day or tomorrow, and pay the quarter in advance, and do the necessary acts, —I should suppose the medical certificate annexed to the former memorial will answer—your reply by bearer will oblige.' Eleanor Story was admitted in March 1843 and discharged as 'relieved' in June.[72] Her three months' stay in the hospital obviously had more to do with her brother's reluctance to pay the fee demanded than with the nature of her illness. That a brother was the single relative most likely to commit a patient, whether male or female, to St Patrick's is hardly coincidental. Social mores dictated that parents and spouses should care for ill children or husbands and wives, but the onus upon siblings, particularly brothers, to care for each other was much less strong. Robert Story's attitude, expressed so bluntly in his letter, that supporting himself, his wife and children came before the interests of his sister, appears to have been all too common. Sisters admitted by brothers had, in many cases, been ill for many years, but the brothers demonstrated a marked reluctance to pay the level of fees demanded by the governors.[73]

In addition to familial and financial problems, there are several other factors that figure prominently in admissions to St Patrick's in the 1840s. In 1818, under what he termed the 'General and Local Causes of Insanity', Dr Hallaran listed foreign or domestic war, the abuse of spiritous liquors, religious dread and heredity, as the most common causes of insanity. In attempting to account for what he saw as a marked increase in insanity between 1798 and 1809, Hallaran drew attention to both the external war against France and the internal upheavals produced by the 1798 Rebellion. He was in no doubt that national and even international political events had an effect on mental health. The alarms and calamities of war produced unnatural excitement, anxiety and disappointment, which could undermine vulnerable personalities. Hallaran was obviously no nationalist for he particularly blamed the 'prevalence of certain political opinions which are inseparable from our recent history' and 'visionary views, and consequent disappointments' for the increase in insanity that he had observed in Cork. He also acknowledged that economic crises could affect the rate of insanity as well. In recent years, he said, he had seen fewer cases produced by 'political feuds', but there had been a great upsurge in cases caused by 'loss of property' and the 'cessation of employment among the working classes'. Thus Hallaran recognised the sometimes unbearable pressures placed on individuals by economic misfortune, like the depression which followed the end of the Napoleonic Wars in 1815.[74]

Details of admissions before the mid-1830s are too scanty for us to be able to assess Hallaran's view as regards the 1798 Rebellion, the French wars or the post-1815 depression. But there was a major disaster of the type that Hallaran envisaged during the 1840s — this being of course the potato famine. This cataclysm is not obviously reflected in admissions to St Patrick's, however, for the Famine did not affect all sections of Irish society equally. The labouring and small farming classes were most severely hit and these were the groups that were least represented among the hospital's patients. We do, though, find tantalising hints of the Famine in some of the admission forms. Betwen 1845 and 1850, fifteen farmers or close relatives of farmers were admitted to St Patrick's. The term farmer can of course cover a very wide socio-economic spectrum, from the relatively wealthy to the very poor. If the fees charged this group are anything to go by, they were somewhere between the two extremes. Most paid £20 per annum. This was the lowest fee at which St Patrick's would accept a boarder and suggests that these farmers were middling rather than substantial. In June 1846 Charles Isdall, a thirty-five year old Protestant farmer from Co. Longford, was committed to the hospital by his brother at £22 per annum, suffering from 'mental abstraction' brought on by 'distress and want'. In June 1847 Robert Panton, a fifty-six year old Protestant farmer from Co. Wicklow, was committed by his wife at forty guineas per annum, suffering from monomania caused by problems in his business affairs. In August 1848 John Flavelle, a fifty-eight year old Co. Dublin farmer and widower with six children, was committed as a free patient by his son and daughter, suffering from insanity brought on by 'embarrassments' in his financial affairs. Others may have suffered from the more indirect effects of the Famine. Alicia Delany, a forty-seven year old Protestant widow and matron of the Abbeyleix workhouse, was committed by her sister in November 1847 at £20 per annum. She was suffering from mania, said to have been brought on by a fright while she was recovering from fever. The matron of a workhouse in 1847, with famine and fever rampant, would have had more than her fair share of frights and shocks. Louis Burton, a twenty year old Protestant from Stradbally, Queen's Co. (Laois), was committed by his mother in June 1848, at fifty-two guineas per annum. He was refusing to eat while recovering from a severe bout of influenza and had become acutely anxious about his brother and sister who were emigrating to America. In this case we can perhaps catch a glimpse of the distress caused by the break-up of families due to emigration.[75] But, in general, due to the fact that most of St Patrick's patients were drawn from the middle classes and from Dublin, the Famine left relatively little impression in the hospital's records. This is not to say, however, that Hallaran's emphasis on the role of wars, depressions and disasters in undermining mental health was misplaced. If one were to investigate the admission records of some of the rural public asylums for the years between 1845 and 1850, one might uncover far more evidence in support of his views.[76]

The marked increase in spirit consumption which occurred in Ireland after 1780, Hallaran saw as another prime cause of the growth in insanity, as was the popular preoccupation with religion produced by the revivalist movements of the late eighteenth century. Hallaran felt that those 'of ordinary endowments, however ardent in the pursuit of knowledge, are not calculated for that close investigation of doctrinal points, upon which our most able devines are still widely at variance'. Moreover, 'religious enthusiasm' and the insanity resulting from it he had invariably found to afflict Protestants rather than Catholics. Swift, who had linked madness and the enthusiasm of Protestant dissenters in his satires would almost certainly have concurred in this judgment. In a separate chapter Hallaran discussed at some length the role of heredity as a factor in mental illness. He did not believe that people were born insane, but he recognised a predisposition to insanity in some people which could be activated by 'certain exciting causes'. Thus he strongly urged that: 'Families, in any degree similar, in this respect, should not intermarry.'[77]

An analysis of St Patrick's admission forms for the 1840s certainly confirms Hallaran's claim that drink played a large part, if not in actually causing insanity, then at least in causing committals to asylums. Some 13 per cent of male patients, though only 1 per cent of females, were admitted because of the effects of excessive drinking. If we look more closely at this 13 per cent, we find that they differed from the rest of the males admitted, in generally being married and over forty years of age. Their occupations were varied, ranging from shopkeeping to medicine to the Church, both Catholic and Protestant. A fairly typical case was that of William Lardner, a forty-one year old, married, surgeon, who had worked in Portugal, Spain and Poland. The application for his admission, made in August 1845, came from his mother, Mary Anne Lardner of Aungier Street, who told the governors: '. . . my son . . . has been residing with me for the last nine months during which time he has been mentally afflicted and unable to contribute to his own support—his malady is daily getting worse and his general demeanour more violent (so much so as to keep me and my daughter in constant apprehension)'. Lardner was diagnosed by two doctors as suffering from monomania brought on by intemperance. They confirmed that his condition was deteriorating and his manner becoming 'furious'. He was admitted as a second-class boarder at £20 per annum in September 1845, transferred to the free list at his mother's request in November 1846, and finally discharged as recovered in August 1848.[78] In this case, as in the case of Thomas Larkin, it was not the onset of Lardner's illness that precipitated his admission to St Patrick's, but rather the threat that he was coming to pose to the safety of his family. Presumably, like Mary Larkin, Mary Anne Lardner was prepared to care for her son at home while this was at all possible. Again this case illustrates Finnane's point that people were not committed to asylums by their families simply because they were mentally ill. Aggravating factors, like financial problems or threats of violence, which disrupted family life, were what actually precipitated committals.

St Patrick's had some success in treating the victims of alcohol, for most were discharged as recovered or, at least, relieved. Drug addiction seems, however, to have proved a more difficult problem, though it was far from being a common one. Only two addicts are recorded as having been admitted in the 1840s: one addicted to opium and the other to mercury. The former was a woman: Maria Walsh, a thirty-six year old, unmarried Catholic from Rathmines, admitted as a second-class boarder in May 1845 by her brother. He described himself as being engaged in commerce, but Maria as having 'no particular occupation'. She had been ill for about four years and had spent three months in St Patrick's in 1841. She was finally discharged, after her second admission, in 1852, but, despite seven years of treatment, she was still considered to be unrelieved. The mercury addict, William Glascock, fared rather better, being discharged as relieved after only three months in the hospital. He was a forty year old, married, customs officer from the island of Jersey, committed by his brother, a Rathmines book-keeper. But it may well have been that the demands of his family or his job did not admit of him staying any longer once he had shown signs of improvement.[79]

That a significant number of cases of alcohol abuse should be found in St Patrick's records is hardly surprising, but it is surprising to find two cases admitted in the 1840s claimed by relatives to be suffering from the deleterious effects of teetotalism. James Lendrum a forty-eight year old Catholic widower and 'dealer in soft goods' from Capel Street, was committed by his son in June 1845. According to the admission form, he had been suffering for twelve months from religious mania and from delusions that peope were trying to rob him, brought on by 'sedentary habits' and by having become a teetotaller. The other 'victim' of teetotalism came from a rather different background. She was Eliza McKittrick, a forty-five year old, unmarried, 'old light Presbyterian', from Co. Antrim. She was committed by her brother, a woollen draper, who described her occupation as 'sewing, knitting, reading and household affairs'. As for her illness this was characterised as 'generally unhappy and discontented' though 'quite easily managed' and it was ascribed to her being 'too retired' and 'too much devoted to religious subjects and teetotalism'. Obviously in both these cases, one Catholic and one Protestant, we are in fact dealing with an intense religious commitment, of which teetotalism was but a reflection.[80]

In 1818 Dr Hallaran had identified 'religious dread as one of the principal causes' of insanity. In fact it was widely believed at the time that what Hallaran termed 'perverted ideas of religion' could form both a cause and a concomitant of mental illness. As a result, the Irish district asylums set up after 1817 were often reluctant to appoint chaplains and this was particularly so in Ulster, where sectarianism was a further complicating factor. Doctors and administrators feared that the introduction of religious instruction into asylums would only aggravate the disorders of many patients. The government overrode this judgment and insisted upon the appointment of chaplains, but it was many years before the Belfast asylum could be persuaded to implement this decision.[81]

If we take all instances in which religion was mentioned, even as a minor cause or aspect of illness, in relation to patients admitted to St Patrick's in the 1840s, we find that it figured in 11 per cent of cases. This is obviously a significant percentage, though perhaps less than one might have expected given Hallaran's remarks. Hallaran also claimed, as noted earlier, that in his many years' experience in Cork he had never come across the case of a Catholic afflicted with 'mental derangement' due to 'religious enthusiasm'. Joseph Robins in his recent study of insanity in Ireland has also identified a close connection between mental illness and Protestant revivalism. According to Hallaran, among Protestants, it was the dissenters who were particularly prone to insanity and moreover they often exhibited 'vivid extremes of sensorial action . . . an inverted picture of their former conceptions'. As patients they generally proved 'the most obstinate, and the least disposed to submit to the necessary modes of treatment', as a result of which they were 'peculiarly liable

to returns of the complaint'. The evidence from St Patrick's admission forms does not, however, bear out these assertions. In the
1840s, of those admitted suffering from a disorder associated with
religion, 32 per cent were Catholics. In terms of Catholics in the
hospital's population, this means that they were somewhat over-
represented among those afflicted with 'religious dread'. Nor
among Protestants were dissenters predominant. In the 1840s the
majority of Protestants admitted St Patrick's due to 'religious mania'
were the members of the Established Church. Though, as the vast
majority of Protestants in the hospital were also members of this
Church, this fact may not be particularly meaningful. Overall,
however, the evidence from St Patrick's admissions in the 1840s
does strongly suggest that 'religious derangement' was not restricted to dissenting Protestants as both Hallaran and Robins imply. [82]

Robins also remarks that a disproportionate number of clergy and
religious were to be found in asylums. If this were true, presumably
St Patrick's would have had a particularly large group given its
traditional links with the Established Church. But, although clergymen and their relatives were usually admitted free, they do not form
an especially large group among the patients at this time. Clergymen made up 5 per cent of admissions in the 1840s, which put them
behind teachers, clerks and farmers and slightly ahead of doctors
and lawyers. All were Church of Ireland clerics, except for the Rev.
Michael Caraher from Armagh, a parish priest committed in 1845 by
his brother because of his violence and heavy drinking. Only one
was suffering from a disorder associated with religion: he was the
Rev. John Galvin from Rathgar in Dublin, who was said by his
brother in 1850 to be afflicted with melancholia and religious mania.
Most, however, had more worldly problems, like over-work and
financial difficulties; one young curate from Kilkenny had become
depressed after a romantic disappointment; while a clergyman from
Dublin had been in various private asylums for seventeen years
after murdering his father and uncle and threatening to kill his
wife. [83]

Hallaran's claim that a hereditary disposition was a major cause of
insanity also appears, at first glance, not to be borne out by the
admission records of St Patrick's; only 4 per cent of admissions, just
seven cases, were labelled as hereditarily insane in the 1840s. Yet,
there were several instances of members of the same family being
admitted to St Patrick's, even with the same disorder, who were not
categorised as suffering from a hereditary illness. [84] The cause of
illness was, however, generally entered on the admission form by
the relative seeking to commit. Presumably, few relatives were

willing to admit that insanity was a hereditary family trait and thus figures for hereditary disorders are probably grossly understated.

By the 1840s St Patrick's was certainly more prosperous financially then it had been in the past, partly as a result of good management by its masters, Patrick Campbell and James Cuming, and partly through its new policy introduced in 1830-31 of accepting more boarders and fewer free patients. A great deal of work had also been done between 1810 and 1840 on the hospital building and grounds, aimed mainly at creating a more pleasant and comfortable environment for patients. The governors believed, or at least hoped, that such improvements would have a beneficial effect upon the troubled minds of the hospital's inmates and would produce more cures. Yet, a quick survey of the outcomes of cases of patients admitted during the 1840s graphically illustrates the shortcomings of the policy of moral management. Only 27 per cent of those admitted during this decade were eventually discharged as recovered, while 13 per cent were discharged as unrelieved, 19 per cent spent at least ten years in the hospital and more than a third—38 per cent to be exact—actually died there. The reports of the government's lunacy inspectorate, begun in 1843, revealed that the vast majority of patients were regarded as incurable and plans then being mooted to turn St Patrick's into a teaching hospital probably foundered upon this obstacle. But, if the failures of moral management were not enough, the lord chancellor's insistence in 1843 that the governors cut fees drastically, though not initially a problem, was in the long run to create grave financial difficulties as well. The 1850s thus witnessed the beginning of a period of serious decline, which culminated in the early 1890s with proposals to close St Patrick's down.

CHAPTER FOUR

Swift's Hospital: The Years of Decline, 1850-1899

The oldest institution for the insane in Ireland is the chartered St. Patrick's Hospital, founded by Dean Swift, and generally known by his name ('Swift's Hospital'). . . . It should have been, under proper management, the Bethlem, if not the Morningside, of Ireland, and its miserable history is a sufficient commentary on the whole of the specialty in that country. . . . In former times the management is understood to have been entirely clerical, and to have been by no means free from scandal, nor has it been very much better in quite recent years, though other elements are now represented on the board. . . . It is not very clear what has become of the Dean's grant. . . . The institution was one of the latest strongholds of the worst forms of restraint. . . . Surely if the great Dean could have foreseen the vile inhumanity with which his charity would have been misused, he would have struck out of his epitaph that mysterious sentence which has ever since moved the wonder and pity of his readers. We cannot but feel a bitter indignation would still tear his heart asunder could he know that the asylum, founded under his will and bearing his name, would have been the last, in English-speaking lands, to relinquish the treatment by barbarous cruelty of the afflicted, with whom he had so deep a sympathy.[1]

ADMINISTRATION, STAFF AND FINANCE

The second half of the nineteenth century proved a particularly difficult period for St Patrick's Hospital. In the 1850s price inflation following the Famine dramatically increased the cost of maintaining patients, while at the same time the governors were prevented from raising boarders' fees by the lord chancellor's 1843 decree that fees should not exceed forty guineas per annum. By 1863 the hospital's financial situation had become so serious that the board was forced into severely restricting the numbers of free patients. Only when the lord chancellor sanctioned a significant fee rise in 1866 was the situation eased. But another financial crisis occurred after 1879 as the country sank into a major depression. This time, however, it wasn't so much income from fees that was affected as income from rents. Agitation by tenants and a series of land acts passed from 1881 onwards considerably strengthened the hand of the tenant *vis–à–vis* the landlord. For St Patrick's Hospital the land war and its aftermath meant a significant decrease in estate revenue. But, while it struggled with rising costs and diminishing income on the one hand, on the other the hospital was under increasing pressure from parliament, and particularly from the new home rule MPs, to modernise and improve its facilities. Generally the government, in the persons of the two lunacy inspectors based in Dublin Castle, had been understanding of St Patrick's problems. But, when two new and more active inspectors were appointed in 1890, they quickly concluded that

> the present governors would carry out [Dean Swift's] intentions with greater faithfulness, and with greater charity to the unfortunate beings to benefit whom his money was be-queathed, by disposing of the present institution and seeking a more suitable locality at a little distance from the city, and there founding another St Patrick's Hospital which might truly be called a sanatorium for the restoration of the mental health of those whom Dean Swift was so anxious to benefit.[2]

For a time it looked as though the hospital, in the form that it had existed for nearly one hundred and fifty years, would disappear.

During such difficult times St Patrick's obviously needed able and determined leadership. But, unfortunately, such leadership was frequently lacking. Aside from any consideration of the abilities of those who filled key positions, the simple fact was that there was a much higher turn-over of such people after 1850 than before. For instance, while three masters served the hospital between 1800 and 1850, there were seven between 1850 and 1900. Similarly, only sixteen elected governors sat on the board between 1800 and 1850 compared with twenty-nine between 1850 and 1900.

In the case of some of the governors it may well be that they simply did not have the time to devote themselves to the hospital's increasingly intractable problems. After 1850 a growing number of businessmen joined the clerics, lawyers, landlords and politicians who had previously dominated the board. Presumably it was hoped that such men would bring their financial acumen to bear upon matters like falling revenue. In the late nineteenth century Dublin had few thriving industries and thus the businessmen who joined the board represented a narrow range of interests. Several were directors of railway companies (Sir Ralph Cusack, R. O. Armstrong, Robert Warren, F. B. Ormsby); two were managers at Guinness's Brewery (W. P. Geoghegan, C. D. La Touche); two were directors of the Bank of Ireland (Robert Law, J. R. Stewart); while a further two were agents for the estate on the south side of the city owned by the earl of Pembroke (J. E. Vernon, Robert Colvill).

After 1850 the demands made upon the governors' time by hospital affairs increased, while simultaneously the number of governors declined. Medical representation on the board disappeared altogether with the abolition of the offices of state physician and surgeon general and, for forty years after 1846, the office of dean of Christ Church was held either by the dean of St Patrick's Cathedral or by the archbishop of Dublin, thereby effectively eliminating another *ex officio* governorship. In the 1850s there seems also to have been problems with the attendance levels of the elected governors, for several who seldom attended appear to have been asked to resign. At the same time attempts were being made to keep the governors in closer touch with the affairs of the hospital. In the early 1850s there were even instances of patients, wishing to be discharged, appearing in person before the board to argue their cases, rather than the governors simply relying on the opinions of the visiting medical officers. In 1857, however, the medical officers were requested to submit monthly reports on the state of patients. But, perhaps most importantly, in 1862 it was decided to appoint at least one and preferably two governors each month to act as 'visiting governors'. Their task was to inspect the hospital regularly, to consult with the master regarding admissions and to inform their fellow governors of any problems. From about 1860 it was therefore no longer considered enough for a governor to sit on the board for years, or till death, while attending the occasional meeting. Being elected to a governorship of St Patrick's Hospital continued to be regarded as an honour, only to be conferred on men of power and status, but it was an honour that now demanded greater amounts of time and energy. It is not surprising therefore to find that after 1850 a significant number of governors resigned their positions after a few years, rather than serving for life as had been the common practice during the previous hundred years.[3]

Medical representation on the board was restored in 1887 with the election of Sir John Banks, an eminent physician, with an interest in mental illness. A former president of both the Royal College of Physicians in Ireland and the British Medical Association, Banks was Regius Professor of Medicine at Dublin University and a physician to the queen in Ireland. Some doctors at the time were reluctant to certify patients for admission to an asylum as prosecutions for wrongful confinement were not uncommon, but Banks seems to have had no qualms: admission forms surviving from the 1870s show that he regularly recommended the admission of patients to St Patrick's Hospital. Perhaps his most important contribution as a governor, however, was his proposal in 1897 that the size of the board be increased by the addition of three new elected governorships. This had the effect of bringing membership up from twelve to fifteen and of further tilting the balance in favour of elected governors. Instead of holding a majority of seven to five, under Banks's proposal, they would hold one of ten to five. Banks himself wanted the new governors to be 'men of business training and who had leisure to devote to the interests and objects of the institution'. A supplementary charter was required to put this proposal into practice. But, when it was secured, the election for new governors which followed in 1898 produced, not businessmen, but a land agent and two doctors. The doctors were Dr Samuel Gordon and Sir Thornley Stoker, the hospital's visiting physician and surgeon. This secured the positions of the visiting medical officers, which, as we shall see later, had been under challenge. It did not, however, produce the businessmen whom Banks felt the hospital most needed at the time.[4]

But, whether they were businessmen or doctors or clergymen, the governors were part of a network, allied by family, by land or by occupation. We saw such networks operating earlier in the cases of Anglo-Irish landed families, like the Beresfords, Ponsonbys, Verschoyles, Fosters and Shaws. By the latter part of the nineteenth century the networks had become, if anything, even more complex. Governors were linked, not just through family connections and land holding, but increasingly through occupation. For example, the governors J. E. Vernon (1867-81) and Robert Colvill (1897-1923) were agents for the Pembroke estate. W. H. F. Verschoyle, whose mother was a Foster, succeeded his father as agent for St Patrick's estates in 1878, having previously trained in the Pembroke estate office under Vernon. Colvill, who was also a director of the Bank of Ireland, lived at Coolock, Co. Dublin, with his brother, James, who was chairman of the Great Southern and Western Railway Company. F. B. Ormsby, also a governor of the hospital (1895-1917), was secretary of the company. Coolock in fact produced a number of governors, including Sir Edward Borough (1849-60), agent for the Dublin militia, of which Sir Robert Shaw was colonel; Robert Law (1849-55), a governor of the Bank of Ireland; and the Rev. J. C. Irwin (1889-1928), who was the rector of the parish. Nearby, at Raheny, lived Sir Ralph Cusack (1869-96), son of Surgeon Cusack and chairman of the Midland Great Western Railway Company. Two other directors, R. O. Armstrong (1881-96) and Robert Warren (1876-94), were also governors of the hospital. Notable Anglo-Irish families, like the Beresfords, Trenches and Plunkets, continued to be represented on the board, but largely through the *ex officio* clerical governorships. Among the elected governors urban men of business came to predominate at the expense both of Anglo-Irish landed families and of clergymen. In 1850 four out of the seven elected governors had been clergymen, but, by the end of the century, there were only two clergymen among the ten elected governors. Given the seriousness of the financial problems that St Patrick's faced in the second half of the century, it doubtless needed all the business acumen that it could muster.[5]

In the first half of the century the hospital had been fortunate in its masters: after the problems created by Dyton and Cottingham in the 1780s, Mahony, Campbell and Cuming had served faithfully for over seventy years between them. But, among those who occupied the position from the retirement of Cuming in 1858 to the appointment of Dr Leeper in 1899, ill health, premature death and neglect of duty took a sorry toll. In 1858 Cuming had been succeeded by his son-in-law, John Trench Gill. The appointment was a logical one: Gill was already resident apothecary in the hospital and his wife, Jane, had been filling the position of matron since 1853 due to the illness of her mother. Catherine Cuming died in 1858 and this presumably precipitated James Cuming's retirement. As master and matron John and Jane Gill received £150 and £100 per annum respectively, as well as free accommodation, light and heat.[6]

The appointment of Gill in 1858, however, had one particular significance which was nowhere referred to by the board. As well as being an apothecary, Gill was a physician, having been trained at the University of Aberdeen. He was thus the first medically-qualified master. Subsequently all masters have had medical qualifications. As we saw in the previous chapter, the philosophy of moral management, which prevailed in asylums during the first half of the century, was not based on medical criteria. It followed that doctors were not essential to its implementation. But the medical profession, particularly in the person of Dr Francis White, the first inspector of lunacy, fought to increase its say in the public asylums. This battle first took the form of an effort to increase the power of visiting medical officers over the lay manager; later, attempts were made to ensure that only qualified medical practitioners were appointed to the office of manager, or resident physician as it came increasingly to be called. This of course inevitably led to conflicts between visiting and resident doctors, until eventually visiting medical officers were done away with altogether. During the 1850s Irish asylum management was gradually being taken out of the hands of lay men and given to doctors. In appointing Dr Gill as master in 1858 St Patrick's was moving with the times.[7]

Unfortunately, however, Gill died suddenly in October 1859, barely a year after his appointment. The board quickly replaced him with Dr Francis Robinson, a surgeon, while Mrs Gill continued in the office of matron. But, in the event, Robinson's seven years as master were to prove particularly difficult. The hospital was experiencing serious financial strains which we shall look at in more detail later. The situation was not helped by the fact that Robinson was frequently absent from his duties due to poor health. In 1862, for instance, he applied for leave on medical grounds, presenting the board with certificates signed by the visiting medical officers, Drs Croker and Hamilton, and by Dr John Banks, who fifteen years later was to join the board as a governor. Robinson said he was suffering from a 'severe illness occasioned by rheumatism, too close application to my duties, and an injury received from a patient'. Banks certified that Robinson was 'in a very delicate state of health' and recommended that he 'leave town at once' as 'he is at present unequal to the discharge of his duties at Swift's Hospital'. Robinson took himself off to Co. Cork for five weeks. In his absence the office of master was filled by his brother Richard, also a surgeon, who appears to have been already living in the hospital and acting as assistant master. Two years later, in June 1864, Francis Robinson again sought leave on medical grounds. In the same month the hospital was inspected by Dr John Nugent, one of the lunacy inspectors, accompanied by Richard Robinson. Nugent was unusually critical, complaining that some attendants were shabby in appearance and their rooms were not made up and that he had seen a donkey grazing in the female airing sheds. He also found a man, whom he thought to be a patient, sleeping in a room full of rubbish. In fact this turned out to be the apothecary, sleeping amid the tools of his trade. The board was obviously unhappy with Nugent's report and it wrote to the ailing Francis Robinson seeking an explanation. Clearly, with the master frequently absent, standards in the hospital were declining.[8]

In September 1865 Richard Robinson was again reporting to the board on his brother's behalf and in November at a special meeting a medical certificate from Dr Banks was tabled which said that the master was 'seriously ill' and should 'leave town for some time'. Francis Robinson was given leave of unspecified length and his brother appointed in his place. Three months later, in February

1866, Dr Banks was able to report that the master was now fit to return to work as 'resident medical officer'. But, rather than welcoming Robinson's recovery, the board resolved that his leave should be continued indefinitely and that his brother, Richard, who was also recovering from a 'severe illness' should leave the hospital 'upon convalescence'. Until further arrangements could be made, the governors ordered that the 'entire management of the hospital be entrusted to Mrs Gill' and that 'no member of Dr Robinson's family be permitted in any way to interfere with the management of the hospital or the arrangement thereof'. The board was obviously very dissatisfied with the performance as master of both Francis and Richard Robinson. It was determined to rid itself of Richard completely and, though Francis was not dismissed, it was clear that the board had no wish for him to continue as master. Both brothers resisted attempts to remove them from the hospital. It was not till July 1866 that Richard left and not till November that Francis could be persuaded to submit his resignation. The fact, however, that the governors agreed to return his security deposit, though resisting his demands for monetary compensation, suggests that they did not consider him guilty of any serious irregularity, beyond being medically unfit for the job. Robinson's successor was Edmund Lawless, a naval surgeon who had distinguished himself in the Crimean War.[9]

At this November 1866 meeting the visiting medical officers also expressed complete satisfaction with Mrs Gill's management of the hospital during the previous nine months and the board awarded her a gratuity of £40 in appreciation of her services. Jane Gill had in fact become the backbone of the hospital: it was she who held it together, and not only during the absence of the master. We don't know her age, but she was probably under twenty when her father was appointed master in 1835; she took over the matronship from her ailing mother in 1853, though she had very likely acted as an assistant to her mother even before that date; in 1858 she was formally appointed matron and held the office till her retirement at the end of 1885. Her association with the hospital thus extended over a period of fifty years. The board of governors obviously had complete confidence in her, to the extent of entrusting her with the entire management of the institution—and on more than one occasion. The first time, as we have seen, was during Robinson's absence on sick leave in 1866; the second was when Lawless died suddenly in 1879; and the third was in 1883 when the then master, Dr Rice, was injured by a patient. In later years Mrs Gill's health was not strong. In 1878 there had been an outbreak of smallpox in the hospital and Mrs Gill had contracted the disease from her servant and been seriously ill. The following year she took charge of the hospital after Lawless's death. But, on Dr Rice's appointment, the governors gave her indefinite leave in order to recover her health and in 1883 they allowed her an assistant in the person of her niece, Jane Fernside. By 1885 Jane Gill was receiving £120 a year, only £20 more than the salary she had been appointed at, but on her retirement she was given a generous pension of £60 a year, while her successor as matron, Mrs Hodson, started on a salary of only £80. At their February 1886 meeting the governors paid tribute to Mrs Gill's 'untiring energy', her 'careful performance of her many onerous duties' and her 'kind and judicious' treatment of patients. An illustration of the latter quality was evident in January 1886 when a Mr Blood secured the governors' consent to remove his sister from the hospital and 'place her for the present with Mrs Gill who at his request has kindly consented to receive her'. Mrs Gill had taken a house in Bray, next door to her sister Mrs Fernside, and, although not licensed as a private asylum keeper, she may well have 'received' other former patients from St Patrick's. Relatives, like the governors, obviously had confidence in her 'judicious' treatment.[10]

But, perhaps the clearest sign of the board's confidence in Mrs Gill occurred much earlier, in 1867, to be exact. In September of that year Mrs Gill was given a month's leave and the money to pay her expenses to visit asylums in England. On previous occasions the board had paid for masters to inspect English asylums: James Cuming, Mrs Gill's father, had gone in 1842 and Dr Robinson had been sent in 1860. But the fact that in this case the matron, and not the newly-appointed master, Dr Lawless, was sent, was a striking indication of Jane Gill's key position in the affairs of the hospital. The visiting medical officers consulted her about patients and expressed admiration for her skill in dealing with them. It was she who, in 1864, began hiring carriages to take patients for drives in the country. The board thoroughly approved of this initiative, though it did insist that the patients pay their own expenses. The architect consulted Mrs Gill about repairs and renovations and she had a say in plans to re-build the kitchen and laundry in the 1860s. Jane Gill thus appears to have had more influence on the affairs of the hospital than any other housekeeper/matron, either before her time or since. But the regulations under which St Patrick's operated never envisaged such a major role for the matron. Mrs Gill was usurping some of the functions of the master and in fact her prominence, particularly in the late 1860s and early 1880s, was a reflection of the shortcomings of the men who filled the office of master at the time.[11]

Dr Lawless served as resident medical officer from 1866 till his sudden death in 1879 from 'apoplexy'—probably a stroke. The appointment of Dr William Rice as his successor signalled the beginning of further troubled years for the hospital. Partly this was the result of the economic depression which struck the country in 1879 and of the ensuing land war. But, during the early 1880s, the governors also became very dissatisfied with the performance of the hospital staff. In 1883 Rice and Jeremiah Smith, the store clerk, were reprimanded for 'want of vigilance and irregularities which have caused serious losses.' In 1884 Dr Rice was dismissed, though the board decided that publicly it should be said he had resigned. Early in 1885 Smith and the accountant, John Butler Yeats, were also dismissed. Smith had served the hospital for twenty-eight years, while Yeats had been accountant for thirty-two and his father for six years before him. Dr Rice's request for a reference and Smith's for compensation and more time to find another home were refused by the board. But in Yeats's case the governors relented somewhat. They expressed satisfaction with his work and allowed him to serve till the end of the year. Yeats, who was a relative of the poet W. B. Yeats, was a part-time accountant, being also employed as a clerk in Dublin Castle. But for Rice and Smith, who were full-time resident officers, dismissal meant the loss of their jobs and their homes and, moreover, without a reference, both would have had difficulty in finding another position. The hospital was in serious financial trouble in the early 1880s: in 1883 its overdraft at the Bank of Ireland reached an unprecedented £2,000 and in 1884 one ward had to be closed down. Yet, it is difficult to discover what exactly were the 'irregularities' which led to the dismissals of Rice, Smith and Yeats. There is mention of substantial discrepancies in the accounts for provisions supplied in 1883 and 1884, and in 1885 the board decided to write off these losses. The master and clerk may have been held responsible for the discrepancies and it may have been felt that a part-time accountant did not have enough time to devote to the hospital's accounts. Certainly Yeats was replaced in 1886 by a full-time accountant.[12]

The main reason why it is hard to trace exactly what happened in 1883-5 is that a vital piece of the evidence has been destroyed, and destroyed deliberately. At the board meeting held on 4 December 1883 the governors apparently set out their grievances against Rice, plus directions as to how he should conduct himself in future. But the minutes of this meeting have been removed from both the draft and formal minute books. Only a note remains, written in 1890 by the then accountant, George Manders, stating that pages are missing and speculating that they 'probably contained something about the conduct of Dr Rice, the master'. Like Manders, all we can do is speculate as to Rice's failings. Rice himself protested strongly against his 1883 censure, calling it in a letter to the board 'unde-served' and asking to be furnished 'with the names of my accusers, as well as with the particulars of their charges' so that he might have a 'fair opportunity of defending my character, which has been so grossly and wantonly assailed'. There are, however, scraps of information in the minute books that allow us at least to make an informed guess as to the charges levelled against Rice and as to who his chief accusers were. The special meeting of the board which reprimanded Rice and Smith, the store clerk, in November 1883 also appointed Jane Fernside as assistant matron and 'diet clerk'; the latter position gave her charge of the distribution of foodstuffs. Perhaps Mrs Gill, who as matron was responsible for the manage-ment of the kitchen, was aware of irregularities in the supply of provisions and wanted her niece to keep an eye on the situation.[13]

We can only speculate as to whether or not Mrs Gill was one of Rice's 'accusers', but we do know that he did clash with the visiting surgeon, Dr Thornley Stoker. Stoker, brother of the theatrical manager and author of *Dracula*, Bram Stoker, was one of the leaders of his profession in Dublin: he served as president of the Royal College of Surgeons in Ireland between 1894 and 1896 and in 1895 he was knighted for his services to medicine. Rice was by no means as eminent, but he was a physician, unlike his predecessors Robinson and Lawless, who had been surgeons. Relations between physicians and surgeons had traditionally been difficult, with the physicians regarding themselves as the senior members of the profession. In Irish asylums at this time, as already noted, there were frequent clashes between visiting and resident medical offic-ers. Thus, both as a physician and a resident medical officer, Rice was likely to be at odds with the visiting surgeon. In 1884 the dispute between Rice and Stoker concerned the treatment of a patient called Singleton. In July Rice told the board that Singleton was 'in a weakly state from not having sufficient food—the meat being either raw or burnt to a cinder'. Rice's letter was referred to Stoker. But, by the time his reply was laid before the next board meeting, Singleton was dead. Stoker reported that death was due to 'exhaustion, which so frequently terminates cases of chronic mania'. As for the question of food, Stoker was adamant that Singleton 'refused his food because he was dying—and did not die because he refused his food'. There were, however, problems in the kitchen and Rice's criticism of the food may well have been justified. The cook, Mrs Connor, who had held the position for forty years, was by 1884 old and ill: she had been suffering from severe rheumatism for more than ten years and seems frequently to have been unable to carry out her duties. After the disagreement between Rice and

Stoker over the Singleton case, the board asked Jane Gill to report on the state of the kitchen. As a result of Mrs Gill's investigation the cook was retired in 1885 on a pension of five shillings a week.[14]

The year 1885 marked something of a watershed, for it saw the departure of the master, matron, accountant, clerk and cook, all of whom, except for the master, had served the hospital for more than twenty-five years. Rice was replaced as resident medical officer by Dr John Moloney, who filled the position till 1899 when he was put in charge of the new auxiliary hospital that the governors had recently purchased at Lucan. Moloney did not make a marked impression upon the hospital, but he appears at least to have been more reliable than his immediate predecessors.

The prominent position occupied by Mrs Gill between 1858 and 1885 and the shortcomings of most of the masters of that period rather obscure the fact that the status of master, or resident medical officer, was actually growing, while that of matron was declining. This is evident from their respective salaries. Dr and Mrs Gill were employed in 1858 at salaries of £150 and £100 per annum; these salaries having remained unchanged since 1816 and 1824 respectively. But, when Mrs Gill retired in 1885, she was only receiving £120 per annum, while Moloney, the new resident medical officer, started in the same year on a salary of £300. Ten years later he was receiving £500 per annum, yet the matron's salary remained £100. Thus the matron's salary had been virtually stationary for seventy years, while that of the master/resident medical officer had increased more than threefold. This dramatic divergence simply reflected the fact that during the second half of the century the master and matron were no longer regarded as a team working in tandem. It is no coincidence, for example, that Mrs Gill was the last matron to be the wife of a master. By the 1870s the practice of appointing husbands and wives to the offices of asylum manager and matron had virtually ceased, for, as lay managers became medical superintendents and rose in status, it became socially unacceptable for their wives to occupy the lowly position of asylum matron. Indeed, some writers on the subject felt that neither superintendents nor their families should even reside in asylums. The view was put succinctly by an English observer in 1877:

> The circumstances of the superintendent's wife acting as matron involves a sacrifice of social position injurious, if not fatal, to success. It is above all things indispensable that medical superintendents of asylums should be educated gentlemen; and if that is to be the case, their wives cannot be matrons. Indeed, it is inconceivable that a man of position and culture

would allow his family to have any connection with an asylum.[15]

As an 'educated gentleman', the resident medical officer of St Patrick's had a much superior status to the old lay master, inside the hospital as well as outside. New regulations and bye-laws issued in the late 1880s, in the wake of Rice's departure, first use the term 'medical superintendent', which quickly superseded that of resident medical officer. The word, superintendent, clearly implied more power and, under the new regulations, the superintendent was given authority to 'superintend and regulate the whole establishment'. Although the accountant, secretary and store clerk had responsibility for accounts, record books and provisions, the medical superintendent still exercised 'general supervision' over all such matters. The matron's inferior status was likewise made very clear. The 1889 bye-laws directed that she 'shall reside in the hospital, and shall exercise immediate superintendence over the female department, but in position and authority subordinate to the resident medical superintendent, to whom she is to report daily . . .'[16] So, even with regard to the female patients, who in the past appear to have been viewed as largely the matron's responsibility, her subordination to the male superintendent was spelled out unequivocally.

After Jane Gill's retirement her successors never again had an opportunity to take over some of the responsibilities of the medical superintendent. The most serious challenge to his authority came, not from the matron, but from the two visiting medical officers. We have already seen that there were clashes between Rice and Stoker over the treatment of patients. Initially it seems that the governors had envisaged the resident medical officer as a mere agent for the visiting medical officers: he would draw their attention to patients in need of treatment and carry into effect whatever treatments they recommended. But the change in title to that of superintendent suggested greater responsibility and this was confirmed by the 1889 bye-laws, which 'entrusted [the medical superintendent] with the moral and general medical treatment of . . . inmates'. They further laid down that the visiting medical officers were to attend the hospital on alternate days. On arrival they were to consult with the medical superintendent and then, in his company, to visit all physically ill patients, as well as those under restraint and those newly admitted. At least once a fortnight, again with the medical superintendent, the visiting officers were to examine the mental condition of every patient. When a patient was being considered for discharge, the visiting officers were to examine the patient 'in conjunction with' the medical superintendent and to 'consult' with him as to what action if any should be taken. Finally, the visiting medical officers were also to attend the hospital when called on by the medical superintendent 'and to afford such advice and assistance as may be required of them, whether to patients, officers or servants'. The use of words like 'advice' and 'assistance' makes clear that in such cases the visiting officers were to act in a supporting role to the medical superintendent.[17]

Despite their declining significance, elections for the positions of visiting medical officers were hotly contested. In 1875, for instance, there were five candidates for the job of visiting surgeon and only after four meetings held over a six-month period, with rare attendances by the archbishop of Armagh and the lord chancellor, did Dr Thornley Stoker emerge as the winner. But at the next election, caused in 1889 by the death of the visiting physician, two governors tabled a motion recommending that he not be replaced. Sir Ralph Cusack, the son of a former visiting surgeon, argued that the public asylums, with an average of 450 patients each, had only one medical officer and so St Patrick's, with a mere ninety patients in 1889, hardly required two. But Sir John Banks, the only doctor on the board, in alliance with several of the clerical governors, was able to defeat the motion. The position of visiting surgeon lapsed in 1912 with Stoker's death and that of visiting physician in 1932 with the death of Dr R. A. Hayes, who had been elected in 1899.[18] But, although the position of visiting medical officer lingered on well into the twentieth century, the 1889 bye-laws had clearly signalled the beginning of the pre-eminence of the medical superintendent in the area of patient care and treatment.

In 1872 the staff of the hospital, aside from the master, matron and visiting medical officers, were given a pay rise; at the time the staff numbered approximately fifty (see p. 167).

One notable employee who does not appear on this list is the hospital's secretary–chaplain. Until 1852 one of the governors had acted as secretary to the board, but from 1852 to 1899 the position was filled first by the Rev. W. P. H. Dobbin and then by the Rev. J. A. Dickinson, both of whom were also chaplains at Steevens Hospital. The chaplaincy at Steevens had been endowed by Stella and so it was doubtless considered appropriate that the chaplain should also serve Swift's hospital. After 1899 the office of secretary was amalgamated with that of accountant and this new office of secretary/registrar became the main administrative position in the hospital—as it still is today. But, prior to 1899, the secretary had generally been a clergyman and in 1851 the board resolved that the secretary should read prayers daily for those patients who were

REVISED PAY SCALES FOR STAFF, 1872

	Present Pay	Future Pay after 3 Years' Service
	£	£
Mr. Yeats, Accountant	50	60
Mr. Smith, Store Clerk	30	40
Gardener	21	22
Head Attendant	18	22
Two 2nd Class Attendants each	15	19
Four 3rd Class Attendants each	15	18
Night Attendant	12	15
First Gate Porter	12	15
Second Gate Porter	10	13
Hall Porter	10	15
Sweeper	12	12
Librarian	6	8
Head Nurse	20	23
One 2nd Class Nurse	15	18
Two 3rd Class Nurses each	12	15
Laundress	17	20
Cook	15	18
Store Maid	8	10
Four Laundry Maids each	6	8
Twenty Ward Maids each	6	8
Two Kitchen Maids each	6	8
Total	526	659[19]

members of the State Church. To facilitate this they ordered the purchase of three dozen Bibles and a similar number of prayer books. As in other asylums, however, the governors were fearful lest religious services should aggravate the disorders of some of the patients. Thus the visiting medical officers were asked to report which patients might benefit from participation in such services. St Patrick's did not have its own chapel and so selected patients were permitted to attend the chapel at Steevens Hospital. But careful selection and supervision did not always exclude violent behaviour: in 1874 St Patrick's was presented with a bill from Steevens for glass broken by its patients. Patients of other denominations could if they wished attend churches in the neighbourhood, but only under the supervision of an attendant. In 1890, however, the new lunacy inspectors, Drs O'Farrell and Courtenay, strongly urged the appointment of a Catholic chaplain to say mass once a week in the hospital. Priests from St James's parish occasionally visited patients, but it was not till 1924 that the priest of the parish was formally appointed as Catholic chaplain to the hospital.[20]

St Patrick's patients seem in fact to have been better provided with secular reading matter than with religious instruction. We saw that there was reference to a library in the hospital in the 1840s and from the 1850s a librarian, who also acted as a clerk, was employed. In 1888 Fanny Stoney, a former governess, was appointed to this position and filled it till 1899. Her appointment is particularly interesting as from 1874 to 1888 she had been a patient in the hospital. Patients certainly helped with cooking, sewing, cleaning and gardening, as such occupations were considered therapeutic, but this is the first recorded instance of a patient, or former patient, being officially employed and paid for her services. It was by no means, however, to be the last such instance. Fanny Stoney, under the supervision of the secretary, bought books, magazines and bookcases for the library. Unfortunately, though, there is no record of her purchases in the 1890s.[21] What does survive is a list, mainly of periodicals, recommended by the visiting medical officers for purchase in 1853.

PERIODICALS AND BOOKS TO BE PURCHASED FOR THE LIBRARY, 1853

Saunders News Letter (Dublin, daily)
Sharpes Magazine
Parlour Library
Chambers Journal (Edinburgh, popular science and arts)
Dublin University Magazine (monthly, literary)
Household Words (London, weekly, ed. Charles Dickens)
Illustrated News (London, popular news and events)
The Weekly Warder (Dublin)
Scott's Novels (Sir Walter Scott's Waverley novels)
Athenaeum (London, weekly, literary review)
Quarterly Review (Edinburgh, Tory literary and news review)
Layard's Works
Literary Gazette (London, weekly, book reviews).[22]

If all, or even most, of these works were purchased, then the library would have been well stocked with the main Dublin, London and

Edinburgh arts and science reviews. In terms of novelists, Scott and Dickens were obviously favourites, though the *Dublin University Magazine* would have given patients access to many of the leading Irish writers of the period as well. If they wished to or were able to, patients could have kept abreast of popular tastes in literature, the arts and science. We do not know to what extent patients used the library, though the need to employ a librarian does suggest a substantial volume of business.

The 1872 pay scales show that by then the keepers were being referred to, in the case of males, as attendants, and, in the case of females, as nurses. In fact, a number of the, to our ears, rather blunt terms reminiscent of prison, which had been used in the eighteenth and early nineteenth centuries, were falling out of use by mid-century. Along with 'keepers' went 'lunatics', 'idiots', 'paupers' and 'cells'. Such words were being replaced by a terminology more suggestive of a hospital. But, although the term 'keeper' may have been dropped, the duties of the position do not seem to have changed much. According to the hospital's 1889 bye-laws the attendants and nurses were to see that patients were properly washed and dressed in the mornings; they were to 'contribute all in their power, both in and out of doors, to their amusement and occupation'; and at night they were to ensure 'that due regard [was] paid to their comfort'. Attendants and nurses were responsible for the 'safe keeping of patients' and in the event of an escape were liable to dismissal. They were never to leave patients 'unguarded', nor were they themselves to be absent from the hospital without the permission of the medical superintendent. Their children were 'on no account . . . to reside in the hospital'. They were not to accept money from patients or their relatives on pain of 'immediate dismissal' and they were particularly to avoid using 'any harsh or intemperate language to patients'. Instead, they were 'to contribute to that system of moral government upon which the value of the institution depends'. Much emphasis was placed on the cleanliness and dress of the patients. Attendants and nurses were 'to pay particular attention to the clothing and becoming appearance of the patients'. The Victorian view that clean and tidy dress reflected a well-ordered and healthy mind obviously prevailed. Women patients particularly caused concern if they dressed in an unusual or untidy manner. As Elaine Showalter has written, the sanity of women patients 'was often judged according to their compliance with middle-class standards of dress'. It was the responsibility of the ward maids, who served both the male and female wards, to ensure that rooms and corridors were clean and that dirty bedding and clothing were delivered to the laundry. At 9 p.m. in winter and

10 p.m. in summer the night attendants took over. Till 6 a.m. they had to patrol all parts of the hospital, keeping the 'strictest vigilance'. Shortly after Dr Leeper was appointed medical superintendent in 1899 he produced a timetable of daily duties which reveals the long and rigidly ordered days worked by the attendants and nurses. When reading this we should keep in mind that staff were not entitled to holidays or sick leave; indeed, it is difficult to discover any time-off that they were entitled to.[23]

As well as long hours of work, the staff also had to endure poor and often unhealthy living conditions. Most of the staff were obliged to live in the hospital, but no adequate purpose-built accommodation was provided for them before the twentieth century. Keepers' rooms had been installed on each corridor when the hospital was built and extended in the eighteenth century. A hundred years later, however, these could only accommodate a fraction of the staff. The female staff, both nurses and ward maids, seem to have suffered most from the accommodation shortage. In the 1860s, for instance, many of the ward maids were living in extensions to the gate lodges on Steevens and Bow Lanes. These seem to have been particularly unhealthy places, for in 1866-7 the visiting medical officers complained about the amount of sickness, particularly influenza and diarrhoea, that they were being called upon to treat among the ward maids living in the gate lodges. Not till 1884, however, were the ward maids transferred to new accommodation. This turned out to be no. 1 ward, the male basement ward which had had to be closed due to lack of funds. But, in the past, it had often come in for criticism as too damp and dark. It may, however, have been better than the gate lodges. Even the gate keepers and their families appear often to have been ill. There were no toilets in the lodges and after Arthur Beattie, one of the gate keepers, died of typhoid in 1870, the medical officers urged that WCs be installed. Yet the other gate keeper died in 1876 of unspecified causes and the wife of Martin Hynes, Beattie's successor, was repeatedly ill before her death in 1883. The hall porter also contracted typhoid in 1881, but he appears to have recovered. Aside from the ward maids and the gate keepers, another particularly sickly employee was the store clerk, Jeremiah Smith, who lived with his family in a house in the hospital grounds. Between 1872 and his dismissal in 1885, Smith, his wife and children suffered a succession of illnesses, including asthma, diarrhoea, gastric fever, scarletina, measles, whooping cough, jaundice, rheumatism and various skin infections. There were as well a number of unspecified disorders. In December 1884, a month before his dismissal, three of Smith's children were down with typhoid, one so severely that for a time his life was despaired of. In the same month, J. B. Yeats, the accountant, who was also about to be dismissed, was being treated for constipation. One wonders if their health improved after they left the hospital. Winters inevitably produced outbreaks of respiratory disorders. In October 1865 the master reported that six of the servants were confined to bed and one had been removed to the Richmond Hospital. The 'prevailing illnesses' were influenza, bronchitis, diarrhoea, rheumatism and catarrhal infections. We shall look more closely at the health of the hospital when we consider the patients, but it is worth noting that the stress of the job took its toll on some of the staff in psychological as well as physical terms. A number of nurses had to be treated for 'nervous' and 'hysterical' disorders, while in 1898 the governors agreed to pay five shillings a week for a year to the mother of Nurse Mooney, 'who after twenty five years service has become insane'.[24]

The general impression one gains from reading the hospital's records is that the employees, or servants as they were called, did a difficult job, often under very trying conditions. There were dismissals from time to time: in 1857 the store clerk, John White, and a nurse were dismissed for 'improper conduct'; in 1862 a keeper was dismissed for assaulting another and 'creating a riot', while at the same time a nurse was dismissed for 'negligence'; in 1888, in a rare case, an attendant was dismissed for injuring a patient. In 1886 and 1887 several attendants were fined for drunkenness, particularly at night: one who was drunk on New Year's night had his pay for 1886 reduced by £5. This spate of incidents of drunkenness occurred immediately after the departure of Dr Rice and suggests that staff discipline may have broken down during his tenure of office. But more common are records of pensions and gratuities granted for long service and details of illness and injury suffered by the servants in the conduct of their duties. In 1862 Richard Dunne, the head attendant, who had been employed for eighteen years was given a gratuity of £40 on his retirement. He had been 'disabled from ill health and injuries received in the discharge of his duties'. Attacks by patients on staff seem to have been relatively common: in November 1864 two male patients 'violently assaulted' two attendants, 'severely injuring' them; in December a male attendant received 'a severe scalp wound'; while in April 1865 a recently-admitted male patient 'severely' injured an attendant and another patient. Nor were the masters immune from attack: in 1862, when applying for sick leave, Dr Robinson had given injury caused by a patient as one of the reasons, while in December 1883 Dr Rice was off work for nearly a month due to a knee injury inflicted by a patient.[25]

Nurses and attendants at St Patrick's worked long hours for low pay, though the fact that they were entitled to free lodging, clothing, food and medical attention, does make comparisons with other wage-earners difficult. Not until 1896 did a union for asylum attendants begin to organise in Ireland and then it was fiercely resisted by superintendents and governors. Yet the staff of St Patrick's was probably no worse off than the staff in the public asylums. In 1873 male attendants in the district asylums were receiving on average £17.10.0 per annum, while females received about £9.15.0. In St Patrick's, under the revised pay scales of 1872, attendants' pay ranged from £15 to £19 per annum, while that of nurses ranged from £12 to £18. Thus St Patrick's continued the tradition of paying its female staff more than the public asylums. In 1899, under Dr Leeper's timetable, attendants and nurses worked approximately a fifteen-hour day, but in the district asylums thirteen to sixteen-hour days were common. Important changes in asylum staffing began to occur after 1890, in both St Patrick's and the district asylums. By the 1880s asylum doctors had concluded that their institutions could be run more effectively only with better trained staff. The Medico-Psychological Association, a body set up in the early 1840s to represent asylum doctors in both Britain and Ireland, devised a handbook for attendants and offered a certificate of proficiency in 'mental nursing'. Asylum doctors in Ireland began in the 1890s to encourage their attendants to master this handbook and to gain certification. At St Patrick's the spur to change was provided by the new lunacy inspectors, Drs O'Farrell and Courtenay. Noting in 1891 that many of the female patients were old and ill, Courtenay urged the hospital to employ a trained nurse. At the same time he said he felt that the 'governors should strive to obtain a higher class of candidates as vacancies occur' and to this end that 'they should consider if the scale of wages offered is such as to attract eligible candidates'. The wages that Courtenay then quoted showed little or no increase over those set in 1872. One of the basic principles of the Victorian asylum was, as already noted, the strict separation of the sexes. Courtenay was thus particularly critical of the practice in St Patrick's of having women clean the male wards. In 1893 he described this as 'subversive of discipline, morality, and order'. Moreover, with a salary of only £6 per annum: 'How can it be expected that persons suitable to have charge of the insane can be obtained for such a sum?' He urged the governors to do away with ward maids in the male wards. Their work, according to him, could be done by the male attendants, helped by the patients, and the money thus saved used to improve the wages of the remaining staff.[26]

The governors responded slowly to these suggestions, but the pace of change picked up noticeably with the appointment of Dr Leeper in January 1899. A trained nurse was employed from 1894 and wages were increased, particularly those of the ward maids. But Leeper immediately set up classes for nurses to prepare them for the exam in mental nursing. Three nurses who had obtained their certificates of proficiency by December 1899 had their pay increased to £20 per annum. In May two new night nurses were employed at £15 each and in October two new attendants were employed at £35 each. The inspectors had also strongly urged the employment of a head attendant to supervise the other attendants. This office had certainly existed in the 1860s and 1870s, but it seems to have been allowed to lapse during the financial stringency of the 1880s. In August 1900 Leeper was given permission to employ a head attendant at the substantial salary of £60 per annum. In February of that year he had already recommended that Nurse Eynthoven, who had gained her certificate in mental nursing, be appointed head female attendant. We shall look more closely at Leeper's reforms in the next chapter. Suffice it to say here that, within months of his appointment, the term 'servant' was being added to the list of obsolete words at St Patrick's, as he set out to create for the first time a trained staff.[27]

From the mid 1850s to the mid 1870s Ireland enjoyed a period of growing prosperity. Agricultural prices were high, though there were several bad seasons in the early 1860s, and the incomes of both farmers and labourers rose. Better communications, with the coming of the railways from 1834, opened up new markets and stimulated industry and commerce in the towns. Although population declined, demand grew and prices rose accordingly. This prosperity was certainly modest by British standards and unevenly distributed—Belfast, for instance, with its linen and ship-building industries fared far better than Dublin—but it contrasted sharply with the destitution, starvation and death of the 1840s.[28]

For those, however, who could not increase their incomes, rising prices created economic hardship. In 1843, under pressure from Dr White and Lord Chancellor Sugden, the board of St Patrick's agreed to set forty guineas as the maximum fee for a boarder. But, as prices rose dramatically in the 1850s, the governors found that their expenditure was coming to exceed their income. Detailed accounts for the 1850s do not survive, but the following table comparing selected contracts entered into by the board in 1852 and 1862 gives some indication of increases in the cost of provisions.

PRICES OF PROVISIONS FOR THE HOSPITAL, 1852 AND 1862

	1852	1862
Mutton	$4\frac{1}{2}$d lb	$6\frac{3}{4}$d lb
Beef	3d lb	$5\frac{3}{4}$d lb
Pure New Milk	$4\frac{3}{4}$d gallon	$7\frac{1}{2}$d gallon
Beer	17/- barrel	16/- barrel
White Soap	30/- cwt	44/- cwt
Dip Candles	5/- dozen lbs	6/6 dozen lbs
Mould Candles	5/6 dozen lbs	7/- dozen lbs
Starch	3/6 stone	4/6 stone
Oaten Straw	1/2 cwt	2/8 cwt
Tea	3/9 lb	3/5 lb
Soft Sugar	36/- cwt	47/- cwt
Patna Rice	16/- cwt	22/- cwt
Sherry and Port Wine	£1.2.0 dozen bottles	£1.4.0 dozen bottles
Whiskey	8/- gallon	15/- gallon.[29]

Not only was the cost of living rising rapidly, however, but the hospital was also coming under government pressure to spend large sums of money on repairs and rebuilding. A commission of enquiry set up in 1857 to look into Irish lunatic asylums had been critical of the conditions existing in St Patrick's and in March 1859 the lord chancellor, Joseph Napier, made an unheralded inspection of the hospital. In his subsequent report Napier commented particularly on the poor state of the laundry, on the lack of a dining hall, on the dampness of the flagged floors and on the generally dreary appearance of the building. The governors were obviously stung by such official criticism and their response was sharp:

> . . . they are obliged to proceed very gradually [they said] in all their improvements, for they have no aid from parliament, and are obliged therefore to meet every outlay by rigid economy; having thus hitherto avoided trespassing on their capital. That the institution was not originally placed in a more airy locality, and erected on a plan characterised by greater cheerfulness, is to be lamented, if it could have been helped—It is however irrelevant to compare modern institutions built at the national

expense, with this edifice erected long ago and at private expense—And the board of Swift's Hospital only have to rejoice, that now and then they are able to accommodate the numerous applicants from other hospitals, a decided preference being shown for this institution by the friends of the patients.[30]

Irritation and defensiveness vie with each other in this minute, which the board instructed its secretary to forward to the lord chancellor. The rather exasperated tone is probably a fair reflection of the governors' attitude to the mounting problems which they faced. For, while the government demanded modernisation, it offered no financial aid. It was in fact in the middle of pouring large sums into the building of more district asylums: six were opened in the 1850s and another six in the 1860s. The governors of St Patrick's had to find more money themselves. To do this they had three possible options: they could increase boarders' fees; they could raise rents on their estates; or they could draw on the capital that they had invested in government stock before 1843. In fact they did all three.[31]

In August 1859 the board told its agent, J.J. Verschoyle, that, due to price rises, rents on the Saggart estate would have to go up. Unfortunately, however, the following three years saw a sharp agricultural depression. Crop yields were extremely low in 1860, 1861 and 1862 and in 1861 wet weather ruined the hay crop upon which the Saggart tenants particularly relied. In general terms this was only a temporary setback to the growing agricultural prosperity, but it couldn't have come at a worse time for the hospital. In 1860 and again in 1863 Verschoyle warned the board that rents were going to be hard to collect due to the effects of bad weather. So, just when the governors needed the rents to be paid on time, just when in fact they wanted to increase the rents substantially, the tenants were finding it extremely difficult to pay at all. Obviously the estate could not provide the additional revenue that the hospital needed both to modernise itself and to keep up with price inflation.[32]

Pursuing its second option for increasing income, the board resolved in November 1859 to approach the lord chancellor with a request that it be allowed to raise fees above the maximum level fixed in 1843. In June Maziere Brady had replaced Napier in the office. He does not seem, however, to have been particularly sympathetic to the board's plight. In November 1860 the governors raised the maximum fee to £45 'in consequence of the increase in the price of provisions'. Presumably Brady had sanctioned the rise;

however, it was far too modest to have much impact on the hospital's deteriorating financial situation. But, shortly before, the board had already resorted to its third option: in October 1860 it had ordered the sale of £2,500 worth of stock both to pay off its £1,800 overdraft at the Bank of Ireland and to finance renovations.[33]

Following the official criticism voiced in 1857-9 the governors had to decide what improvements needed to be made. At the urging of Dr Hatchell, one of the lunacy inspectors, they agreed in September 1860 to send the new master, Dr Robinson, to England to inspect hospitals there. Robinson visited, among others, Derby, Stafford, and York county asylums, the Friends Retreat at York, Hanwell, and in London, Bethlem and St Luke's. On his return he presented the board with a long list of suggested improvements. Some were cosmetic and relatively inexpensive, like painting the corridors in warm colours, instead of whitewash, and ornamenting them with 'pictures, statuettes, and busts on plaster consoles—flowers, creeping plants, singing birds, aviaries and aquariums'; papering the 'sleeping rooms'; replacing the scanty and 'rude' furniture with more plentiful and comfortable couches and seats; and providing a billiard table and bagatelle board. But others were far more substantial and expensive: for instance, Robinson recommended that a new kitchen be built, that the corridor windows be enlarged, that a WC be installed in the lodge where the female servants slept, that the sewers be improved and that a large water tank be installed both to flush the drains and to provide water in case of fire. Robinson had also inspected a number of Irish asylums, including the Richmond, the Central Criminal Asylum at Dundrum and the district asylums at Cork and Maryborough (Port Laoise), but in them he told the board: 'I did not see anything worthy of bringing to your notice . . .'. Despite his poor view of the Irish district asylums, Robinson had nevertheless provided the governors with a lengthy and expensive list of improvements. His recommendations, in conjunction with those of the lord chancellor, meant that in 1861 the governors were faced with the tasks of replacing their hundred-year old kitchen and laundry and of overhauling the toilets and sewers.[34]

Substantial renovations were undertaken in the 1860s, as we shall see when we come to discuss the building, and large sums of money were expended: some £3,000 between 1859 and 1868. In this context one can probably more readily appreciate the governors' concern at Dr Robinson's absences and their decision in 1866 to replace him with a healthier and more effective master. The year 1866 in fact saw something of a financial crisis, which emerges clearly from the accounts.

INCOME AND EXPENDITURE, 1865-6 AND 1866-7

Income	1865-6	1866-7
	£	£
Estate Rental	2,775	2,900
Interest on Stock	554	554
Boarders' Fees	3,205	3,580
Casual Receipts	563	248
Total Income	7,097	7,282
Expenditure		
Living Expenses of Patients	4,468	5,187
Living Expenses of Staff	1,340	1,535
Salaries and Wages	1,076	1,040
Stationery	47	41
Law Expenses	43	56
Extraordinary (inc. repairs)	441	1,576
Total Expenditure	7,415	9,435
Deficit	318	2,153[35]

As well as having to pay for a new laundry and kitchen in 1865-6, in 1866 the governors paid £1,170 for the 'gentleman's garden', the two acres of land between the hospital and Steevens Lane which had been leased from the Trench family since 1816. The only way the governors could finance such enterprises was by the sale of stock: in addition to the £2,500 worth which was sold in 1860, another £5,000 worth was sold in 1866-7.[36]

In August 1866 the board resolved to make another approach to the lord chancellor over the fees. Francis Blackburne had replaced Brady as lord chancellor in July and perhaps the board thought Blackburne, who had advised it in 1836 regarding the Ponsonby lease, might be more sympathetic to its plight. A committee, consisting of Dean West, Dr Sadleir and Cotter Kyle, was set up to investigate the question of fees. The committee reported back to the board in November. It reviewed the whole issue by noting that, up until 1843, the hospital had been making a profit, amounting to £600 per annum in 1843, and that this profit had been invested. In November 1866 the hospital had some £18,000 invested in government stock. When the hundred guinea and sixty guinea boarders were removed in 1843 and the maximum fee set at forty guineas, the initial effect had been minimal, as the average annual cost per patient was £34.11.0. But, with price inflation, by 1866 the average cost per patient was around £47 and the hospital was losing about £360 every year. It was as a result of the committee's report that

£5,000 worth of stock was sold in 1866-7 in order to clear the hospital's overdraft and to provide funds for improvements and land purchase. More importantly, however, the committee strongly urged that the 1843 ceiling on fees be discontinued and that any profit arising from fees be used to 'facilitate the admission of poorer patients to the full extent of the accommodation afforded in the hospital'. This time the lord chancellor agreed to the governors' request and, after lengthy negotiations, a new schedule of fees was introduced early in 1868. Patients were divided into four classes: the first paid a minimum of £100 per year, the second a minimum of £75, the third a minimum of £50 and the fourth paid £25 and under.[37]

Yet, even with this fee increase, accounts prepared by J. B. Yeats in 1869 showed that the hospital was still losing substantial sums of money on the boarders.

PATIENT ACCOUNTS, 1868-9[38]

Average cost per patient for the year ending 31 March 1869, £52.18.0

Total Cost of 124 boarders	£5,590
Total fees paid by 124 boarders	£3,419
Total loss on boarders	£2,171
Total cost of 36 free patients	£1,923
Total loss on 160 patients	£4,094
Fee arrears owing	£ 490

The problem was that, of the 124 boarders resident in the hospital in 1869, only nineteen paid more than £52.18.0; 105 of them paid less than this sum and were thus being subsidised out of hospital funds. Yeats estimated that income from rents, interest on stock and other sources amounted to nearly £3,600, which left an annual deficit of around £500. The governors financed this deficit and also the costs of renovation by selling stock. Between 1860 and 1869 over £8,000 worth of stock was sold, reducing the hospital's capital from over £20,000 to around £12,000. Obviously, though, this strategy could not continue indefinitely. If, when all its capital had been consumed, the hospital was still operating at a deficit, it would rapidly become insolvent. The only way out of this impasse was for the governors to eliminate the deficit on operating costs by reducing expenses and increasing the revenue derived from patients. In the early 1870s this is exactly what they set about doing.

The governors had always devoted much attention to ensuring

fees were paid and any arrears that had accumulated were recovered. In the 1870s this became their main order of business. In
1873 they decided to remove any patient more than six months in
arrears.[39] But such action was not as easy as it sounded. In the past,
threats had frequently been made to return patients in arrears to
family or friends, or, failing that, to send them to the workhouse.
The hospital's solicitors, the Rookes, were kept busy communicating with the families of patients in arrears. But the board seems to
have been most reluctant to carry out either threat. Expulsion of a
patient was not a pleasant procedure and, moreover, it usually
meant the end of any hope of recovering the arrears. Also,
frequently patients had been in the hospital for decades and the
relatives and guarantors who had originally signed the bond for the
fees were dead or untraceable. Sometimes the hospital itself had lost
the bond. In these circumstances the governors did not have very
strong legal grounds for demanding payment. If families flatly
refused to accept elderly relatives, whom they may never have even
seen, the hospital authorities could hardly leave the patient on the
doorstep. In a few cases patients were sent to the Richmond Asylum
or to the workhouse. But such action did not reflect well upon the
reputation of the hospital, which was supposed after all to be a
charity hospital catering for those who could not pay the full cost of
their care.

The board thus faced major problems in its attempts to recover
arrears and enforce regular payment in future. In 1876 it sought the
legal opinion of the attorney-general, George A.C. May, on the
question of the removal of patients. May in his response warned the
governors that if they retained a patient for whom fees had not been
paid, then it would be difficult for them to recover the cost in the
courts. If a patient was not paid for in advance, as specified in the
bond, then the governors had 'their remedy within their own
hands. Their obvious course is to remove a patient who has been
received as a paying patient, but for whom payments are no longer
made.' May, rather naïvely, did not envisage great problems in
returning a patient to his or her relatives. 'I think [he said] the
proper course would be where the lunatic has relatives, to give them
notice that at a given time, the patient would be left with them, and
to send him to them accordingly, of course under proper care—the
responsibility of not receiving the patient would then rest with his
relatives.' If no relatives or friends could be traced, the attorney-
general recommended that the relieving officers of the poor law
union should be notified with a view to removing the patient to the
workhouse. May was in effect telling the governors to have patients
removed who could not pay immediately and thus avoid the

accumulation of arrears. It was a harsh formula and not really workable in practice. However, in his concluding sentence, May put his finger on the basic weakness in the governors' position as regards boarders: 'The governors no doubt are quite aware that the foundation is a charity, and that the whole income of their lands etc. should be applied to the maintenance of nonpaying patients.' Here was the problem: under their 1746 charter the governors had not been empowered to accept paying patients and thus it was, to say the least, arguable whether they had any legal right to enforce payment. Not till 1889 was the situation finally regularised with the granting of a supplemental charter allowing the board to do what it had in fact been doing for 130 years—that is, charge some of its patients fees.[40]

As well as seeking to maximise revenue from fees, the governors also tried to save money by economising. In 1870 a committee of three governors was appointed to inspect the building and recommend ways of curtailing expenses. What the committee recommended is not recorded, but steps seem to have been taken to reduce the cost of provisions supplied to the hospital. In 1871, for instance, the board decided for a trial period to feed some of its patients on tinned Australian lamb and mutton. The hospital's butcher's bill had always been substantial and this step was clearly intended to reduce it. But, the following month, the medical officers recommended against the purchase of further tins, for unspecified reasons, and the experiment came to nothing.[41] Greater savings, however, could be achieved by reducing the numbers of free patients and of boarders paying less than the annual per capita cost for patients. In 1870 and 1871 this is what the governors did.

PATIENTS ACCOUNTS, 1868-71[42]

	1 Apr. 1868-31 Mar. 1869	1 Apr. 1869-31 Mar. 1870	1 Apr. 1870-31 Mar. 1871
Average Annual Cost Per Patient	£52.18.0	£53.7.6	£52.5.9
Paying more than average	19	20	29
Paying less than average	105	94	82
Free	36	36	33
Total	160	150	144
Deficit on Patients	£4,094	£3,906	£3,415

By reducing the numbers of boarders paying less than the annual average cost per patient, and increasing those paying more, over a period of two years the hospital was able to reduce its deficit on patients by over £600. In 1870-71 income from the estate, interest and other sources was £3,449, which just covered the cost of maintaining 144 patients. Thus, by careful management and strict economising, the hospital could cover its operating costs. But, such management entailed a significant reduction in the number of patients and particularly in those patients able to contribute little or nothing towards their expenses. At the same time there was little margin for error. Any major demands upon the governors' resources, like the need for repairs to the building, or any decline in revenue, due to poor harvests and unrest on the estate, could easily tilt the balance, throwing the hospital into a serious financial crisis.

THE ESTATE

In the 1850s and 1860s St Patrick's was hard hit by a combination of rising prices, restrictions on its ability to raise boarders' fees and the need for costly renovations to its century-old building. In the early and mid 1860s substantial amounts of government stock, which formed the hospital's capital base, had to be sold to cover costs. Fee rises in the late 1860s eased the situation somewhat, but, only by reducing the number of patients and economising on services in the early 1870s, were the governors able to make ends meet. In 1879, however, Ireland was hit by a major economic recession, which led to widespread agrarian unrest. In the difficult economic and political circumstances of the 1880s St Patrick's fragile financial stability collapsed completely.

In discussing the impact of the Famine on the governors' Saggart estate, we saw that, despite a desire to consolidate small holdings, the percentage of holdings of less than five acres did not alter greatly: it fell from 50 per cent in 1840 to 43 per cent in 1870. If there was amalgamation in the thirty years after the Famine, it in fact occurred among the larger rather than the smaller tenants. By 1870 some 900 acres, or about half the estate, was held by only two tenants. One of these, holding around 650 acres, was J. J. Verschoyle, the governors' land agent since 1826. Verschoyle, who had land adjoining the estate, began acquiring land on the estate in the 1830s. The governors appear to have co-operated in Verschoyle's expansionist moves, or at least they placed no obstacles in his path, for it was obviously in their interests to have such a reliable and prosperous tenant.[43]

But questions arose, as they had in the Ponsonby case, as to whether or not Verschoyle's leases breached the provisions of the charter relating to land dealings. In June 1880 the board received a letter from W. J. Corbet, the newly-elected home rule MP for Co. Wicklow, asking a series of questions about Verschoyle's leases. Corbet said that he intended to raise the issue of Irish asylums in parliament and indeed he was uniquely qualified to do this, for, up until his resignation in 1875, he had been chief clerk in the lunacy inspectors' office in Dublin Castle. Corbet's letter was quickly followed by one from the Castle itself. T. H. Burke, the under-secretary, wrote reiterating Corbet's queries. If Corbet asked questions in parliament, then the Castle obviously wanted to ensure that the chief secretary was well prepared to answer them.

Corbet asked five questions, demonstrating considerable acquaintance with the hospital's affairs. Were there any leases on the estate exceeding thirty-one years, the limit set by the charter? Did any fee farm grants exist? Had leases been given to anyone 'concerned in the execution of the trust', or their relatives? If any such breaches existed, when did they occur? And finally, and most damningly, was not the agent married to a daughter of the late Dean Pakenham, a governor of the hospital? These were astute questions, for the charter had certainly been breached in the Ponsonby case, with a lease at an undervalued rent going to a trustee representing the family of one of the governors. In Verschoyle's case too, the evidence seemed persuasive, for he held leases exceeding the limits fixed by the charter and was both an employee of the board and a relative of one of the governors.

The governors directed their reply to Burke, not to Corbet, but, in the course of this, they regretted that,

> . . . a gentleman holding the position of a member of parliament should have thought fit on information so inaccurate, not to say unfounded, to have addressed to them a letter containing a grave imputation upon two gentlemen of the highest honour, the one [a] dignitary of the church, long deceased, always respected in life, the other fortunately alive and able to give the most distinct and emphatic contradiction to the charge.[44]

And indeed, J. J. Verschoyle submitted answers to Corbet's queries, which the governors passed on to Burke, while contenting themselves with merely rehearsing the provisions of the charter, and flatly denying that they had been breached. As authority for this denial they gave the word of their solicitor, Rooke, and Verschoyle's letter. In this Verschoyle explained that there had been four leases on the estate, covering some 750 acres, granted before the governors' purchase and renewable for ever. In 1831 and 1838 he and his father had bought three of them from their holders for £5,600 and in 1856 he had exercised his right, under the Leases Conversion Act, to convert these into fee farm grants. Thus, strictly speaking, the governors themselves had never made a lease for longer than thirty-one years; they had simply inherited the longer leases. Verschoyle further said that in 1849 he had married a grand-niece of Dean Pakenham. But the leases had been purchased in the 1830s, well before his marriage and even before Pakenham had joined the board. Verschoyle was obviously interpreting the restrictions in the charter on land holding as applying only to governors—'members of the corporation'—and their relatives, not to employees like himself. As we shall see, he probably had legal grounds for this opinion. Verschoyle further asserted that 'no lease has ever been granted since I became agent to or in trust for any person in any way concerned in the execution of the trust'. The key phrase here is 'since I became agent': Verschoyle had succeeded his father as agent in 1826; the undervalued Ponsonby lease had been made in 1825.[45]

Verschoyle and the governors were thus able to answer Corbet's questions and the matter seems to have gone no further, though Corbet, until he left parliament in 1892, remained an important critic of Irish asylums, both public and private. But the board and its agent appear disingenuous to say the least. They side-stepped the issue of the Ponsonby lease, which was a blatant breach of the charter. They did not mention the fact that in 1830 the lord chancellor himself had expressed grave reservations about the four perpetual leases at Saggart. He said he thought their existence was contrary to the charter and that the estate should be sold off. Nor did they make clear that Verschoyle had other holdings aside from the leases acquired in the 1830s. As late as 1862 he had bought the lease of a tenant called Hornidge, who held eighty-two acres for thirty-one years beginning in 1840. When Verschoyle sought their approval for this step, the governors were quite aware that a breach of the charter might well be involved and so they referred the matter to their barrister, Charles Shaw. Shaw's reply suggests that he regarded the case as a difficult one. He said he thought the charter would not be breached, but he suggested that Hornidge draw up a sub-demise or sub-lease. Shaw did not explain his opinion, but it appears he did not consider that the restrictions in the charter applied to the agent. Nevertheless, he thought it safest if Verschoyle was a sub-tenant of Hornidge's, rather than a direct tenant of the governors.[46]

The governors' response in 1880 leaves one with the clear impression that they were not happy to have their land dealings held up to public scrutiny and they particularly resented being questioned by a Nationalist MP. For the truth was that, in the

Ponsonby case at least, the charter had certainly been breached. In fairness to Verschoyle, however, it should be said that he does not appear to have exploited his position for personal gain quite as blatantly as Ponsonby did his. There is no suggestion, for instance, that he paid a lower rent for his holdings than the governors could have got from another tenant, and he invested large sums in improvements, like buildings and drainage. But his leasing of around one-third of the estate, while he was the governors' agent and married to a relative of one of the governors, certainly did look, at first sight, like the sort of corruption that Swift had feared. The provision in the charter distinctly stated that no lease should be made to, or in trust for, 'any person who shall at the time of the making thereof be a member of the said corporation, or any way related or allied, either by consanguinity or affinity to any person who shall be a member of the same'. The key phrase of course was 'at the time of the making thereof'. Both Ponsonby and Verschoyle argued that they were not governors nor related to governors 'at the time of the making' of the leases in question. Ponsonby was considered to have breached the charter because the lease, though granted before he joined the board, was renewed on more favour-able terms and then sold, while he was governor. Verschoyle's case was not as clear-cut as this: he was never a governor and his leases were acquired from other tenants rather than directly from the board. But he was certainly related to a governor, if distantly, from his marriage in 1849 till Dean Pakenham's death in 1864. He and the governors, backed by the legal opinion of the hospital's barrister, however, seem to have been convinced that the charter had not been breached. And in 1880 the hospital's inquisitors, both in the House of Commons and in Dublin Castle, accepted this interpretation.

The estate rental books, begun in 1840, cease in 1870 and thereafter it is more difficult to chart the history of the hospital's estate. It is clear, however, that Saggart was hard hit by the deteriorating economic conditions of the late 1870s. In 1875 the governors had decided to have the rents re-valued as, due to the increased prices for farm produce, they felt the rents were too low. Between 1840 and 1870 rents at Saggart had risen by about 30 per cent, which was modest considering the great increase in rural prosperity that had occurred in the decades after the Famine. Just three years later, in 1878, however, the picture was very different. J. J. Verschoyle was reporting that the bad weather in the summer and autumn of the previous year had been disastrous: the potato crop was 'a total failure', 'oats did not fill' and 'hay was so badly saved, it brought a low price'. In these difficult circumstances the seventy-three year old Verschoyle successfully sought the governors' permission to appoint his young son, William, as co-agent, to carry out those duties which required physical exertion. This assistance was certainly needed. In 1879 the weather and the crops were even worse and by October the governors were complaining bitterly at the small amount of rent money that they had received.[47]

In the absence of rent rolls, the growing crisis can perhaps best be traced by studying the balance in the hospital's account with the Bank of Ireland. This account had been started in the 1830s and the rents, collected every March and September, were paid into it. Out of it were paid the hospital's running costs. This was of course in keeping with Swift's wish that the estate should be used to support the hospital. The account had been overdrawn at times in the past, notably during the 1860s, when, as we have seen, price inflation, combined with a ceiling on boarders' fees, had led to serious financial difficulties. But never had the hospital's overdraft been as large or as prolonged as in the early 1880s.

BANK OF IRELAND ACCOUNT: MONTHLY BALANCES, 1879-85

Year	Number of months in debit	Maximum monthly debit Balance £	Maximum monthly credit Balance £
1879	2	182	1,043
1880	5	564	344
1881	11	944	7
1882	12	1,265	—
1883	12	2,381	—
1884	7	964	450
1885	1	19	1,347

As this table makes very clear, by 1882-3 the hospital was in a crisis, with a continuous and growing deficit. In January 1883 a sub-committee of the board was set up to enquire into the falling income and the rising expenditure. As a result of its investigations £2,000 worth of stock was sold in August and another £1,000 worth in January 1884 and the proceeds used to clear the overdraft. But drastic economies were also obviously needed: thus, one male ward was to be closed down completely, no work was to be undertaken without the governors' permission, unless it was urgent, and no new patients were to be admitted. We need also to remember that the years 1879-84 marked the tenure of Dr William Rice as master. In November 1883 he and the store clerk were reprimanded for causing the hospital 'serious losses'; in October 1884 Rice was dismissed; in February 1885 both the store clerk and the accountant were also dismissed; while in August 1885 the governors decided to write off unspecified 'discrepancies' in the 1883 and 1884 accounts for provisions. Although the exact nature of Rice's mismanagement is not clear, it presumably contributed to the serious deficits in the hospital's bank balance during the years 1881 to 1883.[48]

Problems on the estate, however, did not merely consist of bad weather, poor crops and rent arrears. The economic problems of the late 1870s had helped produce a major political crisis in the form of what is known as the land war of 1879 to 1882. Charles Townshend, in an important study of political violence in Ireland since 1848, provides a helpful summing up of the nature and impact of the land war when he writes:

> The series of events which are generally known as the land war form a pivotal point in the development of modern Ireland at several levels. Fundamentally, and incontrovertibly, the land war created a revolution in land tenure: it forced the British government first to invert the legal relationship between land-lord and tenant, and finally to deploy state funds and machinery to bring about a substantial transition to peasant proprietorship. More generally, and debatably, it focused the political awareness of the previously unpoliticized rural population, and created a new consciousness of collective strength.[49]

The land war inspired the British prime minister, William Gladstone, to introduce a major land act in 1881, which, in effect, established a system of dual ownership of land. Under the act a land commission was set up to facilitate sale to tenants by lending them the purchase money on generous terms. Subsequent acts passed in 1882, 1885, 1887, 1888, 1891 and 1896 increased the money available and extended the terms. The 1881 act also set up a land court to which tenants could take their rents for adjudication. Initially it was the land court rather than the commission to which the hospital's tenants resorted. The act became law in August 1881 and in October the court opened for business. In December a petition from the Ferns tenants seeking a rent reduction was laid before the board, while in February 1882 it received a request from the Saggart tenants for their rents to be fixed by the land court. In response to these petitions the governors set about employing their own valuers to assess the fairness of their rents. The lack of rent rolls, however, makes it impossible to chart in any detail changes in rents during the 1880s. But clearly, the tenants did exercise their new right to take their cases to the land court over the heads of the governors. In

May 1883, for instance, William Verschoyle reported that he had appealed against two decisions of the court: one lowering a rent by 11 per cent per annum; the other leaving a rent unchanged. The appeals were settled out of court, with the reduction being cut to a mere 2 per cent and the other rent being raised by 11 per cent. Despite their success in these cases, the governors were eventually forced into conceding substantial rent reductions. Further economic difficulties in the mid-1880s led to increased pressure from tenants for reductions. Under the so-called plan of campaign, organised by leading home rule MPs between 1886 and 1891, many tenants deliberately withheld their rent from landlords who had refused reductions. There is no evidence that this tactic was employed against the governors of St Patrick's. Nevertheless, in September 1888, they decided to grant rent abatements ranging from 15 per cent to 20 per cent, and up to 25 per cent in special cases, to their Saggart and Ferns tenants.

Such major reductions obviously had serious implications for the hospital's income. In November 1888 a sub-committee was appointed to consider retrenchment. Within ten days it had recommended that no more free patients be admitted, that the minimum fee be set at £65 per annum, that staff vacancies should not be filled till further notice and that no purchases of any kind should be made without the board's approval. As we shall see, while the hospital's tenants gained new rights in the 1880s, its patients suffered from the resulting economies.[50]

But increasingly militant tenants were only one aspect of the hospital's estate problems. The Ferns and Dublin estates posed peculiar difficulties of their own. Saggart and Dublin were managed by various agents employed by the governors: from 1799 these agents were all members of the Verschoyle family, in whom the governors clearly had considerable confidence. The Symes agency at Ferns was a rather different matter, however. Members of the family were hereditary trustees and agents for the estate under James Symes's 1766 will, which bequeathed the estate to the hospital. It was thus more difficult for the governors to direct and control their actions. By the early 1870s the governors were particularly unhappy at the level of arrears at Ferns. In all they held 1,304 Irish acres at an annual rental of £1,008 per annum. But, after paying various charges that were due on the estate, they only received a little under £600 a year from Ferns. Yet in 1870 the arrears amounted to £472. At Saggart between 1840 and 1870 the governors had been able to raise rents by 30 per cent and reduce arrears by 78 per cent, while on the Dublin estate, rents had gone up 25 per cent and arrears had fallen by 71 per cent. But at Ferns during this period both rent and arrears remained almost stationary. In June 1873 the board rejected Robert Symes's request that the arrears be struck off, complaining that 'the arrears appear to have been carried on from year to year during a period of improvement in the value of land and prices of livestock etc, without any adequate effort to procure the discharge of the amount'. And the governors particularly criticised Symes for not keeping them informed and for allowing sons to succeed to their fathers' farms without taking responsibility for outstanding arrears. Robert Symes replied in a placatory manner, saying that, in response to the governors' letter, he had visited the estate from his home in Wicklow and had talked to the tenants personally regarding their arrears. '. . . their condition is but struggling' he reported,

> as from the light nature of the soil of their farms, quite unsuited for grazing or keep[ing] of cattle. They have chiefly to depend for payment of their rents on their barley crop. However on the whole there is reason to expect that with a moderate pressure a fair decrease in the amount will be effected by the end of the year.

Time in fact proved this to be a decidedly over-optimistic prediction.[51]

Ferns, like Saggart, was hard hit by the poor harvests of the late 1870s. In October 1879 the governors received a petition from their Ferns tenants seeking a six-months rent rebate in order to help them cope with their present difficulties. Symes was asked for his opinion and, though his views were not recorded, on the basis of them, the board rejected the petition. In the midst of these difficulties, in January 1880, Robert Symes died. In his will he bequeathed the agency to his eldest son, Robert W. Symes, a barrister, who had in the past assisted his father in the management of the estate. Symes's succession was not, however, without challenge. William Verschoyle, already the co-agent at Saggart and Dublin, requested that the issue be referred to a full, charter board meeting for consideration, suggesting that he himself was interested in the position. The board went ahead, nevertheless, and in March 1880 appointed R. W. Symes as Ferns agent on a commission of one shilling in the pound, provided he lodge a security of £1,000.[52]

Managing an estate was no easy matter during the land war, and particularly an estate on which the tenants were already seriously in arrears with their rents. Symes quickly reported to the governors saying that he considered the tenants' difficulties genuine and therefore more time should be allowed them to pay. R. W. Symes appears to have been an efficient agent, but his agency was brief for, in September 1881, after only eighteen months in the position, he died. The governors received the news from his brother, Sandham Symes, who, as heir, offered himself as replacement. Discontent at the hereditary nature of the Symes agency had, however, become acute and the governors sought legal opinion. They were told that they could apply to the court of chancery to have new trustees of their own choosing appointed in place of members of the Symes family. As a result, in July 1882, five governors were appointed trustees by the court. In the meantime, the board had written to Sandham Symes informing him that they considered it 'inadvisable' to have the same party acting as both trustee and agent, and they offered him the agency at a shilling in the pound, with a £2,000 security deposit. Symes accepted. But by so doing, he became an employee of the board, like the Verschoyle agents, and thus subject to instant dismissal should his efforts not satisfy his employers.[53]

The governors' decision to exercise more direct control over their Ferns estate quickly proved to have been a very wise one, for, in 1886, they were forced to dismiss Sandham Symes and to hand the agency over to William Verschoyle. Symes had in fact proved to be something of a disaster. Within a year of his appointment arrears had reached an unprecedented £1,750; also, despite repeated requests from the board, he failed to provide detailed or up-to-date accounts; and, after dismissal, it was found that he had not even paid the taxes owing to the land commission. Exactly how much his incompetence cost the hospital is unclear, but substantial sums were certainly involved. Some £600 in tax arrears had to be paid to the land commission in 1887, while Symes himself, admitting to 'carelessness' in the management of the estate, repaid £400 to the board. In 1888, after much discontent among the tenants, William Verschoyle struck off most of the old arrears on their agreeing to pay one year's rent. He also allowed a general rent reduction of 15 per cent and began negotiating a series of fair rent agreements.[54]

The particular problems of the Ferns agency could not have come at a worse time for the governors. They were already having to cope with a general fall in rent income resulting from the economic depression and the land war and also with Dr Rice's mismanagement of the hospital's affairs. Losses at Ferns simply aggravated an already disastrous situation.

Bad weather, poor harvests, discontented tenants and incompetent agents produced serious problems from time to time for the governors on their Saggart and Ferns estates. On the Dublin estate, however, the problems were even more profound and indeed, after the 1820s, virtually continuous. As we have seen, the estate comprised two parts, both bequeathed to the hospital in the latter years of the eighteenth century. There were about seventy properties in the Liberties: in Francis Street and in the lanes behind it, notably Spitalfields, Marks Alley, Walls Lane and Garden Lane. The governors also held a small amount of land along the Grand Canal at Goldenbridge. This was let to four tenants and yielded a rent of only £74 in 1840. Flour and paper mills, a public house and part of the Richmond barracks occupied the site.

When St Patrick's acquired its holdings in the Liberties the area supported a major textile industry, employing numerous spinners, weavers and dyers in small workshops, producing silk, poplin, woollen and cotton cloth. But, by the beginning of the nineteenth century, this industry was in serious decline and, by the 1820s, this decline had become a collapse. Various factors contributed to the problems of the Irish textile industry, but certainly the most notable was the new technology being introduced in England. The mechanisation of spinning and weaving and their concentration in large factories produced cheaper and more plentiful cloth and in so doing destroyed the small-scale textile industry, not only in England but in Ireland as well. For, with the abolition of tariff barriers between the two countries in 1824, cheap English textiles flooded the Irish market. By the early 1840s, on the hospital's estate, only Marks Alley continued to support a small community of silk and poplin manufacturers; Walls and Garden Lanes were given over to provision dealers; Spitalfields to butter and bacon merchants; and Francis Street to a variety of small dealers and trades people.[55]

The governors thus found themselves owning property in one of the most depressed and impoverished parts of the city. Managing such property in order to produce the maximum income for the hospital taxed even the considerable abilities and experience of the Verschoyles. In 1837 J. J. Verschoyle wrote to the board complaining that 100 and 101 Francis Street and 8 and 9 Marks Alley were 'in a dilapidated state and for the most part inhabited by miserable roomkeepers'. Verschoyle was given permission to evict the inhabitants and to advertise for a tenant who would 'rebuild' the houses. Four months later he reported that there had only been one offer for the properties. The governors accepted this and allowed a year free of rent, on condition that the tenant undertake repairs. In 1839 the leases on 109 and 110 Francis Street expired, but one of the houses was partly collapsed and Verschoyle had to have the rest of it demolished. He pointed out to the board that the taxes on the buildings were high in consequence of their 'having formerly been an extensive sugar bakery though now fallen to ruin'. The board instructed him to try and get the taxes reduced 'in consideration of the deterioration of the value of property in the neighbourhood'. In 1840 the two properties were leased for £35 per annum with the first two years being rent free, if the tenant spent £300 on 'good and substantial improvement'. Clearly, it was not in the hospital's interest to allow its properties to fall into ruins and the board frequently gave incentives to tenants to repair decayed buildings. But it was fighting a losing battle in the face of progressive decline of the working-class inner city during the nineteenth century.[56]

DUBLIN RENTS AND ARREARS, 1840-70

	The Liberties		Goldenbridge	
	Rent £	Arrears £	Rent £	Arrears £
1840	372	206	74	266
1845	479	24	59	83
1860	499	27	57	61
1870	499	112	58	26[57]

The above table shows that rents on the governors' Liberties estate increased by about one-third between 1840 and 1870. But most of this increase actually occurred in the early 1840s. After 1845 rents stagnated, properties deteriorated further and it became even more difficult to find tenants willing or able to invest in them. In 1885 Andrew Nolan, who had an interest in 107-109 Francis Street, offered £40 per annum for 110 and 111, plus £100 worth of repairs, provided the first year of the lease was rent free. The governors at first rejected the offer. But Nolan wrote back that his offer was 'more than they are worth as they are in a very bad state of repair', and he went on to say that 'there would not be as much paid for the premises by any other persons who might take them inasmuch as the locality is of very little good to any trade'. He, however, raised his offer to £45 per annum, which the governors accepted.[58]

Notwithstanding Nolan's remarks, two trades do seem to have flourished in Francis Street and the neighbouring lanes after 1850: the sale of drink and the provision of tenement accommodation. Of Nolan's own holdings, 107 Francis Street was a tenement and 110 and 111 were a spirit grocer's business. A comparison of Dublin directories for the early 1840s and early 1890s shows that many of the houses which had accommodated small trades people and dealers in the earlier decade had by the latter one become tenement houses. In 1891 out of about 150 premises in Francis Street, forty-one were tenements and fourteen were spirit grocer shops; in Spitalfields there were ten tenements out of twenty-two premises and in Marks Alley fifteen tenements out of twenty premises. The transformation is particularly clear in Spitalfields, which was almost wholly owned by the hospital. It had developed in the eighteenth century as a centre of the woollen industry, taking its name from a similar area of London. In the early 1840s it already had four houses in tenements, but most of the street was taken up with the businesses of butter and bacon factors or merchants. At 1 Spital-fields was a large bacon market operated by James Lalor; at numbers 15 and 16 a silk weaver and dyer still conducted their businesses. By 1891, however, there were only three factors left, plus a dairy and a storeyard; one house was in ruins, and the rest were tenements. The story was much the same in Marks Alley. In 1843 it had four tenements, but four silk and poplin manufacturers still operated there. In 1885 the governors had leased what were described as 'the houses and ruins known as 4, 5 and 6 Marks Alley' to George Gill for ninety-nine years at only £15 per annum, providing that he spend £150 on repairs within eighteen months. Gill himself lived at number 4, but the other houses were tenements and, by 1891, except for four small dealers and a spirit warehouse, the whole street was in tenements.[59]

The spread of tenements brought with it an often bewildering network of sub-tenancies. The governors usually let two or three houses to one individual, often on a long lease. He or she might die or fall on hard times during the course of the lease, in which case it might be transferred to 'representatives' of the original lessee. This tenant, or tenants, might then sub-let all or part of the property, perhaps on a year-to-year basis. These yearly tenants might then in turn sub-let rooms on a weekly basis. There could thus be two or three layers of tenant—and even as many as five—between the actual owner of the property and the people occupying it. This was almost certainly the situation that existed as regards the hospital's tenements in Francis Street and its adjoining alleys. But such multiple tenancies almost inevitably meant that no one was pre-pared to take responsibility for the upkeep of the property: the actual residents were far too poor, while the various layers of tenants disputed the matter among themselves. The governors, as we have noted, generally demanded that specific sums for repairs be agreed before they would grant a lease. But whether such repairs were always actually undertaken is by no means clear. And, even if they were done at the outset of a lease, the chronic over-crowding in the area, the poverty of the inhabitants, the inadequate sanitation and the failure of the tenants to maintain the houses, meant that, in a relatively short time, dilapidation and decay reasserted themselves.[60]

The governors fully appreciated the desirability of maintaining prosperous businesses in the area and thus preventing their prop-erty from becoming mere slum accommodation. In 1852, for in-stance, they leased two houses in Francis Street to Elizabeth Lalor, who had taken over the Spitalfields bacon market on the death of her husband, James. J. J. Verschoyle strongly supported this decision arguing that, 'it is most desirable to retain as much of the business as possible in that locality'. All was to no avail, however. By 1891 even Lalor's market at 1 Spitalfields had been converted into tenements. Like it or not, the governors of St Patrick's Hospital had become slum landlords.[61]

The three parts of the hospital's estate, Saggart, Ferns and Dublin, all underwent serious difficulties after 1850. Revenue from Saggart and Ferns declined due to rent abatements forced on the governors in the wake of the 1881 land act. At the same time Ferns suffered additional losses caused by the incompetence of its agent. But, on the Dublin estate, particularly that in the Liberties, the problems were rather different: indeed, they were almost the reverse of those posed by the rural estate. In Dublin the governors did not have to deal with militant tenants or with unreliable agents; they had to grapple instead with the slow but inexorable impoverishment of the central city area. While Saggart and Ferns became more prosperous in the 1850s and 1860s and their tenants more demanding, especially after 1879, the Dublin properties and their inhabitants sank into squalor and decay. The governors had a much freer hand in Dublin and showed a greater readiness to evict tenants in arrears. Dublin tenants lacked the organisation and solidarity that their rural counterparts demonstrated when they took reprisals against anyone leasing a farm from which the previous tenant had been evicted. This tactic certainly made the governors reluctant to evict and especially if there was a possibility of persuading the tenant, mainly by financial inducements, to leave voluntarily. But the more ready resort to evictions in Dublin did not solve the estate's problems. By the 1890s, despite the governors' efforts to encourage businesses and to keep their properties in good repair, at least a third of the Dublin estate was made up of slum tenements.

Swift had envisaged the estate as providing the hospital with a substantial and secure income, but he had not—indeed he could not have—foreseen the problems of nineteenth-century Irish landlordism. By the 1880s the estate had become more a liability than an asset. If the hospital was ever to overcome its chronic financial difficulties, it had to find a more reliable source of income than rents from an Irish estate.

THE BUILDING

In January 1899 Dr Richard Leeper was appointed medical superintendent of the hospital and in the following March he took up his duties. On 1 April Leeper presented the governors with a lengthy report, the first of a series of monthly reports, outlining the state in which he had found the institution upon his arrival. The effect that the hospital's long financial crisis had had on the building and grounds is best summed up in Leeper's own graphic words:

> The grounds and garden appear to have been much neglected, the trees unpruned . . . The airing courts . . . unused for years, had become littered with refuse and rubbish, broken glass, old iron, etc. etc. These spaces are tunnelled by rat holes as is a great portion of the garden. The wards and corridors are infested by these animals in great numbers and the rats gain access to the building from the grounds and airing courts. At the end of the gentlemen's garden I find there exists an old privy or closet which is constructed over a cesspool. This has been in constant use and has not been cleaned out I understand for the past five years . . . Similar structures exist on the female side of the house but happily have not been used for years. I would suggest all these be pulled down . . . The disused piggeries at the rear of [the] stable I also wish treated in a similar manner. And the heaps of loose stones and masonry which litter the gentlemen's garden [should] be similarly disposed of. I found two tubs sunk into the ground near to the kitchen in which the offal from the house was thrown. These tubs were surrounded by rats and in a most filthy and unsanitary state . . . I find your board have had fire plugs or taps placed in the corridors, but no hose or pipes are provided which renders such precautions useless in case of fire . . . The outside woodwork of windows etc is rotting for want of paint, the plaster is falling off from walls, especially round the door casings, all of which defects tend to give the institution a dismal and neglected appearance . . . The furniture is in some wards in a very bad state. I have had to remove a great many articles as I considered it highly dangerous to leave the loose legs of sofas and chairs littered about as such things are possible lethal weapons in the hands of the insane. The floors of some of the bedrooms of such patients as are of dirty habits need repainting. As, if this is not done at once, their nightly soaking of urine will rot the flooring which will be expensive to replace. I had to employ a locksmith for some days recently as many of the locks were out of order and urgently needed repairs.[62]

Much of this dilapidation and decay described by Leeper seems to have developed during the 1870s and 1880s. Poor sewerage and drainage had, however, long been a problem and doubtless contributed to the frequent outbreaks of disease that occurred at this time. In November 1852 Dr Croker, the visiting physician, had complained to the board about the smell of the WCs and about the dampness of the flagged floors in the basement wards. As a result, in 1853 the sewers were cleaned out and flagstones were replaced by wooden floor boards. But problems recurred. The medical officers urged further sanitary improvements in 1861 and major work was subsequently undertaken. Yet in April 1885 Dr Thornley Stoker, the visiting surgeon, told the board that the sewerage system was 'most faulty'. Attempts were again made to rectify the problems, but in August Stoker was complaining that, unless an improvement occurred, he feared epidemics of disease in the hot weather. Leeper's 1899 report, however, clearly demonstrates that the problems were not solved, or at least their solution was only temporary. In April 1899, in response to the report, the board set up a sub-committee which ordered a thorough examination of all the hospital's drains. They were found to be 'in a very defective state'. The main drain emptying into the Camac River was 'almost completely closed and was cleared with great difficulty, being full of bricks, stones and quantities of sand, owing to the river Camac being a tidal river and silting up of the river causes rubbish to be washed into drain pipes'. This presumably was why the hospital's drainage system proved so inadequate. But it was not the only problem. The drains themselves were 'laid in a most defective way and the difficulty in clearing the drain was owing to the falling and sinking down of pipes so that several could not run off into the Camac River'. Pipes were laid under the foundations of the building and when these became blocked and burst, their contents seeped into the floors and walls of the basement, creating not only a major damp problem, but a serious health risk as well. Old pipes under the building, left unused after previous attempts at repair, simply provided avenues for rats to enter the hospital. When Leeper had them blocked up the numbers of rats greatly diminished.[63]

The serious deterioration in the state of the building and grounds was probably partly the result of the board's decision to dispense with the services of an architect and this decision was undoubtedly prompted by financial considerations. Sandham Symes, a relative of the board's Ferns agent and architect to the Bank of Ireland, served as architectural adviser to the hospital from 1857 till his retirement in 1882 due to ill health. In the 1850s and 1860s Symes was particularly active, reporting regularly to the board and undertaking a good deal of work. In the 1860s the hundred-year old kitchen and laundry were replaced with new buildings and new equipment. On Symes's and Mrs Gill's recommendations, boilers were put in in place of the open fires which had previously been used for cooking purposes. Bathrooms were also installed: male and female ones being built on each of the three floors. The building, both inside and out, was also painted on several occasion. In 1860 the board decided for the first time to paint the interior in colours, rather than just to whitewash it. The exterior was painted in 1862 and again in 1878 and the wards in 1886. But, no further painting seems to have occurred before Leeper's appointment. So, the exterior windows which he complained were rotting for want of paint, had not in fact been painted for twenty years. Other major improvements also occurred in the 1850s and 1860s. In 1857, for instance, the board employed the Alliance Gas Company to begin the installation of gas lighting in the hospital, while in 1868 the hospital was connected to the new Vartry water supply. Previously water had come from the nearby city basin.[64]

After about 1870, however, work on the building slackened. When Symes retired the board decided not to replace him, though periodically it called on another architect, Rawson Carroll, for his advice. But, while maintenance was neglected, between 1870 and 1899 several important innovations were made. At the urging of Dr Stoker a telephone was installed in 1885, costing £14 for installation and £2 a year for rent. This leap into modernity was not without its problems, however. In 1898 the board instructed the secretary 'to write to the telephone company pointing out how imperfect the instrument in St Patrick's Hospital is'. We have seen that as early as the 1820s and 1830s the governors experimented with various schemes for centrally heating the hospital. None of these proved adequate. But in 1888, under Carroll's supervision, a heating and hot water system was finally installed at the cost of nearly £1,000. The system certainly had teething troubles, but in the long run it proved far more successful than the earlier experiments. The following year, 1889, the governors began the erection of a new gate lodge on the corner of Steevens and Bow Lanes. This entrance replaced the old entrance in front of the main building and it was to remain the major means of entry to the hospital site for nearly a hundred years. But the most important initiative undertaken by the governors during these years was the purchase of an auxiliary hospital outside Dublin.[65]

Even before Leeper's appointment in 1899, the board had been under considerable pressure to make major improvements in the hospital. This pressure, applied from 1890 onwards, came from the inspectors of lunacy. In 1890 Drs G. P. O'Farrell and E. M. Courtenay had been appointed to replace Drs Nugent and Hatchell, who had served as inspectors for forty-three and thirty-three years respectively. In the 1870s and 1880s there was widespread criticism of the inspectors for their slowness and inefficiency. The new, younger inspectors proved to be far more rigorous in fulfilling their duties, as had been intended, and also far more critical of the whole asylum system, St Patrick's Hospital included.[66]

O'Farrell and Courtenay first visited the hospital in July 1890 and, we have seen, they quickly concluded that the governors would carry out Swift's intentions more faithfully 'by disposing of the present institution and seeking a more suitable locality at a little distance from the city, and there founding another St Patrick's Hospital'. They criticised the existing hospital for its 'massive walls, dark corridors, small windows' and for being surrounded by 'lofty buildings, which shut out light and air'. Later reports complained that the furniture was insufficient and shabby, that many of the floors were worn out, that the walls required painting and that ventilation, particularly in the patients' small rooms, was poor. The continuing use of straw bedding and physical restraint were deplored as being more appropriate to the previous century. St Patrick's had 'all the attributes of a prison and none of those of an asylum' and the inspectors concluded that 'it would be impossible for any human power to convert it into a modern hospital for the insane'. In this judgment they obviously did not reckon on the determination of Dr Leeper.[67]

The governors had no wish to close St Patrick's and, in response to the inspectors' criticisms, they sent Dr Moloney to study asylums in Scotland, with a view to suggesting improvements. When Dr Courtenay inspected the hospital again in 1891 he reiterated many of his earlier criticisms. But he did note that the old gate lodge and other dilapidated buildings had been removed from the front of the hospital on Bow Lane and that the new gate was now in operation. He particularly, however, took up one suggestion made by Moloney: that the hospital should obtain a country residence to serve as a convalescent home for patients well on the way to recovery. In the early 1880s patients were sent from St Patrick's to stay in Bray during the summer. The house, 2 Westview Terrace, which Mrs Gill subsequently retired to, was used for this purpose, and there may well have been others similarly employed. But there seems to have been no thought at this time of buying a permanent country or seaside residence.[68]

The governors did not respond immediately to Moloney's and the inspectors' suggestion. The matter became more pressing, however, when the lord chancellor, possibly prompted by the inspectors, threatened to remove chancery patients from St Patrick's unless steps were taken to acquire a convalescent hospital. In 1895 a number of special meetings of the board were held to consider the steps necessary to effect a purchase. The governors first consulted H. P. Jellett, one of the sergeants-at-law and a relative of the then dean of St Patrick's Cathedral, who advised them that a supplement to the charter would be necessary to empower them to purchase another hospital. They also decided to sell £10,000 worth of shares to provide the purchase money and to advertise in the Dublin newspapers for a house on not less than twenty acres of land in Co. Dublin, convenient to public transport. A sub-committee was set up to consider offers. In October the sub-committee reported in favour of Roebuck Castle, Dundrum, then the home of Edward Westby, who owned a large estate in Co. Clare, now part of University College, Dublin. The board decided that £10,000 was a reasonable price for the house. This offer was not successful, however, and in January 1896 the sub-committee recommended Gortmore House (Gort Muire) at Ballinteer, then the home of J. G. Nutting, a businessman and company director; now a conference centre. First £6,000 and then £6,500 was offered for Gortmore, but again, for reasons that are not altogether clear, the sale did not proceed. Perhaps discouraged by these failures, the governors seem to have taken no further action during 1896 and 1897, despite repeated urging by the lunacy inspectors and by the registrar of lunacy, representing the lord chancellor. Finally in April 1898 the board decided to offer not more than £9,000 for St Edmundsbury at Lucan. The following month the governors bought the house for £8,500 from a wealthy American called Nevin.[69]

Roebuck Castle and Gortmore House were both only a couple of miles south of the city centre, in a largely middle-class area of Dublin from which St Patrick's drew many patients. St Edmunds-bury, on the other hand, was seven miles to the west along the river. It was a mile from the nearest railway station, though the Lucan steam tram passed the entrance gates. There were, however, several factors that may have attracted the governors to Lucan and to St Edmundsbury in particular. Lucan in the eighteenth century had been a spa town, with a mineral spring much patronised by Dublin society. In the 1860s and 1870s there had been a small private asylum in Lucan and in the 1880s the spa hotel was revived. So the area had long catered for the physical and mental ailments of the affluent. St Edmundsbury had attached to it some two hundred acres of land, including a farm, which the governors immediately set about operating by employing a steward and purchasing chickens, horses, cattle, sheep, carts, a plough and other farming equipment. A dairy was soon started by the steward's wife and a vegetable garden laid out. In September 1898 the governors were able to sell one hundred barrels of oats, while keeping seventy-five for their own use. Clearly they hoped that, as well as supplying the two hospitals, and thus reducing their very high food bills, the farm would also be profitable commercially. The house itself was large and pleasantly situated, overlooking the river. But much work needed to be done on it, for it lacked both electricity and running water. For nine months, from June 1898 till the first patients were admitted in March 1899, a sub-committee of the board supervised the purchase of furniture, bedding, crockery and cutlery, the employment of staff, the fitting up of a kitchen and major drainage and plumbing work.[70]

There was, however, one fact about St Edmundsbury that must have struck the governors of Swift's hospital forcefully. The house had been built in the late eighteenth century by Edmund Sexton Pery, Foster's predecessor as speaker of the Irish House of Commons. Pery, whose family came from Limerick and who had been largely responsible for the development of the new town of Limerick, resigned the speakership in 1785 and was raised to the peerage as Viscount Pery. But the area was one that Swift would have been very familiar with, for he was a friend of the Vesey family, who were the main landlords and who had developed the spa. In fact he had helped Agmondisham Vesey, a former Irish accountant-general, with the affairs of the estate, though subsequently they fell out over politics.[71] Lucan, given its associations both with Swift and with convalescence after illness, must thus have seemed a most appropriate location for St Patrick's auxiliary hospital.

But St Edmundsbury was only capable initially of accommodating about fifteen female patients and thus, the overwhelming majority of patients remained in the old hospital on Bow and Steevens Lanes. In considering the history of the hospital at this time, the obvious question which springs to mind is: what impact did the succession of problems that St Patrick's faced from the 1850s to the 1880s have upon its patients and particularly upon the quality of their care and treatment?

THE PATIENTS

Between 1850 and 1900 we are fortunate in having a number of accounts of St Patrick's Hospital provided by outside observers, notably the reports of the lunacy inspectors from 1843 onwards and the investigations of parliamentary committees, in particular that of 1857. Dr Leeper's detailed description of the premises on his appointment as medical superintendent in 1899 is also extremely enlightening, as are some of the comments made by H. C. Burdett in his 1891 survey of asylums throughout the world. The picture that emerges from these various sources is a fairly consistent one, but it is by no means flattering. If the living conditions of patients had improved in the 1820s and 1830s, after 1850 conditions deteriorated considerably. A number of factors contributed to this situation, the most obvious being financial. Rising prices in the 1850s and 1860s, in conjunction with restrictions on fee increases, followed in the 1880s by economic recession, unrest among tenants and falls in rent income, all combined to create a severe financial squeeze. Mismanagement by hospital officers and land agents only exacerbated the situation. At the same time, government and parliamentary critics were demanding that the governors spend large sums of money on repairs, renovations and additions to the building, but no public money was forthcoming to help pay for such expensive undertakings. The critics pointed to the governors' investments and argued that this money should be used to upgrade the hospital. The governors themselves were obviously reluctant to draw too heavily upon their precious captial. Perhaps, given the sorry state into which St Patrick's had fallen, they were over-cautious in this regard. Nevertheless, between 1860 and 1900, they did sell some £20,000 worth of stock and expend the resulting funds on renovations, extensions and additions to both the building and the site.

But financial stringency was only one aspect of the problem faced by the governors after 1850. The Irish public asylums too were experiencing great difficulties, particularly in the last quarter of the century. They were overcrowded and short of funds, but equally problematical was the accumulation in them of elderly, incurable patients and the related failure of either moral or physical treatments to effect cures, except in a small minority of cases. The period from the 1850s to the 1890s was not a happy time for psychiatric medicine. Much of the optimism of the earlier part of the century had dissipated and, under the influence of Darwinian theories, a far more pessimistic view, which particularly stressed the hereditary nature of much mental illness, emerged. David Rothman has written that between the 1850s and 1870s: 'In a majority of mental hospitals the careful balance of moral treatment gave way to custodial care . . .' Rothman is here describing developments in the United States, but his assessment applies equally to Ireland. By the 1870s there were twenty-two government asylums spread across the country with beds for over 7,500 patients. Yet they were full to overflowing with people for whom the medicine of the time could do little or nothing. As government became increasingly reluctant to spend vast sums on an asylum system which had not lived up to expectations, so the institutions fell into decay and the prospects of cure receded even further. The problems of St Patrick's were thus far from unique and can only be properly understood against this background of a general decline in both mental hospitals and psychiatric medicine during the second half of the nineteenth century.[72]

As expenses increased in the 1850s, the governors responded by tightening-up on the admission of patients. In 1853 they set a limit of seventy-five on the number of free patients who would be accommodated in future. Ten years later, in 1863, however, the situation had deteriorated to such an extent that they decided to stop accepting free patients altogether, though this seems to have been only a temporary expedient. In the early 1850s the master was forbidden to admit patients, except on days of board meetings and only with the approval of the governors or the visiting medical officers. The governors also attempted to supervise the medical officers somewhat more closely than in previous years. They began, for instance, interviewing patients themselves in order to decide who was fit to be discharged and they demanded more regular and detailed reports on the medical condition of patients. As a result of this demand, from 1857 into the 1880s brief reports from the visiting physician and surgeon were tabled at most board meetings. These dealt largely with the physical, rather than the mental, health of patients, but as such they do afford us a fascinating insight into the extent and nature of illness in the hospital during the 1860s and 1870s.[73]

The death rate among patients at the time was quite high, though no higher than that in the public and other private asylums. It reached 10 per cent of the resident hospital population in 1884, but during the 1870s it had hovered around 7 per cent. These rates, however, give little idea of the extraordinary extent of both endemic and epidemic disease in the hospital. In 1862, for instance, there were serious outbreaks of influenza, gastric fever, typhus, diarrhoea and ophthalmia; in 1863 four patients died from influenza; influenza struck again in 1864, along with cholera, dysentery and diarrhoea; in 1865 six keepers were ill with respiratory and gastric disorders and there was a death from dysentery; in 1866 there was a major cholera epidemic in Dublin which claimed over one thousand lives, but, although rooms were set aside in the hospital to accommodate cases, none were reported; in 1867 pneumonia and tuberculosis were the main scourges; followed in 1868 by a serious outbreak of diarrhoea, with at least twelve cases. And so the pattern continued into the 1870s: in 1870 typhoid fever and diphtheria claimed four lives; while in 1872, 1875, 1878–9 and 1881 there were outbreaks of cholera, resulting in a number of deaths; and in 1874 and 1878 there were even some cases of anthrax and scurvy. Deaths from pneumonia and tuberculosis increased in the late 1870s and the 1880s and in 1887 the medical superintendent asked the board to provide separate accommodation for TB patients as a means of trying to prevent the disease's spread. The young children of the staff were especially at risk in this unhealthy environment: we have already noted the numerous illnesses suffered by the store clerk's family, while in 1880 one of Dr Rice's children nearly died from scarlatina.[74]

Diseases like cholera, typhoid, dysentery and gastro-enteritis are water-borne and thus we probably need go no further than the hospital's extremely inadequate sewerage and drainage systems to find the causes of them. Certainly the visiting medical officers repeatedly complained about the state of the sewers and the WCs. Until Pasteur and Koch demonstrated in the late 1870s and early 1880s that infectious diseases were spread by micro-organisms, it was widely believed that vapours or miasmas from contaminated sources were responsible. In 1872, for instance, the medical officers were blaming 'sewer odours' for outbreaks of smallpox and erysipelas. Another, almost certain source of infection was the Camac River, which ran along the western edge of the hospital grounds before joining the Liffey near Kingsbridge (Heuston) Station. The hospital's sewage emptied into it—that is when the pipes were not blocked, which they often seem to have been—but so did that of most of Kilmainham. The Camac was in fact little more than a sewer, contributing not only to the serious pollution of the Liffey, but to the spread of infectious diseases among the population living along its banks. Aside from water-borne disease, St Patrick's also suffered periodically from outbreaks of typhus. This was spread by body lice and was usually associated with overcrowded and dirty living conditions. It was also, however, the disease *par excellence* of such institutions as prisons, workhouses and pauper hospitals, known popularly as 'gaol fever'. But it was the endemic respiratory diseases, like influenza, bronchitis, pneumonia and pulmonary tuberculosis, that took the most steady toll of lives in St Patrick's. Young people in good health could generally withstand such illnesses, but from the 1850s onwards the hospital's population was an increasingly elderly and ill one. In 1884, for instance, a quarter of the patients were over sixty and, of the 10 per cent who died in that year, all came from this age group. In 1879 the medical officers had complained that too many chronically ill and even dying patients were being admitted: twenty-six patients were admitted in 1879, fourteen of whom eventually died in hospital but, of these, five died within a year of their admission, most from pneumonia or tuberculosis.[75]

In assessing the state of health of the patients in St Patrick's, we need, however, to bear in mind the utterly appalling public health record of the city of Dublin. In 1899, after which the situation did begin slowly to improve, the city had a higher mortality rate than any other major city in Britain, Europe or the United States; one had to venture to Calcutta to find a city that was worse—and even then it was only slightly worse. In the 1860s and 1880s Dublin experienced major epidemics of cholera, smallpox, typhus, measles and scarlatina, while typhoid and TB were endemic. The reasons for this sorry situation do not really concern us here, but, in considering the poor health record of St Patrick's between 1860 and 1890, we need to keep in mind that the hospital was situated close to some of the most impoverished and unhealthy areas of the city.[76]

Critics of St Patrick's in fact frequently pointed to its location as one of its main problems. By the late nineteenth century the hospital was situated on a small plot of ground, surrounded by high walls, in a densely populated, commercialised section of the city. Aside from the nearby Guinness Brewery, which was inexorably swallowing up most of the open land between James Street and Steevens Lane, tanneries, dairies, cattle dealers and spirit grocer shops all flourished along Bow Lane and the western end of James Street. Aside from the unpleasant smells produced by some of these businesses, cattle yards and dairies constituted serious health hazards; the latter particularly were linked to the spread of typhoid and TB through infected milk. Aside from any threat to the patients' physical health, the hospital's location was also considered most harmful for their mental health. Isolated, rural environments, with plenty of outdoor activity, were thought at the time to be highly therapeutic with regard to diseases of the mind. Statistics presented to parliament in 1878 showed that, on average, Irish public asylums had forty-one acres of land attached to them, while private ones had twenty-four acres. With only about six acres at its Dublin site, St Patrick's was grossly inadequate in this respect. We have seen that in 1890 the lunacy inspectors had recommended the closure of the hospital and its possible transfer to a rural site. This, however, was not a new proposal. In 1870 the previous inspectors had made exactly the same recommendation. Drs O'Farrell and Courtenay particularly were convinced that, with its ancient, out-of-date building and its location on a cramped site in a busy part of the city, St Patrick's Hospital could never provide suitable accommodation or treatment for the insane.[77]

NUMBER OF PATIENTS RESIDENT AT YEAR'S END, 1861-1903

Year	Total	Male %	Female %
1861	141	52	48
1868	140	51	49
1875	113	48	52
1877	102	46	54
1883	101	39	61
1891	92	38	62
1903	118	28	72[78]

The above table, in conjunction with the tables reproduced in Appendix 4, tells us a good deal about the sort of people who were admitted to St Patrick's Hospital in the latter years of the nineteenth century. Several important trends are immediately apparent. The number of patients in the hospital fell by about one-third between 1861 and 1891, the steepest declines occurring in the early 1870s and mid 1880s, when the governors were trying to reduce costs. But, at the same time, the number of female patients increased from just under one-half to nearly two-thirds. There were probably several reasons for this jump in female patients, but the closure of one of the male wards in 1884 and the opening of St Edmundsbury for women in 1899, were undoubtedly important factors. Over 90 per cent of patients were classed as incurable, a significantly higher percentage than in either the public or the other private asylums, where the figures were 77 per cent in 1878 and 79 per cent in 1884 respectively. The patients in St Patrick's were increasingly well-educated, but by 1884 nearly two-thirds had no occupation; a figure that reached 90 per cent in the case of female patients. Some 87 per cent of patients were unmarried, but women were much more likely to be single or widowed than men. The hospital's population was also an ageing one: while only 7 per cent were over sixty in 1869, by 1884 this figure had reached 24 per cent. And, again, women tended to be older than men: in 1884 more than twice as many women as men were over sixty. The ageing of the hospital population also almost certainly contributed to the increasing death rate: thus in 1884, of the 10 per cent of patients who died, all were over sixty. Given the higher number of women in this age group, it followed that the death rate among women patients was significantly higher than among men. Women tended, as they had in the 1840s, to stay longer in the hospital as men were more likely to be taken by their relatives, even if they had not improved or were considered incurable.[79]

Whilst the typical patient admitted in the 1840s had been a male, Protestant, in his twenties or thirties, resident in Dublin city, single or possibly married, dependent upon his family for support or perhaps a professional man, a merchant or a student; the typical patient admitted in the 1870s and 1880s was a female, Protestant, over fifty years of age, resident in the Dublin suburbs, single, possibly committed by a distant relative and almost certainly without employment. This is a change worth investigation. Again, as in the 1840s, we can gain a clearer insight into the experiences of the patients of the last quarter of the century by using the surviving admission forms to study specific cases.

A few examples of women admitted to St Patrick's in the late 1870s and early 1880s, who fit the typical pattern fairly well, may help enliven the profile outlined above. Cherry B. was a sixty year old, single Protestant from Booterstown, committed in December 1875 by her brother, a London physician. She was admitted as a first-class boarder at £65 per annum, which sum equalled her annual income derived from rents in Co. Tipperary. She had been ill for some twenty years and had spent periods in Bellevue and Farnham House, private asylums in Finglas. Her illness was ascribed to the death of her mother and its chief characteristic was hallucinations: she particularly imagined that voices were floating in the air around her. Cherry B. spent ten years in St Patrick's dying there in October 1885 from old age and the effects of diarrhoea. Maria H. was a forty-four year old, single Protestant from Rathgar, committed in May 1880 by her mother. She was admitted as a second-class boarder at £60 per annum. She had no occupation and her income was only £18 per annum, derived from a handful of shares in railway and steam packet companies. She was suicidal and her condition was ascribed to the menopause, though nine years earlier she had spent a period in a private asylum in Rathfarnham. She was discharged from St Patrick's in 1885 as recovered. Eliza C. was a forty year old, single Protestant from Kingstown (Dun Laoghaire), committed in May 1880 by a 'relative by marriage', presumably a brother-in-law, who was a teller with the Bank of Ireland. She was admitted as a second-class boarder at £65 per annum. She had no occupation, but derived £70 per annum from land. She was certified by Dr John Banks as suffering from mania due to 'religious excitement' and had previously spent some time in Farnham House. She is recorded as having been discharged unrelieved in 1883, but she must have been subsequently re-admitted, for she died in St Patrick's in 1887 from tuberculosis.[80]

These cases could easily be multiplied tenfold from the surviving admission forms. Like them, many of the women admitted to St

Patrick's in the 1870s and 1880s came from the middle-class town-ships to the south of Dublin city. Many also had independent incomes derived from rents or from shares in railway companies or banks. But often these incomes were small and would not have been easy to live on. A number of these women were committed by sisters, several by brothers-in-law and some by nieces, nephews or cousins. Presumably many lived with married or unmarried sisters and some may truly have been 'maiden aunts'. Although the women admitted at this time tended, on the whole, to be older than those admitted in the 1840s, like them, they appear often to have been dependent on the goodwill of relatives for their homes. And, as we saw in the 1840s, this goodwill may sometimes have run out. As the three examples above demonstrate, a number of these women had been ill continuously or intermittently for many years and many had previously been admitted to private asylums. Sometimes they were transferred directly to St Patrick's from Farnham, Highfield, Lisle or Esker Houses. In such cases their illnesses were usually firmly established and their relatives were seeking cheaper accommodation. But, of course, this simply added to the numbers of ageing, incurable patients with which St Patrick's was already overburdened.

When we turn to the male patients admitted at this time, the picture that emerges is rather less coherent. In general terms they differed from female patients in being younger, more likely to be married and to work, and less likely to spend long periods in the hospital or to die there. In the 1870s and 1880s around 20 per cent of men admitted were professional men, approximately another 14 per cent were army or naval officers; another 10 per cent were farmers; while clerks, students, merchants and traders made up most of the remainder of those in employment. Significant numbers of male patients were admitted with illnesses ascribed to ovework or ill health. Drunkenness, however, was a much less prominent factor than it had been in the 1840s.

The growth of ill health as a factor causing male admissions leads us on to a consideration of the vexed question of venereal disease. For, if we turn from the admission forms to the hospital's register, we find that of the 375 patients admitted between 1880 and 1899, 33 per cent subsequently died in the hospital and of these deaths 18 per cent were recorded as caused by 'general paralysis'. Of the 375 admissions, in 6 per cent of cases the cause of illness was also given as general paralysis. General paralysis of the insane, or *dementia paralytica*, was the term used to describe the last, or tertiary, stages of syphilis, when, some ten to twenty years after the initial infection, serious degeneration of the nerve fibres in the frontal lobes of the brain occurred. This degeneration often produced bizarre, violent and demented behaviour and sufferers were thus usually confined in mental hospitals. Death generally resulted after three to five years, though there could be marked remissions lasting for months. Not till 1905-6, however, was the connection between syphilis and general paralysis fully established and a blood test developed which allowed a reliable diagnosis of syphilis. Various drugs and other substances were used to treat syphilis, the most notorious being mercury, but only in 1910 was a specific remedy discovered.[81]

The extent of VD in nineteenth-century Ireland is a controversial issue. Contemporary, and also many modern, authorities consider that it was not a serious problem; certainly not in rural areas and even in Dublin the incidence was far less than in comparable British cities. As for general paralysis, Finnane notes that in 1905 26 per cent of deaths in English and Welsh asylums were ascribed to it, compared with only 5 per cent in Irish public asylums. But the evidence from St Patrick's patients' records tends to contradict this view. As mentioned, in the 1880s and 1890s 18 per cent of deaths in St Patrick's were listed as due to general paralysis. In the five years from 1852 to 1856 the figure had been 11 per cent; only old age (30 per cent) and tuberculosis (19 per cent) claimed more patients. A case-book, listing male patients in the hospital between 1899 and 1902, records seventy-four cases, 16 per cent of which were identified as due to syphilis or general paralysis. In another 8 per cent of cases the diagnosis is by no means clear, but could well be general paralysis. Three of the confirmed cases were naval officers, one an army officer, one a pawnbroker and one a commercial traveller. Most died within a short time of admission or were sent to other asylums. The prevalence of military and naval men in this group is not surprising as VD was a particular problem in the services. Joseph O'Brien, in his interesting study of Dublin in the early years of the twentieth century, has argued that the incidence of VD, including syphilis, was much greater than contemporary authorities were willing to admit. In 1880, for instance, over one-third of the troops stationed in Dublin were admitted to hospital suffering from VD and some 20 per cent of these admissions were due to syphilis. But O'Brien thinks it was not only the Dublin garrison that suffered in this manner: through prostitutes the disease spread to the general population. As early as 1792 Dublin had a hospital specially catering for VD patients in the shape of the Westmoreland Lock Hospital in Townsend Street, but from 1821 it would only admit female patients. Because of the stigma associated with the disease, male sufferers were often reluctant to seek treatment and indeed many hospitals would not treat them. Steevens Hospital was unusual in maintaining about a dozen beds for syphilitic patients. Perhaps in the final and demented stages of the illness, some of these patients were transferred to St Patrick's. O'Brien claimed to detect a 'conspiracy of silence', particularly among hospital authorities, to obscure the number of deaths caused by syphilis. There is no obvious evidence of such a conspiracy at St Patrick's. Diagnoses are often not very clear, or even totally lacking, but this applied to illnesses other than general paralysis and is simply a reflection of the hospital's inadequate patient records. Nevertheless, the data from St Patrick's incomplete though it may be, does lend support to O'Brien's view that the incidence of VD in late nineteenth-century Dublin has been underestimated.[82]

If many of the female patients in hospital were elderly and had been ill for long periods and a proportion of the men were in the final stages of syphilis, it is hardly surprising that St Patrick's had few patients considered to be curable. But, if so few were curable, then what did the doctors employed by the hospital do? What treatments, if any, did they have to offer such patients?

The bye-laws introduced in 1889 had specified that the visiting medical officers should attend the hospital on alternate days and 'visit all patients labouring under bodily disease'; at least once a fortnight they were also to 'examine . . . the mental condition of every patient . . . under special medical treatment'. But, considering the type of patient admitted to St Patrick's after 1850 and the medical reports of the 1860s and 1870s, one cannot help but gain the impression that the visiting medical officers spent far more time treating 'bodily disease' than they did wrestling with the mental afflictions of their patients. Dr Leeper, in one of his 1899 reports to the board, while proclaiming his faith in the medical treatment of mental illness, rejected what he termed 'mere housing, feeding and protection'. The obvious implication was that his predecessors had largely abandoned attempts to cure patients and instead simply attended to their physical needs. Indicative of this approach was the fact that, in the 1850s at least, vastly more money was spent each year on purchasing wine, spirits, beer and porter than was spent on medicines: in 1857, for instance, the figures were £554 and £16 respectively. Yet, despite the failure of moral management, there was little that the psychiatric medicine of the period could do for such patients as those in St Patrick's, except to treat their bodily ailments and see to their physical needs. As we shall see, Leeper's drastic solution to the problem was to remove elderly and incurable patients and only to admit those whom he thought the hospital could help, which meant younger people in the early stages of illness. He complained that St Patrick's had come to be regarded as a 'dumping ground for incurables, impecunious and hopeless cases of mental disease, owing to its clerical mismanagement. Most of the applicants [according to Leeper] were very poor and only sought admission because they were so troublesome and impecunious that they were discharged from the private asylums.'[83]

In 1891 Burdett complained particularly about the use of physical restraint in the hospital. Strait-jackets appear to have been employed extensively and the old practice of strapping difficult patients in special chairs still seems to have been common. Burdett's information is not always accurate, but he does suggest that restraint was employed particularly freely under Rice; after Moloney took over in 1885 the situation improved somewhat. Nevertheless, in his 1895 report Dr Courtenay had complained that he had found two suicidal female patients under restraint, with no record kept of when or why this had been done. Similarly in his first 1899 report, Leeper said he had found three or four suicidal women 'habitually subjected to restraint' and even forced to sleep in strait-jackets. He removed them immediately, informing the governors that such treatment was 'entirely obsolete', and he ordered that in future such restraint should only be employed in 'very exceptional circumstances' and on his written instructions. He also confiscated fourteen strait-jackets from the senior attendant and placed them in the matron's charge. Clearly strait-jackets were being used extensively by the attendants, with little or no supervision. Restraint was not only used with female suicides, however, it was also employed in cases of violent males. In discussing the staff, we have already noted that injuries inflicted by patients were not uncommon and some of these injuries were obviously serious. General paralysis patients in a state of dementia could certainly be extremely violent. In 1857 20 per cent of patients in St Patrick's were classed as dangerous and there is no reason to believe that this percentage declined significantly in succeeding decades. Some means of preventing such people from injuring themselves or others was necessary. At times in the past, patients had been confined to their cells or had been very closely supervised by the staff or, in the case of wealthier patients, the governors had insisted that a special attendant be employed by the family to act as a guard. But by the 1890s, strait-jackets seem to have become the preferred means of control. Objections to them particularly centred on the fact that they were out-of-date, or 'obsolete' as Leeper put it. Certainly as early as 1857-8 the commissioners investigating Irish asylums had remarked on the hospital's lack of padded cells, which were considered a more modern and humane means of restraint than chains and straps. But it wasn't till more than forty years later, in 1901 to be exact, that such cells were installed in St Patrick's.[84]

Perhaps the most vivid way to convey the state of the hospital, and especially of its patients, in the latter half of the nineteenth century is to look at the cases of several long-term patients: women, admitted in mid-century, who were still in St Patrick's at the beginning of the new century. Their admission forms tell us something about these women when they first entered the hospital. But medical records are then virtually non-existent till 1899 when Leeper started case-books, which describe in some detail the physical and mental states of every patient. So we have, as it were, a snap-shot of these women in the 1840s and then another taken some fifty years later. It is of course a great pity that all is dark in between; one would like very much to know what, if any, treatments these other women received. Nevertheless, a comparison of the two snap-shots tells a good deal about the patients and their care in the half century between 1850 and 1900.

Mary Anne Ryan was admitted to St Patrick's in April 1847 as a second-class boarder at £20 per annum. She was thirty-three years old; an unmarried, Protestant 'separatist', living with her father, John Ryan, a court crier, in Portland Place. He was distinctly reticent on the admission form, recording simply that Mary Anne had been ill for two years and had spent time in a private asylum at Finglas. As to the nature or cause of her illness, there was no information, beyond the statement that she 'threatens at times to drown herself'. Mary Anne had no occupation, no income and no assets. Unfortunately, we know nothing of the treatment she received in the hospital. But, by 1859, her fees were considerably in arrears and, upon investigation, the hospital's solicitor, Henry Rooke, reported that she had no family and thus the arrears were unlikely to be paid. But she was not removed from the hospital; on the contrary, in 1861 her arrears were struck off and she was transferred to the free list. We hear nothing further of Mary Anne Ryan in St Patrick's records till she appears in the first female case-book begun by Leeper in 1899. Leeper obviously found her case an interesting one for he included three photographs of her with his notes.

> Miss Ryan [he wrote in March 1899] seems to have suffered from chronic delusional insanity. Her room in ward no. 4 is the sight of the hospital, the walls being covered with fantastic drawings done with coal ashes and any bits of colour she has been able to secure. She dresses altogether in white flannel which she makes herself. Her delusions are of a religious type coupled with those of persecution.

Clearly, despite her years of institutionalisation, Mary Anne Ryan remained a vivid personality. In Leeper's photographs she is wearing striking white robes and resembles an Old Testament prophet. In May 1900 she was reported to be 'at times quite happy and cheerful', but she seemed 'not to regard time or realise how long she has been in hospital'. In November 1901 she was in 'good health', despite her eighty-seven years and was eating and sleeping well. But, in the following month, she died suddenly. No cause of death was recorded.[85]

We have rather more background information on Eleanor Murray, who was admitted to the hospital in October 1850 as a first-class boarder at £42 per annum. She was a twenty-five year old, unmarried Protestant from Sligo, committed by her mother, after suffering from melancholia for two or three years. More detail in Eleanor Murray's case comes from a memorial sent to the governors in 1854 by her uncle, Denis Murray, an army surgeon then living in Enniskerry, Co. Wicklow, on half-pay. Denis Murray said that his brother, John, a Sligo apothecary, had died of fever in 1835, leaving a widow, Elizabeth, with seven children aged from eleven months to eleven years. She had little in the way of resources and was largely supported by Denis Murray and by two of her own brothers. But further disasters struck the family in the mid-1840s. One of Elizabeth's brothers died in 1845, as did one of her sons at the age of sixteen, after a long and difficult illness, and in 1847 Eleanor, or Ellen as she was called by her family, also became seriously ill. She did recover, but was almost immediately 'seized with dementia'. For over two years she was treated in her mother's home 'under the best medical advice that Sligo afforded', but she showed no improvement and, indeed, there is a suggestion that she may have become violent. Thus, in October 1850, her mother brought her to Dublin and secured her admission to St Patrick's, with Denis Murray agreeing to pay half her fees. When, however, he 'undertook to meet this demand, he hoped that his unfortunate niece might speedily be restored to health under the kind of care and judicious medical treatment she was sure to have in St Patrick's Hospital, but no amendment has taken place in her case, and the complaint appears to have settled down into confirmed "idiocy" leaving no room for hope of recovery.' Having retired after thirty-five years' service and with a family of his own to support, Denis Murray requested the governors to reduce Ellen's fee to the 'cheapest class of paid patient'. The governors responded by fixing her fee at £30 per annum.[86]

Nothing further is recorded of Ellen Murray until she appears in the 1899 case-book. Presumably, at some stage, her family ceased to pay her fees and she was transferred to the free list, but there is no mention of this. In 1899 she was classed as suffering from melancholia and dementia. She was 'very quiet', but when she did talk it was 'in a very incoherent manner'. By 1902 the medical notes record that she lives a very automatic life, eats when food is placed before her and sleeps when placed in bed'. In 1903 her existence was described as 'vegetative': most of the day she spent sitting in front of the fire, staring vacantly into space. In September of that year she developed gangrene in her right foot and, although this improved, she became progressively weaker and died in October, her death being ascribed to dementia and senile decay. She was seventy-eight years old at the time of her death, having spent fifty-three of those years in St Patrick's.[87]

Our third and final case-study of a long-term patient is that of Elizabeth Grove Grady, who spent longer in St Patrick's than any other patient whose records have survived. She was admitted in May 1845 as a first-class boarder, along with her sister Susanna. Elizabeth was 'about thirty' and Susanna 'about forty'. Both women were described as 'ladies', who had previously been living in England; both were said to have been ill for about three years; and the nature of illness in both cases was given as 'believing herself a person of exalted rank'. In fact their admission forms were identical, except that Elizabeth's was signed by her brother, Thomas, who described himself as a gentleman living at Castleknock, Co. Dublin, while Susanna's was signed by another brother, Henry, a solicitor practising in Baggot Street. Neither sister had any occupation or income, but each was entitled to £1,000 under their father's will. At the time of their admission, however, the will was being contested in the courts. One cannot help but wonder what happened to the sisters' £2,000 inheritance once they had been certified as insane.

Susanna died in St Patrick's a little over a year after her admission, but Elizabeth remained a patient for sixty years. As early as 1856, however, the governors were having considerable trouble collecting Elizabeth's fees from her brothers and in 1863 they refused to pay altogether. By 1867 arrears were over £100, but, after letters from the hospital's solicitors threatening legal action or Elizabeth's removal, Henry Grove Grady offered to pay a mere £10. Yet, although her case was obviously a hopeless one and her fees were not being paid, the governors continued to maintain Elizabeth in the hospital. In 1876 she was suffering from rheumatism and in 1879 she was recovering from a dyspeptic attack. By 1899, when the case-books begin, she was being called 'Miss O'Grady' or alternatively 'The princess'. Leeper classed her as suffering from 'delusions of exaltation' and his notes for January 1902 record that:

Portrait by Sean O'Sullivan of Dr Richard Leeper, medical superintendent of St
Patrick's Hospital, 1899-1941.

Registry of

Number	NAME	Class	Age	Religion	Date of Admission	Occupation or TRADE	PLACE of BIRTH	Place of Abode before ADMISSION	MEDICAL PERSON Certifying	Person signing Security	By whom Recommended

St. Patrick's Hospital.

PROBABLE CAUSE of Illness	How long Ill before Admission.	SPECIES of DISEASE	RELAPSES when and how often they have occurred.	Period of transfer to Convalescent Division.	DISCHARGED			Period and Cause of DEATH	OBSERVATIONS
					RECOVERED	RELIEVED.	Taken by Friends Unrelieved		

Page from the Registry of St Patrick's Hospital 1795-1925, showing admissions from July to December 1844.

A female ward at St Patrick's in 1904: note the attempt to decorate and furnish the long corridors onto which patients' rooms opened.

Patients' drawingroom in 1904: note the potted plants, magazines, writing desk, organ and piano, all intended to create a comfortable, homely atmosphere and provide entertainment for the patients.

Swift's escritoire, in which the hospital's legal papers were kept from 1771 to 1931; one of the benches from the Irish Parliament house in College Green, which came into the governor's possession by means unknown.

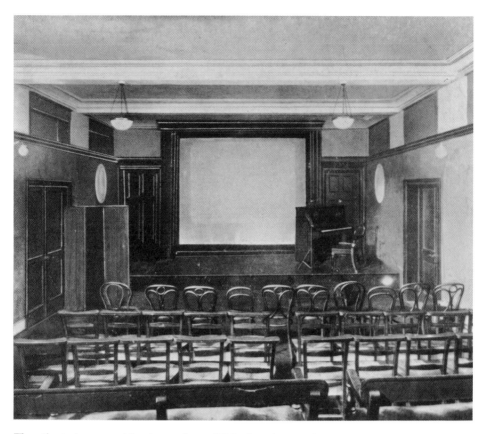

The silent cinema, with piano, about 1928: the silent and then talking pictures were very popular with patients from the mid 1920s till the mid 1950s, when they were superseded by television.

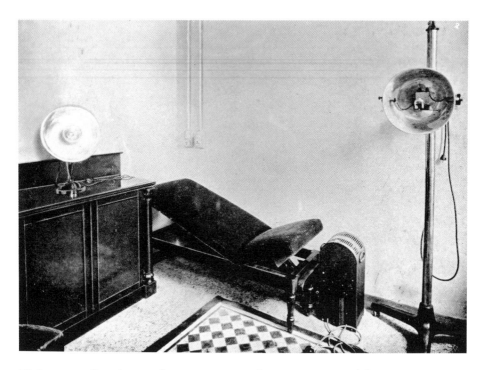

Violet ray, radiant heat and massage room, about 1928: some of the new treatments introduced in the 1920s.

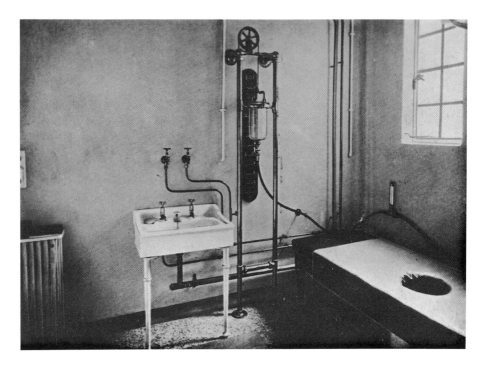

Plombiêre and hydro-therapeutical room, about 1928: water treatment continued, though in rather different forms.

Miss O'Grady still believes she is the princess and is constantly asking about the king's coronation. She imagines he has been crowned already. She is quiet and amiable. General health is fair.

In August 1904 she was still 'usually good humoured' and was dispensing 'favours and titles to all those whom she considers have been kind to her'; several of the staff had been knighted. She was 'very little trouble' and it is clear, even from these brief and dispassionate notes, that she was something of a favourite with the staff. But early in 1905, at the age of ninety, she contracted bronchitis and in May she died, the cause of death being given as 'chronic delusional insanity and senile decay'.[88]

Although Mary Anne Ryan, Ellen Murray and Elizabeth Grove Grady spent far longer in St Patrick's than the average patient, they are nevertheless fairly typical of the sort of long-term, elderly patient that the hospital accommodated in the 1890s. After fifty years, all three had lost touch, not only with their families, but with life outside the walls of St Patrick's. Elizabeth Grove Grady certainly seems to have maintained an intense, if deluded, interest in the affairs of royalty, but Mary Anne Ryan had lost all sense of time and Ellen Murray was little more than an automaton. Ellen had clearly succumbed to the effects of institutionalisation, but it is interesting to see that the other two had not: both, despite, or even perhaps because of, their delusions, remained distinctive and interesting personalities. Yet, by the 1890s, there was nothing that the hospital could do for any of them: Leeper's notes, for instance, make no mention of treatment, beyond mere physical care. We do not know what, if any, treatment they received in the early years of their residence in the hospital, but clearly it had had little or no effect. By the 1890s, and probably earlier, these women were simply being housed, clothed, fed and cared for by the hospital; they were not being treated for their mental disorders. As the government inspectors, Leeper and Burdett all attested, by the 1890s St Patrick's was an asylum, caring for a small group of mainly geriatric inmates; it was not a hospital actively seeking to cure its patients and return them to the outside world.

There is little doubt that the half century after 1850 marked a low point in St Patrick's history. The hospital staggered from financial crisis to financial crisis as the building became more and more dilapidated and patient care deteriorated seriously. Burdett's harsh description, reproduced at the begining of this chaper, had, despite inaccuracies, much truth in it. It should, however, be remembered that Burdett, who demonstrated for the time a not uncommon

Englishman's sense of superiority to all things Irish, had little appreciation of, let alone sympathy for, the many problems that the board of governors faced. The simple fact was that St Patrick's had never been properly financed. Swift's estate was utterly inadequate to the tasks of building and operating a charity hospital. Right from the outset, various expedients, like charging some patients fees and seeking government grants, had had to be resorted to in order to open the hospital and keep it operating. But these were makeshift measures at best. Charging fees, for instance, was not sanctioned either by Swift's will or by the hospital's charter and yet it was essential to the hospital's survival. Critics, like Lord Chancellor Sugden, Dr Francis White and the 1857-8 commissioners of enquiry, were unhappy at the thought of a charity hospital charging fees and building up a capital reserve. But the attempt made in the 1840s to put a ceiling on fees simply helped produce a financial crisis in the 1860s. Presumably the governors did not seek a new charter empowering them to charge fees because such an innovation would have been directly contrary to Swift's wishes and thus unlikely to receive official approval. The commissioners, who investigated Irish asylums in 1857, certainly concluded that: 'From the terms of the Dean's will there can be no doubt that no payment was contemplated on the part of the patients'.[89] Aside from patient fees, the hospital's other principal source of revenue was rent from property. This at least was sanctioned by the will and the charter. But the growing crisis in Irish landlordism during the nineteenth century made estate management an extremely difficult and far from financially rewarding undertaking.

Thus by the last quarter of the nineteenth century, the hospital's problems had reached a peak and even the election of a group of influential businessmen to the board seems to have produced no solution. By the late 1880s the possibility of closure was looming large. Yet there were a number of developments in the 1880s and 1890s which, in time, were to open the way to a far better future for St Patrick's and its patients. The land acts of these years held out the possibility that the hospital's estate could be sold on reasonably favourable terms and the resulting capital invested in a more lucrative manner. At the same time, the governors were able to secure a number of important amendments to their ancient charter, which did away with many of the restrictions under which they had laboured for so long. The main amendments were contained in the first supplemental charter, granted in 1888. The board sought it at a time of major financial crisis, which convinced even the lord chancellor, Lord Ashbourne, that the provisions of Swift's will at last needed amendment. The new charter confirmed the 'object of the charity' to be the care and treatment of 'poor persons who are or shall be idiots or lunatics', but, at the same time, it empowered the governors 'to charge such fees as they shall think fit to any person'; the money to be used in 'support of the inmates of the hospital generally'. The charter also allowed the governors to pay whatever salaries, wages and pensions they saw fit, thus doing away with the provision that restricted such payments to not more than one-fifth of the annual income. In addition the board could hold or lease land in perpetuity or for any term of years it wished; it was no longer limited to a maximum term of thirty-one years. And it could also sell any amount of such land and invest the funds in stocks and shares. The board was thus at last permitted to operate in an unfettered manner financially: to charge fees, to pay wages and to trade in land and shares in whatever way it considered best for the interests of the hospital. The other two supplemental charters have been mentioned already: the first, granted in 1895, empowered the governors to buy a convalescent hospital in Co. Dublin using the £10,000 that they had invested; while the second, granted in 1897, allowed the creation of up to three new elected governorships.[90]

So, despite the gloomy picture of St Patrick's and its affairs painted by observers in the 1890s, the hospital entered the new century, in some respects at least, on a hopeful note. The land acts, in conjunction with the supplemental charters, gave the governors an opportunity to solve, or certainly alleviate, the institution's chronic financial problems. But the major catalyst of reform was the new medical superintendent appointed in 1899, Dr Richard Leeper.

CHAPTER 5

Leeper's Hospital, 1899-1941

The eighteenth century hospital
Established by the tears of Madam
Steevens, who gave birth, people said, to
A monster with a pig's snout, pot-head.
The Ford turned right, slowed down. Gates opened,
Closed with a clang; acetelyne glow
Of headlights. How could Maurice Devane
Suspect from weeping-stone, porch, vane,
The classical rustle of the harpies,
Hopping in filth among the trees,
The Mansion of Forgetfulness
   Swift gave us for a jest?

Tall, handsome, tweeded Dr Leeper
Inspecting the mindless at a glance
Quick-striding, always ready to leap,
A duffering Victorian; . . .

One afternoon, he looked in dread
Into the ward outside. The beds
Were empty. Quiet sunshine glowed
On the waxed floor and brass. He hurried
Across to the high window, stood
On the hot pipes to see the view.
Below there was a widespread garden,
With shrubberies, walks, summerhouses.
He stared in wonder from his bars,
   Saddened by the boughs.[1]

TRANSFORMATION: FROM ASYLUM TO HOSPITAL

Richard Leeper came from a family with strong links to the Church of Ireland. He had trained in Dublin as a surgeon, spent some years as AMO at Dr Eustace's private asylums, Hampstead and Highfield, in Glasnevin, and, immediately prior to his appointment at St Patrick's, had been in charge of a workhouse asylum at Rathdrum in

Co. Wicklow. As well he was surgeon to the local infirmary and, in his own words, 'did the usual carpentry surgery of cutting off limbs irreparably damaged by accidents and such like'. An acquaintance was later to write that: 'Dick Leeper, beside being a doctor of more than ordinary skill, was one of the best shots and fishermen in that super-sporting county of Wicklow . . . probably also a good man to hounds in the hunting areas of that county's diverse country . . .'[2] In addition to being a sportsman, Leeper was a dedicated amateur naturalist and the patients of St Patrick's were later to benefit from his knowledge through lectures he gave on birds and other wildlife. Leeper, who was in his mid thirties at the time of his appointment, had gained a favourable reputation by his work at the Rathdrum asylum. Dean Jellett of St Patrick's Cathedral and Sir Thornley Stoker, with whom Leeper had trained, seem to have been behind his selection as superintendent. The opening of St Edmundsbury, the death of Dr Gordon, the visiting physician, and the appointment of Stoker as a governor, all of which occurred in 1898, opened the way for the re-organisation of the medical staff. A subcommittee was established, which recommended Dr Moloney's transfer to Lucan to head the new hospital there and Leeper's appointment to the position at St Patrick's.[3] Leeper immediately set about the task of reforming the hospital. In the first five or six years of his tenure of office, he devoted his considerable energies to a number of basic, but vital tasks: the renovation of the old building and the cleaning up of the site; the upgrading of the staff; and the replacement of old and chronic patients with curable cases, whose families were prepared to pay handsomely for first-rate treatment.

The inspectors, Drs Courtenay and O'Farrell, with strong support from J.M. Colles, the lord chancellor's registrar of lunacy, had already commenced the process of reform in the eight years before Leeper's appointment. Their main achievement was undoubtedly persuading the governors to buy an auxiliary hospital at Lucan. But the huge and expensive task of completely overhauling the old hospital was also begun. The old gate lodge and collection of sheds at the front of the building were removed and the new elegant stone lodge completed on the corner of Bow and Steevens Lanes; work was begun on re-plastering and re-flooring the patients' prison-like bedrooms; some of the rooms were provided with furniture and many of the old iron bedsteads, bought in the 1830s, were replaced with new ones of a sort used in the district asylums; the old straw ticks gave way to hair mattresses; and records of restraint and seclusion were kept for the first time. But progress was slow and the inspectors' reports frequently expressed frustration that more was not being done. 'Laying aside all consideration for the insane,' wrote Courtenay in 1891, 'and looking on the establishment merely as a mercantile concern, the governors must see the importance of rendering the institution attractive to the public'. If appeals to altruism did not spur the governors on sufficiently, then the inspectors were not above appealing to their commercial instincts: better facilities would justify higher fees and higher fees would help cover the cost of better facilities.[4]

But it was only with Dr Leeper's appointment early in 1899 that the pace of reform began to match the inspectors' expectations. As we have seen, Leeper began almost immediately to submit detailed and highly critical reports on the state of the hospital to the governors. But privately his views seem to have been even more critical than these reports would suggest. Many years later, in 1938, he wrote a long letter to the then board describing his experiences and impressions on his arrival at St Patrick's. This letter is admittedly somewhat rambling and repetitive, but it provides a vivid insight into the state of the hospital in 1899, when, we should remember, a campaign to improve the building had been under way for at least eight years. Leeper's letter is obviously written by an old man, looking back over many years, but most of the information in it is perfectly consistent with, if more outspoken than, the reports he was submitting to the board at the time and thus it is worth quoting at some length. Leeper said that he had been told to arrive at the hospital on a Saturday night, but his rooms

> were so thick with dust that no one could breathe in them. The late resident medical superintendent had taken off his carpets, leaving a one-inch layer of thick dust on the floors. No one was here to receive me, and I had to try to breathe in the boardroom. Well, after a time, I got my rooms habitable and I then found just what I am telling the board. The date was *1899!* Just remember this date. The hospital was just about 150 years old, and behind the times. Many of the patients were bedded on *straw*, just fancy that, in 1899!! The wards were bereft of all decorations or suitable furniture. Rats ran along before me as I went round, and the patients—in straw ticks—glared at me out of their straw environment, in their cells. No lights, except stable lanterns, in the hands of the night staff, enlightened the bedrooms, opened by a large deadshot lock key, as large as a small bunch of fire irons.

Leeper was in no doubt as to who was responsible for the deplorable state into which St Patrick's had fallen:

> It was [he went on] an eighteenth-century asylum, which was totally neglected by the board of governors, who were entirely

composed of a lot of Irish Church clergymen, who came, board-day after board-day, to do jobs and admit the off-scourings of the Irish private asylums here, at the request of their own partisans. They granted admissions, ignoring all the while that this hospital was from its foundation entirely undenomina-tional and given to the nation by royal charter . . . Burdett, in his history of the hospitals and asylums of the British Isles, then published, holds up the governors of this hospital to extremely hostile criticism, and justly so . . .

While continuing to express considerable hostility towards the clerical governors, Leeper at the same time acknowledged that some of the businessmen elected to the board during the 1890s had been instrumental in reforming the hospital.

It was not at all to my credit that I started the modernisation of the hospital, because the old divines had been eliminated and a new board had been appointed. Mr Ormsby, Mr Christopher La Touche, Mr William Geoghagan and Mr Robert Colvill had been appointed governors, and to them and Sir Thornley Stoker really belong the credit of purging the Augean stable, with merely myself as a very willing assistant. The old board of jobbers and clerical ignoramuses used actually to sit as a board and never even see the medical superintendent, so intent were they all to job in some friend of theirs, almost always a hopeless lunatic who had been bled dry in some private asylum near Dublin . . .

If Leeper was scathing in his remarks about some of the governors, he was equally scathing in his assessment of the hospital's staff:

The male nursing staff consisted of a lot of old soldiers, who were recruited from an old soldiers' society in York Street. They were bribed by pints of porter to carry up the coal to the wards and were said to co-habit with three old sluts who were employed to take down the straw soiled each night by the straw tick bedded patients. No lights except hurricane hand lamps were used, but they may have delighted in darkness because of their deeds of evil . . . When I came here, there was a matron [Mrs Hodson], who occupied the front rooms of this hospital. She was a widow with one paralysed son and another son and daughter. All these lived here at the hospital's expense. She had no knowledge or training of any kind and was the product of the jobbing, old people, who were supposed to be the guardians of the hospital's interests . . . [Generally, according to Leeper, the staff were] just old, illiterate men, and women, who did not know what a temperature meant, and God's poor, afflicted people were left to such as these.

Not only did Leeper concede the justice of Burdett's criticisms, he compared St Patrick's in the 1890s to Hogarth's portrayal of Bethlem Hospital in London in the 1730s. 'Well, I have changed all this,' Leeper told the governors in 1938, and so he did.

The hospital was inspected in both June and December 1899 and a list of improvements was compiled that, in less than a year, exceeded those of the previous eight years. The drainage system had been entirely overhauled, greatly alleviating the problem of rats; the exterior of the building had been painted; many of the old walls and sheds, which cluttered up the small amount of open ground available, had been removed and new gardens laid out; the process of re-decorating the patients' rooms had been accelerated; a new carriage had been purchased to allow twice daily drives to Phoenix Park, and picnics at Lucan had been instituted; a head attendant had been appointed; three nurses had passed the Medico-Psychological Association's exam and the rest of the staff were attending lectures in preparation for it; nurses and attendants had received pay increases and had been provided with their own dining rooms; efforts had been made 'to get rid of some of the old chronic and hopeless patients' and to replace them with patients more likely to benefit from a limited period of residence in the institution; more patients had been encouraged to occupy themselves with work and, particularly in the case of male patients, to help out with repairs and painting; and the inspectors were heartened by the fact that, in the six months from June to December, no patients had been restrained in strait-jackets or confined to their rooms.[5]

In his December 1899 report Leeper summarised his own feelings as to what had been achieved and what more needed to be done. He began with the patients, for, in the midst of all the cleaning, repairing and painting, he had not lost sight of his major objective, which was, as he informed the board, to render 'this institution more extended in its field of usefulness and more fitted for its purpose'; and its purpose, as laid down by its founder, Dean Swift, was to alleviate the plight of the mentally ill. During 1899 seventeen new patients had been admitted, five had died and twenty-five had been discharged, so that the number of patients had fallen from 102 to eighty-nine. Of those discharged, ten were hopeless cases sent to other asylums, but eleven had been discharged as cured and a further four as relieved. Leeper considered this a most encouraging result, particularly given that no restraint had been used. 'The fact that so many have recovered within the year', Leeper told the board, 'is largely owing to the constant medical treatment to which all these patients have been submitted . . . The mere housing, feeding and protection formerly given to lunatics, however careful and systematised, is utterly short of what is now demanded from those whose duty it is to medically tend the sufferers from mental disease.' Here Leeper unequivocally proclaimed his intention of transforming St Patrick's from an asylum for the maintenance of the mentally ill into a hospital for their treatment and cure. He felt that: 'Most cases of mental disease either recover or sink into a condition of chronic insanity within three years from the commencement of their asylum treatment . . .'; and thus he urged the governors to fix a time limit to all admissions. If, after the expiry of this limit, patients had not recovered, then they would be transferred to a public asylum, unless their retention was 'of considerable pecuniary benefit to the hospital'. Leeper was impressed by the scale of the district asylums, telling the board in a later report that the state had provided 'ample, almost extravagant, accommodation for the insane poor', so that the 'retention of a large sediment of incurable, lost and destructive cases is most injurious to a comparatively small hospital, overtaxes its endowment and thereby prevents a more generous treatment of the acute cases . . .' In 1899 he also warned the governors that '. . . a hospital for incurable lunatics gains no reputation . . .' There was little sympathy for the insane in Ireland, he thought, and thus St Patrick's received little money in the way of donations and bequests. Without a government grant or donations or the resources of the rich private asylums, Leeper readily acknowledged that St Patrick's had an uphill battle 'to take, and retain, the position of one of the leading institutions of the kingdom, a position which it held a century ago.'[6]

Leeper seems to have had a well-developed competitive sense, for he viewed other asylums, whether public or private, whether in Ireland, England or Scotland, as rivals. He told the board in his May 1900 report that the private asylums were expending large sums on alterations and improvements and St Patrick's had to keep pace. Moreover, under the Local Government Act of 1898, the new county councils were empowered to build private wards in connection with the district (now county) asylums for the reception of paying and chancery patients. Leeper asked the board's permission to write an account of the hospital, its facilities and admission procedures, which he then proposed to circulate within the medical and legal professions. But, in order to gain favourable publicity for St Patrick's and to outbid its rivals, Leeper needed to be able to present impressive recovery rates. Such rates, however, were depressed by the continuing existence of a significant group of incurables. In July 1901 Leeper informed the board that, out of ninety-three patients then in the hospital, thirty-seven were over sixty years of age. The large number of elderly patients meant a high death-rate, which was hardly calculated to impress prospective patients or their families. In November of the same year Leeper returned to the issue, informing the board that, out of ninety-five patients then resident, fifteen were free and forty-three paid only part of the cost of their maintenance. All the free patients and most of the partially free Leeper considered incurable. They were likely to remain 'for many years to come', he warned, 'a heavy burden on the charity'; and he requested that no more be admitted for the time being. Leeper's attitude may seem a trifle harsh, but he was operating in a world of equally harsh financial realities. Without attracting more and higher paying patients, the hospital could not cover the cost of improvements. Leeper also found that rival asylums were quite ruthless in pursuing a policy of financial gain. In November 1900 he told the board that he had planned to send some of the chronic, free and partially free patients to Scottish and English asylums, not necessarily permanently, but in hopes that a temporary change of surroundings might prove beneficial. But, to his surprise, his proposal met with a universal rebuff. Unless they 'are either a pecuniary benefit to the institution,' he wrote, 'or likely to shortly recover, and thereby raise the annual recovery rate . . .' they would not be accepted. The management of such institutions was obviously conducted 'on the hardest of business lines', Leeper rather sadly concluded.[7] The lesson, however, was that to survive St Patrick's had to operate similarly. The days of providing open-ended, free accommodation to elderly and difficult patients were over. Something of the impact of the hospital's new, more rigorous, admissions policy can be gauged from the tables below.

COMPOSITION OF PATIENTS AT ST PATRICK'S HOSPITAL, 1890-1933

	1890	1899	1901	1919	1933
Total Number	96	89	95	132	155
Free %	22	28	16	4	7
Under Cost %	52	24	45	55	43
At or Over Cost %	24	48	39	41	50[8]

INCOME FROM FEES AT ST PATRICK'S AND
ST EDMUNDSBURY HOSPITALS, 1899-1930

	1899	1916	1930
Total £	5,432	16,244	29,826
Average Per Patient £	53	115	159[9]

If Leeper, on the one hand, tried to persuade the board to operate a much more rigorous admissions policy, on the other hand, he worked tirelessly to improve the living conditions of all patients. In 1890 and again in 1891 the inspectors had singled out the patients' bedrooms as particularly in need to improvement: although the word 'cell' had been dropped, clearly they remained cell-like. The inspectors commented on tiny windows providing inadequate light and ventilation, rough walls, rotten floors, little or no furniture, and old, often broken, beds with straw ticks. The dark and poorly furnished day-rooms and corridors and the decayed gardens were hardly inviting for recreation purposes and thus patients generally spent a great deal of time in their rooms. Lacking dining rooms, they were also fed in these rooms, and the resulting scraps attracted rats. Leeper was fully alive to the detrimental effect of such conditions, telling the governors in 1900 that: 'The absence of light and the prison-like surroundings which exist in old-fashioned asylums [are] most injurious to the patients and tend to diminish their prospects of recovery'.[10]

Initially under pressure from the inspectors and later with Leeper's enthusiastic encouragement, the governors began the huge task of repairing and re-decorating over a hundred patients' rooms. Floor boards had to be replaced; walls cemented, papered and painted; windows enlarged; new beds and furniture supplied; doors repaired and new, modern locks installed. Aside from the sheer amount of work involved and its cost, logistics also posed major problems. Renovations had to be undertaken literally over the patients' heads, but without distressing them or compromising the institution's security. In May and June 1901, Leeper reported that new toilets and bathrooms were being fitted up and that the doors and locks on the male side of the building had all been removed in preparation for the installation of new ones. 'This work has been the cause of great anxiety to me;' Leeper went on, 'and has necessitated my constant personal attention lest accidents or escapes should occur owing to the number of tradesmen having constant access to the wards.'[11]

Perhaps it was for reasons of security, as much as to cut costs, that patients and staff were employed to undertake much of the redecoration. In December 1900, for instance, Leeper asked the board to increase the wages of Nurses Vaughan and Bailey from £10 to £12 per annum. Not only were they competent and 'very kind to the patients', but 'in their leisure moments' they had been engaged in papering the female patients' rooms, at a cost of 5s 10d per room. For the patients, however, such employment was considered therapeutic. In May 1901, after his inspection, Dr Courtenay had commented favourably on the fact that six of the male and twenty-one of the female patients were 'constantly occupied'. Nothing, he thought, 'does more to produce happiness and contentment amongst all classes of the insane than some form of employment'. Leeper only regretted that so few of the men were fit for the tasks of painting and gardening. With a third of them over sixty years of age and a significant proportion suffering from general paralysis, manual labour was clearly beyond most of them. Whilst the nurses were employed in re-decorating, the female patients appear to have been restricted to more 'lady-like' activities such as sewing. Courtenay in 1901 noted that all the clothing needed in the hospital was now being made there. One of Leeper's aims in fact seems to have been to cut costs by making the institution more self-sufficient. Not only was clothing produced, but the farm at Lucan supplied milk, meat and vegetables. Admittedly deliveries were irregular and unpredictable, sometimes leaving the kitchen with no milk or vegetables for days and at other times with a glut. In one week in August 1900 Leeper complained he received twenty-four dozen cabbages, but no peas, beans or fruit. Even so, the supply of fresh vegetables from Lucan marked an improvement over the state of affairs prior to Leeper's appointment. On arrival he had found a number of the male patients suffering from curious skin problems. It was only when he saw what they were being fed that he realised they were in fact suffering from scurvy. A ready supply of lime juice and Lucan vegetables quickly solved this problem. In October 1901 a repairman was employed as Leeper felt it would save the hospital a good deal of money if small-scale repairs could be carried out by a staff member instead of an outside contractor. In similar vein a greenhouse was erected in front of the building so that the hospital would have its own supply of plants and flowers for the wards, even in winter.[12]

As well as more pleasant surroundings and more employment, the patients were also provided with more recreation and entertainment. Drives to and walks in Phoenix Park became a daily occurrence, while groups of three or four male patients were allowed to attend concerts in the city, accompanied by an attendant. But entertainment was also brought to the hospital. In winter, concerts, lantern slide shows and dances were organised, and in summer, garden parties were held every week, with sports competitions on the newly laid out tennis court and croquet lawn. In the summer of 1901 some fifty patients, a little over half of all inmates, were fit enough to attend these gatherings. In the early 1880s convalescent patients were being sent during the summer to stay at a house in Bray. Whether this occurred every year and for how long it lasted is not clear. But, from 1900, the governors began regularly to rent a house, first at Greystones and then at Killiney, for a month every summer. This step had been urged on an initially reluctant board by Dr Colles, a barrister and doctor of law and the registrar of lunacy, who was responsible for chancery patients and who argued that such patients at other asylums enjoyed this privilege.[13] If the governors wanted to attract more wealthy chancery patients, they had to match the facilities of the private asylums. In the event the patients' summer holiday at the seaside proved popular and it was continued throughout Leeper's period of office.

More controversial, however, was the provision of religious instruction for patients. The Rev. J. A. Dickinson, chaplain to Steevens Hospital and secretary to the governors of St Patrick's from 1871 to 1899, read daily prayers and held Sunday services for the patients at St Patrick's. Catholic clergy from St James's parish visited patients occasionally, but on an unpaid basis. Patients who were well enough were also able to attend churches in the neighbour-hood. But the numbers involved were small. In 1901, for instance, out of ninety-three patients, twenty-eight were attending Sunday services in the hospital, while one went to St James's Protestant parish church. Only fifteen of the patients were Catholics and only one was fit enough to attend mass outside. In their 1890 report the lunacy inspectors had urged the governors to appoint a Catholic chaplain to say mass at least once a week in the hospital. But this recommendation was not acted upon and, indeed, it was not until 1924 that the parish priest of St James's was formally appointed chaplain to the hospital at a salary of £50 per annum. When Dickinson retired as chaplain in 1902, Sir Thornley Stoker success-fully moved that the Rev. J. Crawford Irwin, rector of St James's and one of the governors, be appointed chaplain to St Patrick's and the Rev. Charles Benson, rector of Lucan, chaplain to St Edmundsbury. Irwin was paid £50 per annum for conducting weekly services and Benson £20 for making occasional visits.[14] As we have already seen, many asylums, public and private, were reluctant to appoint chaplains and to allow their patients to participate in religious services. They gave way in the end to government pressure, but often only after considerable resistance. St Patrick's was typical in this regard.

Other assorted measures to improve patient comfort and safety included the installation of proper fire-fighting equipment and emergency exits; the construction of more day-rooms on each floor; the renovation of bathrooms and toilets; the introduction of patients' dining rooms; and the fitting up of lifts to transport food from the kitchen. This latter measure is typical of the simple, but significant, improvements made by Leeper. Previously food had been carried by the nurses and attendants from the kitchen in the basement to the patients' rooms. With around one hundred patients having to be served, this was a large and time-consuming task. It meant, on the one hand, that food was often cold before it reached the patients and, on the other hand, that patients were left largely unattended while the staff were engaged downstairs in the kitchen. Lifts delivering food upstairs greatly simplified the whole procedure. Leeper also overhauled the hospital's diet, mainly in order to make it more varied. Unfortunately we have no details of the diet at this time, though doubtless the farm at Lucan provided an important new and cheaper source of meat and vegetables. In connection with the changes in meal arrangements, Leeper also asked the board for permission to purchase three clocks. He said that these were 'urgently needed' to ensure that meals were served on time.[15] The apparent lack of clocks in St Patrick's before 1900 is very revealing. It suggests that, up until then, time was considered of little importance in the hospital. One might go so far as to fancy that, when patients were admitted, time, in essence, stopped for them. To patients considered incurable and likely to spend the rest of their lives in St Patrick's, time had no meaning. In a sense, perhaps Leeper's greatest achievement was to re-introduce time into the hospital, and thus to bring the place back into harmony with the outside world. To patients receiving treatment and with the expectation of cure, time was a real and vital aspect of their lives.

As we have seen, the inspectors were especially pleased with Leeper's refusal to use restraint, in the form of strait-jackets, on difficult patients. But he did institute other measures to control them. In 1901 two padded-rooms were installed in the hospital. They cost the considerable sum of £235 to fit up, as specialist workmen had to be brought from London for the job. But Leeper told the board that, if the hospital was to treat acute cases in the early stages, when there was a good chance of recovery, rather than as long-term, chronic cases, then padded-rooms were essential. Later, difficult patients were often simply confined to bed, though

St Patrick's padded cells remained in use up to the 1950s. Leeper also tackled the old problem of segregating the more difficult and destructive cases: a problem largely created by the hospital's design. Over the previous century attempts had been made at different times to introduce segregation, but, in the end, the indiscriminate mixing of patients had always reappeared. In 1900 Leeper converted the end of ward No. 3, on the top floor of the male wing, into what he termed an 'observation dormitory'. It was easier to watch such patients in dormitory-style accommodation than in single rooms and thus to prevent them doing damage to themselves or to their furniture and bedding. The main drawback to this innovation does not seem to have emerged till many years later, when, in 1925, a highly disturbed female patient committed suicide by jumping from a top floor bathroom window. In his report on the incident the then inspector, Dr D. L. Kelly, criticised the hospital for housing suicidal patients on the top floor. Nevertheless, the introduction of segregation, after so many abortive attempts in the past, was a major step forward in dealing with violent patients.[16]

Aside from renovating the old hospital building and admitting more curable patients for fixed periods, Leeper's other prime task was the upgrading of the staff. In this regard he was in the forefront of the movement to reform Irish asylums. Staff training had begun in English and Scottish asylums in the 1880s, with the Medico-Psychological Association's handbook for attendants being published for the first time in 1885. Irish asylums were slow to follow: the Richmond in Dublin began training in the 1890s, but even as late as the 1920s many county asylums still employed large numbers of untrained staff. St Patrick's, also, was in advance of other private asylums, for, after attending the M.P.A.'s annual meeting in London in 1900, Leeper was able to tell the governors that the training schemes at St Patrick's and the Stewart Institution were the only ones at Irish private asylums recognised by the association for the purposes of its proficiency certificate.[17]

When Leeper took up his duties early in 1899, he found a totally untrained staff that had not received a pay rise for nearly thirty years. In 1890, in their first report, the new inspectors of lunacy noted that the staff consisted of six attendants, one night attendant and four ward maids to care for thirty-six male patients; and three charge nurses, two night nurses and ten nurses and ward maids to care for sixty female patients. In addition there was a cook, two kitchen maids, five laundresses, one hall maid and a work woman. The offices of head nurse and head attendant, which had existed in the 1870s, had obviously disappeared. The three charge nurses were each responsible for one of the female wards, but their duties seem to have over-lapped those of the matron. Certainly in 1899 Leeper found that there were feuds between the matron, Mrs Hodson, and the charge nurses over who should do what. As we saw in the previous chapter, Leeper immediately set up a training scheme to prepare both nurses and attendants to sit for the M.P.A. exam in mental health nursing. He also employed a head nurse and a head attendant and discharged the 'old women', as he called the ward maids employed to clean the male wards. In their place he engaged three new male attendants. So, at last, female staff had been removed from the male wards and a complete segregation of the sexes was achieved. The new head attendant Leeper recruited in England, during his visit for the M.P.A. 1900 annual meeting. In fact a significant number of new staff employed at this time came from England, presumably because it was easier to find trained staff there than in Ireland. The new head nurse, Marie Eynthoven, was, however, drawn from the hospital's existing staff. In 1902 she replaced Mrs Hodson as matron and also assumed the office of storekeeper or steward. Leeper felt that the hospital would function more efficiently if the offices of head nurse, matron and storekeeper were all held by the one person. He also insisted that detailed records of clothing, bedding and linen issued from the store should be kept. Apparently this had not been done in the past by the storekeeper and thus much of the hospital's supply could not be accounted for. Matron Eynthoven was clearly a success, for she continued in the position till 1937: making her one of the longest serving matrons in the hospital's history.

At St Edmundsbury between 1899 and 1905 there were some fifteen to seventeen female patients, mainly chancery and high fee-paying patients. They were cared for by a nursing staff consisting of a matron, a head nurse, six nurses and a night nurse. When the first matron, Jean Glegg, was appointed late in 1898 at £75 per annum, the governors specified that she be a 'qualified surgical and mental nurse.' She was followed in 1901 by a Miss Sneyd and in 1905 by Helena Golding. Matron Golding had previously been assistant matron at the Bloomfield Retreat, the private asylum run by the Quakers in Dublin, and so presumably had considerable experience in mental health nursing. She served at St Edmundsbury till 1929.[18]

By employing already qualified nurses or putting his own staff through a training programme, Leeper was able to upgrade the female staff quickly. In December 1900 the inspectors were already commenting on the 'great improvement in staff'. Out of sixteen nurses at St Patrick's, eight were fully trained. But the picture was by no means as impressive as regards the male attendants: only two out of fourteen of them had their certificates in mental nursing. The male staff in fact proved something of a problem for Leeper, Soon after his appointment in 1899, he was complaining of the poor quality of the attendants: one had recently allowed a patient to escape; another was, in Leeper's word, 'eccentric' in behaviour; while a third was refusing to undertake night duty. A year later Leeper was reporting to the board that the attendants were very 'unsettled' and had at one stage refused to work. In response he 'dismissed two of the ring leaders; and the remainder . . . returned to work'. In fact, by the end of 1901, according to the inspectors' report, 'almost all the male attendants [had] been changed'. Given the claim made in his 1938 letter, that the male attendants were mainly corrupt old soldiers, it is not surprising that Leeper sought to get rid of most of them at the earliest opportunity. But, at the same time, he was determined to improve staff living conditions and pay. Over a period of two or three years he urged the governors on numerous occasions to increase the pay of both nurses and attendants to at least the level prevailing in the public asylums and also to offer incentives to those who gained their certificate in mental nursing. Unless this was done, he warned, St Patrick's would lose its newly qualified staff to other asylums offering better pay. Eventually, in a rather piecemeal fashion, new pay scales did emerge: attendants received £20 to £24 per annum, charge attendants £25 to £35; and the head attendant £60; while nurses received £12 to £20, with charge nurses being on the highest scale; night nurses £15; and the head nurse £40. In addition an extra £2 per annum was offered to those who passed the M.P.A. examination. These pay scales were on a par with those prevailing in the county asylums and certainly marked an improvement over those prevailing before 1899, under which attendants received from £15 to £22 and nurses/ward maids from £6 to £18.[19]

It wasn't only the nursing staff, however, who received pay rises. In 1901 there were six laundry maids, each being paid £9 per annum. But, on closer investigation, Leeper found that three of them had been receiving porter in lieu of wages. He asked the board to stop this practice immediately and instead to pay all six £10 per annum. The large number of male general paralysis patients then in the hospital meant that there was a great deal of 'foul laundry' and that the laundresses' work was 'onerous'. The laundry itself Leeper found to be in a 'deplorable state', with the boilers, which had been installed in the 1860s, worn out, so that no hot water was available. These had to be completely replaced.[20]

Leeper also urged the board to take out insurance to cover itself against accidents to staff and to introduce a staff pension scheme. As we have seen, the governors often did grant pensions, but they were regarded as a privilege, for which the retiring staff member had to petition, and not as a right. It was not till 1905 that the board moved to take out accident liability insurance and then only after an accident to the cook had led to a claim against the hospital. As for staff superannuation, a comprehensive scheme was not introduced till 1914. But, the county asylums had begun a pension scheme only in 1909, so St Patrick's was not far behind in this regard. The county asylums had made this move partly as a result of pressure from newly-formed staff unions. There is no evidence of trade union activity at St Patrick's at this time, but, as we shall see, after 1914, the formation of unions among both the nursing and the labouring staff was to lead to major changes in management-staff relations at the hospital.[21]

As well as giving a great deal of attention to the duties and salaries of the staff, Leeper also gave consideration to his own position as both superintendent and resident medical officer. He clearly found his administrative duties excessively demanding: the words 'strain' and 'anxiety' figure frequently in his early reports to the board. In his 1938 letter, Leeper admitted frankly:

> My life was one of constant strain. If I went for an hour into town, or to see a friend, I never knew what catastrophe awaited me when I returned to the hospital. I was solely responsible, for, although the board paid for one consultant surgeon and one consultant physician, these two officials were wholly irresponsible as regards the treatment, or management, of the hospital, but could be called if any physical illness occurred. Physical illnesses were rare, but suicidal obsessions and impulses always were here and the medical superintendent alone was responsible. For such serious responsibilities no assistance, or advice, was obtainable from anybody . . . After coming here for the first few months, I felt I could not endure the very awful life I had committed myself to. After my life in Wicklow, it was almost unbearable, but I felt I had got a job to do and I did my best to forget my former happy life and to do my best for the poor people I found myself amongst. My wife helped me in many ways, in . . . trying to humanise the wretched wards.

In September 1900, about eighteen months after his appointment, he thanked the board for agreeing to grant him a month's paid leave every year and to pay for a locum to replace him. Previously the medical superintendent had had to petition the board for leave each year and to pay for his own replacement. He then went on:

> Since entering on my duty here I have felt keenly the constant strain and responsibility of such an anxious post . . . I find it

exceedingly difficult at times to devote that amount of time that is now considered necessary to the medical treatment of the insane, so much am I occupied in the administrative work of the hospital and so constantly engaged in interviewing friends of the patients and their relatives; and others constantly calling for information in connection with the hospital and its work.

He suggested the appointment of an assistant medical officer (AMO) who would be able to devote more time to the care of patients and to maintaining detailed patient records. The board accepted his recommendation, but it was not till over a year later, in November 1901, that Dr Michael Curran was appointed the first AMO at St Patrick's. The delay, Leeper felt, was due to the fact that the salary offered, £150 per annum, was not high enough to interest many suitable candidates. The board, however, refused to raise it. The AMO was appointed initially for twelve months and, in the early years, most left after the end of this time. Only with the appointment of Dr H. R. C. Rutherford in 1906 was a more permanent occupant for the position found; Rutherford served till 1925.[22]

In March 1902 Dr John Moloney, who had moved to St Edmundsbury in 1899 to make way for Leeper, resigned. In his 1938 letter Leeper said that Moloney in fact had been asked to resign by the governors, when he informed them that he intended to marry one of his former patients. The board, expressing its 'entire satisfaction' with Leeper's performance, offered him the superintendentship of St Edmundsbury, as well as St Patrick's, at a salary of £550 per annum, plus free fire, light, vegetables, eggs, butter and milk.[23] Leeper accepted 'very reluctantly' at the urging of Sir Thornley Stoker and on condition that the board employ an AMO at St Edmundsbury. His first visit there confirmed his worst fears:

All the present farm buildings were dilapidated and almost roofless. The house was lit by glass bowled paraffin lamps. The matron [Miss Sneyd] was a very kindly lady, who had no previous experience of mental disease. The former matron [Miss Glegg] had been dismissed for intemperance. Only one nurse of any mental experience had been employed, and she had been dismissed, I think . . . from the county asylum service. Two or three of the patients had fallen out of the bedroom windows, and one lady patient had sustained a fracture of her hip, which lamed her for life . . . The water supply for domestic purposes, WCs and bathrooms depended upon an old pumping arrangement, worked by a horse, who was driven round and round, and so pumped water, which was seldom quite sufficient. The walls of the garden were all crumbling to pieces and also the walls around the place.

So from 1902 Leeper shouldered much of the work of repairing and renovating St Edmundsbury, as well as managing the main hospital.

Despite his complaints that much of his time was taken up with administrative duties, Leeper did find time to exercise an active interest in his profession. He attended meetings of the M.P.A. in London and eventually went on to become president of the organisation; he gave a series of lectures to staff at St Patrick's preparing them for the M.P.A. exam; and he also seems to have conducted his own research into mental illness. In 1901, for instance, he asked the board for money to buy equipment to enable him to continue his 'pathological work in connection with mental disease'; in 1904 a microscope was also bought at his request. Leeper's interest is also obvious from the patient case-books. He had begun these in 1899 in order to have a continuous record of changes in each patient's condition. It was generally the responsibility of the AMO to keep them up-to-date. But Leeper inserted in them photographs of patients, often to illustrate oddities of dress and behaviour, and also pictures of brain sections he had made during post-mortems. Leeper's pathological work would thus seem to have consisted of microscopic examinations of brain abnormalities. This is almost certainly the first attempt to undertake real scientific research into mental illness at St Patrick's. In 1904 the governors also allowed Leeper to give clinical instruction, 'provided he exercises due care to preserve the due privacy of patients'. This is probably another first: the first occasion on which St Patrick's could claim to be a teaching hospital.[24]

Leeper's interest in the brain and its pathology was in keeping with one of the main trends in late nineteenth and early twentieth century psychiatry. A succession of great German neurologists had laid the basis for a rigorous study of abnormalities of the brain, particularly in relation to psychotic illness. Wilhelm Griesinger (1817-69), for instance, had argued that brain damage or disease was the key to all mental disorders; the great Emil Kraepelin (1856-1926) had made many important contributions, including the identification of *dementia praecox* and manic depression as the two major forms of psychosis; while Eugen Bleuler (1857-1939) went on to revise the whole concept of *dementia praecox* and to introduce the new classification of schizophrenia. Aside from this work in Germany, the period 1890 to 1914 also saw significant advances in France, with J. M. Charcot's (1825-95) and Pierre Janet's (1859-1947) investigations into hysteria and hypnosis; in England, with the publication in 1897 of the first volume of Havelock Ellis's (1859-1939) study of the psychology of sex; and, most notably, in Austria, with Sigmund Freud's (1856-1939) first publications exploring, through dreams, jokes and slips of the tongue, the workings of the unconscious mind. Much of this latter work, including Freud's, was not to have any real impact in the English-speaking world till after the psychic traumas created by the First World War. Kraepelin's work had, however, included important studies of the symptoms of general paralysis of the insane and it is probable that syphilis and its effects on the central nervous system were the main areas in which Leeper was interested. His early reports make clear that he was shocked by the large number of general paralysis patients in the hospital. In such circumstances an interest in neuro-syphilis would be natural. Aside from brain abnormalities and general paralysis, what his other research interests were is, unfortunately, not clear from the surviving documentation.[25]

Some measure of Leeper's achievement in the first few years of his superintendentship can be gauged by a glance at the prospectuses that the hospital published in 1902 and 1905. In 1902 the governors were able to issue a prospectus for St Edmundsbury, setting out the advantages of the institution, with flattering extracts from the inspectors' 1899, 1901 and 1902 reports. 'So different is everything from the traditions of Irish asylums for the insane', boasted the board, 'that one can hardly realise that this delightful place is to be used for such a purpose.' Photographs illustrating the brochure showed the spacious drawing room, the well-furnished reading room, the dining room, with formally set table, and the extensive grounds and woods. The governors' confidence in St Edmundsbury was made clear in 1905 when they decided to erect a villa in the grounds for eight male patients and again in 1910 when they bought Woodville, a 126 acre farm, adjoining the St Edmundsbury grounds.[26]

By 1905 the board felt ready to produce a similar brochure for St Patrick's itself. This was illustrated with photographs of the staff, the ward corridors, a drawing room, the billiard room and the newly-laid out gardens and croquet lawn, and it included extracts from the inspectors' 1903 and 1904 reports. Said the governors:

> For a metropolitan asylum [St Patrick's Hospital] can lay just claim to be well off, both for extent and situation, as any similar institution in the United Kingdom. Ample space is afforded for exercise . . . The buildings are extensive . . . The dietary is liberal and varied . . . The recovery rate has been over 53 per cent on all admissions for the past five years . . . The patients

are allowed to receive visits from their relations weekly
... They can also receive at all times the visits of their
respective clergymen ... Entertainments, both indoor and
outdoor, are frequently given ... A large staff of trained,
experienced, and certified nurses and attendants is maintained
... Numbers of insane persons of the upper and middle
classes have been treated [though persons] of all ranks have
been continuously received in [St Patrick's] since its
foundation ...

While advancing the merits of the institution, the governors,
however, did not hide the financial strains that it was forced to
operate under. They admitted that, 'in times past', St Patrick's had
been 'heavily weighted by incurable cases'. Moreover, 'the action of
the late land laws [had] reduced the value of the endowments of the
hospital' and 'in recent years' it had been rated and taxed by the
Dublin corporation. The governors made clear that the hospital
needed more patients from the 'upper and middle classes' and, in a
plea to doctors, they urged an end to the 'deportation of Irish
patients to Scotch and English asylums, in no sense superior to their
own ...'[27]

But, even higher paying patients could not cover the cost of all the
reforms made between 1899 and 1905. A major change in the
hospital's method of financing its work was essential.

THE SALE OF THE ESTATES

We saw in the previous chapter that during the 1880s an alliance of
discontented tenants and home rule MPs had been instrumental in
pressuring the British government into passing a series of land acts.
At first these acts had aimed essentially to give tenants a greater say
in matters relating to their holdings, particularly as regards the level
of rents. But, by the late 1880s, land purchase acts were reaching the
statute books. Under these the government offered to lend tenants
the money with which to purchase their holdings from the landlords. At first the landlords were reluctant to sell, partly because
they did not consider the terms offered very attractive. But in 1903
the Wyndham Act, in addition to facilitating the sale of whole
estates instead of individual holdings, held out to landlords the
incentive of a bonus, in the form of a percentage of the purchase
price. Some of the tenants' leaders, notably Michael Davitt, opposed
the act as being too favourable to the landlords. Yet, in practice, the
Wyndham Act proved highly successful, opening the way for a
flood of sales. Between 1903 and 1909, when compulsory sale was

introduced, over a quarter of a million holdings were purchased by their tenants for some 28 million pounds.[28]

If the hospital's tenants had been eager in the early 1880s to have their rents adjudicated by the land court, from 1903 they showed an equal eagerness to buy their holdings. In December of that year tenants from both the Saggart and Ferns estates petitioned the board of governors on the subject of land purchase. The governors replied that they were 'not at present anxious to part with their estates'. When both groups of tenants petitioned again in 1905 the governors sought to placate them by offering generous rent reductions ranging from fifteen to twenty-five per cent.[29] It might have appeared that the board was not the least interested in selling its estate, but the contrary was in fact true. The governors were well aware that, if the many recent reforms undertaken were to be maintained and hopefully extended, then it was vital that the hospital should be put on a far more secure financial footing. The reforms, notably the purchase of St Edmundsbury, had been paid for out of the hospital's investments. But, by 1905, this reservoir of funds was almost exhausted and thus both a more substantial and a more reliable income was desperately required. The admission of more short-term, high fee-paying patients after 1899 certainly boosted the revenue derived from patients. But, with the political climate favouring tenants' rights over landlords' incomes, there was no way that the estate revenue could be boosted similarly. The board's estate sub-committee was thus given the task of deciding if it would be more advantageous as regards income for the hospital to sell the estate and invest the resulting monies in stocks and shares.

In a report discussed by the board at its January 1906 meeting, the sub-committee came out strongly in favour of sale under the terms of the Wyndham Act. With prices for holdings ranging from 21.54 years to 27.69 years of the annual rent charge, plus a 7 per cent bonus, the sub-committee reckoned the governors would receive £56,582 for their Saggart estate. Invested at $3\frac{1}{2}$ per cent interest, this capital sum would yield an annual income of £1,980—the current annual rental for Saggart was £1,930. The sale of the Ferns estate, after the payment of the various substantial charges that encumbered it, would yield £15,697. If invested, this sum would produce an annual income of £566, compared with the current rental income of £570.[30] Thus the hospital could derive an income from investments equivalent to that derived from the estate. Moreover investments would not require the constant, expensive and time-consuming management that was necessary for the estate. Increasingly throughout the nineteenth century it had been the estate and its problems, and not the hospital and its patients, that had dominated board meetings. So, by ridding themselves of their estate, the governors would not only secure a potentially greater and more reliable income, they would also free themselves from the onerous burdens of Irish landlordism.

Most of the Saggart and Ferns estates appears to have been sold off between 1906 and 1908. Information on Ferns is rather scanty, but, by December 1908, eighty-five agreements had been sealed with Saggart tenants, involving a total purchase price of a little over £46,000. The sale of some parts of the estate, however, proved a far more protracted process. The Walsh holding, one of the largest, was not sold till 1920, when it realised over £5,700; while the 120 acres held by Major William Verschoyle Campbell, who succeeded his uncle, W. H. F. Verschoyle, as land agent in 1941, was acquired by the land commission for £2,000 as late as 1937.[31]

The governors were paid by the land commission partly in cash and partly in stock which they sold and re-invested. By 1916, when the hospital published its first annual report, it had investments with a face value of over £50,000, mainly in Irish and English railway companies and Canadian and Australian stock. These investments were divided into three groups, according to the hospital's main financial needs: interest on the largest, or endowment, group was used to buy more stock; interest on the pension group provided revenue to pay staff pensions under the scheme set up in 1914; while interest on revenue investments produced money towards the day-to-day running costs of the institution.[32] These investments, largely resulting from the sale of Saggart and Ferns, provided a vital financial cushion, ensuring that even if St Patrick's, St Edmundsbury and the farm lost substantial sums of money, the hospital would not face the sort of financial catastrophe that had loomed on several occasions between 1850 and 1900.

Aside from interest on investments and patient fees, the other main source of revenue continued to be rents. In the 1920s, for example, the hospital was getting around £800 a year from its property. Some of this came from the estate in Dublin, which had not been sold along with the rural estates. The main stumbling block to sale was the Ashbourne Grammar School which owned the head rent of the Francis Street area. In 1921 and again in 1935 the governors made strenuous efforts to persuade the school to agree to sale: in the latter year they actually offered the estate, valued at £4,700, to the school for £3,000. But the school would neither allow the hospital to sell the estate to someone else, nor agree to buy it itself. Meanwhile the properties continued to deteriorate. By the early 1930s the rents from Francis Street hardly covered the £210 annual head rent owed to the grammar school. Moreover the Dublin corporation was moving to acquire derelict sites in Spitalfields and to condemn houses in Francis Street. In such cases the hospital was only entitled to paltry compensation. Some of the Goldenbridge property had been acquired in 1930 by the corporation for housing and road widening schemes with minimal return to the hospital. So, whereas the hospital had ceased to be a substantial landlord by 1914, the seeming intractable problems of the Dublin estate continued into the 1930s and beyond.[33]

The governors, however, were not only engaged at this time in divesting themselves of land, they also purchased a small but crucial amount. As we saw in Chapter 2, the original hospital building had been constructed on a mere half acre of land provided by Steevens Hospital. Subsequently some twelve to thirteen acres had been leased from several landlords, notably Steevens, the Trench family and the corporation. The hospital was thus not only short of land, but such land that it had was held on a far from secure basis. The Trench land, comprising the gentlemen's garden and fronting Steevens Lane, had been purchased in two lots in 1866 and 1889. In 1911, after Steevens Hospital had served them with a notice to quit, the governors decided to purchase the land to the north that they had leased since 1816. This was acquired in 1912 for £1,100. The lease on the corporation land fronting Bow Lane to the west expired in 1911, and, though the governors wished to buy the site, the corporation would only agree to another thirty-one year lease. But in 1915 the hospital was able to extend its grounds further by buying from Guinness's Brewery for £2,000 the area known as Christchurch Fields which lay to the northwest. Part of this was then leased to Steevens in exchange for a portion of the old graveyard. These purchases finally secured the hospital's position after over 150 years at the site. They would suggest that all thought of moving the whole institution to the country—a proposition seriously entertained in the 1890s—had finally been abandoned. Certainly when Leeper urged the governors in 1911 to purchase the land leased from Steevens, he informed them that he had consulted Rooke and Rooke, who were of the opinion that the charter precluded such a move. Under the provisions of Swift's will, enshrined in the charter, St Patrick's had to be located 'near' Steevens. During this period the governors also consolidated their position at Lucan by purchasing the 126-acre Woodville farm from Lord Annaly for £2,600. They did not want the property, which adjoined St Edmundsbury, falling into the hands of another institution, such as a school, and they also wished to increase the size of their farm.[34]

If the first five years after Leeper's appointment in 1899 saw major reforms in the admission procedures, living conditions and staffing of the hospital, the decade before 1914 saw equally crucial changes in the financing of the institution. On its sites at Dublin and Lucan it now had a far more secure and reliable income with which to pursue its operations. Such new-found strength was moreover to be crucial in helping the hospital weather the political and economic storms of the decade after 1914.

WARS AND REBELLIONS: THE HOSPITAL UNDER FIRE

If the sale of most of the estate freed the governors from having to deal with the demands of increasingly militant tenants, the spread of trade unionism in Ireland after 1900 created a new problem for them: that of militant workers. In the past hospital employees had been hired, fired, paid, fined and pensioned, all at the governors' discretion; the workers themselves had little or no say in the matter. The nursing staff were called 'servants' and, like domestic servants in middle- or upper-class homes, they were expected to live-in and to work long hours and, after the 1830s, were very poorly paid for their efforts. They were treated in fact as unskilled labour and physical strength and good health were the basic qualifications for the job. Yet St Patrick's never seems to have had much difficulty in finding such staff. Given the lack of employment opportunities for unskilled workers in late nineteenth-century Dublin, most were probably grateful for a secure, full-time job of any sort. Leeper's upgrading of the staff, however, altered this situation. Nurses and attendants with the Medico-Psychological Association's certificate were trained workers and not mere labourers and, if the hospital wanted to retain such skilled staff, it had to offer them more attractive wages and conditions. At the same time that the hospital was upgrading its staff, trade unions were beginning to reach out to groups like asylum workers and manual labourers, who had not previously been organised. Associations of asylum workers had existed in Ireland since the 1890s, but it was not till 1917 that an Irish Asylum Workers Union was formed.[35] Earlier, in 1909, the Irish Transport Workers Union, later the Irish Transport and General Workers Union (ITGWU), had been established in Dublin by dockers and carters, under the leadership of Jim Larkin. From then till Larkin broke away in 1924 to form the Workers Union of Ireland, the ITGWU was to the fore in organising unskilled and semi-skilled workers. The growth of such unions was undoubtedly assisted by the political upheavels of the period 1914-1922. The First World War, for instance, took away 200,000 young workers, 49,000 of whom never returned, and left in their wake a labour shortage, which strengthened the bargaining power of the unions.

The outbreak of the war in August 1914 also led to severe price inflation and this was the most immediate impact that the fighting had on the hospital. Between 1915 and 1920, after which inflation began to ease, the cost of provisions and groceries for St Patrick's (excluding St Edmundsbury) increased by 105 per cent, fuel and light by 125 per cent, while salaries and wages went up by over 90 per cent. Fuel, mainly in the form of coal, rose particularly sharply in price: Tedcastle's prices doubled between 1913 and 1916. But, with three miles of heating pipes in the old building alone, the hospital needed at least seven tons of coal a week. Price was not the only problem, however, for by 1918 rationing had been introduced and the hospital had to justify its consumption to the Coal Controller's Department.[36]

Price inflation not only hit the hospital, but also its staff, leading to demands for pay rises. In 1915 the governors introduced a war bonus: a sum paid to staff, over and above their annual wages, for the duration of the war, in order to compensate them for price increases. But this measure did not head off discontent, as the bonus fell short of the inflation rate. Initially the most militant of the hospital's employees were the farm labourers at Lucan. In July 1914, just before the outbreak of war, thirteen of them petitioned successfully to have their weekly wage raised to sixteen shillings a week. A little over a year later, in October 1915, the governors awarded them one shilling a week extra, plus five shillings a month in the form of a war bonus. But in November 1916 the labourers petitioned again, this time for eighteen shillings a week, plus five shillings a month, and, after a short strike, the governors gave in to their demands. This would seem to be the first occasion on which any of the hospital's employees staged a strike. Apparently it occurred without direct union involvement for negotiations were conducted between the governors, Leeper and the men. Six months later, however, when the farm labourers demanded another pay rise, they were represented in their dealings with the board by the ITGWU. By October there had been no response from the board and so the men staged their second strike in twelve months. But they called it off two days later when Leeper explained to them that the governors would take no action pending the setting up of an agricultural wages board promised by the government. In December the new board awarded the men twenty-five shillings a week, which both they and the governors accepted.[37]

This agreement was short lived, however, for, in March 1918, the men were on strike again after the ITGWU demand for thirty shillings a week had been rejected by the governors. If granted, this would have amounted to a 100 per cent pay rise in less than four years, yet in fact it would barely have enabled the men to keep pace with price inflation. The cost of living index, set at 100 in 1914, had reached 203 by 1918 and continued to rise till in 1920 it was 249. But in 1918 the governors decided that Leeper, representing the hospital, should join the Co. Dublin Farmers Association, an organisation of landowners, and that they should abide by the association's policy, particularly with regard to wage rates. Clearly the hospital, facing a powerful union on its own, was feeling somewhat isolated. If its labourers had found strength in numbers, by joining a farmers' union, the hospital was merely following their example. Thereafter the governors accepted the outcome of negotiations between the ITGWU and the farmers' union and, as a result, labourers' wages rose to thirty-two shillings a week in 1918 and forty-three shillings in 1920. These were certainly substantial increases, but the Lucan farm was making healthy profits between 1916 and 1920 due to the high cost of agricultural produce and the lack of foreign competition. One economic historian has suggested that the income levels attained by Irish farmers in the south in 1919-20 were not substantially exceeded till the 1950s. Only when losses began to accumulate, as prices fell drastically after 1920, did the governors begin seriously to resist pay rises and eventually in fact to demand pay cuts.[38]

The nursing staff were slower to organise than the farm labourers and far less ready to resort to the strike weapon. In 1916-17, after agitation by the attendants, they received pay rises to compensate them for inflation and in 1920 pay scales were revised, mainly to eliminate the war bonus.

NURSES AND ATTENDANTS ANNUAL PAY, 1917 AND 1920

	Nurse		Attendant	
	1917	1920	1917	1920
	£	£	£	£
On appointment	10	20	20	30
After one year	15	23	25	33
On Prelim.Cert.	20	26	30	36
On Final Cert.	25	30	35	40
Charge/Night	30	35	45	50[39]
	+ 25% bonus		+25% bonus	

Staff in the public asylums seem to have been more militant, for, between 1917 and 1924, the Irish Asylum Workers Union led a series of bitter strikes for better conditions. In 1919, for instance, the staff of the Monaghan asylum barricaded the building, raised the red flag and, cheered on by the patients, held off nearly 200 police for several days until persuaded to negotiate. But, when the nursing staff at St Patrick's sought union representation, they turned to the ITGWU rather than to the Asylum Workers' Union. Pay was not the only issue that concerned them. In 1923 the ITGWU was pressing the governors to introduce shorter working hours. The union was also keen to establish a closed shop for it informed the governors that, if non-union staff had not joined the union by 12 June 1923, 'penalties' would be imposed. The governors seem to have ignored this demand and, after 1923, splits in the union movement plus deteriorating economic conditions undermined the strength of organised labour. Nevertheless, the eight or nine years after 1914 had witnessed the hospital's employees, whether labouring or nursing, organising and, for the first time, exerting their power, mainly in support of demands for better pay. The old days, when the governors or the medical superintendent could simply dictate to the staff, were gone for good.[40]

The unionisation of the staff was a major development, yet it was somewhat overshadowed by the dramatic political upheavals of the years 1916 to 1922, notably the Easter rising, the Anglo-Irish war and the civil war. As in the past, in the case of events like the 1798 rebellion, the Napoleonic wars, the Famine and the land war, St Patrick's Hospital was by no means immune from the vicissitudes of Irish history. Despite high walls and restricted access, neither the building nor the patients could escape the turmoil that the rising and the civil war particularly brought to Dublin city.

Appendix 6 consists of a copy of Dr Leeper's report to the board concerning the hospital's experiences during the 1916 Easter rising. Some of the bitterest fighting of that bloody week took place in and around the South Dublin Union: the old workhouse, now the site of James's Hospital. The workhouse commanded the main road between Dublin city and the Royal Hospital at Kilmainham, the headquarters of the British army in Ireland, and was also close to both the Richmond and Islandbridge barracks. By interdicting this route the rebels, led by Eamonn Ceannt and Cathal Brugha, hoped to disrupt the dispatch of reinforcements to the city centre and to isolate the army headquarters. The British, on the other hand, were equally determined that the link between the capital and Kilmainham should be kept open. But, although numbering only about forty men, the insurgents held out in the face of ferocious attack from Easter Monday till the following Sunday, when the general surrender took place. As well as mounting an assault from James Street, the British kept the site under almost continuous fire from the Royal Hospital to the north-west, from Rialto to the south and from Kingsbridge (Heuston) Station to the north. It was during these fusillades that the top storey of St Patrick's Hospital was hit. As Leeper indicates in his report, when the British attempted to fire on the workhouse from Kingsbridge, the hospital was directly in the line of fire and thus found itself in the centre of a battlefield. Both sides also made effective use of snipers. In such circumstances, one can understand Leeper's admiration for the elderly chaplain, the Rev. J. C. Irwin, and the carters, John Lane and John Tully, in making repeated trips to the hospital at the risk of their own lives. Leeper probably welcomed the presence of Irwin as much because he was one of the most senior governors as because he was a chaplain. For, as he says, perhaps a trifle melodramatically, the responsibility of possibly having to decide whether to surrender or defend the hospital was an onerous one and belonged more properly to the governors than to himself. If Leeper was shaken by his experience under fire, one can only wonder at its effect on the already precarious mental health of his patients.[41]

The governors responded to the ordeal of Easter 1916 by taking out substantially increased insurance to cover the threat of fire to the two hospitals and the farm buildings. By 1921 they were again sufficiently alarmed by the political state of the country to invest in more insurance. They insured the farm van, the two motor cars and cash in transit to and from the bank, with Lloyds of London against loss, through 'riot, civil commotion etc.' This proved a wise move. A year later, in July 1922, the governors were unable to meet in the hospital on the 3rd, owing to 'conflict between nationalist troops and irregulars'. This is a reference to the fierce fighting between pro- and anti-treaty forces that took place in Dublin during late June and early July 1922, and which marked the outbreak of the civil war. From 28 to 30 June the Four Courts, occupied by a republican garrison, had been shelled and machine-gunned by the national army. The firing, however, was often wildly inaccurate. A number of shells, for instance, landed in the grounds of the Royal Hospital, much to the annoyance of the British army officers, who still had their headquarters in the building. Unlike 1916, St Patrick's does not seem to have been hit on this occasion, but the fighting would have been clearly visible from the hospital building. In his report of 1 July 1922 Leeper informed the governors that:

> During the week past there has been continuous firing about the place and the rest of the patients has been greatly broken by the nightly cannonades and machine-gun fire about the hospital. So far no one in your service has been injured, but many have run great risks coming and going in the discharge of their duties.

After the destruction and fall of the Four Courts, the republicans occupied large parts of Sackville (O'Connell) Street and sporadic fighting continued across the city during the first week of July. Snipers roamed the rooftops and a number of non-combatants were shot down in the cross-fire. That the governors did not want to travel to the hospital for their meeting in such circumstances is hardly surprising.[42]

When they were finally able to assemble at the end of the month, they noted, tactfully, in their minutes, that St Edmundsbury's Laundanlette car had been 'removed' by 'armed forces'—the word 'armed' was written in to replace 'government', which had been crossed out. The 'removal' of the car had obviously not occurred peacefully, for the driver, Michael McDonald, was in Steevens Hospital as a result of the incident. The car was not recovered and in November the board decided to launch a claim for damages against the provisional government. Nor was McDonald able to resume his duties: by February 1923 the board was paying him a pension of twenty-six shillings a week. But, although the hospital had been under fire in 1916 and, to a lesser extent, in 1922, McDonald seems to have been the only casualty that it sustained.[43]

The effect of these events on the mental health of the patients is, however, another matter. In September 1922, during the civil war, Leeper was compaining that:

> The constant firing around the city is very distressing to many of the patients and affects many who suffer from delusions of persecution in a marked manner. Almost every night there is constant firing in Bow Lane and all about the buildings on James Street.

Hallaran, in the context of the 1798 rebellion, had argued that wars and rebellions had a detrimental effect upon the mental health of certain susceptible people. A perusal of the hospital's patient register and case-books for the period from 1914 to 1923 provides much evidence in support of this view. During the war a number of soldiers were admitted suffering from the effects of their combat experience. English asylums at the time were full of the victims of what was called 'shell shock', and in fact it was the medical profession's rather reluctant recognition of the reality and serious-ness of this disorder that gave a much-needed boost to psychiatric medicine and, in particular, to the theories and techniques of psychoanalysis. In Ireland, however, domestic upheavals com-pounded the problem. Actually, there were more patients admitted to St Patrick's due to the effects of the 'Sinn Fein rebellion', 'disturbances' and the 'condition of the country' than there were due to military service. But war work certainly took its toll: for instance, a number of workers in munitions factories were admitted in 1917-18. And even the armistice brought its problems: Alice H., a thirty-six year old, Protestant cook from Pembroke Road, admitted in May 1919, had been suffering from 'acute excitable mania' since 11 November 1918, caused, according to the patient register, by 'the sudden excitement of peace being proclaimed'.[44]

Between 1914 and 1918 soldiers, war workers, women with sons or husbands at the front and Dubliners, who had experienced the 1916 rising at first hand, all figured significantly in admissions. But the insecurities and anxieties of the immediate post-war years in Ireland also took a heavy toll. The following cases provide a fair example of the sort of problems that the hospital was called upon to treat during the years that saw the birth of the new Irish state. Hugh M., a thirty-five year old, Catholic postman from Newry, was admitted in March 1921 suffering from 'delusions' after being 'held up' three times while on duty; John F., a fifty-three year old, Catholic farmer from Strokestown, Co. Roscommon, was admitted in November 1922 with 'mania' brought on by 'raids'; Thomas S., a forty-eight year old, Catholic 'collector', living in Parnell Square, was admitted in March 1923 in an over-excited state, the 'result of a beating from crown forces'; John G., a forty-seven year old, Protestant former resident magistrate from Mullingar, was admitted in June 1923 suffering from 'delusions' brought on by the 'anxiety' of his duties as a magistrate; George S., a twenty-eight year old, Protestant farmer from Colooney, Co. Sligo, was admitted in September 1923 suffering from 'delusions' caused by 'visits from armed raiders'; while Patrick S., a thirty-nine year old, Catholic tailor from Kells, Co. Meath, was admitted in December 1924 with 'mania' due to 'internment during political disturbances'. Farmers appear to have suffered particularly during these troubled years, as the table below suggests:

FARMERS ADMITTED TO ST PATRICK'S, 1916-24

Year	Farmers as % of Total Male Admissions
1916	5
1917	15
1918	11
1919	17
1920	30
1921	37
1922	40
1923	39
1924	8

Although their illnesses varied, most were ascribed in the patients' register to 'worry' associated with the state of the country or their business affairs or both.[45]

Another group particularly susceptible to mental breakdown in the face of political upheaval were 'gentlewomen', that is women from affluent backgrounds, either among the Anglo-Irish gentry or the successful Dublin professional and commercial classes. Two such women were admitted to St Edmundsbury in 1919. Vilma De R., a fifty-one year old Catholic from Burlington Road, was admitted by her husband in September 1919 in an extremely depressed and suicidal state and died in St Edmundsbury three months later. She suffered from vivid delusions, which took an interesting form. She heard shooting going on constantly round the house, was convinced that men were trying to break in and believed that the room she was in was full of the heads of murdered people, including her husband. At night she claimed a jazz band played on the roof and that tumbrils passed up and down the corridor. Given the virtual war raging in Ireland in 1919, it is not hard to understand that a wealthy, disturbed woman should have delusions involving armed attacks on her house and tumbrils passing to and fro in the middle of the night. Another woman with interesting delusions was the Hon. Mrs Hugh H., a forty-seven year old, American widow from Co. Wicklow, admitted by her brother-in-law, Lord W., in February 1919. She had been ill since 1915, suffering from 'chronic delusional insanity', and she remained a patient in St Edmundsbury till her death from cancer in 1941. Her delusions were also by no means inexplicable. According to the case-book, she claimed her husband had been murdered by the butler and she lived in constant fear of the 'domestics', whom she was convinced were plotting to claim her life as well. Attacks on big houses and their occupants became more prevalent after 1919, but even in 1919 Anglo-Irish families were leaving the country in substantial numbers. Most were from the west; few from Co. Wicklow. Yet, it is hard to believe that Mrs H.'s fear of her domestic staff was not influenced by the hostility that many Irish people, and particularly nationalists, felt for the old landlord class.[46]

With a significant number of inmates suffering from delusions of persecution produced by the violence of the times, it is no wonder that Leeper became alarmed for patients' mental health when the hospital was under fire in 1916 and 1922.

IN A NEW STATE: GROWTH AND CONSOLIDATION

The Irish Free State officially came into existence on 7 December 1922, but its future was not really secured till May 1923 when the republicans announced a ceasefire, thus ending the bitter civil war. Although, as individuals, most of the governors had probably not been sympathetic to the nationalist cause, as a board, they quickly adapted to the new political reality. Late in 1923, for instance, they decided to buy £10,000 worth of stock in the first national loan of the Free State government, although the interest rate was a relatively low 5 per cent. This decision to invest money in the new state was a striking gesture of confidence and commitment. In the event the loan was over-subscribed and the governors were able to obtain only £9,000 worth of stock. But in 1927 they secured a further £2,000 worth of shares in the second state loan and in 1932 £3,000 worth in the third.[47]

The break with Britain affected the board most directly through the abolition of the office of lord chancellor. The lord chancellor had always been the most senior of the *ex officio* governors and, by virtue of his responsibility for chancery lunatics, he had been closely involved in the hospital's affairs. Lord chancellors like Newport (1739-57), Clare (1789-1802) and Sugden (1841-6) had all played important roles at critical times in St Patrick's history. In the new state the lord chancellor was replaced by the chief justice, who presided over the supreme court, the highest court of appeal. The governors were anxious to add the chief justice to the board, but in order to do this they first had to have their royal charter recognised by the new government. There were of course many institutions in Ireland at the time deriving rights and privileges from royal charters issued by various British monarchs. To regularise this state of affairs, the Dáil passed in 1926 the Adaptation of Charters Act, which recognised such charters and provided for their adaptation to the new circumstances prevailing in the Free State. The governors of St Patrick's quickly moved to obtain an order under the act from the executive council, or cabinet, substituting the chief justice for the lord chancellor on their board.[48]

The first chief justice was Hugh Kennedy, a barrister and former king's counsel, who had acted as the main legal adviser to the provisional government and had been the first attorney general of the new state. Kennedy played a key role in advising Michael Collins and later William T. Cosgrave on the multitude of complex legal issues arising from the ending of British rule. He had also been a member of the committee which drafted the 1922 constitution. Fortunately for St Patrick's, Kennedy took a keen interest in the hospital's affairs. In 1925, before he had been formally added to the board, he inspected St Edmundsbury, which largely housed chancery patients, for the chief justice had inherited the lord chancellor's responsibilities as regards these patients. He actually attended his first meeting as a governor in July 1926 and, till his death ten years later, he regularly chaired board meetings and acted on more than one occasion as visiting governor.[49] He was probably more active on the hospital's behalf than any lord chancellor since Sugden in the 1840s. On his death he was succeeded as chief justice by Timothy Sullivan, while at about the same time the president of the high court, Conor Maguire, was elected to fill a vacancy on the board. When Maguire himself became chief justice in 1946, he moved from an elected to an *ex officio* governorship. Thus St Patrick's was well served by the leading judges of the new Irish state.

In 1937 the governors established a sub-committee to examine the hospital's bye-laws, with a view to eliminating those considered obsolete. In its report this committee suggested, among other things, that a casting vote be given to the chairman of the board, that new *ex officio* governors be selected to replace the archbishops of Armagh and Dublin, who were unable to attend regularly, and that the board forfeit its power to dismiss senior hospital employees without notice or explanation. Clearly this was an attempt to bring the board of governors into line with changing circumstances, and particularly to eliminate governors who were not active in the hospital's affairs. The board seems to have hoped to replace the archbishop of Armagh with the archdeacon of Dublin. A number of archdeacons had served as elected governors over the years. There is no indication of who the board was proposing to replace the archbishop of Dublin with, but it is probable that the governors, as well as hoping to improve attendance, aimed to reduce Protestant clerical influence. Of the five *ex officio* governors, all except the chief justice were senior Protestant clergymen. The board may have wanted to replace the archbishop of Dublin with a layman, or, even possibly, with a senior Catholic cleric. The hospital's solicitors, Rooke and Rooke, hoped that these changes could be brought about by an executive order under the Adaptation of Charters Act, as had been the replacement of the lord chancellor in 1926. But the Department of the President of the Executive Council decided that a private bill in the Dáil would be necessary for such major amendments to the charter. In light of this judgment the governors decided only to pursue such revisions as could be undertaken within their existing powers. This effectively ruled out any change in the composition of the board, and in fact its structure has remained the same to the present day.[50]

Notwithstanding these changes, or attempted changes, there was actually a remarkable degree of continuity in the management of St Patrick's, and indeed of other mental hospitals, in the years after 1922. The two lunacy inspectors were replaced in 1923 by a single inspector, Dr Daniel Kelly, and, as we have seen, the chief justice took over the role previously exercised by the lord chancellor as regards chancery lunatics. In 1925 a commission was set up to investigate relief offered to the sick and destitute poor, including the mentally ill. Leeper gave evidence to this enquiry. But, although it issued a fairly critical report, at least as far as the state mental hospitals were concerned, no major action was undertaken till the passing of the Mental Treatment Act in 1945. In fact, as regards mental hospitals, the first twenty years of Irish government saw little more than a continuation of the system created under British rule.[51]

Despite the addition of the chief justice and the president of the high court, and the abortive attempt to remove the Protestant archbishops, continuity was also the hallmark of St Patrick's board of governors. Members of the so-called Protestant ascendancy continued to be dominant. In the 1920s and 1930s the elected governors included two archdeacons of Dublin; Captain Anthony Maude, who had replaced Thomas Greene as secretary of the representative body of the Church of Ireland; five former British army officers, including Major John Cusack, a grandson of Surgeon Cusack; three land agents, including Richard Maunsell, who was active in various organisations representing landlords' interests; a number of company directors; and also, for the first time, a stockbroker. The connection with Guinness's Brewery was also maintained, notably in the persons of Henry Seymour Guinness, assistant managing director of the company and a senator in the new Irish parliament, and Sir John Lumsden, chief medical officer of Guinness's dispensary. In 1938 Leeper's son-in-law, H.S. McClelland, a solicitor, was also added to the board.

During these years, however, two of the most interesting governors were descendants of Swift. St Patrick's had begun by maintaining close connections with the Swift family: its first master, William Dryden, and its first visiting surgeon, John Whiteway, were both relatives of the Dean, while on the minus side, its chief debtor for many years was Deane Swift. But, by the beginning of the nineteenth century, these links had largely been severed, though John Pomeroy, the board's treasurer from 1810 to 1833, was a distant relative by marriage. The Swift connection was not resumed till 1909, when Ernest Godwin Swifte K.C. was elected to the board, and 1921, when John Gordon Swift MacNeill K.C. was also elected. These two make an interesting study in contrasts, reflecting perhaps some of the contradictions inherent in their illustrious ancestor. Swift MacNeill was a distinguished jurist, a professor of constitutional law, first in King's Inns and later University College, Dublin, and the author of a number of works on Irish legal and political affairs. He was also, perhaps surprisingly, nationalist MP for Donegal South from 1887 to 1918. This makes him the first and only former home rule MP to sit on the board of governors. Sir Ernest Swifte, as he became in 1921, had rather different sympathies. He was also a barrister, but had been a Dublin police magistrate for many years. He is chiefly remembered today as the magistrate whose banning of a meeting organised by Jim Larkin during the 1913 Dublin transport strike led to serious clashes between police and people in Sackville (O'Connell) Street, known as Bloody Sunday, and the jailing of both Larkin and James Connolly.[52]

It is possible that Dr Leeper, although not a member of the board, may have had a hand in the elections of both Swifte and Swift MacNeill, for he was deeply interested in the hospital's history and particularly in its connection with Swift. It was largely through his efforts that the hospital acquired its important collection of Swift memorabilia. The governors, originally being composed of Swift's executors, had inherited most of the papers relating to his estate. For many years these were of more than academic interest, for it was on the basis of them that the governors struggled to recover Swift's loans. Most of Swift's possessions were distributed among his friends or sold, but, in 1771, being in need of 'a press for containing deeds and papers', the governors acquired 'the founder's escritoire', or writing desk. Presumably Dean Corbet gave permission for it to be used and it was moved from the Deanery to Marsh's Library. There it remained till 1829, when, the governors having decided in the previous year to hold their meetings at St Patrick's, it was moved to the hospital, where it has remained ever since.[53] Up until the 1920s then, the writing desk was the only substantial object, actually having belonged to Swift, that the hospital owned. But after 1920 Leeper began acquiring memorabilia, with the intention of establishing a Swift museum in the hospital.

At present the hospital has four portraits of Swift. One, of unknown authorship and date, was presented to the hospital by Sir Ralph Cusack in 1882, but the other three were acquired through Leeper's efforts. In 1925 the governors authorised him to pay not more than sixty guineas for portraits of Swift, Stella and Vanessa, belonging to Major Connellan of Coolmore, Co. Kilkenny; while in 1932 Leeper, then president of the Royal Medico-Psychological Association, presented the hospital with a copy of Charles Jervas's portrait in the National Gallery, London, on the association's behalf. Finally, in 1937, Leeper presented another portrait, one he had obtained 'many years ago' for £25 at an auction in Delville, Glasnevin, formerly the home of Swift's friend, Dean Delany.

Leeper clearly kept an eye open for auctions of 'Swiftiana'. In 1926 he paid £22 for a bust of Swift from Lucan House. In 1931 he was authorised to pay £7.10.0 at an auction for two examples of Wood's half pennies and in the same year he paid £10 for a wooden tea-caddy, with a portrait of Stella, formerly belonging to Mrs Delany. But, as well as purchases, Leeper was also able to persuade owners of 'Swiftiana' to donate material to the hospital. The most important donor was Mary Swift MacNeill, J. G. Swift MacNeill's sister. Neither brother nor sister had married and Mary Swift MacNeill wanted the family's collection of Swift memorabilia to go to a public institution. The hospital, given its association with Swift, the fact that her brother had been a governor and that Leeper was establishing a museum devoted to Swift, seemed the ideal recipient. She donated a miniature of Swift in a locket said to have belonged to Stella; a silver coffee pot and stand, a replica of a lost original presented by John Gay to Swift, who had given him the idea for *The Beggars Opera*; and Swift's silver snuff box. The executors' papers already provided the hospital with an important collection of Swift documents and so most of Leeper's acquisitions were pictures or objects. But in 1934 a codicil to Swift's will, written by Alexander McAulay in the late 1730s and endorsed by Swift, came up for auction in London. The original will had been destroyed in the Four Courts in 1922. The governors were naturally anxious therefore to secure the only surviving portion of the document that led to the establishment of the hospital. Fortunately they were able to do this for the sum of £25. Leeper had also at some stage acquired Swift's watch and in 1942, just after his death, his daughter donated this to the hospital in his memory. Thanks to Leeper's efforts, when Maurice Craig organised an exhibition in 1948 to celebrate the hospital's bicentenary, nearly a third of the material exhibited in the Royal College of Physicians in Dublin came from the St Patrick's own collection.[54]

The flurry of purchases and donations that took place in the early 1930s was probably partly inspired by the fitting up of a new boardroom for the governors. The board had previously met in one of the rooms on the ground floor at the front of the building. But in 1930-31 the governors, at Leeper's urging, asked W. M. Mitchell and Sons to fit up the former ladies drawing-room in Thomas Cooley's west wing as a boardroom. It was in their new, stately, panelled boardroom that the governors chose to display their impressive collection of 'Swiftiana'. At the same time the secretary/registrar moved into new offices beside the boardroom. Swift's writing desk, which had stored the hospital's most valuable documents for over 150 years, was superseded by a steel safe and, according to Albert

Coe, the registrar, 'the litter of two hundred years' was clearly away. What this 'litter' consisted of is not made clear, but it is doubtful that a student of the hospital's history would have dismissed two hundred years of accumulated documents as 'litter'.[55]

It is worth noting in this context that the hospital contains another interesting collection of historic objects, which have their own peculiar relationship to Swift. In the boardroom today and in the corridors outside are several benches which originally came from the Irish House of Commons in College Green, now the Bank of Ireland. How or even when the hospital acquired these is a mystery. The only reference to them contained in the governors' minute books deals with an abortive attempt in 1883 to sell them to Cecil Guinness, when the hospital was in the midst of a major financial crisis. The most likely source for the benches, however, is John Foster, who, at the time of the Act of Union, was both speaker of the Irish House of Commons and a long-serving governor. Foster had certainly helped the hospital on several occasions when it sought grants from parliament to defray the cost of repairs and extensions. As speaker, although he had personally opposed the Union, he would presumably have had a major say in the disbursement of the furnishings of the former commons chamber. Given Swift's poem 'The Legion Club', which ridiculed the Irish parliament by comparing it to a madhouse, it seems somehow appropriate that a number of the MPs' benches should have found a home in Swift's own hospital for the mad.[56]

After the extensions to St Patrick's built by Thomas Cooley in 1778-83 and Whitmore Davis in 1789-93, which increased its capacity to 150 patients, no major additions occurred for over one hundred years. The purchase of St Edmundsbury in 1898 and the erection of a villa for male patients in its grounds in 1905-7, allowed the hospital to accommodate around twenty-five extra patients at Lucan. But, at the main site in the city, the number of patients had declined progressively. The closing of the damp basement wards, plus the commandeering of patients' rooms to provide additional staff, treatment and recreational facilities, combined to reduce the hospital's capacity. By 1916 St Patrick's had accommodation for only around 115 patients. Leeper was eager to extend the old building, particularly to cater for more male patients, who were out-numbered two to one by women. In 1916, therefore, the governors authorised their architect, A. G. C. Millar, to erect extentions to the two original wings of the hospital. These contained bedrooms, bathrooms and day-rooms for some fifteen patients and were built at a cost of £5,000. Despite delays caused by strikes, the additions were largely completed by Easter 1916—just in time to come under fire from British soldiers in Kingsbridge Station. A further extension, to provide accommodation for about thirty male patients, was built in 1934-6 by W. M. Mitchell at a cost of £9,000. But, perhaps the most interesting additions to St Patrick's at this time were not the extra bedrooms provided in 1916 and 1936, but the new treatment facilities erected in the 1920s.[57]

In 1928 a new central block was built for electrical, dental, surgical and water treatments. The following year a solarium wing was added and in 1932 a foam bath was installed. A number of these additions reflected new developments in the physical treatment of mental illness and they illustrated Leeper's desire to keep the hospital abreast of new techniques. He himself was appointed examiner in mental diseases in the National University in 1924. In 1931 the Royal Medico-Psychological Association met in Dublin and a reception for the visitors was held at St Patrick's; the following year Leeper was elected president of the body. Leeper made frequent trips to England to attend meetings of the association and also to study the workings of English mental hospitals; in 1935 he visited Paris to investigate diathermy. Short-wave diathermy, which involved the application of electric currents to produce heat in the deeper tissues of the body, was employed to treat both schizophrenia and general paralysis. Violet ray therapy was also used at St Patrick's in cases of melancholia and schizophrenia; hydrotherapy and massage were used to counter alcohol and drug addiction; while continuous baths were employed to calm manic patients. This latter technique was of course an old one, but it was still popular in the 1920s and 1930s. Strait-jackets and padded rooms were also resorted to in such cases. Leeper, however, never seems to have been very keen on these methods of restraint and in 1928 Dr Kelly, the government inspector, reported that he was tending rather to confine both highly manic and highly depressed patients to bed.[58]

In 1924 a pathologist was employed by the hospital to study specimens taken from patients and to advise on sepsis. In 1927 a dentist was also added to the staff. He saw all patients on admission and twice a year thereafter. His employment reflected the belief that bad teeth could aggravate certain disorders, notably schizophrenia. The removal of teeth and also of tonsils became common practice in the hospital. Clearly Leeper's approach to mental illness was essentially a physical one: he believed that disturbances of the mind usually reflected bodily problems, and thus required medical treatments. Syphilis and its resulting general paralysis of the insane was a good example of this physical model. To combat tertiary syphilis Leeper, during the 1920s made extensive use of malaria therapy.

Infected mosquitoes or blood were imported by special delivery from England and the patient bitten or inoculated a number of times with the *plasmodium malariae*. Subsequent nursing and medical care of such patients demanded considerable skill if the disease was not to progress too far. But, experiments in Austria had found that a third of syphilitics so infected experienced complete remission. At the time, however, the process by which this occurred was not really understood.[59]

In 1932 Florence Shegog was employed by the hospital as a masseuse and in 1935 she began occupational therapy (OT) and gymnastics classes twice a week for the female patients. For, while Leeper put great stress on what Dr Kelly termed 'active medical treatment', he also appreciated the need to provide patients with recreation and amusement. In 1924 wireless sets were bought for both St Patrick's and St Edmundsbury and in the following year the governors decided to build a cinema in St Patrick's. This was designed by A. G. C. Millar and completed in 1926 at a total cost of £2,400. It was equipped with a Gaumont silent film projector and proved an immediate success: in 1929 Dr Kelly described it as 'the greatest source of interest and amusement'. Unfortunately no record seems to have survived of what films were actually shown. The advent of talking pictures in 1929 quickly put the hospital's cinema out of the date however, and in 1935 the governors authorised Albert Coe, the registrar/secretary, to inspect the equipment recently installed in Grangegorman Hospital (formerly the Richmond Asylum) to show talking pictures. On receiving Coe's favourable report the governors decided to spend £335 on similar equipment for St Patrick's.[60]

During the 1920s Dr Kelly praised not only the cinema, but also the ample supply of books and magazines, the regular gramophone record recitals, the indoor games, the drives undertaken in the hospital's two cars and the provision of a summer holiday house in Killiney. But in 1933 and again in 1934 he lamented that few patients were actively involved in work or even in hobbies. Several of the female patients did needlework and assisted in the laundry and on the wards, while a handful of the men were also engaged in ward work and in gardening. The old view that the mentally ill benefited from productive work, or at least creative recreation, still clearly held sway. It was probably as a result of Kelly's comments that in 1935 the hospital started OT and gymnastics classes. By 1938 nearly a quarter of all patients were attending these classes. As for treatments, 43 per cent were receiving massage, electrical or water therapy and a further 17 per cent short-wave treatment.[61]

The table immediately below illustrates some important features of

THE PATIENTS, 1905-28

	1905	1916	1923	1928
Number admitted	40	41	64	54
Number discharged	33	29	51	38
Number died	8	9	10	8
Number remaining 31 December	115	139	158	166
% of recoveries on admissions	52	54	47	42
% of deaths on daily average number resident	6	6	6	5
% over 65	37	24	21	8
Number of voluntary boarders (over 60) remaining 31 December	2	—	3	7 [62]

STATE OF THE HOSPITAL, 1937-8

	St Patrick's	St Edmundsbury
Patients		
Total Number	153	24
Free	4	—
Under Cost	84	18
Weekly Cost per Patient	£2.19.9	£7.1.9
Weekly Fee per Patient	£2.13.3	£6.2.2
Weekly Loss per Patient	£0.6.6	£0.19.7
Number Admitted Annually	79	8
Voluntary Boarders Admitted	47	—
Total Discharged	74	9
Discharged Recovered	40	?
Staff		
Number of Nurses	29	10
With Final RMPA Cert.	17	7
Number of Attendants	18	6
With Final RMPA Cert.	9	1

Finances

	£
Net Loss on Working Accounts:	
St Patrick's	3,463
St Edmundsbury	1,198
The Farm	61
Total Loss	4,722
Annual Income:	
Investments	4,503
Rents	358
Total Income	4,861
Surplus	139 [63]

St Patrick's and St Edmundsbury during the last years of Leeper's superintendentship. Firstly, on its basic function of caring for the mentally ill, the hospital lost substantial sums of money: some £4,500 per annum. Patient fees did not even cover the cost of patient maintenance, let alone other expenses, like salaries and wages. Free patients had been almost totally eliminated, but the majority of patients continued to pay less than the actual cost of their upkeep. St Patrick's, in this regard, thus lived up to its claim to be a charitable institution. It was only the income from investments that allowed the whole enterprise to remain solvent. Secondly, the first table shows that there was quite a high turnover of patients each year, so the number of long-term patients would have been relatively small. The recovery rate, in terms of admissions, was of the order of 40 to 50 per cent, which, at the time, was considered highly satisfactory. These statistics apply only to certified patients, but, under Leeper, the hospital had also begun admitting what were termed voluntary boarders. These were patients who agreed to enter the institution without being formally certified as mentally ill by two doctors. At first their numbers were small, but, by the end of the 1930s, they made up around one-third of admissions. Voluntary boarders usually suffered from less serious problems than certified patients and thus had a significantly higher turnover: in 1928, for instance, eleven were admitted and eight discharged during the course of the year. By extending the hospital's facilities to such patients, the governors considerably increased the scope of St Patrick's activities. This was very much in line with Leeper's policy of trying to attract people for whom there was a good chance of cure, rather than allowing the hospital to become full of elderly, difficult and incurable patients, as had happened in the nineteenth century. In opening the hospital to less seriously ill people, the governors were in advance of the public sector, for it was not until the Mental Treatment Act of 1945 that provision was made for voluntary admissions to the public mental hospitals.[64]

Over and above statistics, accounts, minutes and reports, in order to gain an impression of what life was like in St Patrick's in the 1920s and 1930s, we are fortunate in having several first-hand accounts. One of these accounts is that of a member of the medical staff, which will be discussed in the next chapter; another is that of a patient. Most of our sources for St Patrick's history reflect the views of those, like the governors, the medical superintendent and the lunacy inspectors, who were engaged in managing the hospital. The admission forms also sometimes afford us access to the views of patients' families. But the patients themselves are tantilisingly silent; although interspersed among the pages of the case-books are occasional letters, drawings and scraps of verse. A rare exception to this state of affairs, however, is the poet, Austin Clarke, who was admitted to St Patrick's in 1919 suffering from 'melancholia' and was discharged a little over a year later as 'relieved'. In 1966 Clarke published a long poem, entitled *Mnemosyne Lay in Dust*, which, amidst accounts of memories and dreams, included a number of vivid cameos of hospital life from the patient's point of view. Such a first-hand description is of course very valuable but, nevertheless, it needs to be treated with some caution. We must remember firstly, that it is a work of art, not a factual account; it does not aspire to accuracy of detail. Secondly, the poem appeared more than forty years after the events it deals with occurred. For both these reasons, the work's factual accuracy must remain in doubt. Even given these reservations, however, the poem still offers a fascinating perspective on hospital life. For one thing, it refers to and describes staff and patients by name. In Clarke's view—he goes by the name of 'Maurice Devane' in the poem—Dr Leeper is 'Tall, handsome, tweeded', 'quick-striding' and, as his name implies, 'always ready to leap'. But, at the same time, in the eyes of the young patient, the nearly sixty year old doctor is a 'duffering Victorian'. When 'Maurice' refuses food, it is Leeper, who, with the help of four attendants, force-feeds him by inserting a tube down his throat. Dr Rutherford, the assistant medical officer, is to 'Maurice' 'mad-eyed', but 'agreeable in word'. Clarke also offers a number of telling sketches of male patients: one, with 'the rage of syphilis . . . in his brain'; another, a 'dangerous lunatic', a 'machine in need of constant supervision'; and a third, who 'claimed he was the bastard/ Of George the Third'. The poem goes on to describe briefly, but often vividly, small scenes of everyday hospital life: the night attendants on winter evenings sitting around the fire and discussing the latest sporting results; an elderly patient dirtying his bed and having it changed by an attendant; male patients wandering aimlessly round the garden; 'Maurice' being confined to a padded cell in the middle of the night; and later being taken for a walk in Phoenix Park by an attendant. *Mnemosyne Lay in Dust* is undoubtedly an idiosyncratic view of St Patrick's, but it does convey various features of patient life from the patient's perspective; a perspective different from, but no less valuable than the ones found in the governors' minute books or the superintendent's reports.[65]

Leeper was medical superintendent of St Patrick's for over forty years and his identification with the hospital was such that, from being popularly called Swift's hospital, it became known during his tenure of office as Dr Leeper's hospital. Moreover, this change of name represented a real change in the nature of the institution: from a decaying home for elderly incurables, firmly rooted in the past, St Patrick's became, under Leeper's guidance, a hospital making serious attempts to keep abreast of modern developments in treatment and to apply these to its patients. Leeper re-introduced psychiatric medicine into St Patrick's, which, in the decades immediately prior to his appointment, had merely been caring for the basic physical needs of patients. Many of the treatments employed by Leeper have subsequently been superseded, if not actually discredited, but this fact should not detract from his very considerable achievement. As has been suggested, the decision to purchase clocks for St Patrick's can be seen as symbolic of the reforms that Leeper instituted: when time was re-admitted to St Patrick's, so was hope. Treatments may not have always lived up to expectations and recovery rates may seem low by present-day standards, but, nevertheless, most of Leeper's patients lived in hopes of eventual recovery and discharge. The same, however, could not be said of most of their nineteenth-century predecessors.

In 1934 Leeper's wife, Elizabeth, died and, although he remained actively engaged in the hospital's affairs, her death was a bitter blow from which he never really recovered. He himself died in 1941, at the age of seventy-eight. Dr Kearney, the government inspector of mental hospitals, doubtless spoke for many when, in a report on St Patrick's, he praised the 'wonderful advances' that had been made under Leeper and 'deeply deplored' his loss to the hospital.[66] The obvious question that arose in the wake of Leeper's death was, who could possibly replace him?

CHAPTER 6

St Patrick's Opens its Doors, 1942-1977

Canst thou not minister to a mind diseas'd;
Pluck from the memory a rooted sorrow;
Raze out the written troubles of the brain;
And with some sweet oblivious antidote
Cleanse the stuff'd bosom of that perilous stuff
Which weighs upon the heart?[1]

In the minutes of a board meeting held on 30 July 1956, there is a small item towards the end of the agenda, which records that the medical superintendent recommended, and the governors agreed, that the doors leading from the ground floor corridor into male ward no. 2 and female ward no. 5 should be replaced by mahogany ones with glass panels and no locks, at a cost of £58.[2] This decision at first sight may seem only of interest to the hospital's carpenter, but in fact it was to prove revolutionary—probably more important to St Patrick's than the advent of moral management in the early years of the nineteenth century or Leeper's reforms in the early years of the twentieth. For, in the 200 years up to the mid 1940s, the most enduring and characteristic feature of the hospital had been its locked doors. Theories about mental illness and modes of treatment might change, but what did not change was the need to confine the mentally ill in a physically restricted and secure environment. Restraint had certainly in many ways become less rigorous: chains had given way to straight-jackets and then to padded rooms and finally, under Leeper, to simple confinement in bed. Nevertheless, the basic principle that those disordered in mind, who might conceivably do damage to themselves or to other people, should be physically constrained, remained. So, although the terms mental or psychiatric hospital superseded words like madhouse or asylum, St Patrick's was far removed from the sort of hospital that treated bodily disorders. Its high walls, locked doors and barred windows remained all too reminiscent of a prison.

But in the 1940s and 1950s, mainly as a result of the introduction of new drugs, which afforded greater control than ever before of violent or bizzare behaviour, the prison-like aspects of the hospital began to disappear rapidly. In 1956, as mentioned, the ward doors were replaced by unlocked ones. Actually, though, this was only one step, albeit a significant one, in a process that had begun ten years before: the locks were removed because, after 1946, they had ceased to be used. Not only were the internal communicating doors within the hospital opened, but also the gates on to the outside world, which had previously been manned by a uniformed gate-keeper. During the late 1940s patients and public came to enjoy much the same degree of access to St Patrick's as they enjoyed to other types of hospital. And, as a result, far greater numbers of people passed voluntarily in and out of St Patrick's doors; most spending weeks rather than years under treatment. In this way the hospital lost much of its former aura of mystery and menace and became instead a familiar and more readily accepted part of people's lives. Those working in the hospital, who lived through the change from the locked and enclosed institution of the 1930s and early 1940s to the open hospital of the 1950s and 1960s, remember it as very dramatic and also as extremely exhilarating.

One man was largely responsible for this transformation of St Patrick's: Dr (later Professor) J. N. P. Moore, who served as junior assistant medical officer from 1938 to 1941 and then as medical superintendent from 1946 to 1977. A recent medical graduate recovering from tuberculosis, Moore found the regime at St Patrick's in the late 1930s congenial, if rather limited. The rigours of a junior position in a busy general hospital would almost certainly have told upon his health. In fact, when he sought employment at St Patrick's, he thought it wise not to mention his illness in case it was held against him. But Dr Leeper proved to be more interested in his abilities as a fisherman than in his health. Actually, as Leeper was to explain to Moore when they knew each other better, the two were by no means unconnected. Leeper, a keen sportsman himself, believed that an interest in natural history and outdoor activities was essential to the stability and well-being of anyone embarking on the 'hazardous career' of psychiatry. St Patrick's was congenial to someone in Moore's position simply because the work was not time-consuming nor particularly demanding. He described his feelings at the time in an article reflecting on his career, written in 1986:

> Like so many people in those earlier days, I became a psychiatrist by chance rather than by choice—in my case, a refugee from the common life-threatening scourge of the time, pulmonary tuberculosis. Relegation to patient status was a humiliating, if eventually salutary, experience which gave me a new understanding of the way people feel when they fall victim

to a serious and socially isolating illness. The sense of shame, the feelings of rejection, the threat of relapse, the fear that detection will alienate friends and limit the prospects of employment, have much in common with the reactions of young people who, today, develop psychiatric illness. Liberation from this shamed secrecy did not come about from any sudden access of enlightenment and tolerance in the community, but from the fortuitous discovery of efficient antidotes to the tubercle bacillus.[3]

Not only did Moore recover his health at St Patrick's, but he also had time to study for and obtain his diploma in psychiatric medicine.

He worked under Leeper and with Robert Taylor, the senior assistant medical officer. Taylor was responsible for the female patients and Moore for the male. Every morning each did the rounds of his side of the hospital, checking on the patients. One of them was then on duty alternate afternoons. At night the night nurses and attendants took over and calls to the doctors were rare. In remembering these years now, Professor Moore stresses how little could be done for patients, beyond caring for their physical health and safety, assessing their condition, encouraging an interest in occupation and recreation and offering comfort and counselling to relatives. Yet, even in such discouraging circumstances, the hospital staff often exhibited great dedication to the care of the patients. Moore recalls that perhaps his most unpleasant duty was to tube-feed extremely depressed patients, who would not otherwise have taken food at all. Keeping such people alive, however, was about all Moore could do for them — he had no way of bringing them out of their stupor. A number of the treatments begun in the 1920s continued in use, while, at the same time, Dr Leeper remained open to innovatory techniques. The operating theatre, dental surgery and hydrotherapy department were used extensively, particularly to combat hidden infections, which were believed to lie behind many illnesses. But, perhaps the most dramatically successful therapy of the time was the treatment of tertiary syphilitic infection, or general paralysis, with benign tertian malaria. This hazardous procedure was eventually superseded by the use of antibiotics, but during the 1920s and 1930s it did offer hope to patients faced otherwise with a painful death.

But, although the life of a young doctor in St Patrick's in the 1930s was comfortable and comparatively easy, it was at the same time profoundly frustrating. For psychiatric medicine seemed to have little or nothing to offer a great many very ill patients. Freud and his assorted disciples and rivals had certainly made notable advances in understanding neurotic disorders, while the neurologists had taken equally great strides in revealing both the functions and malfunctions of the brain. Yet the causes of many disabling psychotic illnesses, such as schizophrenia and severe mood disorders, remained obscure and treatments were often non-existent, or, at best, only partially effective. Aside from diagnosing, physically caring for these cases and hoping for spontaneous remissions, the medical staff of mental hospitals could do comparatively little. Thus, while the therapeutic aspect of such institutions had certainly made advances since the beginning of the century, the custodial aspect still remained strong. Moore remembers often being dispirited by the number of patients for whom he could apparently do nothing. Spontaneous remissions did, however, occur, even in unlikely cases, and these were frequently a source wonder and inspiration.

> My first enthusiasm for my new work in its strange setting [Moore writes] was occasioned by observing a melancholic man who had been in hospital for more than a year, deeply depressed and agitated, tortured by guilty ruminations over past 'misdeeds'. He was transformed overnight to a jovial, outgoing, competent human being, his new zest for life apparent in his concern to get back to his neglected family and business.

> This type of spontaneous transformation without any special therapeutic intervention, leavened the load of apathy, withdrawal and despair, so prominent a feature of the symptomatology in the hospital wards in those days. Mood change and its effect on behaviour in all its variations has remained the great fascination of my clinical experience.

Moore left St Patrick's late in 1941 to take up a position at the Crichton Royal Hospital in Dumfries, Scotland. There, over the next five years, he says, he really became a psychiatrist—something he felt he had not quite achieved at St Patrick's. Crichton Royal had on its staff during the war a number of eminent psychiatrists, many of whom had been forced to flee their homes in Germany and Austria to escape the advance of fascism. The director of clinical research at the hospital was Professor Willy Mayer-Gross from Heidelberg, whom Moore has described as a 'giant among psychiatrists'. At Crichton Royal, Moore was exposed to the latest thinking and the newest therapeutic techniques, all of which he was to take back to St Patrick's after the end of the war.[4]

While Moore was mastering new ideas and methods in Scotland,

St Patrick's was struggling to adjust to the death of Leeper and also to the problems caused by the Emergency, as the Second World War was termed in neutral Ireland. When Leeper died the governors' vote of sympathy clearly expressed a deep and genuine sense of loss: it recorded that 'they all felt they had lost a great personal friend'. But the loss to the hospital of the man who had guided and dominated it for over forty years was perhaps even more severe. The fact that Leeper's death occurred in the midst of major national and international crises only succeeded in compounding the problem. The governors quickly decided that, 'in the present abnormal world conditions', no applications for the position of medical superintendent should be invited and instead they offered the post to Taylor, who had been acting in Leeper's place during his illness.[5] Though a competent and conscientious doctor, Taylor lacked Leeper's dynamism and charisma. He was essentially a cautious and conservative man, not likely to embark on major reforms or new initiatives. Yet it has to be said that he was also severely constrained by the exigencies of the Emergency.

Cut-backs became the order of the day. By 1941 coal was in short supply and the hospital had to introduce drastic conservation measures. Taylor restricted patients' baths to two days a week. At the same time attempts were made to cut back on the clothing supplied to staff. The matron at St Patricks' was asked to make do with two dresses a year instead of three, as her counterpart at Lucan already had to do. The board also decreed that: 'No underclothing, commonly called 'undies', shall, in future, be issued to any new appointments of nurses, maids or cooks.' Such penny-pinching measures could, however, prove counter-productive. The question of 'undies', for instance, rumbled on for years. The staff complained to their union and, as late as 1945, the Workers' Union of Ireland (WUI) was writing to the board demanding that the practice of providing new staff with 'undies' be resumed. The governors, however, remained adamant.[6]

Considerably more serious was the question of whether patients should be evacuated from Dublin in order to avoid the risk of aerial bombing. Just after the outbreak of war, in October 1939, Leeper had recommended that the hospital begin to practise the evacuation of patients from the upper floors to the basements, although, at the same time, he conceded that it was 'not clear what would be the position in the basements . . . in the event of fire and the use of gases'. The alternative was to evacuate the patients to Woodville House on the Lucan estate. Yet, as the house had no water, light, sewers or cooking facilities, this seemed hardly feasible. In 1941, on the night of the bombing of North Strand, patients did indeed have to be evacuated from the top to the ground floor, the windows of which were sandbagged. This experience revived the whole question of Woodville House as a safe alternative to St Patrick's. Early in 1942 Taylor was reporting to the board in some detail on plans for the move and the inspector of mental hospitals, Dr Joseph Kearney, was asked to look over the building and to report if it could be fitted up as a hospital. Nothing appears to have come of these proposals, however. Perhaps Kearney's report was unfavourable or perhaps, as the threat of further bombing diminished, it was felt that such a radical step was no longer called for.[7]

As well as shortages and the fear of bombing, Taylor and the governors also had to cope with a prices/wages spiral, similar to, though not as severe as, the one that had hit the hospital during the 1914-18 war. As prices increased due to shortages, so staff through their unions demanded pay rises to compensate them. This time, however, it was often not within the governors' power to refuse. Cost of living bonuses were awarded to most of the staff in 1940 and again in 1943. In the latter instance bonuses ranging from one to seven shillings a week were recommended for the nursing and domestic staff by the Wages Advisory Tribunal, while at the same time the Agricultural Wages Board raised the wages of farm workers by four shillings a week. These decisions added £733 a year to the hospital's wages bill, without the governors having much say in the matter. In August 1944 the WUI led some 5,000 Co. Dublin farm labourers in threatening a strike if they did not receive another four shillings a week extra, plus shorter working hours. The farmers met and, after some uncertainty, agreed to the union's demands and again the hospital had little alternative but to follow suit.[8]

Despite pay increases to workers at Lucan, the farm actually remained profitable during the Emergency. Albert Coe, the hospital's secretary, reported to the board in 1943 that, if St Patrick's had had to buy the produce supplied by the farm in 1942, it would have cost an extra £520. Moreover, Coe argued that the farm allowed 'controlled continuity of food supplies . . . during the war emergency'. More serious financial problems, however, arose with regard to the patients, and particularly to those at St Edmundsbury. Patient numbers had fallen off sharply in 1940 and 1941, presumably due to the upheavals of the time, and fee income declined accordingly. At the same time bad debts among the existing patients were on the rise. In May 1940 the board raised fees to four guineas a week at St Patrick's and eight guineas at St Edmundsbury and, at the same time, it appealed to the high court to increase the fees of those patients who were wards of court, many of whom were accommodated at Lucan. The following month the court responded by agreeing to pay an extra £1,000 per annum for ten patients. Nevertheless, one of the governors still seriously suggested that the board should consider giving up St Edmundsbury as an uneconomic proposition. The hospital certainly lost substantial sums of money on its wealthy patients, who were in fact supposed to subsidise those less well off. In 1938, for instance, it was losing 19s 7d a week on each of the twenty-four patients at St Edmundsbury compared with a loss of 6s 6d a week on each of the 153 patients at the main hospital in Dublin. By 1944 the loss per patient at Lucan had leapt to nearly two guineas a week, while that at St Patrick's had reached ten shillings. Overall the hospital's financial situation deteriorated seriously during the early years of the Emergency, before recovering somewhat in 1944 and 1945, as the table below reveals.[9]

FINANCIAL STATE OF THE HOSPITAL, 1938-44

	1938 £	1941 £	1944 £
Losses on hospital & farms	4,762	6,873	6,152
Profits from shares, rents etc.	6,131	5,536	5,275
Overall working profit/loss	+1,369	−1,366	− 877[10]

The financial stringencies of the Emergency, plus Taylor's basically conservative approach, meant that the first half of the 1940s was for the hospital a time of stagnation. Yet Taylor was aware of important new methods of treatment coming into use in the late 1930s and early 1940s and attempts were made to introduce some of them into St Patrick's. Leeper had certainly always been interested in innovations and continued so even into his last years. Thus, in 1939, he was reporting to the board on his experiments with a new drug, called cardiazol. He was giving it, with promising results, to four patients suffering from 'schizophrenia or dementia praecox which [was] regarded as entirely due to hereditary mental defect, and [has] baffled all previous modes of treatment . . . ' Yet, with disarming honesty, Leeper conceded that: 'This treatment is based on no sound scientific basis, and seems to be a mere shot in the dark, and is very drastic, but offers the only hope we have of alleviating the needs of these hopeless cases.' Taylor, however, was less prepared than Leeper to attempt mere 'shots in the dark'. In December 1942 he presented the board with a report on electro-convulsive therapy (ECT) which had been first used on patients in Italy in 1938 and, since its introduction to England in 1940, had become extremely popular, particularly in the treatment of severe and long-term depression. Taylor was authorised to buy the necessary equipment for St Patrick's at a cost of £55. In his annual report the government inspector, Dr Kearney, complimented the hospital on this step, but some of the staff seem to have been less enthusiastic about it. In 1943 the WUI was complaining about the extra work entailed for its members in carrying patients back to their beds on stretchers, after they had received the 'new "shock" treatment'. Nevertheless, despite the unpleasantness of the technique for both staff and patients, its initial results were encouraging, as it did appear to relieve severe depression in many cases and even to offer aid to those suffering from schizophrenia. Although subsequently much criticised and, to some extent, superseded by drugs, ECT still continues in use today as an effective way of relieving intractable melancholia or the exuberance of severe elation.[11]

In September 1945 the board asked Taylor to investigate an even more contentious new method of treatment. This was pre-frontal leucotomy: the surgical severing of the frontal section of the brain. The technique had been developed by a Portuguese neuro-surgeon in the mid-1930s and by the early 1940s had become very popular in the United States, where it was used to treat a variety of problems, from schizophrenia to homosexuality. When Taylor reported back to the board in December, however, the governors decided to postpone the matter for twelve months. This delay was probably due to financial considerations as much as to possible doubts about the efficacy of the procedure. For, at about the same time, the board planned and then decided to cancel celebrations of the bicentenary of the hospital's charter, which fell in August 1946. It was probably felt that in the circumstances of 1945-6 the hospital had little to celebrate. With the advent of Dr Moore, however, leucotomy was introduced into the hospital and in 1948, somewhat belatedly, an exhibition and reception were held and a commemorative book published to mark the two hundredth anniversary of the granting of the first charter.[12]

In retrospect the years 1945-6 now seem rather like 'the dark before the dawn'. The ending of the Emergency undoubtedly eased some of the hospital's most immediate financial problems, while the passing of the Mental Treatment Act in 1945 opened up major opportunities for all psychiatric hospitals. But, at St Patrick's, changes in staff were the real key to rejuvenation. In March 1945 Albert Coe, aged seventy-one, resigned after thirty-two years as secretary. He had clearly found the job onerous in recent times and commented in his letter to the board that the previous three years had been the 'most difficult of fulfilment' he had ever experienced.

Coe was replaced by Robert McCullagh, who had held a series of senior administrative positions in the Great Northern Railway, the deputy chairman of which was J. B. Stephens, a member of the board.[13] McCullagh recalls that Coe seemed in some ways like a relic from a long past era. He would not, for example, allow a telephone in his office and so had to be called by means of a buzzer to take telephone messages in the front hall. McCullagh found his administrative and accounting procedures equally antiquated: the register of patients operated on a system that had first been introduced in the 1830s. Patients' names were entered chronologically rather than alphabetically and this meant that if one did not know the month and year of admission, tracing a patient could be a time-consuming process. Professor Moore has termed McCullagh's appointment as 'truly serendipitious', for, apart from his administrative skills, McCullagh was a lively, popular and devoted member of the hospital staff. He joined enthusiastically in the reorganisation of St Patrick's, although for him personally it meant long hours of extra work. In addition to his many duties at the hospital, McCullagh also found time to pursue a career as a singer with various Dublin choirs and musical societies. Through his good offices the hospital was treated to many fine concerts and operettas, and music thus became an important part of the social life at St Patrick's. Moreover, he never failed to spread the good news of the changes at the hospital among his wide circle of friends, leading Moore to term him 'a supreme ambassador' for St Patrick's.

McCullagh's cheerful and tireless efforts were undoubtedly crucial during the late 1940s and early 1950s, when the hospital was undergoing a major transformation. Other members of the staff also rose to the demands of the occasion, but it has to be said that there were some who did not. There were serious problems, for instance, with several matrons. One at Lucan had to be asked to resign after constant friction with her senior staff; her successor was then unfortunately soon forced to resign due to health problems. Meanwhile, at St Patrick's the matron was threatening legal action over her resignation. Some of the staff were simply set in their ways and unable to adapt to new ideas and techniques. Not until the appointment in 1947 of Eileen Herbert, who had worked with Moore in Scotland, was a matron for St Patrick's found who could successfully guide the more conservative nursing staff through a period of major reform.[14]

The most important staff change, as far as the hospital's future was concerned, was the replacement in 1946 of Dr Taylor by Dr Moore. Taylor submitted his resignation in July 1946 and Moore, who had obviously impressed the board during his term as AMO, was quickly appointed his successor at a salary of £1,500 per annum. One of Moore's first administrative acts was to open the hospital's gates on to the outside world—a gesture of profound symbolic, as well as practical, significance. He also began to break down the traditional division between the male and female sides of the hospital, opening the doors between the two and encouraging the mixing of men and women during occupational and recreational activities. This breaking down of divisions did not apply only to patients, however; it also extended to the staff. The male and female nursing staff were united under the control of the matron. The chief male nurse, James McTear, became an enthusiast for the new system and magnanimously accepted subservience to the matron, but other members of staff were much less cooperative: several, mainly male nurses, resigned. Trained in the simple restrictive practices of the early years of the century, they could not accept a more open and trusting, and thus more demanding, regime. Given her augmented role in managing the nursing staff, the matron became crucial to the success of Moore's reforms. Kathleen Draper, the matron on his arrival in 1946, proved unsympathetic to his ideas, but Eileen Herbert was, according to Moore, 'a cheerful, enthusiastic reformer'. When in 1951 she resigned to marry Dr Maurice O'Connor Drury, the senior AMO in charge of St Edmundsbury, she was succeeded at St Patrick's by Anne Kelly.[15] Only twenty-eight years of age at the time of her appointment, Matron Kelly had qualified, like her predecessor, at Crichton Royal and was thoroughly imbued with the new modes of mental care and treatment. During her long tenure of office lasting over thirty years, the training of nurses at St Patrick's was systematically reorganised and put on a par with that practised in general hospitals.

Almost immediately Moore also set about applying the new methods of treatment that he had learnt in Scotland, in particular ECT, insulin shock therapy, leucotomy, and then, in the 1950s, new forms of chemotherapy. The impact of these techniques was almost immediately obvious, mainly in the rapid increase in the turnover of patients and in the numbers resident in the hospital. St Patrick's had always been a small hospital, particularly compared to some of the large public mental hospitals built in the nineteenth century. This had probably saved it from some of the problems of overcrowding and institutionalisation which had plagued the state institutions. But it also meant that the number of people benefiting from its services, at any one time, was relatively small. At the end of 1938, for instance, the two hospitals in Dublin and Lucan between them had only 178 patients, while during the course of the year there had been 111 admissions and 100 discharges. Yet Leeper had proudly informed the board that this was the highest admission rate during his forty years as superintendent. Over the six years of war-time emergency these figures, if anything, declined, for, when Taylor resigned in July 1946, the two hospitals had only 158 patients and admissions and discharges were both running at about eight per month. Just ten years later, however, in April 1956, patient numbers had reached 283, while in the month of March alone 106 patients had been admitted and 130 discharged, and by December 1962 these figures were 330, 168 and 195 respectively. Thus, in less than twenty years, patient turnover had increased astronomically: the hospital was admitting and discharging *each month* far more patients than it had previously treated *in a whole year*.[16] The graphs below provide a pictorial indication of this increase.

This extraordinary rise in the numbers of people being treated in the hospital certainly does not reflect some sudden epidemic of psychiatric illness during the 1950s. Rather it reflects a greater popular awareness of and openness about such illness; the marked success of new methods of therapy, particularly drug therapy; and, not least, easier access to St Patrick's resulting from Moore's open-door policy. More patients of course meant greater expenses, but more patients also meant an increase in fee revenue for the hospital: between 1950 and 1962 revenue from fees went up by 192 per cent, though fees themselves only rose by 80 per cent. The board was able to limit fee rises, despite considerably increased expenditure on patient services, partly due to the fact that, from 1952 onwards, patients with voluntary health insurance (VHI) were entitled to benefit for the first six weeks, and later the first thirteen weeks, of their stay in the hospital. But benefit, even during the weeks that it operated, often fell far short of the actual level of fees, for, until 1961, VHI benefit for mental illness was lower than that paid in respect of clinical or surgical illness. Between 1957 and 1961, for instance, when up to 60 per cent of patients were covered by VHI benefit amounted to £2.16.0 a week, while fees ranged from seven to eight guineas a week. And even when benefits for all types of illness were equalised in 1961, St Patrick's patients only received an increase of one guinea per week, still leaving them far short of the hospital's fees. In most cases the patient's family had to make up the difference, although where particular hardship was involved, the governors continued to exercise their traditional charitable role and to subsidise patients. Yet, although VHI did not wholly cover patient expenses, the decision taken in the 1950s to accept mental illness as an insurable risk, plus the subsequent decision to treat mental and physical illness as the same for insurance purposes, set an extremely important precedent and undoubtedly contributed to

Admissions, Discharges and Outpatients, 1945-69

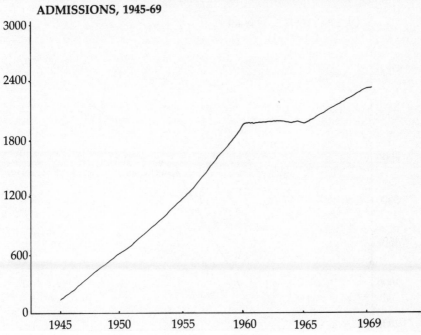

ADMISSIONS, 1945-69

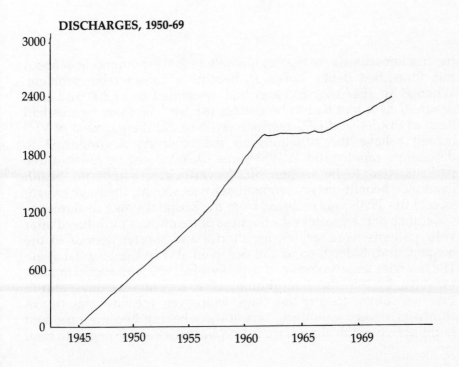

DISCHARGES, 1950-69

OUTPATIENTS, 1959-69

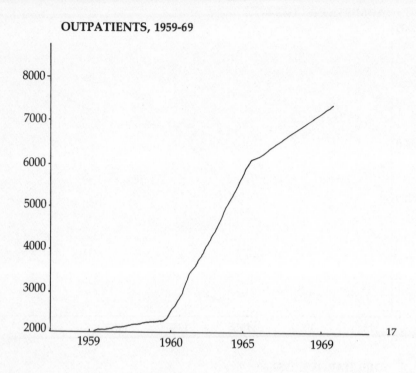

the franker attitudes to mental illness which were emerging at about this time. Bad debts, however, became a considerable problem. Whereas in 1947 overdue fees had amounted to £2,800 and £156 worth of debt had had to be written off; by 1952 these figures had leapt to £17,500 and £722 respectively. Nor did the payment of VHI benefit relieve the situation; on the contrary, it continued to deteriorate rapidly and in 1958 some £3,200, owed by ninety-three patients, had to be written off. Nevertheless, except for health insurance benefit, no government aid was sought; the huge expansion of the 1950s was financed from the hospital's own resources.[18]

Because of the greater effectiveness of treatments introduced after 1946, patients were staying for shorter and shorter periods in the hospital and, indeed, some did not even stay in the hospital at all. The average length of stay of a patient in 1950 was approximately 145 days; by 1957 this had plummeted to seventy-five days; and in 1967 was down to fifty-five days. Moreover, the vast majority of admissions were voluntary, certification having become rare, and as the above graph shows, from 1959 St Patrick's also began to treat people on an out-patient basis. In 1959 an out-patients department was built in the grounds of the hospital at a cost of some £7,000. It was staffed each afternoon on a rota basis by doctors from St Patrick's and patients were charged a small fee, which in 1962 ranged from 2s 6d to a guinea. Beginning with 2,000 patients in the first year, by 1968 the department was treating 7,500 patients a year.[19]

Right from the start Moore had been anxious, not only to open the hospital to the public, but also to expose the hospital's doctors to a far greater range of people and disorders. From his own experience of the closed hospital of the 1930s, he knew that doctors, living and working for years with a small and largely unchanging group of people, could become as narrow and institutionalised as their patients. He sought to counteract this problem in a variety of ways. One way, of course, was to increase the turnover of in-patients and also to open the hospital to out-patients. But there were other ways as well. In 1947 he persuaded the governors to rent consulting rooms, first in Baggot Street and later in Fitzwilliam Square, where he and later other senior members of the medical staff could see private patients.[20] Not only did this get the doctors out of the hospital and supplement their salaries, but it offered opportunities to publicise the hospital and to recruit new patients. Moore, though, was not solely interested in the sort of people who might wish to attend discreet consultations in Fitzwilliam Sqaure, he was also keen to extend psychiatric services to the city's many public and voluntary hospitals.

Dr Leeper had acted as an honorary consultant to the Meath Hospital and, on his appointment in 1946, Moore was asked by the board of the Meath to continue in the same capacity. He thus began to hold a weekly out-patients clinic at the Meath and to refer more serious cases for in-patient treatment at St Patrick's. As patient numbers expanded he was joined by junior colleagues from St Patrick's, for whom Moore considered the Meath clinic good experience. From under 500 cases in 1952, the clinic's clientele rose to 4,500 ten years later and, by 1968, had reached 5,500. The formation of the Federation of Dublin Voluntary Hospitals in 1961 gave further scope to St Patrick's to extend its services to other hospitals and in 1967 it became an associate of the federation. As a result, members of the medical staff were assigned to the Adelaide, Baggot Street, Sir Patrick Dun's and St James's Hospitals to provide weekly out-patients clinics and on-call consultations to in-patients. Dr Moore also acted on an *ad hoc* basis as a consultant to Dr Steevens Hospital, a door having been made in the wall between the two hospitals for his personal use. St Patrick's closest involvement with another hospital, however, was not with its next door neighbour, Steevens, but with its huge near neighbour, St James's.[21]

In 1961 the minister for health appointed a Commission of Inquiry on Mental Illness, under Mr Justice Seamus Henchy of the supreme court, to investigate psychiatric services in Ireland and to recommend necessary changes. The commission's report, published in 1966, made a variety of wide-ranging recommendations. In particular it stressed the need for the integration of psychiatry with general medicine through the introduction of psychiatric units into general hospitals. It also recommended that private mental hospitals, like St Patrick's, should be involved in providing services for the health authorities. On the basis of these proposals the governors of St Patrick's entered into an agreement with the eastern health board, with the approval of the department of health, to run a fifty-bed in-patient unit at St James's Hospital and to provide out-patient and community care for the Dublin postal districts 6, 8 and part of 14. The health board supplied the premises, in the grounds of James's as well as meals and some services, while St Patrick's provided the nursing and medical staff.[22]

The establishment of this unit, combined with the emphasis that the 1966 report had placed on the need for improved psychiatric training, also opened the way for much closer links between St Patrick's and Trinity College, Dublin. In 1947 the governors had approved a proposal to make St Patrick's a fully-fledged teaching hospital and soon medical students from the Colleges of Physicians and Surgeons and from the School of Physic at Trinity College were attending ward rounds and lectures at the hospital. But these arrangements were taken a step further in 1968-9 when the boards of St Patrick's and Dublin University decided that a chair of academic psychiatry should be established within the university, the holder of which would be a consultant at St Patrick's and based in the new unit at St James's Hospital. At the same time the board of the university decided to designate the medical director of the hospital a clinical professor of psychiatry. These steps amounted to a considerable upgrading of Trinity's psychiatric research and training facilities. Both the hospital and the university were fortunate in their first appointment to the chair of academic psychiatry. The new professor was Peter Beckett, a cousin of the playwright Samuel Beckett and a graduate of Trinity College medical school, who had trained and practised in the United States. Beckett was instrumental in establishing the organised post-graduate training of young doctors in psychiatry, first in Dublin and later, in cooperation with the Royal College of Psychiatrists, throughout the country. But his sudden death within only five years of his appointment robbed the cause of psychiatric education in Ireland of one of its most able champions. Nevertheless, St Patrick's ties with Trinity College have continued and, indeed, over the years have been further strengthened. All medical directors since Moore have automatically, on appointment, become clinical professors of psychiatry in the university, while the directors of the clinic at James's have been appointed professors of psychiatry. Moreover, since 1977, two non-medical Trinity professors have served on the board of governors, thus significantly enlarging the connections between the hospital and the university.[23]

The rapid increase in the numbers of patients being treated in St Patrick's after 1946 and the diversification of the hospital's activities had significant implications for staffing. The number of medical, nursing and administration staff increased rapidly, and the hospital was faced with the question of where to put these people, for most of the staff were still required to live in. St Patrick's in the past had never provided purpose-built staff accommodation; junior doctors, nurses, attendants and domestics had been housed in whatever spare space offered itself. This had often meant living in dark, damp basement wards or in unsanitary, overcrowded gate lodges. As late as 1953 nurses at St Edmundsbury were still living in the gate lodge, which was described as 'very damp'.[24] But, during the 1950s, at long last, this unsatisfactory state of affairs was rectified. As the list below indicates, the hospital embarked on a major programme of construction and purchase.

NEW STAFF ACCOMMODATION, 1950-61

		Cost £
1950-1	Matron's flat built at St Patrick's	1,960
1950-1	Nurses home bought, Salmon Pool, Islandbridge	10,381
1950-6 1960-1	Medical superintendent's house at Lucan bought and extended	11,836
1953	Riverside House, Islandbridge, bought	3,588
1953-4	Fonthill, Lucan, bought for junior doctors	19,910
1954-6 1959-60	Nurses home, St Patrick's, built and extended	18,361
1955-7	Nurses' flat built over cinema	6,528
	Expenditure on staff accommodation	72,564[25]

The 1950s saw, in addition to better staff accommodation, major changes in the pay and conditions of service of the nursing staff. In 1946 the pay scales were structured in much the same way as they had been since the beginning of the century, with increases being awarded to those who obtained the Royal Medico-Psychological Association's certificates and to night and charge nurses. The pay of female nurses ranged from £30 to £100 per annum and, upon marriage, nurses, and indeed matrons as well, had to resign. Single male attendants received from £40 to £115 per annum, while married men were paid from £40 to £131. In addition, all were entitled to free board and lodging, free uniforms and three weeks' annual leave a year on full pay. Although the pay was poor and the requirement to live in restrictive, St Patrick's was able to retain many of its staff for long periods. In 1955, for instance, nurses Annie Branigan and Lily Hickson were presented with clocks by the governors to commemorate their service of fifty-four and fifty-one years respectively. Neither, it should be noted, was asked to retire, nor did they show any eagerness to do so, though both must have been in their seventies. At the same time the cook, Mary Caffrey, did retire after over fifty years with the hospital. An even more striking example of length of service was revealed in 1958 when Patrick Cleary, who had been an attendant since October 1900, retired at the age of eighty-four. Although Professor Moore remembers, during his period as an AMO in the 1930s, being impressed by the patience and care with which such ageing nurses treated their often very difficult patients, by the 1950s staff appointed at the beginning of the century were rapidly giving way to much younger, better paid and better trained nurses. By 1956 pay for female nurses had increased significantly to between £130 and £300 per annum, while male nurses (the term attendant having been dropped) were receiving from £150 to £330, with an annual allowance of £130 for those who were married. The WUI had been active in the late 1940s and early 1950s in pushing for better pay for the nursing staff, while the interests of the domestic staff were vigorously represented by the Irish Women Workers Union. But Moore himself was anxious that the hospital attract new and able staff and, in order to do this, he knew St Patrick's pay had to be at least on a par with that offered in state hospitals like Grangegorman.[26]

Below is a list of the qualifications for employment and conditions of service of female nurses operating in 1952:

QUALIFICATIONS FOR EMPLOYMENT, 1952

1. Candidates must be unmarried and not contemplating marriage.

2. Their ages should range from eighteen to twenty-five.
3. They should have attained the national schools' seventh standard, though preference will be given to candidates with a secondary level education.
4. They must be recommended by their parish clergyman and the principal teacher of their school, plus one other responsible person and, if previously employed, they must produce a testimonial from their employer.[27]

CONDITIONS OF SERVICE, 1952

1. On appointment all nurses must serve six months on the temporary staff, then, if a vacancy exists and a physical fitness exam is passed, the nurse will be appointed to the permanent staff.
2. The period of training for the final certificate of the General Nursing Council is three years and it must be obtained within four years of the nurse's first temporary appointment or her services will be dispensed with. (In 1961 it was decided that nurses who did not qualify within four years could be appointed as nursing assistants.)
3. Nurses obtaining their final certificate must continue on the hospital staff for twelve months after the exam.
4. The services of all nurses shall cease at the end of four years, but the board will have discretion to offer permanent appointments to qualified staff. (Later, nurses during their first four years with the hospital were designated 'student nurses' and qualified nurses with permanent positions were termed 'staff nurses'.)

These conditions of service clearly reveal the evolution of the concept of a student nurse: a nurse appointed on a temporary basis for three to four years, during which time she (and indeed he) was learning psychiatric nursing and preparing to pass exams. When Leeper started nurse-training in 1899, a course of lectures lasting a few months was sufficient to get staff their certification and many who, for whatever reason, failed or did not sit the exam remained on the staff, though penalised by lower pay. But, as the years passed, so training became more prolonged and more demanding. In 1935, when the first register of psychiatric nurses was commenced by the Irish Nursing Council, the hospital's school of nursing was recognised as a registered training school. By the 1950s, as we have seen, training entailed a three to four year course and no nurse could be appointed to the permanent staff without certification. In less than fifty years psychiatric nursing had thus been transformed from little more than unskilled labour into a complex and demanding profession.[28]

The growing demands of training placed a heavy burden on the staff, medical as well as nursing, and they had to be increased to deal with it. As well as student nurses, the staff had to supervise medical students, who came to work for a mandatory period on the wards and in the out-patients department, and also trainee psychiatrists, who, in addition to their clinical work, had to attend lectures in preparation for exams for membership of the Royal College of Psychiatrists. Many psychiatrists have over the years done all or part of their training at St Patrick's and many have gone on to pursue distinguished careers in Ireland or abroad. Some, however, continued at or returned to St Patrick's after their training. Among the more notable of these have been Dr Maurice O'Connor Drury, who rose from AMO to be deputy director of the hospital. Initially, however, Drury had read philosophy at university, obtaining a first at Cambridge. There he forged a close, and indeed a life-long, friendship with the great Austrian philosopher, Ludwig Wittgenstein, for whom he became both executor and biographer. Despite his psychiatric training, Drury continued his interest in philosophy, occasionally giving lectures to philosophy students at Trinity College. In November 1948 Wittgenstein came to Dublin, having resigned his position at Cambridge, and spent nearly a year in cottages in Counties Wicklow and Galway. He was struggling, in the face of ill health and depression, to write his last major work, *Philosophical Investigations*, which, when it was finally published in 1953, quickly became one of the landmarks of twentieth-century philosophy. In Dublin he took a room in Ross's Hotel (now the Ashling), in Parkgate Street, just across the river from St Patrick's, intending to stay for only a short time in order to see Drury. But here, in this rather unlikely setting, buoyed by Drury's friendship and by discussions with Moore, the great philosopher at last found the peace of mind with which to advance his work. He stayed in fact until July 1949 and made far more progress on his book that he had anticipated.[29] Drury worked at St Patrick's for over twenty years, though perhaps his greatest contribution was made at St Edmundsbury, to which he and his wife, the former matron Eileen Herbert, moved in 1951. He was particularly interested in the theory and practice of hypnosis and used this technique, with considerable success, in the treatment of many disabling fears and phobias.

Other figures who have been prominent among the medical staff in recent decades have included Moore's successors as medical director: P. J. Meehan (1978-83), Karl O'Sullivan (1983-8) and Anthony Clare (1989-). Dr Meehan joined the staff in 1956 as a

Two photographs of the front of St Edmundsbury, Lucan, bought as an auxiliary hospital by the governors in 1898: in about 1902 and today with new extension.

Patients' drawingroom and diningroom at St Edmundsbury, 1902.

Portrait by Derek Hill of Professor J. N. P. Moore, medical director of St Patrick's Hospital, 1946-77.

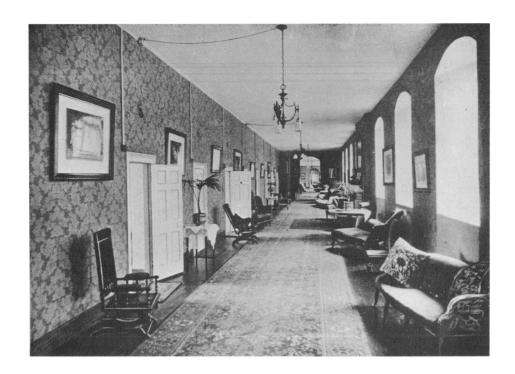

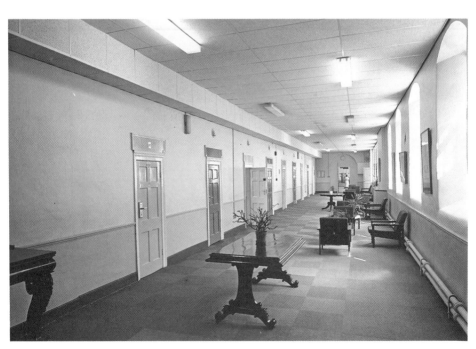

A female ward about 1946: the carpet seems not to have changed since 1904, though the rest of the furnishings have. Below, the former ground floor female ward today: now used as doctors' offices.

The boardroom: created in the early 1930s from the female drawingroom and displaying some of the governors' collection of Swiftiana.

The Swift Centre: built in the early 1980s at the rear of the hospital, opening on to Steevens Lane, and providing extensive day-care facilities.

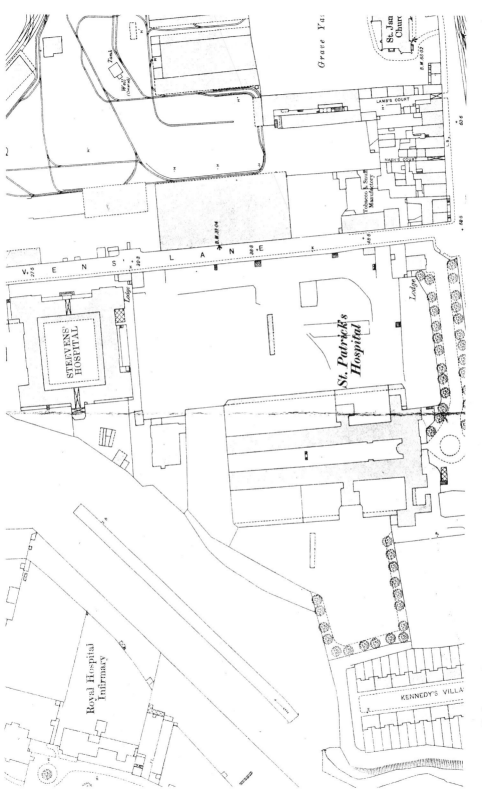

Ordnance Survey map of the hospital site in 1909 showing the original elongated U-shaped design still very much intact.

HOSPITAL GROUND PLAN

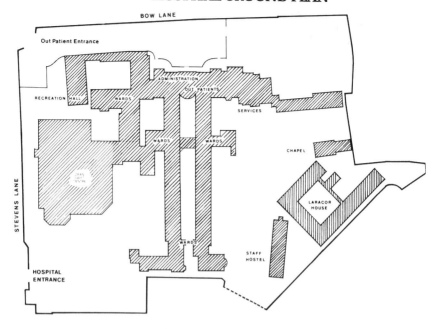

Ground plan of the hospital site today, showing the new Dean Swift Centre.

junior AMO and worked closely with Moore before succeeding him as director in 1978. Since 1983 he has served as one of the hospital's associate medical directors. In the next chapter we shall say more about Meehan's major contribution to St Patrick's. But not all the senior medical staff have served continuously at the hospital. Dr O'Sullivan trained at St Patrick's, as well as filling the office of medical director, but, both before and after that appointment, he pursued a distinguished career in psychiatry in Canada. He was replaced by Dr Anthony Clare, who also trained at St Patrick's, but who, prior to his appointment as director, had been professor of psychiatry at St Bartholomew's Hospital in London and a well-know writer and broadcaster on mental health matters. Like Drs O'Sullivan and Clare, many of St Patrick's graduates have chosen to practise overseas, notably in England, the United States, Canada and Australia. Clearly the plan to turn St Patrick's into a major centre for psychiatric training, first mooted unsuccessfully in the 1840s, has now been fully realised.

In the 1950s and 1960s there were important additions to the staff which reflected the increasing scope and variety of the hospital's services. In 1955 a social therapist was appointed to organise social activities for the patients; in the past this task had been undertaken by matrons and doctors on a rather random basis. But from 1955, dances, concerts, lectures and fêtes became far more regular. The annual summer fête was particularly important, not only as a means of raising funds, but also as a way of publicising the hospital's work. In 1960, for instance, it included tours of the building, plus talks and films about mental illness, alcoholism and psychiatry. At the same time that a social therapist joined the staff, a psychiatric social worker was also appointed, especially to help patients and their families deal with the practical problems associated with illness and hospitalisation. The occupational therapy department was expanded in 1956 to offer a wide range of handicrafts, while a physical fitness instructor was also employed. In 1958 Moore decided that the hospital should have its own chaplains, rather than just relying on the services of the clergy of St James's and Lucan parishes. These 'spiritual advisers', would, ideally, have some training or experience in dealing with the particular problems of the mentally ill. With the approval of Archbishop McQuaid, Fr Joseph Erraught, a Jesuit, was appointed as the first spiritual adviser to the hospital's Catholic patients. The archbishop also approved plans for a new chapel at the hospital, which was opened in 1966.[30]

While treating a variety of psychiatric disorders, there is one problem that St Patrick's has particularly focused on and this is alcoholism. The hospital's interest grew party out of Moore's experience in Scotland in the mid 1940s. Soon after the ending of the war, in 1946, Mayer-Gross made a visit to the United States to see what new developments in the field of psychiatry had taken place there during the years of conflict, when scholarly and scientific communication had been difficult. Moore remembers that:

> On his return he held a staff meeting and told us that the most impressive therapeutic advance he had encountered in his travels was at a meeting of an organisation called Alcoholics Anonymous, run by patients suffering from alcoholism and exclusive to sufferers from this tragic disease. A few months later on return to Dublin, I was requested one evening to see a member of this organisation. He proved to be a cheerful, burly, American who introduced himself as Conor, his first name, in conformity with the rules of his organisation. He told me that he had come over especially from America to the land of his forebears to spread the news about Alcoholics Anonymous. After some discussion and on the strength of Mayer-Gross's recommendation, I introduced him to a recently admitted patient with a long history of alcoholism and personal disaster. He was named Richard Percival and that week, along with Conor, he formed the first Alcoholics Anonymous group in these islands and, I believe, in Europe.[31]

In 1960 Percival was appointed a social worker at St Patrick's, with specific responsibility for alcoholic patients, and later he became the first director of the Irish National Council on Alcoholism. The hospital remains closely associated with AA and INLA to this day, when at least 25 per cent of admissions are for alcoholism. The director of the alcoholism programme for many years has been Dr John Cooney, who in addition to this work, was from 1963 to 1984 the medical director of the Mental Handicap Service of the Daughters of Charity. As well he was largely instrumental in the establishment of the Friends of St Patrick's Hospital in 1979 and in assembling the hospital's impressive collection of modern art.[32]

Along with treatment and training, research is the other key area of St Patrick's activities. At present, helped by the Friends of the hospital, research is being undertaken in such areas as seasonal variation in mood, biochemical patterns in depressive illness, the effectiveness of group therapy and the bases of alcohol dependence. In the mid 1970s, prior to the formation of the Friends, a development committee, chaired by Lady Goulding and Charles J. Haughey TD, raised nearly half a million pounds to finance the erection of a scientific and clinical research unit. This building provided the hospital with up-to-date, purpose-built research facilities for the first time, and allowed a considerable expansion of the research programme.[33]

In considering the roles of individuals, whether doctors, nurses or administrators, who contributed to the enormous changes that occurred at St Patrick's after 1946, we should not overlook the role of the board of governors. As pointed out in Chapter 3, St Patrick's was unusual among hospitals in the eighteenth and nineteenth centuries in having a relatively small board of governors, which took an extremely active role in the hospital's affairs. Although governors served in an honorary capacity, in the sense of not being paid for their efforts, they were not honorary in the sense of being expected to do very little. On the contrary, at different times over the past two centuries, governors who did nothing for the hospital were usually politely asked to resign. And the same remains true of the twentieth-century board. For, still today, St Patrick's is run, not by doctors or bureaucrats, but by a handful of unpaid governors, who generally receive little or no public recognition. With regard to the developments that took place at St Patrick's after 1946, the board of governors was no mere rubber stamp: a number of governors, drawing on their particular expertise, initiated, organised and supervised important changes. Godfrey Goodbody, governor from 1940 to 1959, Irish manager of the Friends Provident Insurance Company and a member of the notable Dublin Quaker family, was instrumental in the hospital's purchase in the early 1950s of both Salmon Pool and Fonthill houses, which provided much needed staff accommodation.[34] The Wardell family, well-known tea merchants, have served the hospital long and well: firstly in the person of John M. Wardell, governor from 1930 to 1973, who was chairman of the board for many years; secondly in the person of his son, C. V. Denis Wardell, elected in 1959, who is the current chairman; and thirdly in the person of his grandson, Trevor Wardell, elected in 1989. Other governors have put their expertise at the hospital's disposal. Jeffery B. Jenkins, elected in 1953, the head of W. and R. Jacob, the biscuit manufacturers, has used his considerable engineering and architectural knowledge to good effect in supervising much of the building that has occurred at the hospital in recent decades, in conjunction with Edward Byrne, the able and long-serving clerk of works; while John Wilson-Wright has made a notable contribution to the hospital's farming and general business policies. A former governor who occupies a truly unique position is Valerie, Lady Goulding, the first and, so far, the only woman to have been elected to the board. As already mentioned, drawing on her considerable abilities as a fund-raiser, she initiated and ran an appeal in the mid 1970s which raised the large sums needed to provide the hospital with up-to-date research facilities. In so doing Lady Goulding demonstrated to her fellow governors the value of well-managed fund raising campaigns—a lesson they have subsequently much benefited from. Among the *ex officio* governors, the Very Rev. Henry Lewis-Crosby, dean of Christ Church Cathedral from 1938 to 1962, made an especially valuable contribution by his regular attendance at meetings and minute attention to hospital affairs. Although some of Swift's plans for his hospital proved impractical, mainly because he left insufficient money to allow it to operate wholly as a charitable institution, with regard to the board of governors, reality has more closely approximated his wishes. To this day, despite the medical profession's predominant role in psychiatric care, the small group of governors, created in perpetuity by the 1746 charter, continues to be St Patrick's principal organ of management. The governors leave questions of treatment to the doctors, but all other matters concerning the hospital's affairs are still firmly in their hands.

Attempts made after 1946 to 'normalise' hospital life were thoroughly endorsed in 1960 by the government inspector of mental hospitals, Dr B. M. Ramsay. He complimented the hospital's staff, remarking that they had 'succeeded in creating a way of life which approaches, to a great extent, that of people living in the outside community'. One apparently small, but in the long term highly significant, step towards bringing the hospital into line with the world outside its walls was the installation in 1955-6 of television sets in both the Dublin and Lucan hospitals. The patients were said to be 'delighted' with this new mode of entertainment and, indeed, within a year the hospital's cinema had to be closed due to the competition of television.[35]

Attempts to provide entertainment for the patients had a long history, going back at least to the early years of the nineteenth century when the master began to invite first class boarders to his rooms for games of whist. But, during the 1950s, serious attempts to inform, educate and train patients, to help them cope with the demands of life outside the hospital, also began to be undertaken. Moore thought it important that the patients know something about mental illness and the various methods of treatment; and he felt that they should also know something of the history of the hospital. Robert McCullagh, the secretary, who was particularly interested in Swift, was persuaded to lecture new patients on the founding of St Patrick's, while Moore, and later other members of the medical staff, talked about psychiatric illness and treatment. Eventually the 'Morning Lecture', given each morning by one of the staff on a particular aspect of mental health and followed by a question-and-answer session, became an essential part of hospital routine. Moore himself has described the morning lecture thus:

> The day's therapeutic programme at St Patrick's begins with the morning lecture and a form of group therapy, I believe, unique to the hospital. Each morning at 9.30 a.m. a member of the staff on a three-week rotation basis gives a short didactic lecture on some aspect of psychiatry. This is followed by an open-forum type discussion when questions range far and wide and every conceivable aspect of illness and health and human activity come up for discussion. Such topics as depression, schizophrenia, the treatments we use, the running of the hospital, the organisation of the hospital day, family relationships, going home, what to tell the boss, the neighbours, or a future boy- or girl-friend, are examples of recurring topics for discussions. ... Patients show they are deeply interested and avid for information and respond to factual answers and explanations. The staff learn much from these talks too, and many useful changes in the hospital routine have followed discussions at these meetings. The morning lectures are the best and most punctually attended functions in the day's programme.[36]

In 1982 Drs Meehan and Cooney inaugurated a biennial series of lectures on aspects of mental health and the hospital's work, given in the evening by the staff, aimed at the general public. Again in the words of Professor Moore, such information, when 'simply, sensitively and honestly given', is the 'best antidote to the inevitable fears and forebodings which accompany [mental] illness'. In 1986 some of these lectures were published in book form, under the title *All in the Mind: Approaches to Mental Health*. More practical skills were provided by the Rehabilitation Institution. This was originally set up to help ex-TB patients re-train and re-enter the work force, but by the late 1950s it was undertaking a similar service for ex-patients of St Patrick's. Eventually the hospital's after-care and rehabilitation facilities would extend to sheltered workshops, a day-care centre, a hostel and group homes.[37]

In 1959 an out-patients department and recreation hall were opened at St Patrick's. In line with their new policy of opening the hospital's gates to the public and of publicising the institution's work, the governors held a large reception to mark the event. Some four hundred people attended, including the then minister for health, Sean MacEntee. Moore and McCullagh held a press conference; a marquee was erected in the grounds, where refreshments were served to the music of a band; and several speeches were made, including one by the chief justice, Conor Maguire, a governor for over twenty years. After the opening, performed by Professor Mayer-Gross from Moore's *alma mater*, the Crichton Royal, some ninety of the guests went on to the Gaiety Theatre for a performance of Denis Johnston's play about Swift, *Dreaming Dust*.

During the ceremony Moore made an interesting speech, summing up some of his ideas about the role of the hospital in the community. But firstly he praised the courage and foresight of the governors in being prepared to spend large amounts of capital, 'accumulated in times of prosperity in the past', on new buildings and facilities. The 'interest on this capital had kept the hospital doors open in lean years in the past' and Moore knew that by spending it now the governors were running a distinct financial risk. Nevertheless, he was convinced that what was lost in terms of investment income, would be replaced by 'a handsome dividend in the form of an even happier hospital and hastened recoveries'. He then went on to warn that:

> For too long we have lived in isolation behind the same high walls and locked doors which sheltered our patients. We are only beginning to recognise that our responsibilities to our patients do not begin when they enter hospital, or end when they have been discharged: prophylaxis, after-care, and rehabilitation must play an increasing part in the psychiatry of the future . . . Emotional problems are so universal and affect so intimately every branch of life, that we need, not so much more specialists, and certainly not more hospital beds, but more out-patient facilities, more expert treatment of patients in their own homes, more social clubs, more schemes for training handicapped people, and more universal recognition that the mentally ill are not a race apart—but merely ourselves in a different set of circumstances.[38]

Perhaps no clearer nor more eloquent declaration of St Patrick's commitment to the new, more open and varied methods of treatment could be found than this.

Moore had great faith in the new forms of physical treatment and of chemotherapy introduced in the 1940s and 1950s. In his 1986 reflections he wrote:

> Apart from difficulty in visualising the old-time hospital and its residents, the young psychiatrist may find it difficult to imagine the incredible sense of enthusiasm and optimism experienced by hospital personnel with the advent of the physical methods of treatment . . . Electroplexy, insulin therapy and chemotherapy, apart from the dramatic symptom relief they often achieved, provided a great incentive to therapeutic endeavour. Hospital morale was elevated, we felt we were real doctors and nurses again, who could determine events rather than wait

passively for them to happen. In the mid 1950s I remember reading a paper on the new chemotherapy and saying 'I have never taken either chlorpromazine or reserpine, but these drugs have done me an immense amount of good through their effects on my patients. I am a more confident doctor, and in particular, I can make friends with my schizophrenic patients'. Of course we were too optimistic and our brightest hopes were not fulfilled . . . [Nevertheless] physical treatments in psychiatry must rank among the great achievements of modern medicine. It would be inconceivable to turn the clock back and try to run a hospital service without their aid. Locked doors, excessive sedation and prison-like supervision would of necessity return, in the interests of patients' safety. [39]

He felt that many of the problems associated with such treatments, which created something of a backlash in the 1960s and 1970s, had arisen from 'lack of care and sophistication in their application. Faulty diagnosis, inappropriate dosage, insensitive technique, inadequate follow-up (specially the latter) are more frequent causes of disappointment and failure than the limitations of the methods themselves.'

But in his 1959 speech Moore clearly demonstrated his belief that the physical and chemical treatments, of themselves, were not the complete answer to the problem. As he said, the hospital's responsibility did not begin when patients were admitted nor end when they were discharged. The residential hospital was at the centre of a large wheel and radiating out from it were a whole range of other facilities offering treatment, education, training, support and advice to individuals, before, during and after their time in hospital. And of course there were increasing numbers of people who took advantage of the hospital's facilities and services without ever actually taking up residence in it.

At the end of a paper on new methods of treatment being tried at St Patrick's, which was delivered to a conference in the early 1950s, Moore remarked that, in his more optimistic moments, he aspired to answer Macbeth's plaintive cry:

Canst thou not minister to a mind diseas'd;
Pluck from the memory a rooted sorrow;
Raze out the written troubles of the brain;
And with some sweet oblivious antidote
Cleanse the stuff'd bosom of that perilous stuff
Which weighs upon the heart?[40]

Nearly forty years later, a historian can perhaps hazard the judgment that his optimism was by no means misplaced.

CHAPTER 7

The Era of Community Care, 1978-1989

Hospitals should not be seen as isolated facilities outside community care but as part of the community provision.[1]

But we need a more informed public and a more sympathetic medical profession. We need, too, a greater share of the available resources if the developments in the community necessary to avoid the institutionalisation of vast numbers of patients in large, unsavoury and dilapidated mental hospitals are to take place . . . While a modern psychiatric hospital today stands as a testimony to Swift's foresight, the mentally ill of Dublin and Ireland remain a challenge to all of us . . .[2]

St Patrick's Hospital was conceived in the 1730s, planned in the 1740s and built in the 1750s. These decades, which saw the establishment in Dublin of at least half a dozen other hospitals, marked the beginning of the city's emergence as a major European medical centre. Some 250 years later, however, the 1980s have witnessed the closure of many of these early hospitals. Most of those that were older than St Patrick's, like Jervis Street and Dr Steevens, have gone, and today probably only the Rotunda, which first opened in 1745 in a house in what is now South Great George's Street, has a longer history.[3] But, if the 1980s have seen moves in Ireland to close small, eighteenth-century hospitals, they have also seen moves, not just in Ireland but throughout the western world, to close large, eighteenth- and nineteenth-century mental hospitals. One would therefore expect that a small, elderly, Dublin mental hospital would be doubly under threat. And so it would seem for, in 1984, in a report entitled *The Psychiatric Services; Planning for the Future*, a government study group came out strongly in favour of a shift from hospital-based to community-based care. The study group focused on the provision of new accommodation in the community: houses, flats, lodgings and hostels, and envisaged hospitals as only a last resort. Its report also continued the emphasis, placed by the Commission on Mental Illness's 1966 report, on the need to develop psychiatric units attached to general hospitals, rather than to perpetuate large, isolated asylums.[4].

At various times in the past St Patrick's has faced crises: often these have been of a financial nature; but at other times they have centred more on the hospital's role and its capacity to adapt to changing modes of treatment. Now, in the last quarter of the twentieth century, as St Patrick's approaches its two hundred and fiftieth anniversary, it is facing a crisis of the latter sort, for one is inevitably drawn to ask: how is it coping with the new orthodoxy of community care? Will St Patrick's go the way of its next-door neighbour, Dr Steevens Hospital, or can it accommodate community care and find a role for itself within a new, less hospital-oriented system?

Although patients are staying for shorter and shorter periods in psychiatric hospitals[5] and many of the larger and older hospitals are closing down, the demand for psychiatric care is not diminishing; on the contrary, year by year it continues to grow. Psychiatric facilities, whether hospitals, clinics or day-care centres, are treating more and more people. Clearly there is a perceived need within the community for a great deal of psychiatric care; a need which is increasing rather than declining. St Patrick's faces the issue of how it should cater for this need without hospitalising people as it was built to do. Thus, not only its methods of treatment, but its physical facilities have to be adapted to cope with new modes of care.

Already under Professor Moore in the 1950s the hospital had begun re-orienting its facilites more towards out-patient care. As noted in the previous chapter, an out-patients' department was opened in 1959 and ten years later it was treating over 7,000 people every year. In 1975, at the opening of the new research unit and admissions facilities, Moore had observed that:

> In all branches of medicine today there is concern that hospital-isation has become such a crippling economic burden to the individual and to the state that it should be reduced to a minimum within the limits of safety and efficiency. It is more important than ever that illnesses should be diagnosed early, and more people treated in their own homes. In psychiatry, too, we are all agreed that the principles of community-based medicine should be put into practice. For this reason I should like to stress that we are not adding to the number of hospital beds. Rather we are providing conditions for the more efficient use of hospital services when the need for them arises.

And the need would arise:

> For example, when special investigations are required, when close observation is desirable, when specialised treatments are indicated, when patients no longer can cope with their work or

their environment, and sometimes to give much needed respite to a troubled family scene. Stay in hospital should be as brief as is consistent with the relief of the symptoms and the rehabilitation of the patient.[6]

Another major step away from in-patient care was taken in the late 1970s and early 1980s under Moore's successor, Dr P. J. Meehan. This was the building of the Swift Centre. Meehan, as we have seen, had joined St Patrick's staff in 1956 as a junior AMO and by the late 1960s he had risen to be Moore's deputy. Shortly after succeeding Moore in 1978, Meehan with Dr John Cooney, the associate medical director, and several of the governors visited a number of countries to investigate the provision of day-care facilities. The governors were keen to extend and modernise the hospital. Thus a major building programme was planned and carried out, particularly under the supervision of Jeffery Jenkins and Desmond Bradley, which involved additions to St Patrick's and the renovation of St Edmundsbury. A day-care centre, as well as offering improved in-patient facilities, would allow the hospital to treat more patients without actually admitting them and, in a period of severe price inflation with the cost of hospital beds sky-rocketing, it was vital that alternatives to hospital admission should be developed. But the decision to introduce day-care was not taken for solely financial reasons. A day-care centre would also allow St Patrick's to develop further its behavioural therapy programmes, for, in terms of treatment, the hospital was increasingly exploring modes of changing people's behaviour without resort to drugs. Physical treatments like chemotherapy and ECT certainly continued in use, particularly for those suffering from more serious disorders who required admission to the hospital, but behaviour modification through psychological and social therapies, which could be conducted on an out-patient basis, was increasingly resorted to. Thus the Swift Centre, opened in 1985 by the then minister for health, Barry Desmond, contained counselling and group therapy rooms, a lecture theatre, kitchens and enlarged OT facilities, as well as the hospital's alcoholism unit, plus provision for ECT treatment and research.[7]

As part of their building programme, the governors also formulated plans to replace some of their older patient accommodation with new, more up-to-date facilities. The hospital did not want to increase the number of its beds, but rather to transfer patients from eighteenth- or nineteenth-century wards to comfortable, modern accommodation. This programme is still in train, though the Swift Centre project included the provision of new wards. Under

Meehan's successor as director, Dr Karl O'Sullivan, the hospital set about emphasising its link with its founder by giving new wards names with Swiftian associations. Thus, in 1984, wards 7, 8 and 9, which had been added to the original six, became Stella, Kilroot and Delany; the new 33-bed admission ward became Vanessa and the convalescent unit was named Laracor. As we saw in Chapter 2, the governors had originally named wards after the hospital's early benefactors. This practice does not seem to have caught on though, for soon the three male and three female wards were simply being designated by numbers. The introduction of names in the early 1980s thus constituted a return to the governors' original intentions of the 1740s and 1750s.

During O'Sullivan's five years as medical director substantial renovations were also undertaken at St Edmundsbury. It had originally taken wealthy, convalescent patients from St Patrick's, though in time patients began to be admitted there directly. Lucan offered a more secluded, private and restful environment than that found in the main hospital in Dublin. But as facilities were improved at St Patrick's, so convalescent patients became increasingly reluctant to transfer to Lucan. St Edmundsbury had not been designed as a hospital. It was a large, rambling house, which made observation of patients, whether for treatment or security purposes, difficult. Moreover washing and toilet facilities were poor and few patients had their own rooms. The governors thus decided that an addition to the original house, providing high-class accommodation in single rooms, each with its own bathroom, was required. As a result a unit with forty-four single rooms and three double rooms was built and the old house then renovated to offer communal and treatment facilities. Under O'Sullivan's direction a more structured programme of therapy was also introduced into St Edmundsbury, so that the hospital is now able to treat a wider array of patients than ever before.

Today St Patrick's has beds for somewhat over 400 patients; 320 at the main hospital, fifty at St Edmundsbury and a further fifty at James's Hospital. The hospital admits some 3,000 patients each year; approximately one-third of these are first admissions, while some three-quarters are from the Dublin/Meath/Kildare/Wicklow area. The out-patients' department receives over 6,000 visits each year. The psychiatric unit at James's Hospital, which offers in-patient treatment to the Dublin South Central area and has its own out-patients' department, is still staffed by St Patrick's, though staffing is gradually being taken over by James's. Currently the total staff of St Patrick's is around 400, nearly half of these being nurses. St Patrick's continues to train both doctors and nurses. In fact the hospital is now one of the largest centres in the country for the training of psychiatrists, psychiatric nurses and, also, for general practitioners wishing to become more familiar with clinical psychiatry. It offers, in addition, post-graduate training placements in psychology and social work and continues to give undergraduate teaching in psychiatry to medical students from Trinity College, Dublin.

With regard to treatment, in recent years St Patrick's has been developing a wide range of specialist programmes—an approach that was pioneered by Dr John Cooney in his treatment of alcoholics. Aside from the alcoholism programme, the hospital also has treatment programmes for mood disorders, sexual dysfunction, bereavement, eating disorders, marital problems and social difficulties. These programmes are generally organised by consultant psychiatrists aided by teams of ancillary workers. The approach is multi-disciplinary and holistic, with—in addition to psychiatrists— nurses, social workers, counsellors, psychologists, therapists and even physicians contributing to the programme. The aim is to create a scheme of treatment appropriate to the needs of each individual patient. These needs may be psychological, physical, social or vocational; in other words, the whole person is catered for. In the early, often acute, phase of the disorder, in-patient care may be required, at least for a short period, but thereafter all treatment is conducted on an out-patient basis. Such treatment can take a variety of forms, including individual, group or family therapy, chemotherapy, ECT, relaxation, recreational and occupational training. As well as offering a wide variety of therapies, St Patrick's also treat a considerable range of disorders: around 50 per cent of the patients admitted to the hospital suffer from affective or mood disorders, including depression, manic-depression and grief reactions; approximately 25 percent are treated for alcoholism; while 12 per cent are classed as schizophrenics, and about another 7 per cent have neurotic problems, including phobic and stress-related complaints.

Perhaps the best summary of the hospital's current general approach to psychiatric care is contained in a lecture that Dr Meehan gave in the 'All in the Mind' series, which was published in book form in 1986. Having an association with St Patrick's extending over more than thirty years and involving a variety of medical posts from a junior one to the most senior, Meehan is probably uniquely qualified to describe the hospital's present approach to treatment. Like Moore before him, Meehan emphasises that in certain cases a brief period of in-patient care may be called for.

Admission to hospital may be indicated sometimes in cases

other than those involving a major psychiatric illness. For example, if the presenting complaint is unusual and a clear-cut diagnosis not easy to make, a period of observation and assessment, possibly supplemented by refined testing pro- cedures would be indicated and this can usually only be done in a hospital setting . . . In addition, in those cases where alcohol is a serious problem, the personal and inter-personal, psycholo- gical and physical life of the individual can be so disturbed that expert detoxification in hospital followed by specialised psycho- logical treatment may be necessary for recovery. Lastly, a small number of those with more disabling forms of the minor breakdowns may need in-patient care. This applies mainly to those whose ability to cope with ordinary living is seriously impaired by the nervous condition.[8]

The first step in in-patient care is to make a complete physical and mental assesment of the patient: his or her illnesses and disabilities, personal history and current problems. If appropriate, the patient's family might be involved and a social worker or a psychologist called upon for assistance. Meanwhile the nursing staff will be monitoring the patient's physical and mental condition in hospital and reporting to the relevant doctor. As Meehan observes: 'This threefold approach—establishing a picture of the problems pre- sented, helping the individual to get to know the nursing and medical staff and having a plan of treatment organised—may take the best part of a week during which the person concerned is confined to bed as a rule.'[9] In most cases treatment will be along physical and psychological lines. Thus, for instance, people suffer- ing from depression may be treated with anti-depressant drugs or with ECT. Once such physical treatments have brought about some improvement and the patient is able to get about again, he or she will be encouraged to participate in the daily activities of the hospital. Group discussions, lectures, physical training, games and handicrafts are all intended to stimulate the patient and to help revive his or her physical and psychological functioning. With such an approach, most people admitted to St Patrick's are likely to have lost the worst of their symptoms after four to six weeks. But, they will still probably be afflicted with anxiety, lack of confidence or problems in emotional communication. Here psychological therapy for either individuals or groups, conducted on an out-patient basis, can help teach the person new and healthier attitudes and modes of behaviour.

While for some hospitals the 1980s have been years of contraction and even of closure, for St Patrick's they have been a period of redevelopment and refinement. The governors have spent substantial sums on upgrading and modernising their facilities: replacing old wards with new, more comfortable, ones and providing much expanded services for out-patients. At the same time, modes of treatment have been refined. Specialist programmes utilising the skills of a range of trained staff have been developed to treat a variety of disorders. Thus St Patrick's continues to care for a large number of patients, though many never take up residence in the hospital and those who do usually only stay for a matter of weeks. Dr Meehan has drawn a fundamental distinction between the treatment of physical and psychological illness on the basis of rest versus activity. 'It is well known', he says '. . . that rest is the basis of treatment for any physical disorder, but can be highly detrimental in the management of psychiatric illnesses.' In cases of psychiatric illness, once the acute symptoms have eased, 'activity, stimulation and involvement with others is the sheet-anchor of treatment. . . '.[10] St Patrick's does not offer patients rest and asylum from the demands of the world; on the contrary, through its treatment programmes, it seeks to offer them enhanced involvement.

But, as we have seen, in the past, withdrawal from the community was the very *raison d'être* of institutions like St Patrick's. During the eighteenth and early nineteenth centuries they tended to resemble prisons, for they were places where 'lunaticks' could be locked in 'cells' under the control of 'keepers'. During the nineteenth century the terminology changed as mental hospitals came to be viewed as 'asylums', places of refuge, where the 'insane' could live out their lives, protected by 'attendants' from the rigours of the outside world. But, in the second half of the twentieth century, there has been a reaction against the idea of the mental hospital as a place of withdrawal, cut off from the community. This reaction has been an extreme one, with calls for the total abolition of mental hospitals. Instead of being hospitalised, the 'mentally ill' are to be 'cared for' in the 'community'. Here the terminology is perhaps suggestive of a family looking after its weaker members. But is the community a family? The term 'community care' certainly has a warm glow about it, as doubtless did the term 'moral management' in its day. The moral managers were in reaction against the perceived cruelty of the eighteenth-century madhouses. But moral management failed, for the kindness and comfort offered within the walls of asylums attracted patients rather than relieved them and so the nineteenth-century mental institutions became overcrowded and unmanageable. Returning the mentally ill to the 'care' of the community will certainly rid us of the evils of huge, expensive and decaying asylums, but, as with the theory of moral management, we may be in danger of swapping one problem for another. Before the erection of institutions to confine the mentally ill, they wandered the streets and countryside as beggars or were confined at home by their families, who were often incapable of looking after them properly. Obviously, no one would wish to return to this state of affairs, though in parts of the United States and Britain community care does seem to have amounted to little more than turning disturbed people out into the street without support of any kind. In 1976, with regard to England, Professor Anthony Clare lamented that:

> The running-down of the large mental hospitals has not been accompanied by a significant development of community based resources. Instead, there has been over-crowding in the hospitals, a rise in the number of homeless and poorly housed people, and a shift of people from the mental health and into the prison services. The result of such inept planning has been the debasement of the concept of 'community care'.[11]

Such developments certainly do not accord with the theory of community care, but then theory and practice are all too often prone to diverge.

Perhaps St Patrick's offers something of a compromise as regards the problems of community care. As David Cohen suggests in the quotation prefacing this chapter, hospitals should no longer be viewed as existing in opposition to the community. In the past they certainly were, but today they need to be part of the community services. St Patrick's, with its relatively small size, its stress on short term in-patient treatment and its highly-developed programme of out-patient care, has achieved something of a balance between the advantages of the hospital and those of the community. Today none of its patients are likely to become victims of institutional neurosis, but equally they are not likely to be sent out into the community to fend for themselves without adequate support. Mental hospitals have had a stormy and often rather grim history, as the story of St Patrick's amply demonstrates. But closing them down will not solve, and probably not even ease, the problem of mental illness. Some doubtless are too large, too run down or too inconveniently located to be serviceable in the future, but others, like St Patrick's, can and should continue, in conjunction with community-based facilities, to make a valuable contribution to the care and rehabilitation of the mentally ill.

APPENDIX 1

Extracts from Swift's Will and the Charters

A. SWIFT'S WILL, 1740

In the Name of God, Amen. I Jonathan Swift, Doctor in Divinity, and Dean of the Cathedral Church of St. Patrick, Dublin, being at this Present of sound Mind, although weak in Body, do here make my last Will and Testament, hereby revoking all my former Wills . . .

Item: I give and bequeath to my Executors all my worldly Substance, of what Nature or Kind soever (excepting such Part thereof as is herein particularly devised) for the following Uses and Purposes, that is to say, to the Intent that they, or the Survivors or Survivor of them, his Executors, or Administrators, as soon as conveniently may be after my Death, shall turn it all into ready Money, and lay out the same in purchasing Lands of Inheritance in Fee-simple, situate in any Province of Ireland, except Connaught, but as near to the City of Dublin, as conveniently can be found, and not incumbered with, or subject to any Leases for Lives renewable, or any Terms for Years longer than Thirty-one: And I desire that a yearly Annuity of Twenty Pounds Sterling, out of the annual Profits of such Lands when purchased, and out of the yearly Income of my said Fortune, devised to my Executors as aforesaid, until such Purchase shall be made, shall be paid to Rebecca Dingley of the city of Dublin, Spinster, during her Life, by two equal half-yearly Payments, on the Feasts of All-Saints, and St. Philip and St. Jacob, the first Payment to be made on such of the said Feasts as shall happen next after my Death. And that the Residue of the yearly Profits of the said Lands when purchased, and until such Purchase be made, the Residue of the yearly Income and Interest of my said Fortune devised as aforesaid to my Executors, shall be laid out in purchasing a Piece of Land, situate near Dr. Stevens's Hospital, or if it cannot be there had, somewhere in or near the City of Dublin, large enough for the Purposes herein after mentioned, and in building thereon an Hospital large enough for the Reception of as many Idiots and Lunaticks as the annual Income of the said Lands and worldly Substance shall be sufficient to maintain: And, I desire that the said Hospital may be called St. Patrick's Hospital, and may be built in such a manner, that another Building may be added unto it, in case the Endowment thereof should be enlarged; so that the additional Building may make the whole Edifice regular and compleat. And my further Will and Desire is, that when the said Hospital shall be built, the whole yearly Income of the said Lands and Estate, shall, for ever after, be laid out in providing Victuals, Cloathing, Medicines, Attendance, and all other Necessaries for such Idiots and Lunaticks, as shall be received into the same; and in repairing and enlarging the Building, from Time to Time, as there may be Occasion. And, if a sufficient Number of Idiots and Lunaticks cannot readily be found, I desire that Incurables may be taken into the said Hospital to supply such Deficiency: But that no Person shall be admitted into it, that labours under any infectious Disease: And that all such Idiots, Lunaticks and Incurables, as shall be received into the said Hospital, shall constantly live and reside therein, as well in the Night as in the Day; and that the Salaries of Agents, Receivers, Officers, Servants, and Attendants, to be employed in the Business of the said Hospital, shall not in the whole exceed one Fifth Part of the clear yearly Income, or Revenue thereof. And, I further desire that my Executors, the Survivors or Survivor of them, or the Heirs of such, shall not have Power to demise any Part of the said lands so to be purchased as aforesaid, but with Consent of the Lord Primate, the Lord High Chancellor, the Lord Archbishop of Dublin, the Dean of Christ-Church, the Dean of St. Patrick's, the Physician to the State, and the Surgeon-General, all for the Time being, or the greater Part of them, under their Hands in Writing; and that no leases of any Part of the said Lands, shall ever be made other than Leases for Years not exceeding Thirty-one, in Possession, and not in Reversion or Remainder, and not dispunishable of Waste, whereon shall be reserved the best and most improved Rents, that can reasonably and moderately, without racking the Tenants, be gotten for the same, without Fine. Provided always, and it is my Will and earnest Desire, that no Lease of any Part of the said Lands, so to be purchased as aforesaid, shall ever be made to, or in Trust for any Person any way concerned in the Execution of this Trust, or to, or in Trust for any Person any way related or allied, either by Consanguinity or Affinity, to any of the Persons who shall at that Time be concerned in the Execution of this Trust: And, that if any Leases shall happen to be made contrary to my Intention above expressed, the same shall be utterly void and of no Effect. And I further desire, until the Charter herein after mentioned be obtained, my Executors, or the Survivors or Survivor of them, his Heirs, Executors, or Administrators, shall not act in the Execution of this Trust, but with the Consent and Approbation of the said seven additional Trustees, or the greater Part of them, under their Hands in Writing, and shall, with such Consent and Approbation, as aforesaid, have Power, from time to time, to make Rules, Orders, and Regulations for the Government and Direction of the said Hospital. And, I make it my Request to my said Executors, that they may in convenient Time apply to his Majesty for a Charter to incorporate them, or such of them as shall be then living, and the said additional Trustees, for the better Management and Conduct of this Charity, with a Power to purchase Lands; and to supply by Election such Vacancies happening in the Corporation, as shall not be supplied by Succession, and such other Powers as may be thought expedient for the due Execution of this Trust, according to my Intention herein before expressed. And when such Charter shall be obtained, I desire that my Executors, or the Survivors or Survivor of them, or the Heirs of such survivor, may convey to the Use of such Corporation in Fee-simple for the Purposes aforesaid, all such Lands and Tenements, as shall be purchased in manner above mentioned. Provided always, and it is my Will and Intention, that my Executors, until the said Charter be obtained, and afterwards the Corporation to be thereby incorporated, shall out of the yearly Profits of the said Lands when purchased, and out of the yearly Income of my said Fortune devised to my Executors as aforesaid, until such Purchase be made, have Power to reimburse themselves for all such Sums of their own Money, as they shall necessarily expend in the execution of this Trust. And that until the said Charter be obtained, all Acts which shall at any Time be done in Execution of this Trust by the greater Part of my Executors then living, with the Consent of the greater Part of the said additional Trustees, under their Hands in Writing, shall be as valid and effectual, as if all my Executors had concurred in the same.

The Last Will and Testament of the Revd Dr Jonathan Swift (reprint, Dublin, 1984), pp.1-5

B. THE CHARTER, 1746

After rehearsing the provisions of Swift's Will, the Charter went on:

To the Intent therefore that the said Charity may be duly conducted in all succeeding Generations, and the pious Design of the said Testator the more effectually carried on: Know Ye, That we of our especial Grace, certain Knowledge, and mere Motion, by, and with the Advice and Consent of the most Reverend Father in God our right trusty and right intirely beloved Councellor, John, Archbishop of Armagh, Primate of all Ireland; and our right trusty and well beloved Councellors, Robert, Baron Newport, of Newport, our chancellor of our said Kingdom of Ireland; and Henry Boyle, Esq. Speaker of our House of Commons in our said Kingdom of Ireland, our Justices General, and General Governors of our said Kingdom of Ireland; and according to the Tenor and Effect of our Letters under our Privy Signet and Sign Manual, bearing Date at our Court at Saint James's the seventh Day of May One Thousand Seven Hundred and Forty-six, in the nineteenth Year of our Reign; and now inrolled in the Rolls of our high Court of Chancery in our said Kingdom of Ireland; Have granted, ordained, declared, constituted, and appointed, and we do, by these Presents, for Us, our Heirs and Successors, grant, ordain, declare, constitute, and appoint, that the Archbishop of Armagh for the Time being; our right trusty and well beloved Councellor Robert, Baron Newport of Newport, our Chancellor of our said Kingdom, and the Chancellor or Keeper of our Great Seal of our said Kingdom for the Time Being; the most Reverend Father in God our right trusty and right intirely beloved Councellor, Charles, Archbishop of Dublin, and the Archbishop of Dublin for the Time Being; the Right Reverend Father in God, Thomas, Bishop of Kildare, Dean of our Cathedral of Christ-Church, and the Dean of Christ-Church for the Time Being; the Dean of our Cathedral of Saint Patrick's, Dublin, for the Time being; Robert Robinson, Esq. our State Physician, and State Physician of our said Kingdom for the Time Being; John Nicholls, Esq. our Surgeon General, and our Surgeon General of our said Kingdom for the Time Being; and the said Henry Singleton, our Chief Justice of Common Pleas in our said Kingdom; Eaton Stannard, Recorder of the City of Dublin; Patrick Delany, Doctor in Divinity; James Stopford, Doctor in Divinity, Vicar of Finglass; James King, Doctor in Divinity, Prebendary of Tipper; John Gratton, Clerk, late Prebendary of Clonmethan; and Alexander M'Aulay; and such others as shall from Time to Time be nominated and elected to supply Vacancies in Manner herein after mentioned; shall be from henceforth one Body Politick and Corporate, and to have Continuance for ever by the Name of the Governors of Saint Patrick's Hospital, Dublin, and that, by the same Name they shall have perpetual Succession, and that they and their successors by that Name, shall be able and capable, in Law, to purchase and take to them and their successors, in Fee Simple, any Lands, Tenements, or Hereditaments, in our said Kingdom of Ireland, not exceeding in the Whole the clear yearly Value of Two Thousand Pounds Sterling; and further, that they may take and receive any Sum or Sums of money, Goods, Chattels, or personal Estate, whatsoever, that shall to them be given, granted or bequeathed, the yearly Rents and Profits of such Lands, Tenements, and Hereditaments, and the yearly Interest and Income of such personal Estate, until the same be laid out in purchasing real Estate of Inheritance in Fee Simple; to be by them expended for the Uses and Purposes of said Will.

And our Will and Pleasure is, that the Executors abovenamed, or the Survivors or Survivor of them, or the Executors of such Survivor, shall grant and assign to the said Corporation the Residue of the Effects, bequeathed to them as aforesaid, that shall remain in their Hands, after discharging thereout the Funeral Expenses and Debts of the said Testator, and such Legacies as by the Intention of the Testator are to be thereout discharged, together with their necessary Expenses and Disbursements in the Execution of the said Will: such Residue and the Interest and the Income thereof, to be laid out by the said Corporation, according to the true Intent and Meaning of the said Will.

And we do hereby grant and ordain, that the said Corporation by the Name aforesaid, shall be able and capable, in Law, to sue and be sued, plead and be impleaded, in any of our Courts, and other places whatsoever, and before any Judge, Judges, or Justices whatsoever, in all Manner of Suits, Complaints, Pleas, Causes, Matters, and Demands of whatsoever Kind, Nature, or Form they be, and all other Matters and Things, to do in as full, ample, and effectual Manner, as any other Body Politick or Corporate within our Realm of Ireland may, or can do.

And we do hereby give and grant to the said Corporation to have a common Seal, with such Stamp and Inscription to be made and ingraved thereon as they shall think proper; and that it shall be lawful for them and their Successors to change, break, alter, and renew the same at their Pleasure.

And for the better conducting the said Charity, we ordain and appoint, that the said Corporation shall have four quarterly Meetings of the Members thereof; that is to say, upon the first Mondays in May, August, November and February, in every year in all future Times at such Place or places in the City or Suburbs of Dublin, as they or the greater Part of them shall think proper; and may have such other general Meetings and at such Times and Places as the greater part of the Members of the said Corporations shall from Time to Time think fit to appoint; and whatever shall be done at any general Meeting of the said Corporation by the greater Part of the Members then and there convened, (such greater Part not being less than Three in Number) shall be, and shall be deemed and taken to be, the Act of the whole Corporation, and shall be as valid to all Intents and Purposes as if all the Members thereof were present and consenting thereto, (the making of Leases, and Election of Members, only excepted.)

And that the said Corporation, at their First general Meeting, shall elect a Treasurer, Secretary, and such other Officers as they shall find needful, to continue until the First Monday in November next thereafter, and until others be chosen to succeed them; and that at the Time of such Election, an Oath shall be administered by any Member of the Corporation, who shall be appointed for that Purpose by the Majority of the Members then and there assembled, to such Treasurer, Secretary, and other Officers, for the due and faithful Execution of their respective Officers; which Oath such Member so appointed as aforesaid, is hereby impowered to administer.

And we do further direct and appoint, that at the General Quarterly meeting of the said Corporation, to be held upon the first Monday in November, in all future Time, there shall be a new Election of Persons to serve in the respective Offices aforesaid, or the former Officers continued, as shall be thought most convenient; and at every such new Election, such Oath as aforesaid shall be administered, in Manner abovementioned, to the Officer or Officers so elected or continued; and the said Corporation are hereby impowered, at any general Meeting to remove any of their Officers for Misdemeanors; and upon the Death or Removal of any of them, to choose others to succeed in their Places.

And to the Intent that the said Corporation may have perpetual Succession, and that their present Number may for ever hereafter be supplied, kept up and preserved, we do ordain, grant, and appoint, that whensoever any Member thereof shall happen to die, the Survivors of the Persons constituting the said Corporation, shall remain incorporate by the Name aforesaid, to all Intents and Purposes, as if all the Members thereof had continued. And upon the Death of any Member (other than the Lord Primate, Lord Chancellor or Keeper of the Great Seal of Ireland, Lord Archbishop of Dublin, Dean of Christ-Church, Dean of Saint Patrick's, State Physician, and Surgeon General of Ireland, all for the Time Being) some fit Person, whose most usual Place of residence for three Years at the least then next preceding, has been in the City or Suburbs of Dublin, shall, in convenient Time, at a general Meeting of the said Corporation, be elected in the Room and Place of such Member so dying by the greater Part of the Members then and there convened;

such greater Part not being less than seven; whereof the Lord Primate, Lord Chancellor, or Archbishop of Dublin, for the Time Being, to be always one.

And our Will and Pleasure is, that all Leases, to be made by the said Corporation, of any Lands, Tenements, or Hereditaments, shall be made at some one of their quarterly Meetings, by the greater Part of the Members then present, and also with the Consent and Approbation of the Lord Primate, Lord Chancellor, Archbishop of Dublin, Dean of Christ-Church, Dean of Saint Patrick's, our State Physician, and Surgeon General of Ireland, for the Time Being, or the greater Part of them; under their Hands in Writing, indorsed upon every such Lease: and that every such Lease shall be of Lands, Tenements, or Hereditaments, in Possession, and not in Reversion or Remainder; and shall be made for a Term not exceeding Thirty One Years; and not dispunishable of, or for any Manner of Waste; and upon every such Lease there shall be reserved the best yearly Rent, that can reasonably be had or gotten for the Premises thereby demised; without any Fine to be had or taken for the same: And that no such Lease shall at any Time be made to, or in Trust for any Person who shall at the Time of the making thereof be a Member of the said Corporation, or any way related or allied, either by Consanguinity or Affinity to any Person who shall then be a Member of the same; onto, on in Trust for any Person who shall then be Treasurer or Secretary of the said Corporation, or bear any other Office under the same, or be any way related or allied either by Consanguinity or Affinity to any such Officer.

And we will and ordain, that all Leases which shall be made by the said Corporation, according to the true Intent and Meaning of these Presents, shall be good and valid; and that all Leases or Writings, purporting to be Leases, or Agreements for Leases of any Lands, Tenements, or Hereditaments, belonging to said Corporation, that shall be contrary, in any Respect, to the true Intent and Meaning hereof, shall be absolutely void and of no Effect.

And we do hereby for us, our Heirs and Successors, grant unto the Corporation at their said quarterly Meetings, in all future Time, and at no other Meetings, full Power to make such Rules and Ordinances, and from Time to Time, to alter the same, as they shall think proper for the good Government of the said Corporation, and Management of the Affairs thereof, and to give such Instructions, Directions, and Salaries, as they shall judge reasonable, to their Treasurer, Secretary, and such other Officers as they shall think fit to employ.

Provided that such Rules, Ordinances, Instructions, and

Directions, be not repugnant to the Laws then in Force within our said Kingdom of Ireland, nor contrary to the Intention of the said Testator expressed in the said Will as herein above recited; and that the same be approved of and confirmed by the Lord Chief Justice of our Court of Chief Place, or of Court of Common Pleas in Ireland, or by the Lord Chief Baron of our Court of Exchequer in our said Kingdom for the Time being.

And provided that the said Salaries of Officers to be employed by the said Corporation, shall not in the Whole, at any Time, exceed one Fifth Part of the clear yearly Profits, Interest, and Produce, of the real and personal Estate to them at that Time belonging.

And we do hereby further ordain and direct, that the said Corporation do, at their first general Meeting, nominate and appoint Seven of their Members to be a Committee, to meet upon the first Tuesday in every Month or oftener, as Need shall require. And the said Committee, or any Three or more of them, are hereby impowered to carry into Execution, all such Rules, Ordinances, Instructions, and Directions, as shall from Time to Time be made and confirmed in Manner abovementioned; such Committee to continue till the first Monday in November next following the first said Meeting of the said Corporation; at which Time, and on every first Monday in November yearly, the said Corporation shall nominate Seven of their Members to be a Committee for one Year then ensuing, for the Purposes aforesaid.

Provided always, and we do hereby expressly declare our Royal Will and Pleasure to be, that it shall not be lawful for the said Corporation at any Time, by any Act of theirs, to diminish their annual Income, whether the same shall arise from real or personal Estate, but that they shall at all Times confine their annual Expences and Disbursements to their annual Income. And whatsoever Sums of Money shall come to them by Gift or Bequest, shall, in convenient Time, be lent out at Interest, or laid out, from Time to Time, in purchasing Lands, Tenements, or Hereditaments, until such Time as their clear yearly Income shall amount to Two Thousand Pounds Sterling, unless the Disposal of such money be otherways directed by the Donor . . .

The Charter of His Majesty King George II, for Erecting and Endowing St Patrick's Hospital . . . (reprint, Dublin, 1798) pp. 7-15

C. SUPPLEMENTAL CHARTER, 1888

. . . Know ye therefore, that we of our special Grace, certain knowledge and mere motion, by and with the advice and consent of our Lieutenant General and General Governor of Ireland, and

according to the tenor and effect of our Letter under our Privy
Signet and Royal Sign Manual, bearing date at our Court at Saint
James, the 22nd day of October, 1888, in the 52nd year of our Reign,
have granted, ordained, and declared, and by these presents We do
hereby grant, ordain, and declare that the said Charter of Incorporation of the Governors of Saint Patrick's Hospital, Dublin, granted
by our said Ancestor, King George the Second, shall from henceforth, save as hereby varied and amended, remain in full force.

Object of the charity

And we ordain and appoint that the said Hospital shall continue
and be for the dieting, lodging, clothing, and maintaining poor
persons who are or shall be Idiots or Lunatics, and for supplying
them with medical and surgical assistance, medicine, and all
manner of necessaries without fee or reward.

Provided always, that it shall be lawful for the said Governors to
charge such fees as they shall think fit to any person or persons who
or whose relatives or Guardians shall consent and agree to pay the
same, such fees when received to be included in the annual income
of the said Hospital, and to be applied for the maintenance, care,
and support of the inmates of the Hospital generally.

Provided further, that nothing shall prevent the governors of the
said Hospital, if they shall think it advisable so to do, from
supplying extra articles of comfort to the patients for whom fees
shall have been paid as aforesaid.

Salaries of officers and others

And further, that the said Corporation may, notwithstanding
anything in the said original Charter to the contrary, from time to
time fix for, appoint, and pay to its officers, nurses, and servants,
such salaries and wages or pensions, or annual allowances or
donations in lieu thereof, as shall seem to them just and reasonable,
and as the income from time to time of the said Corporation may
suffice to pay, and make such rules and regulations as they shall
think fit for the due discharge of their duties by such officers,
nurses, and servants, omitting the oath in the original Charter
mentioned.

Bye-laws

And further, that it shall and may be lawful for any Members of the
said Corporation, not being less than 5 in number, by Summons (to

be served, until the making of the Bye-Laws hereinafter mentioned, in the manner before the granting of these Presents used for summoning Meetings of the said Corporation, and after the making of such Bye-Laws in the manner to be thereby provided), to convene the said Corporation, and at the said Hospital or elsewhere to hold Assemblies in order to treat and consult upon all matters concerning the Government of the said Hospital and the management of its properties and affairs; and that the said Corporation so to be convened and assembled, or the major part of them, may make, ordain, constitute, appoint, and establish such Bye-Laws as to them shall seem requisite for the regulation, government, and advantage of the said Corporation and its properties and affairs, and for the management of the said Institution, its servants and patients and may alter, annul, revoke, and abrogate any Bye-Laws so made: provided always, and it is our will and pleasure, that all such Bye-Laws be approved by our Chancellor of Ireland, the Lord Chief Justice of Ireland, and the Master of the Rolls in Ireland, or their successors in office, or any two of them, and so as such Bye-Laws be agreeable to the Laws and Statutes of our Realm and the said Charter . . .

Purchase of lands

And also that they, the said Corporation, and their successors for ever (by the name aforesaid) shall be able and capable in Law to purchase, have, hold, take, receive, and enjoy to them and their successors, in fee or in perpetuity, or for a life or lives, or for any term or terms of years, or for any other tenure, any manors, lands, tenements, rents, annuities, pensions, tithes, or other hereditaments whatsoever without any limit.

May hold funds and securities

And that the said Corporation and their successors for ever (by the name aforesaid) may take and receive any sum or sums of money, or any stocks, funds (whether public or private), or any securities for money of what nature or kind soever, or any manner of goods or chattels that shall be to them given, granted, devised, or bequeathed by any person or persons, or given or granted by any body politic or corporate capable of making a gift or grant thereof for the use of and benefit of the said Hospital.

Investment of funds

And that the said Governors or Corporation may, in their discretion, either permit any funds, securities, or property of any kind vested in them, or to which they may be entitled, or which may be at any time given, devised, or bequeathed to them, either to remain on the securities in which they shall at the date of the said Letters Patent, or at the time of such gift, devise, or bequest, be invested, or at any time, and from time to time, sell and convert the same, or any part thereof, and lay out and invest from time to time the proceeds of such sale and conversion, or any of the funds of the said Corporation, in the Government Funds of the United Kingdom, or of any of the Government Funds of any of our Colonies or Dependencies, or in the Debentures, Debenture Mortgages, or Debenture Stocks of any Public Body or Corporation duly incorporated by or in pursuance of any Act of Parliament, or by our Charter: provided such securities shall be authorized by the powers for borrowing conferred on such Body or Corporation, or in the Debenture Stocks or Mortgages of any Company which shall for three years next preceding such investment have paid a Dividend on their Original Stocks; or in the purchase of any Lands or Head-rents of Fee-simple Tenure; or upon any of the Securities for which Trustees may lend or invest Trust Funds under the powers conferred, or to be conferred, by any of the Statutes which now or hereafter may be in force in our Realm; and the said Governors or Corporation may from time to time vary and transpose the said investments into or for others of any nature hereby authorized.

May demise lands

And it shall and may be lawful for the said Corporation from time to time, by Indenture under their Common Seal, to demise any of its Lands, Tenements, or Hereditaments for the time being proposed to be demised, and for any Rent and Fine appearing reasonable and just, and so that in every such demise there be contained a covenant by the Lessee for due payment of the Rent, and that such Lease be made to take effect in possession or within six months from the execution thereof, and that the Tenant do execute a counterpart thereof.

May sell lands

And it shall be lawful for the said Corporation, or any Committee appointed, as aforesaid, for the management of the affairs of the said Corporation, from time to time as they shall think fit for the benefit of the said Charity, to enter into Contracts for the Sale of and to Sell all or any part of the Lands, Tenements, or Hereditaments of whatever tenure, corporeal or incorporeal, which now being to, or

shall hereafter be purchased by, given, granted, devised or bequeathed to the said Corporation, upon such terms and subject to restrictions, stipulations, and conditions as to title, or evidence of title, or otherwise, as they shall think fit, and with power to buy in, or rescind, or vary any Contract for Sale, and to resell without being answerable for any loss occasioned thereby; and the receipt of the said Corporation under their Corporate Seal for the purchase-money shall be a sufficient discharge to the purchaser or purchasers, who shall not be bound to see to the application of the purchase-money or any part thereof, or be answerable or responsible for the loss or misapplication thereof: and the said Corporation or Committee shall hold the proceeds of any sale under the power hereby given after payment thereout of all costs and expenses properly and necessarily incurred upon trust for the said Charity, in the same manner in all respects as if the same formed part of the Capital Funds of the said Corportion . . .
Supplemental Charter of St. Patrick's Hospital . . ., (Dublin, 1889), pp. 4-9

D. SECOND SUPPLEMENTAL CHARTER, 1895

. . . And whereas the said Governors have by a further Petition to our present Lieutenant General and General Governor of that part of our United Kingdom of Great Britain and Ireland called Ireland dated the 5th day of August 1895 represented and set forth that in order to increase the usefulness of the said Charity and to adapt the means and accommodation employed and provided in the said Hospital for the treatment of persons objects of the said Charity to the improved methods now adopted for the treatment of idiots and lunatics as well as to develop and improve the working of the said Hospital and the augmentation of its funds it was expedient to obtain a House and grounds in the Country near Dublin which could be used as an adjunct to the said Hospital and where particularly the class of lunatics whose prospects of recovery was more hopeful and those approaching convalescence could be placed and where the Patients could have the advantages of better air and more cheerful and healthy surroundings and further as in the said Petition set forth. And whereas the Governors are now possessed of the following funds principally derived from the accumulation of fees received from paying patients in the said Hospital and from the accumulation of the surplus rents of their Estates not required in past years for the purposes of the Hospital that is to say the sums of seven thousand one hundred and eighty pounds four shillings and nine pence, $2\frac{3}{4}$ p.c. stock, and three thousand pounds of the like stock the said sums being hereinafter referred to as the accumulated fund. And whereas the said Petitioners by their said further Petition having prayed that our Lieutenant General and General Governor of Ireland would recommend to us that we would graciously be pleased by our Letters Patent under the Great Seal of Ireland to grant a Supplemental Charter to the said Hospital for the purposes hereinafter mentioned . . .

Know ye therefore that we of our special Grace certain knowledge and mere motion by and with the advice and consent of our Lieutenant General and General Governor of Ireland and by and with the advice of our counsel learned in the law or some of them do hereby grant ordain and declare that the said charter of Incorporation of the Governors of Saint Patrick's Hospital Dublin granted by our said ancestor King George the Second as varied and amended by our Supplemental Charter dated the 9th day of November in the 52nd year of our reign and the said Supplemental Charter shall from henceforth save as hereby varied and amended remain in full force respectively.

And we ordain and appoint as follows:–

Power to obtain new Hospital or Asylum as an adjunct to the said Hospital

The Governors of St. Patrick's Hospital Dublin may acquire by purchase or on Lease for a term of not less than 21 years with or without a power of surrender at the end of every 3 years and with power if required in the due administration of their trust to sell lease or surrender the same a proper site in the County Dublin within seven miles from the City of Dublin for a Lunatic Asylum with out-offices and grounds to be used worked and maintained in connection with or as an adjunct to the said Hospital and out of the revenues of the same and may either alter and adapt any existing House or buildings upon the lands so to be acquired or may erect new buildings thereon for the purposes aforesaid and from time to time as occasion may require effect such structural or other alterations in or additions to the buildings so acquired or erected as they may think proper and may apply a sufficient sum or sums of money out of the said accumulated fund or out of any other sums which may have been similarly accumulated for all or any of the purposes last aforesaid and for furnishing and equipping such new Hospital with all necessary furniture requirements and conveniences for the proper and effective working thereof.

Name of the new hospital or asylum

The said New Hospital or Asylum shall also as well as the said Parent Hospital be called "Saint Patrick's Hospital Dublin" and wherever the words "Saint Patrick's Hospital Dublin" "the said Hospital" or "the Hospital" or "the said Institution" or "the Institution" are used in the said Charter or Supplemental Charter they shall be deemed to include such new Hospital or Asylum as well as the said Parent Hospital whenever the context admits thereof.

Amendment of leasing power in supplemental charter

The Leasing Power in the said Supplemental Charter shall be amended by inserting after the word "hereditaments" in the said power the following words viz. "for any term commensurate with the term or interest of the said Corporation in the said lands tenements or hereditaments." . . .
Second Supplemental Charter of St. Patrick's Hospital . . . (Dublin, 1896), pp. 4-6

E. THIRD SUPPLEMENTAL CHARTER, 1897

. . . And whereas the said Governors have by a Petition to Our present Lieutenant General and General Governor of that part of Our United Kingdom of Great Britain and Ireland called Ireland dated the 3rd day of May 1897 represented and set forth that in order to the more efficient transaction of the business of the said Hospital and to facilitate its management it was expedient that the Governors should be empowered to increase the number of Governors from twelve to fifteen . . .

Know ye therefore that We of Our special Grace certain knowledge and mere motion by and with the advice and consent of Our Right Trusty and Well Beloved Councillors Our Justices General and General Governors of Ireland and by and with the advice of Our Council learned in the law or some of them do hereby grant ordain and declare that the said Charter of Incorporation of the Governors of Saint Patrick's Hospital Dublin granted by Our said Ancestor King George the Second as varied and amended by Our two Supplemental Charters dated respectively the 9th day of November in the 52nd year of Our reign and the 5th day of December in the 59th year of Our reign and the said Supplemental Charters shall from henceforth save as hereby varied and amended remain in full force respectively.

And we ordain and appoint as follows:–

Power to increase the number of the members of the Corporation

The Governors of Saint Patrick's Hospital Dublin may from time to time at their discretion and notwithstanding any restriction in that behalf contained in their original Charter of Incorporation increase the number of the Members of the said Corporation by the election of a new member or new members provided always that under no circumstances shall the number of elected members of the said Corporation exceed ten nor the total number of the members of the said Corporation exceed fifteen: The qualifications and mode of election of such new member or new members as aforesaid shall be in every respect the same as now exist or shall hereafter be lawfully provided in reference to the election of new members of the said Corporation in substitution for members dying or resigning.
Third Supplemental Charter of St. Patrick's Hospital . . ., (Dublin, 1897), pp. 4-5.

APPENDIX 2

The Governors of St Patrick's Hospital,
1746-1989

A. EX OFFICIO GOVERNORS

Lord Chancellor

1746-1757   Robert Jocelyn, Baron Newport (1755 Viscount Jocelyn)
1757-1767   John Bowes (1758 Baron Bowes of Clonlyon)
1768-1789   John Hewitt, Baron Lifford (1781 Viscount Lifford)
1789-1802   John Fitzgibbon (1789 Baron Fitzgibbon, 1793 Viscount
            Fitzgibbon, 1795 Earl of Clare)
1802-1806   John Mitford, Baron Redesdale
1806-1807   George Ponsonby
1807-1827   Thomas Manners-Sutton, Baron Manners
1827-1830   Sir Anthony Hart
1830-1835   William Conyngham Plunket, Baron Plunket
1835   Sir Edward Sugden
1835-1841   Lord Plunket
1841   Sir John Campbell (1841 Baron Campbell)
1841-1846   Sir Edward Sugden
1846-1852   Maziere Brady
1852-1853   Francis Blackburne
1853-1858   Maziere Brady
1858-1859   Joseph Napier
1859-1866   Maziere Brady
1866-1867   Francis Blackburne
1867-1868   Abraham Brewster
1868-1874   Thomas O'Hagan (1870 Baron O'Hagan)
1875-1880   John Thomas Ball
1880-1881   Lord O'Hagan
1881-1883   Hugh Law
1883-1885   Sir Edward O'Sullivan
1885   John Naish
1885-1886   Edward Gibson (1885 Baron Ashbourne)

1886	John Naish
1886-1892	Lord Ashbourne
1892-1895	Samuel Walker
1895-1905	Lord Ashbourne
1905-1911	Samuel Walker (1906 Sir Samuel Walker)
1911-1913	Redmond Barry
1913-1918	Ignatius O'Brien (1916 Sir Ignatius O'Brien, 1918 Baron Shandon)
1918-1921	Sir James Campbell (1921 Baron Glenavy)
1921	Sir John Ross

Chief Justice

1926-1937	Hugh Kennedy
1937-1946	Timothy Sullivan
1946-1962	Conor Maguire
1962-1972	Cearbhall O Dalaigh
1972-1974	William O'Brien Fitzgerald
1974-1985	Thomas F. O'Higgins
1985-	Thomas Finlay

Archbishop of Armagh

1746-1764	George Stone
1765-1794	Richard Robinson (1777 Baron Rokeby)
1795-1800	William Newcome
1800-1822	Hon. William Stuart
1822-1862	Lord John George Beresford
1862-1885	Marcus Gervais Beresford
1886-1893	Robert Bent Knox
1893-1896	Robert Samuel Gregg
1896-1911	William Alexander
1911-1920	John Baptist Crozier
1920-1938	Charles Frederick D'Arcy
1938	John Godfrey Fitzmaurice Day
1938-1959	John Allen Fitzgerald Gregg
1959-1969	James McCann
1969-1980	George Otto Simms
1980-1986	John Ward Armstrong
1986-	Robin Eames

Archbishop of Dublin

1746-1765	Charles Cobbe
1765	Hon. William Carmichael

1766-1771 Arthur Smyth
1772-1778 John Cradock
1778-1801 Robert Fowler
1801-1809 Charles Agar, Viscount Somerton (1806 Earl of
           Normanton)
1809-1819 Euseby Cleaver (1811 of unsound mind, Archbishop
           Brodrick of Cashel coadjutor)
1820-1822 Lord John George Beresford
1822-1831 William Magee
1831-1863 Richard Whately
1863-1884 Richard Chenevix Trench
1884-1897 William Conyngham Plunket, Baron Plunket
1897-1915 Joseph Ferguson Peacocke
1915-1919 John Henry Bernard
1919-1920 Charles F. D'Arcy
1920-1939 John A. F. Gregg
1939-1956 Arthur William Barton
1956-1969 George O. Simms
1969-1977 Alan Alexander Buchanan
1977-1985 Henry Robert McAdoo
1985-   Donald Caird

Dean of Christ Church Cathedral

1746-1761 Thomas Fletcher, bishop of Kildare
1761-1765 Richard Robinson, bishop of Kildare
1765-1790 Charles Jackson, bishop of Kildare
1790-1804 George Lewis Jones, bishop of Kildare
1804-1846 Hon. Charles Lindsay, bishop of Kildare
1846-1864 Henry Pakenham, dean of St. Patrick's Cathedral
1864-1872 John West, dean of St. Patrick's Cathedral
1872-1884 R. C. Trench, archbishop of Dublin
1884-1887 W. C. Plunket, archbishop of Dublin
1887-1908 William C. Greene
1908-1921 Harry Vere White
1921-1938 Herbert Brownlow Kennedy
1938-1962 Henry Lewis-Crosby
1962-1967 Norman David Emerson
1967-1988 Thomas Noel Desmond Cornwall Salmon
1989-   John T. F. Paterson

Dean of St Patrick's Cathedral

1746   Gabriel James Maturin
1747-1775 Francis Corbet

1775-1794	William Cradock
1794	Robert Fowler
1794-1810	James Verschoyle
1810-1817	John William Keatinge
1817-1828	Richard Ponsonby
1828-1842	Henry Richard Dawson
1842	Robert Daly
1843-1864	Henry Pakenham
1864-1889	John West
1889-1902	Henry Jellett
1902-1911	John Henry Bernard
1911-1924	Charles Thomas Ovenden
1924-1933	Hugh Jackson Lawlor
1933-1935	Thomas Arnold Harvey
1935-1950	David F. R. Wilson
1950-1958	William Cecil de Pauley
1958-1968	John Ward Armstrong
1968-	Victor G. B. Griffin

State Physician

1746-1770	Robert Robinson
1770-1803	Robert Emmet
1803-1826	James Cleghorn
1826-1840	Alexander Jackson

(At various times the office of state physician was held jointly by two doctors, but the senior only of these sat on the board of the hospital.)

Surgeon General

1746-1767	John Nicholls
1767-1783	William Ruxton
1784-1787	Archibald Richardson
1787-1813	George Stewart
1819-1854	Sir Philip Crampton

B. ELECTED GOVERNORS

1746-1754	Rev. John Grattan (prebendary of St. Patrick's Cathedral)
1746-1755	Eaton Stannard (recorder of Dublin; 1754 prime

serjeant-at-law)

1746-1759   Rev. Dr Thomas King (1731-59 vicar of St. Bridget's parish; prebendary of St. Patrick's Cathedral)

1746-1759   Henry Singleton (1740 chief justice of common pleas; 1754 master of the rolls)

1746-1759   Rev. Dr James Stopford (1727 vicar of Finglas parish; 1753-9 bishop of Cloyne)

1746-1767   Alexander McAuley (barrister; 1761-6 M.P.; judge of the Dublin consistory court)

1746-1768   Rev. Dr Patrick Delany (1728 chancellor of St. Patrick's Cathedral; 1744-68 dean of Down)

1754-1756   Benjamin Bowen (Dublin alderman)

1755-1779   Anthony Foster (1737-66 M.P.; 1766-77; lord chief baron of court of exchequer)

1756-1762   Rev. Dr John Wynne (rector of St. Mary's Donnybrook; 1730-62 precentor of St. Patrick's Cathedral)

1759-1783   Sir Richard Levinge

1761-1763   Sir William Cooper

1761-1814   Colonel Thomas Cobbe (of Newbridge, Swords)

1763-1788   Rev. Dr Isaac Mann (1757-72 archdeacon of Dublin; 1772-88 bishop of Cork)

1763-1805   Rt. Hon. John Beresford (1760-1805 M.P.; 1780-1802 chief commissioner of revenue)

1767-1773   George Smith (barrister; baron of the court of exchequer)

1768-1773   Rev. William Blashford

1773-1791   Rev. Dr John Lyon (curate of St. Bridget's parish; prebendary of St. Patrick's Cathedral)

1773-1798   Rev. Dr Thomas Paul (rector of St Thomas's parish)

1779-1828   John Foster (1768-1821 MP; 1785-1800 speaker of the Irish house of commons; 1821 Lord Oriel)

1783-1794   Rev. Dr Thomas Hastings (1764-94 prebendary of St. Patrick's Cathedral; 1785-94 archdeacon of Dublin)

1790-1828   Rev. Dr Robert Fowler (1794-1813 archdeacon of Dublin; 1813-41 bishop of Ossory)

1791-1814   Rev. Dr Henry Walsh (prebendary of St. Patrick's Cathedral)

1794-1798   Rev. Dr James Verschoyle (1794-1810 dean of St. Patrick's Cathedral; 1810-34 bishop of Killala)

1798-1819   Hon. and Rev. William Beresford (1794-1819 archbishop of Tuam; 1812 Baron Decies)

1798-1828   Rev. Thomas Cradock (rector of St. Audoen's; prebendary of St. Patrick's Cathedral; librarian of Marsh's Library)

1805-1833   Hon. and Rev. John Pomeroy (rector of St. Ann's parish; 1832 Viscount Harberton)

1814-1818   Rev. James Saurin (1813-18 archdeacon of Dublin; 1819-42 bishop of Dromore)

1814-1849   Sir Robert Shaw (of Bushy Park, Terenure; 1804-26 M.P. Dublin city; 1815-16 lord mayor of Dublin)

1818-1851   Rev. Thomas Russell Cradock (rector of St. Nicholas Without; librarian of Marsh's Library)

1819-1851   Rev. Dr John Torrens (1818-51 archdeacon of Dublin)

1828-1843   William Peter Lunel (businessman; director of Bank of Ireland)

1828-1867   Rev. Thomas Kingston (vicar of St. James's parish)

1828-1869   Sir Robert Shaw (of Bushy Park, Terenure; amateur photographer)

1833-1849   George Carr (barrister; director of the Bank of Ireland)

1849-1855   Robert Law (governor of the Bank of Ireland)

1849-1860   Sir Edward Borough (army agent)

1849-1866   Rev. E. S. Abbott (rector of St. John's parish)

1851-1855   Rev. William La Poer Trench

1851-1864   Rev. Dr John West (1851-64 archdeacon of Dublin; 1864-89 dean of St. Patrick's Cathedral)

1855-1856   James Robert Stewart (land agent; governor of the Bank of Ireland)

1855-1873   Rev. Richard Barton (rector of St. Michael's parish; prebendary of Christ Church Cathedral)

1857-1860   Rev. W. H. Tighe (dean of Ardagh; 1860 dean of Derry)

1860-1880   William Cotter Kyle (barrister; M.I.R.A.; secretary of the board of education)

1860-1902   Rev. Dr Ralph Sadleir (rector of Castleknock; prebendary of St. Patrick's Cathedral)

1866-1867   Hon. George Handcock

1866-1909   Thomas Greene (secretary of representative body of the Church of Ireland)

1867-1881   John Edward Vernon (1835-87 agent for Pembroke estate)

1868-1887   George Woods Maunsell (barrister)

1869-1896   Sir Ralph Cusack (1845 barrister; 1858-80 clerk of the crown, court of chancery; chairman Midland Great Western Railway Company; son of Surgeon Cusack)

1876-1894   Robert Warren (barrister; director Midland Great Western Railway Company)

1881-1889   Rev. Thomas Tomlinson (rector of St. James's parish)

1881-1896   Richard Owen Armstrong (director Midland Great

Western and Dublin, Wicklow and Wexford railway companies)

1887-1908 Sir John Banks (physician-in-ordinary to the queen in Ireland; 1880-98 regius professor of medicine, T.C.D.)

1889-1928 Rev. J. Crawford Irwin (rector of Coolock parish; rector of St. James's parish)

1895-1917 Francis B. Ormsby (secretary Great Southern and Western Railway Company)

1896-1908 Christopher Digges LaTouche (head brewer at Guinness's Brewery)

1896-1921 William Purser Geoghegan (head brewer at Guinness's Brewery)

1897-1923 Robert Colvill (agent for Pembroke estate; director of the Bank of Ireland)

1898 Dr Samuel Gordon (1889-98 visiting physician to St. Patrick's Hospital)

1898-1912 Sir Thornley Stoker (1876-1912 visiting surgeon to St. Patrick's Hospital)

1902-1917 Rev. Dr Robert Walsh (rector of Donnybrook; 1910-17 archdeacon of Dublin)

1905-1908 Sir James LaTouche

1908-1918 Rev. W. C. Greene (former dean of St Patrick's Cathedral)

1909-1927 Sir Ernest Swifte (barrister and magistrate)

1909-1933 John Arthur Maconchy (businessman)

1915-1918 George P. Stewart

1917-1923 Dr George Scriven

1917-1932 Henry S. Guinness (manager of Guinness's Brewery; Free State senator)

1917-1935 Captain Anthony Maude (of Belgard Castle, Clondalkin; land agent; 1910-35 secretary of representative body of the Church of Ireland)

1918-1929 Richard E. Maunsell (land agent; director Property Defence Association)

1918-1932 Rev. Thomas S. Lindsay (rector of Malahide; archdeacon of Dublin)

1921-1929 J. G. Swift MacNeill (Q.C.; 1887-1918 home rule M.P. Donegal; professor of law, U.C.D.)

1923-1938 William F. Moloney (of Guinness's Brewery)

1923-1944 Christopher D. Evans (director Great Southern Railway Company)

1926-1929 Major J. H. W. Cusack (of Abbeyville, Malahide; Royal Irish Fusiliers; grandson of Surgeon Cusack)

1927-1940   Brigadier-General Henry Twigg
1929-1944   Sir John Lumsden (chief medical officer, Guinness's dispensary; commissioner of St. John's ambulance brigade; physician to Mercer's Hospital)
1930-1932   Robert H. R. Stewart (land agent)
1930-1973   Captain John M. Wardell (businessman; chairman of the board of governors)
1932-1938   Rev. R. H. Bodel (rector of Castleknock)
1932-1942   Sir William Haldane Porter
1932-1961   Gerald F. C. Hamilton (land agent)
1933-1937   Hon. Brinsley Plunket (of Luttrelstown Castle, Clonsilla)
1935-1951   Eden Fitzherbert (stockbroker)
1937-1946   Conor Maguire (1932-6 T.D.; 1936-46 president of high court; 1946-62 chief justice)
1938-1952   Herbert Saunderson McClelland (solicitor, Barrington and Son)
1939-1957   J. B. Stephens (director Great Northern Railway Company)
1940-1959   Godfrey Goodbody (insurance company manager)
1942-1951   Dr Gerald Cecil Dockeray
1944-1953   Cyril Dickinson (secretary Irish Landowners Convention)
1944-1981   Maurice Dockrell (TD; 1960-61 lord mayor of Dublin)
1946   Charles Gavan Duffy (president of high court)
1946-1959   Cahir Davitt (Dublin circuit judge)
1951-1971   Thomas Fitzherbert (stockbroker)
1953-1967   Archibold Robinson (solicitor)
1953-1969   Sir Richard Levinge (of Knockdrin Castle, Co. Westmeath)
1953-   Jeffery B. Jenkins (managing director Jacobs)
1957-1967   Harald Osterberg (Danish consul)
1959-1964   Robert R. B. Jobson (stockbroker)
1959-   C. V. Denis Wardell (businessman; chairman of the board of governors)
1962-1971   Conor Maguire (1932-6 T.D.; 1936-46 president of high court; 1946-62 chief justice)
1964-   John Wilson-Wright
1967-1980   Dr Jeremiah F. Dempsey (general manager Aer Lingus)
1968-1984   Hon. Lady Goulding (director Central Remedial Clinic)
1969-1977   Kennedy Kisch (company director)
1972-1976   Hon. David Nall-Cain
1972-1983   Dr Arthur Hughes (managing director Guinness's Brewery)

1977-1982	Professor David Spearman (Trinity College, Dublin)
1977-1984	Dr T. K. Whitaker (economist)
1980-	William G. L. Forwood (solicitor)
1981-1985	Desmond H. L. Bradley (consulting engineer)
1983-	Angus McDonnell (stockbroker)
1983-	Kevin Wylie (investment banker)
1984-	Professor D. I. D. Howie (Trinity College, Dublin)
1985-	Lt General Carl O'Sullivan
1988-	J. R. William Dick
1989-	Trevor G. D. Wardell

APPENDIX 3

Staff of St Patrick's Hospital, 1746-1989

A. VISITING PHYSICIAN

1746-1770 Robert Robinson (state physician; 1746-70 governor)
1770-1803 Robert Emmet (state physician; 1770-1803 governor)
1803-1825 James Cleghorn (state physician; 1803-26 governor)
1825-1840 John Crampton
1840-1870 Charles Philips Croker
1870-1888 Henry Freke
1889-1898 Samuel Gordon (1898 governor)
1898-1932 Richard Atkinson Hayes

B. VISITING SURGEON

1756-1797 John Whiteway
1797-1800 Clement Archer
1800-1813 John Armstrong Garnett
1813-1861 James William Cusack
1861-1875 John Hamilton
1876-1912 Sir William Thornley Stoker (1898-1912 governor)

C. MASTER/RESIDENT MEDICAL OFFICER/MEDICAL SUPERINTENDENT/MEDICAL DIRECTOR

1746-1756 William Dryden
1757-1783 Timothy Dyton
1783-1787 George Cottingham
1787-1812 Timothy Mahony (1807-12 Robert Mahony, son, assistant)
1812-1835 Patrick Campbell
1835-1858 James Cuming
1858-1859 Dr John Trench Gill (1857-8 resident apothecary; son-in-law of James Cuming)
1859-1866 Dr Francis Robinson (Dr Richard Robinson, brother, assistant)

1866-1879 Dr Edmund Lawless
1879-1884 Dr William Rice
1884-1899 Dr John Moloney (1899-1902 medical superintendent of St. Edmundsbury, Lucan)
1899-1941 Dr Richard Robert Leeper
1942-1946 Dr Robert Taylor (1925–42 assistant medical officer)
1946-1977 Dr John Norman Parker Moore (1938–41 assistant medical officer)
1978-1983 Dr P. J. Meehan (1956-68 assistant medical officer; 1968-77 deputy director; 1983– deputy director)
1983-1988 Dr Karl O'Sullivan
1989- Dr Anthony Clare

D. HOUSEKEEPER/MATRON/CHIEF NURSING OFFICER

1757-1768 Bridget Dryden (wife of William Dryden)
1768-1783 Elizabeth Dryden (Mrs Kinsey; daughter of Bridget Dryden)
1783-1787 Mary Hankison
1787-1824 Dorothy and Elizabeth Hankison (daughters of Mary Hankison)
1824-1835 Catherine Campbell (wife of Patrick Campbell)
1835-1858 Catherine Cuming (wife of James Cuming)
1858-1885 Jane Gill (daughter of Catherine Cuming; wife of Dr John Gill)
1886-1901 Mrs Hodson
1901-1937 Marie Eynthoven
1937-1942 Gladys Williams
1942-1946 Mabel Pogue
1946-1947 Kathleen Draper
1947-1951 Eileen Herbert
1951-1986 Ann Kelly
1986- Michael Connolly

E. SECRETARY/TREASURER/ACCCOUNTANT/REGISTRAR

Secretary

1746-1786 Rev. Dr John Lyon (1773-91 governor)
1786-1794 Rev. Dr Thomas Hastings (1783-94 governor)
1794-1798 Rev. Dr James Verschoyle (1794-1810 governor)
1798-1818 Rev. Thomas Cradock (1798-1828 governor)
1818-1851 Rev. Thomas Russell Cradock (1818-51 governor)
1852-1871 Rev. W. P. H. Dobbin
1872-1899 Rev. J. A. Dickinson

Treasurer

1747-1757	Rev. Dr Francis Corbet (1747-75 governor)
1755-1756	Benjamin Bowen (1754-6 governor)
1757-1777	Anthony Foster (1755-79 governor)
1777-1798	Dr Robert Emmet (1770-1803 governor)
1798-1810	Rev. Dr James Verschoyle (1794-1810 governor)
1810-1833	Hon. and Rev. John Pomeroy (1805-33 governor)

Accountant

1840-1846	Joseph Goslett
1846-1853	George Yeats
1853-1885	John Benjamin Butler Yeats (son of George Yeats)
1885-1889	T. H. F. Newland
1889-1899	George E. R. Manders

Secretary/Registrar

1899-1913	George E. R. Manders
1913-1945	Albert E. Coe
1945-1970	Robert McCullagh
1970-1988	Reginald Crampton
1988-	Noel Breslin

F. LAND AGENT

Saggart, Dublin (from 1791) and Ferns (from 1886)

1746-1756	William Dryden
1757-1776	Bernard Kane
1776-1783	Stuckey Simon
1783-1799	Charles Hamilton
1799-1826	John Verschoyle
1826-1878	John James Verschoyle (son of John Verschoyle)
1878-1941	William Henry Foster Verschoyle (son of J. J. Verschoyle)
1941-1967	W. J. Verschoyle-Campbell (nephew of W. H. F. Verschoyle)

Ferns

1766-1886	Symes family

The Patients: Statistical Tables

ADMISSION FORMS TO ST PATRICK'S HOSPITAL, DUBLIN
1841-1850 & 1874-1883

	1841-1850		1874-1883	
Number of Patients:				
Total Admissions	256		171	
Surviving Forms	178 (69%)		154 (90%)	
Sex:	%		%	
Male	61		43	
Female	39		57	
Religion:	%		%	
Protestants	75		81	
Catholics	25		19	
Marital Status:	Male	Female %	Male	Female %
Married	40	19	28	23
Single	54	75	69	62
Widowed	6	6	3	15
Age:	Male	Female %	Male	Female %
Between 20 & 40	64	61	54	40
Committed By:	Male	Female %	Male	Female %
Father	19	19	21	4
Mother	15	19	15	16
Brother	25	23	24	12
Sister	3	10	6	11
Husband	—	13	—	20
Wife	20	—	12	—
Other	18	16	22	37
Length of Stay:	Male	Female %	Male	Female %
More than 5 years	29	43	9	24

	1841-50		1874-1883	
Discharged:	Male	Female %	Male	Female %
Recovered	27	26	25	40
Relieved	18	24	27	14
Unrelieved	11	6	21	10
Fate Unknown	6	7	10	6
Died in Hospital	Male	Female %	Male	Female %
	38	37	17	30
Cause of Illness:	Male	Female %	Male	Female %
Not Known/Given	30	44	33	32
Over Study/Work	13	3	24	2
Financial Reverses	10	4	5	7
Ill Health	7	13	12	16
Childbirth/Menstrual	—	7	—	12
Drink	13	1	7	5
Drugs	1	1	3	1
Religion	5	6	7	2
Grief	1	6	2	4
'Romantic/Domestic'	4	4	—	1
Heredity	6	2	5	4
'Anxiety/Nervousness'	5	6	—	11
Hysteria	—	2	—	2
'Mental Excitement'	5	1	—	—
'Brain Fever'	—	—	2	—
'Shock'	—	—	—	1

Length of Present Illness:	%	%
Less Than One Week	4	9
1 Week to 1 Month	14	17
1 Month to 6 Months	28	31
6 Months to 1 Year	15	11
1 Year to 5 Years	27	22
5 Years to 10 Years	7	7
More Than Ten Years	4	3

Place of Residence:	%	%
Dublin: County	4	4
City	34	32
Suburbs	14	33

	1841-1850	1874-1883
Place of Residence:	%	%
Leinster (excluding Dublin)	23	13
Ulster	12	3
Munster	6	4
Connacht	3	6
Britain	3	3
United States	—	2
Occupation:	%	%
Private Means	5	23
Dependent on Family	31	28
Professional	29	18
Business	7	6
Trade	11	7
Clerical	5	9
Agricultural	6	4
None Given	6	4

Admission Forms nos 300-599, 1841-53, and nos 920-1150, 1873-87.
(S.P.H.D. 19th century papers, uncat.)

PATIENTS IN ST PATRICK'S HOSPITAL, 1869, 1876, 1884

Numbers:	1869	1876	1884
Resident at 31 December: Male	67 (49%)	54 (49%)	35 (37%)
Female	70 (51%)	57 (51%)	59 (63%)
Admitted during Year	13	18	16
Discharged:			
Total	12 (9%)	12 (11%)	14 (15%)
Recovered	5 (4%)	9 (8%)	0 (-)
Died	4 (3%)	8 (7%)	9 (10%)
Prognosis:			
Curable	5	5	1
Incurable	126 (92%)	99 (89%)	90 (96%)
Marital Status:			
Married	13	12	6
Single	121 (88%)	97 (87%)	81 (86%)
Widowed	3	2	7

	1869	1876	1884
Diagnosis:			
Mania	65 (47%)	34 (31%)	43 (46%)
Monomania	7	—	9
Melancholia	25 (18%)	33 (30%)	28 (30%)
Incoherence	7	10	—
Imbecility	28 (20%)	26 (23%)	11 (12%)
Idiocy	5	4	3
Plus Violent	7	15	6
Plus Suicidal	3	4	—
Age:			
20 to 40	63	40	38
40 to 60	65	42	33
Over 60	9 (7%)	20 (26%)	23 (24%)
Education:			
Well Educated	72 (53%)	83 (75%)	84 (89%)
Reads and Writes well	55	26	8
Ditto Indifferently	3	2	—
Can Read Only	—	—	2
Cannot Read or Write	7	—	—
Occupation:			
Army	8	7	4
Navy	—	—	1
Church	9	6	3
Law	1	2	—
Medicine	3	2	4
Student	9	10	3
In Trade	8	9	—
Farming	5	4	4
Other	13	19	17
None: Male	18 (27%)	8 (15%)	7 (20%)
Female	63 (90%)	44 (77%)	51 (86%)

Nineteenth Report on the District, Criminal and Private Lunatic Asylums in Ireland, 132-43 [C-202], H.C. 1870, xxxiv, 418-29; *Twenty-sixth Report on . . . Asylums,* 104-15 [C-1750], H.C. 1877, xli, 552-63; *Thirty-fourth Report on . . . Asylums,* 110-21 [C-4539], H.C. 1885, xxxvi, 745-55.

The Staff: Dr Leeper's List of Daily Duties, October 1899

ST PATRICK'S HOSPITAL
DAILY DUTIES

a.m.

5.45   The Night Attendants to call the Day Attendants and see that they get up.

6.0   All Day Attendants to be on duty.

6.0   Patients to get up and to be properly washed and their hair brushed. Troublesome Patients to remain in their rooms until all the other Patients are cleaned.

6.30   Attendants' Breakfast.

6.50   The Charge Attendants to see or give instructions for the opening of windows, weather permitting, and the beds opened so as to air; all necessary work to be done in the ward; soiled linen to be taken to the laundry; all utensils to be washed, and slops must be removed as rapidly as possible. As much of the cleaning, etc. as possible to be done before the Patients' breakfast.

8.30   Patients' Breakfast.

9.0   The Patients all to be made tidy and prepared for the exercising ground.

10.15   All galleries and rooms to be in proper order and ready for inspection, and all Attendants neatly dressed, and in uniform, ready to go into the grounds.

12.00   The Patients to return to their respective wards, and to be washed and their hair brushed, ready for dinner.

p.m.

12.15   First Division Attendants' Dinner.

12.45   Second Division Attendants' Dinner.

1.30   Patients' Dinner.

2.45   The wards to be again tidy and the Patients to go into the grounds—the Attendants to arrange between themselves who will precede the Patients into the grounds and who will follow them. No Patients will be allowed in the grounds unless an Attendant be with them.

4.0   The Patients to return again to their wards, and be washed and their hair brushed, ready for tea.

4.15   Attendants' Tea.

5.30   Patients' Tea.

6.15   The troublesome Patients put to bed. Cleaning can often be done after this, which is more difficult to do in the morning when all the Patients are in the wards.

7.30   The Patients who were put to bed first to be visited, wet cases to be induced, if possible, to respond to the calls of nature.

9.0   All patients to go to bed. Those who had gone to bed earlier to be again visited before being handed over to the Night Attendant.

10.0   All Attendants to be in.

10.30   All Attendants to be in their respective rooms.

Attendants' Rooms—the Attendants are not to frequent their own rooms during the day, except when off duty. They are to be kept in a neat and orderly manner, great care being exercised in locking up scissors, razors, knives, and all articles of value or importance. The Medical Superintendent has authority to inspect them at any time, as has also the Head Attendant, who shall report any untidiness to the Medical Superintendent. Twenty minutes are allowed for an Attendant to shave and dress, and put his room tidy—this to be done at the most convenient time between 6.50 a.m. and 10.15 a.m. No two Attendants to be away from the ward at the same time. An Attendant leaving a ward must first ascertain whether others are present, and must notify where he is going to the Charge Attendant, and the probable duration of his absence, in case of his services being required.

Night Attendants—commence their duties at 9 p.m. and have charge of, and are responsible for, the Patients in each ward. This responsibility does not cease, nor must they leave the wards, until the Day Attendants have entered on their duty and their report of the night occurrences duly written out and left at the Head Attendant's office. They should see the Charge of each ward, from whom they will learn the general condition of the Patients, with special particulars respecting those recently admitted, those suffering from epilepsy, excitement, or bodily illness or debility, those manifesting dangerous or suicidal tendencies, and those who from any peculiar circumstances require more than the usual attention.

They shall raise out of bed, and induce to attend the call of nature, at regular intervals during the night, those Patients who are in the habit of wetting or soiling the beds. With some patients one systematic call will suffice, with others it will be found necessary to repeat the call at each visit. Uncleanly habits will be corrected in a large majority of instances by those repeated attentions, which are used with success in the case of children. If a patient quarrels with or disturbs the other Patients in the dormitories and cannot be induced to be quiet, removal to a single room is to be made; if violent, obtain the assistance of the Day Attendant who may be sleeping in that part of the building.

In the event of any Patient destroying his linen or bedding, the torn articles shall be at once removed and other articles substituted. For this purpose the special strong clothes are to be employed. In case of illness, or if there is any doubt as to the Patient's condition, the Medical Superintendent should at once be called.

They shall see that all Day Attendants are in their rooms at 10.30 p.m., and shall report to the Medical Superintendent any irregularity or misconduct committed while they are on duty.

They shall see that the necessary fires are properly attended to, and record their wakefulness and punctuality, on the pegging clocks provided for that purpose, every hour.

At 5.45 a.m. they shall call the Day Attendants and see that they rise, and report to the Charge Attendants anything that has occurred during the night which might call for special supervision or care.

(Signed) RICHARD R. LEEPER
Placard: Daily Duties, October 1899, (S.P.H.D., 19th century papers, uncat.)

St Patrick's Hospital and the 1916 Rising

Dr Richard Leeper's Report to the Governors, 3 June 1916

To the Board of Governors of St Patrick's Hospital, 3 June 1916.

My Lords and Gentlemen,

Owing to the Rebellion no meeting of the Governors has occurred since I last reported to your board on April 1st. Since then the following patients have been admitted — Mrs. Gibson, Miss Briscoe, Band Sergeant Keogh and Miss O'Donovan. The illness of both these last mentioned cases was produced by shock and terror caused by the insurrection and [both] were admitted during the height of the Rebellion. The Army ambulance which conveyed Mr Keogh to the Hospital was fired on whilst conveying the patient to the Hospital. Three patients died all from natural causes. Owing to the disturbances it was exceedingly difficult to bury the remains, and in the case of Rev. H. [?] King-Finley I had to place the coffin for some days in the garden before I could with the valuable help of Mr Irwin [governor and chaplain] have him interred in the parish graveyard. Mr Irwin attended repeatedly at the Hospital during the Rebellion at considerable risk of his life. On my arrival here from Lucan on Easter Monday firing commenced all round this district and continued more or less constantly for 10 days.

At many times the rattle of machine gun fire was often continuous for hours and the bullets came into the wards in several places. The greatest danger was caused to the lunatics by the firing of the soldiers at the Kingsbridge [Sean Heuston Bridge]. Bullets entered the New Wing and raked the top ward on the ladies side. When this began I personally placed barricades and padding material such as mattresses in the windows. It seems most wonderful that none of the patients or nurses were killed as the fire lasted for several hours. A guard of 40 soldiers were at the front gate and I and my wife fed these men as well as we could during the Rebellion.

My great anxiety at first was that the Hospital would be occupied by the Rebels, as was the Union [South Dublin Union Workhouse, now James's Hospital], and if this had been attempted, I would have much wished for your Board's direction as to whether it were best to resist or allow the Rebels to occupy the Hospital. It has been a most trying experience for us all and I cannot but report upon the admirable calmness [?] and attention to their duties which character-ised the conduct of the nurses during the period as they came under fire and their he.ʾ in preventing the patients from becoming alarmed and panic stricken and the discipline of the Hospital disturbed.

We have been in the centre of a battlefield for 10 days surrounded by the armies and this experience is one that few have experienced. Mr Keogh, admitted in a condition of acute mania with homicidal and suicidal tendencies, has recovered and been discharged into his wife's care . . .

During the Rebellion I have had the House Repairer employed in securing with iron bars some windows which were unprotected and now he is cleaning and repainting rooms on the male side which were very dirty, and required repainting for some time.

Dr Colles [registrar of lunacy] visited the Hospital and inspected the places where the bullets entered the wards. I desire to draw your attention to the conduct of your man Tully and also to that of John Lane. These men throughout the Rebellion at great personal risk brought into us the milk from Lucan [the hospital's farm], and sheep and lambs, which I had killed. I would suggest that some honorarium be given them in recognition of their conduct, which was largely responsible for our suffering no hunger, and for the patients being properly fed through the insurrection [John Tully, van man, and John Lane awarded £2 each: Board Minutes, 5 June 1916] . . .

Medical Superintendent's Reports, 1911-17 (S.P.H.D., 20th century papers, uncat.)

Notes

Chapter 1, pp. 1-31

1. John Harvey, *Dublin: a Study in Environment* (reprint, Wakefield, 1972, of orig. edn London, 1949), p. 77.
2. W. M. Thackeray, *The English Humourists; The Four Georges* (reprint, London, 1949, of orig. edn London, 1853, 1861), pp. 27-8
3. [Rev. Francis Mahony], *The Works of Father Prout*, ed. Charles Kent (London, n.d.), pp. 76-7.
4. Irvin Ehrenpreis, *The Personality of Jonathan Swift* (London, 1958), pp. 117-18.
5. James Joyce, *Ulysses* (reprint, Harmondsworth, 1982, of orig. edn, Paris, 1922), p. 45.
6. Norman O. Brown, *Life Against Death: the Psychoanalytical Meaning of History* (reprint, London, 1970, of orig. edn, London, 1959), pp. 163-81. For a recent survey and critique of Freudian interpretations of Swift, see Hermann J. Real and Heinz J. Vienken, 'Psychoanalytic Criticism and Swift: the History of a Failure' in *Eighteenth-Century Ireland*, i (1986), pp. 127-41.
7. Jonathan Swift, *Gulliver's Travels* (reprint with intro. by Michael Foot, Harmondsworth, 1984, of orig. edn, London, 1726), p. 18.
8. Seamus Deane, *A Short History of Irish Literature* (London, 1986), p. 41.
9. J. N. P. Moore, *Swift's Philanthropy* (Dublin [1967]), p. 3.
10. *Jonathan Swift: the Complete Poems*, ed. Pat Rogers (Harmondsworth, 1983), p. 498. (Hereafter *Poems*).
11. Ehrenpreis, op.cit., pp. 125-6.
12. John Boyle, Earl of Orrery, *Remarks on the Life and Writings of Dr Jonathan Swift. . . .* (3rd edn, Dublin, 1752), p. 264.
13. Ibid., p. 279.
14. Ibid., pp. 272-3
15. For examples of some of the popular anecdotes attached to Swift, see A. C. Elias Jr, 'Lord Orrery's Copy of *Memoirs of the Life and Writings of Swift* (1751)' in *Eighteenth-Century Ireland*, i (1986), pp. 117-25. In 1931 Dr Francis Burke of Lower Leeson Street, Dublin, donated a large book of clippings, entitled Swiftiana, to the hospital. This contains articles, notices and reviews from a variety of English and Irish newspapers, magazines and journals ranging from the 1740s to the 1930s, all relating to Swift. It provides a fascinating compendium of both popular and scholarly views of the Dean over a period of nearly two hundred years.
16. W. R. Wilde, *The Closing Years of Dean Swift's Life; . . .* (2nd edn, Dublin, 1849), p. 78.

17. Maurice Craig, *Dublin, 1660-1860* (reprint, Dublin, 1980, of orig. edn, Dublin, 1952), p. 97.
18. T. P. Kirkpatrick, *The Foundation of a Great Hospital: Steevens in the XVIII Century* (Dublin, 1933), pp. 10-11.
19. John Banks, 'The Writ "de Lunatico Inquirendo" in the Case of Jonathan Swift, D.D., Dean of St Patrick's; with Observations' in *The Dublin Quarterly Journal of Medical Science*, new series, xxxi, no. 61 (1861), p. 90.
20. T. G. Wilson, 'Swift's Deafness; and His Last Illness' in *Irish Journal of Medical Science*, 6th ser., no. 162 (June 1939), p. 298.
21. *The Correspondence of Jonathan Swift*, ed. Harold Williams (Oxford, 1965), iv, 258, 545. (Hereafter *Corr.*)
22. Wilde, op.cit., p. 66.
23. Banks, op.cit., pp. 89-90.
24. *Corr.*, v, 207-8, 214-15.
25. Ibid., p. 214.
26. Ibid., p. 214.
27. W. R. Brain, 'The Illness of Dean Swift' in *Irish Journal of Medical Science*, 6th ser., nos 320-1 (Aug./Sep. 1952), pp. 337-45. The pioneering, but still highly readable, study of aphasia is Henry Head, *Aphasia and Kindred Disorders of Speech* (2 vols, Cambridge, 1926); a vivid recent case history, worth comparison with Swift's experience, is given in Oliver Sack's fascinating book, *The Man who Mistook his Wife for a Hat* (London, 1986), pp. 76-80. For other, useful accounts of Swift's health, see T.G. Wilson's two articles, 'The Mental and Physical Health of Dean Swift' in *Medical History*, ii, 3 (July 1958), pp. 175-90 and 'Swift and the Doctors' in *Medical History*, viii, 3 (July 1964), pp. 199-216.
28. *Poems*, p. 487.
29. Ibid., p. 489.
30. For a discussion of the neurotic traits in Swift's personality, see Moore, op.cit., pp. 18-20.
31. For the Augustan view of madness, see Max Byrd, *Visits to Bedlam: Madness and Literature in the Eighteenth Century* (Columbia, S. C., 1974) and Michael DePorte, *Nightmares and Hobby Horses: Swift, Sterne and Augustan Ideas of Madness* (San Marino, Calif., 1974).
32. E. G. O'Donoghue, *The Story of Bethlehem Hospital from its Foundation in 1247* (New York, 1915), pp. xviii, 16-25.
33. For the history of the development of the word, see the *Oxford English Dictionary*.
34. Michel Foucault, *Madness and Civilization: a History of Insanity in the Age of Reason*, trans. Richard Howard (reprint, London, 1985, of orig. English edn, London, 1967), pp. 38-43; George Rosen, *Madness in Society: Chapters in the Historical Sociology of Mental Illness* (Chicago and London, 1968), pp. 160-4.
35. Foucault, op.cit., p. 44; see also M. E. Rose, *The English Poor Law, 1780-1930* (Newton Abbot, 1971), pp. 11-12.
36. For critiques of Foucault's view that a 'great confinement' of lunatics began in the second half of the seventeenth century, see J. G.

Merquior, *Foucault*, Fontana Modern Masters, ed. Frank Kermode (London, 1985), pp. 21-31 and Roy Porter, *Mind-Forg'd Manacles: a History of Madness in England from the Restoration to the Regency* (London, 1987), pp. 5-9, 110-11.

37. J. T. Gilbert (ed.), *Calendar of Ancient Records of Dublin* (Dublin, 1895), v, 321; (Dublin, 1896) vi, 257.

38. Keith Thomas, *Religion and the Decline of Magic: Studies in Popular Beliefs in Sixteenth- and Seventeenth-Century England* (reprint, Harmondsworth, 1978, of orig. edn, London, 1971), pp. 15-16, 172, 351-2.

39. Quoted in Klaus Doerner, *Madmen and the Bourgeoisie: a Social History of Insanity and Psychiatry*, trans. Joachim Neugroschel and Jean Steinberg (London, 1981) p. 26; for Willis, see also Porter, op.cit., pp. 46-7, 176-8.

40. DePorte, op.cit., pp. 6-7.

41. Porter, op.cit., p. 177.

42. Andrew Scull, 'Moral Treatment Reconsidered: Some Sociological Comments on an Episode in the History of British Psychiatry' in Andrew Scull (ed.), *Madhouses, Mad-Doctors, and Madmen: the Social History of Psychiatry in the Victorian Era* (London, 1981), p. 108.

43. Porter offers a persuasive, and probably long overdue, challenge to the portrait of eighteenth-century psychiatry which depicts only cruelty, squalor and ignorance; see Porter, op.cit., pp. 1-15.

44. John Locke, *An Essay Concerning Human Understanding*, ed. J. W. Youlton (reprint, London, 1961, of 5th edn, London, 1706), i, 5.

45 Jonathan Swift, *A Tale of a Tub and other Satires*, ed. Kathleen Williams (reprint, London, 1975, of 5th edn, London, 1710), p. 104.

46. O'Donoghue, op.cit., pp. 235-40, 249-51. For recent, more sympathetic portrayals of Bedlam, see P. H. Allderidge, 'Bedlam: Fact or Fantasy?' in W. F. Bynum, Roy Porter and Michael Shepherd (ed.). *The Anatomy of Madness* (London, 1985), ii, 17-33 and Porter, op.cit., pp. 121-9.

47. Swift, *A Tale of a Tub*, p. 111.

48. Majorie Nicolson and Nora M. Mohler, 'The Scientific Background of "Voyage to Laputa"' in A. Norman Jeffares (ed.), *Swift: Modern Judgements* (London, 1969), pp. 223-37.

49. *Poems*, pp. 551-2.

50. Ibid., p. 554.

51. Irvin Ehrenpreis, *Swift, the Man, his Works, and his Age: Dean Swift* (London, 1983), iii, 819, 827-31.

52. Byrd, op.cit., p. 60; Moore, op.cit., p. 18.

53. Quoted in the Introduction, Swift, *Gulliver's Travels*, p. 15.

54. Thackeray, op.cit., p. 29.

55. DePorte, op.cit., p. 91.

56. T. P. Kirkpatrick, *A Note on the History of the Care of the Insane in Ireland up to the End of the Nineteenth Century* (Dublin, 1931), p. 12.

57. Gilbert, op.cit., vi, 214.

58. Kirkpatrick, *Steevens*, p. 4.

59. Kirkpatrick, *Care of the Insane*, pp. 7-8; Charles McNeil, 'The Hospital of St John Without the New Gate, Dublin' in *Journal of the Royal Society of Antiquaries of Ireland*, 6th ser., 1v (1925), pp. 58-64.

60. Joseph O'Carroll, 'Contemporary Attitudes Towards the Homeless Poor, 1725-1775' in David Dickson (ed.), *The Gorgeous Mask: Dublin 1700-1850* (Trinity History Workshop 2, Dublin, 1987), pp. 64-85; L. A. Landa, 'Jonathan Swift and Charity' in *Journal of English and Germanic Philology*, xliv (1945), pp. 337-50.
61. Joseph Robins, *The Lost Children: a Study of Charity Children in Ireland, 1700-1900* (Dublin, 1980), pp. 11-16; O'Carroll, op.cit., p. 74.
62. Gilbert, op.cit., viii, 507-10.
63. J. F. Fleetwood, *The History of Medicine in Ireland* (2nd edn, Dublin, 1983), pp. 95-104, 205-11.
64. Ehrenpreis, *Dean Swift*, iii, 568.
65. Robins, op.cit., p. 21.
66. *Corr.*, iv, 65-70.
67. Wilde, op.cit., p. 82.
68. *Corr.*, iv, 448, 326, 425.
69. Gilbert, op.cit., viii, 135.
70. Ehrenpreis, *Dean Swift*, iii, 839-40, 856, 900; *Corr.*, v, 274.
71. Gilbert, op.cit., viii, 183.
72. *Corr.*, iv, 319, 366-7.
73. Ibid., v, 24.
74. Kirkpatrick, *Care of the Insane*, pp. 14-15.
75. Joseph Robins, *Fools and Mad: a History of the Insane in Ireland* (Dublin, 1986), p. 49.
76. *The Last Will and Testament of the Revd. Dr Jonathan Swift* (reprint, Dublin, 1984), p. 4
77. *Corr.*, v, 112-13.
78. Ibid., iv, 373-4.
79. Quoted in W. L. Parry-Jones, *The Trade in Lunacy: a Study of Private Madhouses in England in the Eighteenth and Nineteenth Centuries* (London and Toronto, 1972), p. 223.
80. Porter singles out St Patrick's Hospital as evidence that not all eighteenth-century madhouses were places of squalor and cruelty; see Porter, op.cit., pp. 10, 157.
81. *Corr.*, iv, 405-6.
82. Ibid., v, 112-13.
83. Ibid., iv, 296.
84. Ibid., iv, 296-7.
85. *Last Will and Testament*, pp. 2-4.
86. *The Charter of His Majesty King George II, for Erecting and Endowing St Patrick's Hospital; Founded by the Last Will of the Reverend Doctor Jonathan Swift, Late Dean of St Patrick's Dublin; for the Reception of Idiots, Lunaticks and Incurables* (reprint, Dublin, 1798), p. 12.
87. Ibid., p. 15.
88. Vouchers produced by Mr Robert King for Money paid during the time of Dr Swift's Insanity from Nov. 1742 to Nov. 1745 (St Patrick's Hospital, Dublin (hereafter S.P.H.D.), Swift papers, uncatalogued).
89. The Governors of St Patrick's Hospital, Dublin . . . Against . . . Committees of the said Doctor Jonathan Swift and Robert King, Gent.,

To the Right Hon. the Lord Chancellor of Ireland, [Report of] William Wall, 22 June 1748 (S.P.H.D., Swift papers, uncat.)

90. Ibid.

91. The details of Deane Swift's debts are contained in Loftus versus Swift and the Governors of St Patrick's Hospital, Dublin, Outline of Case for the Opinion of Robert French, 26 Apr. 1797; for Denn's debt, see two bonds between Philip Denn of Saggart, Co. Dublin, and Rev. Dr Jonathan Swift, Dean of St Patrick's, Dublin, 30 Sept 1738, 2 Jan 1738/9 (S.P.H.D., Swift papers, uncat.); for Lynch's debt, see P. V. Thompson and D. J. Thompson, *The Account Books of Jonathan Swift* (Newark, N. J., and London, 1984), pp. cxxiv, 310-13.

92. Bond forms for Swift's industry money, nos 1-84 (plus two unnumbered), 1718-44; An Account of Industry Money and Bonds, 7 Dec. 1744 (S.P.H.D., Swift papers, uncat.).

93. An Account of the several Bonds returned by Mrs Land to William Dryden, n.d. (S.P.H.D., Swift papers, uncat.); Minute Books of the Governors of St Patrick's Hospital, Dublin (hereafter M.B.), 7 July 1749; *Last Will and Testament*, pp. 7, 11-12.

94. C. N. French, *The Story of St Luke's Hospital* (London, 1951), pp. 4, 9-10.

95. It should perhaps, however, be pointed out that the 'cells' built in the 1750s are now used for various purposes, particularly as offices — they are no longer used to accommodate patients.

Chapter 2, pp. 32-103

1. Journal of John Moore, Carrickfergus, Co. Antrim, Feb. 1767 (P.R.O.N.I., D 3165/2).

2. Charles Maturin, *Melmoth the Wanderer: a Tale* (reprint, Harmondsworth, 1977 of orig. edn, Edinburgh, 1820), p. 91.

3. Sir Walter Scott, *The Works of Jonathan Swift* (2nd edn, Edinburgh, 1824) i, 527-8.

4. M.B., 29 Aug., 3 Nov. 1746; 19 Nov. 1748.

5. Ibid., 2 Nov. 1747.

6. Ibid., 2 Feb., 6 Mar. 1746/7. Until 1752 Britain and Ireland employed the old style, Julian calendar, according to which the year began on 25 March. In 1752 this was replaced by the new style Gregorian calendar, with the year beginning on 1 January. In the text I have corrected dates between 1 January and 25 March to the new style year, while in these notes I have given both years, with the old style first.

7. Alexander McAulay to Robert King, 12 Jan. 1747/8 (S.P.H.D., 18th century papers, uncat.).

8. M.B., 15 Dec. 1749; 6 Nov. 1752; 6 Feb. 1758.

9. John Warburton, James Whitelaw and Robert Walsh, *History of the City of Dublin. . . .* (London, 1818) ii, 691 note; M.B., 5 May 1755.

10. Plaques were placed on the walls of four of the wards, at a cost of twelve guineas, but the names did not endure and, until quite recently, wards were simply designed by numbers. M.B., 25 Feb. 1750/1; 5 May 1755; *Dublin Journal*, 22-5 Feb. 1752; *The Gentleman and*

Citizen's Almanack, (By John Watson, Bookseller), for the Year of Our Lord 1758 (Dublin, 1758), p. 69.

11. For the recovery of the £200 Boyton and £500 Gore legacies, see M.B., 23 Dec. 1760; 26 Aug. 1753; 25 Jan., 26 Mar. 1788. For the bequests of Henry Gill of Carrickfergus and the Hon. Mrs Jane Bury, see *The Irish Builder*, 1 Apr. 1897, pp.68-71. This article contains a wealth of detailed information on the hospital's history, apparently supplied to the journal by the then medical superintendent, Dr John Moloney.

12. *Dublin Journal*, 8-11 Feb. 1766. I would like to thank Dr Robert Mahony for this intriguing reference.

13. Ian Campbell Ross (ed.), *Public Virtue, Public Love: the Early Years of the Dublin Lying-In Hospital, the Rotunda* (Dublin, 1986), pp.20-2, 25, 97.

14. M.B., 3 Aug., 20 Aug., 24 Nov. 1750; An Account of Sundry Disbursements on Account of the Governors of St Patrick's Hospital by William Dryden, 1750-6 (S.P.H.D., 18th century papers, uncat.).

15. M.B., 4 Feb. 1750/1; 6 May 1751.

16. M.B., 25 Feb. 1750/1.

17. M.B., 24 Feb. 1752; Warburton, Whitelaw and Walsh, op.cit., ii, 691 note; Lease of lands at Kilmainham from the Petty Canons and Choristers of St Patrick's Cathedral to John Worrall, 1748 (S.P.D.H., 18th century papers, uncat.).

18. To the Honorable the Knights, Citizens and Burgesses, in Parliament Assembled, the Humble Petition of the Governors of St Patrick's Hospital, Dublin, 3 Nov. 1755 (S.P.H.D., 18th century papers, boardroom).

19. M.B., 9 Aug. 1756; 23 Dec. 1758; 22 Jan. 1759.

20. Campbell Ross, op.cit., pp. 26-8, 48.

21. Map of the Saggart Estate of the Governors of St. Patrick's Hospital, Dublin, by Thomas Reading, 1751; Survey bill of Jonathan Barker for £240.9.7$\frac{1}{2}$, March 1756; An Account of what the several tenants of Saggart (are willing to abide by) belonging to the Governors of St. Patrick's Hospital with the Observations of the Committee, 1757 (S.P.H.D., 18th century papers, uncat.); M.B., 13 Mar. 1756; 1 July 1757.

22. M.B., 29 July 1757; Rent Roll of the Estate of the Governors of St Patrick's Hospital with an account of the arrears returned by Mr Dryden to and for 25 Mar. 1758 (S.P.H.D., 18th century papers, uncat.).

23. Heads of Disputes among the Tenants of Saggart, n.d. (S.P.H.D., 18th century papers uncat.).

24. M.B., 11 Dec. 1747; 19 Oct. 1749.

25. Ibid. 7 Nov., 15 Nov. 1748; 10 Jan. 1748/9.

26. T. P. Kirkpatrick, *The Foundation of a Great Hospital: Steevens in the XVIII Century* (Dublin, 1933), p. 8; Maurice Craig, *Dublin, 1660-1860* (reprint, Dublin, 1980, of orig. edn, Dublin, 1952), p. 113.

27. M.B., 5 May, 3 Aug. 1747; 24 May 1748; 28 Apr. 1749.

28. Ibid., 11 Dec. 1747; 28 Mar., 18 Apr. 1748; for Levinge's bequest, see also *Dublin Journal*, 20-24 June 1749.

29. M.B., 15 Dec. 1749; 10 Feb. 1748/9.
30. Ibid., 19 Nov. 1748; 10 Feb. 1748/9.
31. In his discussion of the building of St Patrick's Hospital, Maurice Craig identifies Wills as Isaac Wills, a builder who worked on Steevens Hospital and also on St Ann's Church in Dawson Street, but, in his later book on the development of Dublin, he correctly names Michael Wills, and not Isaac, as the builder involved at St Patrick's. Certainly the governors' minute book names Michael Wills as Semple's rival. [Maurice Craig (ed.)], *The Legacy of Swift; a Bi-Centenary Record of St. Patrick's Hospital, Dublin* (Dublin, 1948), pp. 32-3; Craig, *Dublin*, p. 171; M.B., 15 Dec. 1749.
32. J. H. Bernard, *The Cathedral Church of St Patrick; a History and Description of the Building, with a Short Account of the Deans* (London, 1903), p. 33.
33. M.B., 18 Apr., 15 Dec. 1749; Craig, *Dublin*, p. 171. Wills continued, however, to work for the governors: the tradesmen's accounts for fitting up the wards show that he was paid nearly £22 in 1759-60. What he did is not specified, but it is likely that he supervised this work; see M.B., 6 Aug. 1759; 23 Dec. 1760.
34. Offices and Apartments of the following Dimensions in the Plan of George Semple, which are not in Mr Wills's, n.d. (S.P.H.D., 18th century papers, uncat.).
35. *The Diary of John Evelyn*, ed. William Bray (reprint London, 1907, of orig. edn, London 1818-19), ii, 123.
36. E.G. O'Donoghue, *The Story of Bethlehem Hospital from its Foundation in 1247* (New York, 1915), pp. 202-11.
37. M.B., 18 Apr. 1749; 29 Mar. 1751.
38. Ibid., 7 July, 6 Nov., 15 Dec. 1749.
39. [Craig], *Legacy*, p. 33 gives the date as February 1749, but this is according to the old sytle calendar; under the new, it is 1750.
40. George Semple's book of plans and further description of the foregoing design: and the methods intended to be taken in the execution thereof, 2 Feb. 1749/50 (S.P.H.D., 18th century papers, boardroom).
41. Ibid., pp. 17, 22.
42. O'Donoghue, op.cit., p. 244
43. Semple's plans, p. 1.
44. Ibid., pp. 5-6.
45. Ibid., p. 8.
46. M.B., 29 Mar. 1751.
47. Semple's plans, pp. 10-12.
48. O'Donoghue, op.cit., pp. 244-5.
49. Semple's plans, p. 5.
50. M.B., 20 Dec. 1757; 4 Aug. 1762.
51. The construction of the hospital can be traced, in some detail, in the minutes of the board meetings, and also through payments to Semple, recorded in Dean Corbet's accounts; see, in particular, M.B., 7 July, 6 Nov., 15 Dec., 1749; 2 Feb. 1749/50; 5 July 1750; 25 Feb. 1750/

51; 29 Mar., 27 May, 4 Nov., 18 Dec., 1751; 5 Feb., 24 Feb., 25 Apr., 18 July, 3 Aug., 10 Aug., 11 Dec. 1752; 7 May, 29 Nov. 1753.

52. O'Donoghue, op.cit., pp. 212-13.

53. C. N. French, *The Story of St Luke's Hospital*, (London, 1951), pp. 29-30, 38.

54. Fitzpatrick, *Steevens*, pp. 8-10.

55. Rent Roll, 25 Mar. 1758; Rent Roll of the Estate of the Governors of St Patrick's Hospital with an Account of the Arrears due 29 September 1759 (S.P.H.D., 18th century papers, uncat.)

56. Rent Roll, 29 Sept. 1759; M.B., 3 Feb. 1777. Slater already had a paper-mill at Clondalkin and in the 1740s was noted in Dublin for his fine paper. Certainly his rivals, the Joy family, proprietors of the *Belfast News-letter*, who had their own mills in Ulster, seem to have been impressed by his operations; see Mary McNeill, *The Life and Times of Mary Ann McCracken 1770-1866: a Belfast Panorama* (reprint, Belfast, 1988, of orig. edn, Dublin, 1960), pp. 16-17, 22.

57. M.B., 2 Mar. 1774; 28 Aug. 1775.

58. Petition, 3 Nov. 1755; M.B., 9 Aug. 1756; Walter Harris, *The History and Antiquities of the City of Dublin . . .* (Dublin, 1766), pp. 467-9.

59. M.B., 29 July 1757.

60. Ibid; Offices and Apartments in Semple's plan, n.d.

61. M.B., 29 July 1757. It is difficult to make these pay figures very meaningful as we lack detailed information on wages, prices and the cost of living in Ireland during the eighteenth century. Some figures relating to the pay of labourers do survive, however, and, as the keepers at St Patrick's appear to have been regarded essentially as unskilled labourers, there is a basis here for comparison. We know, for instance, that in the 1750s and 1760s builders' labourers in Dublin were earning one shilling per day, while in the 1770s, according to the visiting agricultural expert, Arthur Young, rural labourers earned on average $6\frac{1}{2}$d per day. At about this time the keepers and most of the servants employed by St Patrick's were receiving 4d per day. It might appear from this that the hospital staff were poorly paid, but we need to remember that, on top of their wages, they also enjoyed free food and accommodation. Moreover, their employment was regular and relatively secure, which is more than can be said for that of labourers, whether urban or rural. Thus, although the actual pay was relatively low compared to that of similar workers, employment at St Patrick's had obvious attractions and certainly it would seem that the governors never had any trouble in finding employees. For a brief, though helpful, discussion of the eighteenth-century Irish standard of living, see L. M. Cullen, 'Economic Development, 1750-1800' in T. W. Moody and W. E. Vaughan (ed.), *A New History of Ireland, Volume iv: Eighteenth-Century Ireland, 1691-1800* (Oxford, 1986), pp. 185-7.

62. For two examples of works printed by Dyton in the early 1770s, see C. E. Sayle (ed.), *A Catalogue of the Bradshaw Collection of Irish Books in the University Library, Cambridge* (Cambridge, 1916), i, 341.

63. E. Evans to Rev. J. A. Dickinson, 2 Apr. 1889 (S.P.H.D., 19th century

papers, uncat.). With this letter to the hospital's secretary, Evans enclosed a copy of Nanny McDaniel's obituary in the April 1798 issue of the *Monthly Miscellany; or Irish Review and Register.*

64. M.B., 7 Nov. 1757.
65. Ibid., 23 Dec. 1760; 1 Nov. 1762; 2 Dec. 1767.
66. Ibid., 12 Sept. 1757.
67. Ibid., 19 Sept. 1757; *Universal Advertiser,* 12 and 18 Oct. 1757.
68. M.B., 7 Nov. 1757; 23 Dec. 1758; 22 Jan. 1759.
69. Ibid, 15 Oct. 1757.
70. Ibid., 23 Dec. 1758.
71. Ibid., 4 Aug. 1762.
72. A. P. W. Malcomson, *John Foster: the Politics of the Anglo-Irish Ascendancy* (Oxford, 1978), p. 358.
73. Ibid., pp. 7-8.
74. M.B., 8 May 1780.
75. Ibid., 4 May, 6 June 1772.
76 Ibid., 23 Jan. 1775.
77. Malcomson, op.cit., p. 358.
78. For the personalities and careers of Foster, Beresford and Fitzgibbon, see R. B. McDowell, *Ireland in the Age of Imperialism and Revolution, 1760-1801* (Oxford, 1979), pp. 307-8, 450-51; Thomas Pakenham, *The Year of Liberty: the Great Irish Rebellion of 1798* (reprint, London, 1982, of orig. edn, London, 1969), pp. 65-8, 246-7; Edith Mary Johnston, *Ireland in the Eighteenth Century* (Gill History of Ireland 8, Dublin, 1974), pp. 163, 178-9; David Dickson, *New Foundations: Ireland, 1660-1800* (Helicon History of Ireland 6, Dublin, 1987), pp. 158-62.
79. M.B., 1 Feb. 1797; 11 May, 18 June 1798; 4 Feb., 28 Mar. 1799.
80. Notes on Macdonnel, Butler and McByrnes, tenants on Ferns estate, n.d. (S.P.H.D., 19th century papers, uncat.).
81. These notes were obviously made after the rebellion and they appear to relate to the question of whether or not these tenants' leases, which were due to expire in 1803 and 1808, should be renewed.
82. M.B., 23 Jan, 1775.
83. Ibid.
84. Ibid., 1 Dec. 1769.
85. Ibid., 4 May, 6 June 1772.
86. Ibid., 28 Aug, 1775; 5 Dec. 1777; Bernard Kane's accounts, 12 Oct. 1775 (S.P.H.D., 18th century papers, uncat.).
87. Extracted from the Book of Orders of St Patrick's Hospital [by Rev. John Lyon], 1760-72 (S.P.H.D., 18th century papers, uncat.).
88. M.B., 24 Apr. 1773; 28 Aug. 1775. Emmet also seems to have taken an interest in the affairs of the Ferns estate for, among the hospital's papers, there is a letter from him to the dean of St Patrick's dated 10 May 1798, in which he apologises for not being able to attend the board meeting on the following day and goes on to criticise the Symes agency, recommending that the governors purchase the family's annuity. Given the trouble that the hospital was later to have with its

Ferns agents, this was wise advice; see Dr Emmet to the dean of St Patrick's Cathedral, 10 May 1798 (S.P.H.D., 18th century papers, uncat.).

89. Ibid., 6 Feb. 1776; 8 Dec. 1777; 19 Nov. 1810.

90. Ibid., 1 Feb. 1779; 3 Feb. 1783; 23 Aug. 1792.

91. Ibid., 5 Nov. 1789; D. J. O'Donoghue, *Life of Robert Emmet* (Dublin, 1902), p. 17. In the three years, 1800-02, sixteen meetings of the board are recorded in the minute book, eight of which Dr Emmet attended.

92. M.B., 3 Nov. 1766; 5 June, 13 June, 21 June 1783.

93. Ibid., 7 July, 4 Aug., 30 Sept., 1783; 1 Jan. 1798.

94. Ibid., 16 July 1783; 1 Aug. 1785; 7 May, 15 May, 29 June, 5 Nov. 1787; Deposition of Timothy Mahony, 29 Aug. 1787; Bill of Costs of Henry Betagh, 1787-92 (S.P.H.D., 18th century papers, uncat.).

95. M.B., 26 Mar. 1784; 25 Jan. 1788; 2 Feb. 1801; 8 May 1764; 3 Feb. 1772; 1 May 1780.

96. Ibid., 30 Sept. 1783. The pay increases that occurred between the 1750s and 1780s were quite dramatic, amounting often to the trebling of an employee's wage. As indicated, the increase in the number of patients and the introduction of chamber boarders were major factors contributing to this rise. But, from the scattered figures available, it would seem that in Ireland wages generally rose substantially between the 1720s and 1770s. Thus, if St Patrick's employees were financially better off in the 1780s than they had been thirty years earlier, so were much of the rest of the population. See Cullen in Moody and Vaughan (ed.), op.cit., p. 186.

97. Rental of the Estate of the Governors of St Patrick's Hospital at Saggart in the County of Dublin, 1789-90 (S.P.H.D., 18th century papers, uncat.); M.B., 15 Dec. 1777.

98. Copy of the will of James Symes, 31 Dec. 1766, with Codicil, 2 Jan. 1767 (S.P.H.D., 18th century papers, uncat.).

99. State of account between the Right Hon. the Governors of St Patrick's Hospital and Abraham Symes (appointed by the Trustee) under the Will of the late James Symes for Three years ending 29th September 1797, and One Year ending September 1798 (S.P.H.D., 18th century papers, uncat.).

100. M.B., 11 Feb. 1791; 5 Nov. 1792; Bill of Costs of Henry Betagh, 1787-92; The Governors of St Patrick's Hospital account with Charles Hamilton for one year's rent of their Estate at Saggart, and one year's rent of the Estate bequeathed by Dr John Taylor ending at March, May and June 1796 (S.P.H.D., 18th century papers, uncat.).

101. Report on St Patrick's Hospital by James Verschoyle and Thomas Cradock, 22 Mar. 1799 (S.P.H.D., 18th century papers, uncat.).

102. M.B., 13 Oct. 1768; 7 Nov. 1796; 19 June 1809; 2 May 1814; 15 June 1804; 17 Feb. 1880.

103. Ibid., 1 Feb., 7 Nov. 1796; 4 May 1801; 27 May 1799; 7 Feb. 1803; 1 Mar. 1813.

104. Ibid., 3 Feb. 1806; 20 Mar. 1803; 15 Aug. 1805; Rental of the Lordship

of Ferns . . . 25 Mar. 1799; Rental of the Lands of Lower Ferns . . . from Euseby Lord Bishop of Ferns for 21 Years from 24 June 1804 (S.P.H.D., 18th and 19th century papers, uncat.).

105. For a handy summary of the economic problems of this period, see L. M. Cullen, *An Economic History of Ireland since 1660* (reprint, London, 1978, of orig. edn, London, 1972), pp. 100-05.

106. Rentals of the Estate of the Governors of St Patrick's Hospital at Saggart, 25 Mar. 1813, 25 Mar. 1814, 25 Mar. 1816, 25 Mar. 1817, 25 Mar. 1818, 25 Mar. 1821, 25 Mar. 1822 (S.P.H.D., 19th century papers, uncat.).

107. For the genealogy of the Verschoyle family, see *Burke's Irish Family Records* (London, 1976), pp. 1163-6.

108. M.B., 1 Feb. 1819.

109. Ibid., 15 Mar. 1819.

110. Rental, Saggart, 25 Mar. 1821; Richard Rinkle to the Governors of St Patrick's Hospital, 1 Feb. 1819 (S.P.H.D., 19th century papers, uncat.).

111. M.B., 1 Aug. 1825; 7 Aug. 1826.

112. Craig, *Dublin*, pp. 195-9.

113. M.B., 12 Jan. 1778.

114. [Craig (ed.)] *Legacy*, pp. 36-7.

115. M.B., 7 Apr., 5 May 1781.

116. Ibid., 16 July 1783.

117. Ibid., 22 May 1776; 12 Jan. 1778; 3 Nov. 1781; 15 July 1784.

118. Ibid., 8 Nov. 1788; 4 May, 20 May 1789. Davis, who has been described as a 'rather mediocre architect' also worked for the La Touche family, through whose influence he became overseer of the Bank of Ireland buildings. The decision simply to copy Semple's design may have partly been a reflection of Davis's lack of imagination; see David Dickson and Richard English, 'The La Touche dynasty' in David Dickson (ed.), *The Gorgeous Mask: Dublin, 1780-1850* (Trinity History Workshop 2, Dublin, 1987), p. 23.

119. M.B., 7 Nov. 1785; 25 Jan. 1788; 17 Jan., 23 Aug. 1792.

120. *Report from the Committee . . . for . . . making Provision for the Care of Lunatics and Idiots by Grand Jury Presentments*, p. 2, H.C. 1803-4 (109), iv, 772; *Report from the Select Committee on the Lunatic Poor in Ireland*, H.C. 1817 (430), viii; *Copies of all Correspondence . . . on the Subject of Public Lunatic Asylums*, pp. 17-18, H.C. 1828 (234), xxii, 239-40; W. S. Hallaran, *Practical Observations on the Causes and Cure of Insanity* (2nd edn, Cork, 1818); Mark Finnane, *Insanity and the Insane in Post-Famine Ireland* (London and Totowa, N.J., 1981), pp. 20-26.

121. M.B., 23 Aug. 1792.

122. Report of sub-committee, 22 Mar. 1799 (S.P.H.D., 18th century papers, uncat.).

123. M.B., 2 May, 12 May 1808; 10 Mar. 1809.

124. Ibid., 6 Nov. 1809; 5 Nov. 1810. Parke was a protégé of John Foster, who doubtless recommended him to his fellow governors. He built

the Commercial Buildings in Dame Street in 1796-9, the Royal College of Surgeons in Stephen's Green in 1806, and, after his work at St Patrick's, stables for Foster at his home in Collon, Co. Louth; see Malcomson, op.cit., p. 17 and Craig, *Dublin*, p. 279.

125. M.B., 5 Nov., 19 Nov. 1810. Theophilius Swift was also far from truthful: the report he gave Sir Walter Scott of his father's financial dealings with Dean Swift was, for instance, highly misleading. The evidence shows that Swift was extremely generous to his young cousin, while Deane Swift was simply a poor manager of money; see Sir Walter Scott, *The Works of Jonathan Swift* (2nd edn, Edinburgh, 1824), i, p. 441-3 note. For Theopilius' own strange doings, including his imprisonment for libelling Trinity College, see Constantia Maxwell, *A History of Trinity College, Dublin, 1591-1892* (Dublin, 1946), pp. 150-51 and W. J. McCormack, *Sheridan LeFanu and Victorian Ireland* (Oxford, 1980), p. 4.

126. M.B., 19 Nov., 26 Nov. 1810.

127. Ibid., 26 Nov. 1810.

128. Ibid., 9 Apr. 1811; 16 Apr. 1812.

129. Ibid., 23 Apr. 1812; 14 Feb. 1814. For the problems of the Waterford workhouse and its overcrowded asylum, see *Report from the Select Committee on the Lunatic Poor in Ireland*, pp. 39-42, H.C. 1817 (430), viii, 71-4.

130. *Report from the Select Committee on the Lunatic Poor in Ireland*, p. 45, H.C. 1817 (430), viii, 81.

131. *Third Report from the Committee on Madhouses in England*, pp. 7-9, H.C. 1816 (451), vi, 363-5.

132. M.B., 12 May 1808; 7 Aug. 1815; 2 Nov. 1818; *Report from the Select Committee on the Lunatic Poor in Ireland*, p. 46, H.C. 1817 (430), viii, 82.

133. *Third Report from the Committee on Madhouses in England*, p. 8, H.C. 1816 (451), vi, 364.

134. M.B., 7 Aug. 1815.

135. Ibid., 6 May, 7 June 1816; *Report from the Select Committee on the Lunatic Poor in Ireland*, pp. 45-6, H.C. 1817 (430), viii, 81-2.

136. *Report from the Committee on Madhouses in England*, H.C. 1814-15 (296), iv; Andrew Scull, *Museums of Madness: the Social Organisation of Insanity in Nineteenth-Century England* (reprint, Harmondsworth, 1982, or orig. edn, London, 1979), pp. 78-82.

137. *Third Report from the Committee on Madhouses in England*, p. 8, H.C. 1816 (451), vi, 364.

138. Changes in attitudes to treatment will be discussed more fully in the next chapter, but for useful accounts, see Scull, *Museums of Madness*, pp. 54-75 and Elaine Showalter, *The Female Malady: Women, Madness and English Culture, 1830-1980* (reprint, London, 1987, of orig. edn, New York, 1985), pp. 26-42.

139. M.B., 19 Sept. 1757; 1 Feb. 1762; 30 Sept. 1783; 12 May 1808; 1 Mar. 1813; Report of the sub-committee, 22 Mar. 1799 (S.P.H.D., 18th century papers, uncat.); *Third Report from the Committee on Madhouses*

in England, p. 8, H.C. 1816 (451), vi, 364; *Report from the Select Committee on the Lunatic Poor in Ireland*, p. 45, H.C. 1817 (430), viii, 81.

140. Quoted in Constantia Maxwell, *Dublin under the Georges, 1714-1830* (London and Dublin, 1946), pp. 115-16. For several articles illustrative of eighteenth-century Dublin working-class life, see Dickson (ed.), *The Gorgeous Mask.*

141. M.B., 25 May 1784; 5 June 1820.

142. Ibid., 22 June 1810.

143. Daily Expense of a Boarder at St Patrick's Hospital, n.d. (S.P.H.D., 19th century papers, uncat.); M.B., 7 May 1787; *Third Report from the Committee on Madhouses in England*, p. 8. H.C. 1816 (451), vi, 364. For informative discussions of Irish diets and food costs during the late eighteenth century, see L. M. Cullen, *The Emergence of Modern Ireland, 1600-1900* (London, 1981), pp. 140-92 and R. B. McDowell, 'Ireland in 1800' in Moody and Vaughan (ed.), op.cit., pp. 672-5.

144. M.B., 1 Aug. 1768; 6 May 1771; 6 June 1786; 4 May 1801.

145. Ibid., 28 Aug. 1785; 20 Dec. 1757; 11 Nov. 1815; 10 Apr. 1809; 15 June 1804; *Third Report from the Committee on Madhouses in England*, p. 8, H.C. 1816 (451), vi, 364.

146. M.B., 8 Nov. 1800.

147. *Third Report from the Committee on Madhouses in England*, p. 8, H.C. 1816 (451), vi, 364.

148. *Report from the Select Committee on the Lunatic Poor in Ireland*, p. 45, H.C. 1817 (430), viii, 81.

149. M.B., 8 Nov. 1800; 6 Aug. 1759; 5 May 1760; 23 Dec. 1760; 1 Nov. 1762; 2 Nov. 1767; 6 May 1771.

150. Roy Porter, *Mind-Forg'd Manacles: a History of Madness in England from the Restoration to the Regency* (London, 1987), pp. 178-9, 193-4, 218, 226-7.

151. Hallaran, op.cit., pp. 80, 82-3.

152. Ibid., pp. 71-2, 104-5, 108-9, 129, 137-8, 143, 147.

153. Ibid., pp. 133-6, 163-4. For the development by the Tuke family of moral management techniques at the York Retreat, see Anne Digby, 'Moral Treatment at the York Retreat' in W. F. Bynum, Roy Porter and Michael Shepherd (ed.), *The Anatomy of Madness* (London, 1985), ii, 52-72 and also Andrew Scull, 'Moral Treatment Reconsidered: Some Sociological Comments on an Episode in the History of British Psychiatry' in Andrew Scull (ed.), *Madhouses, Mad-doctors and Mad-men; the Social History of Psychiatry in the Victorian Era* (London, 1981), pp. 105-18.

154. Hallaran, op.cit., pp. 99, 113, 151, 207-8, 166-8, 170-4.

155. M.B., 4 May 1807; 6 May 1822.

156. Ibid., 6. Nov. 1769.

157. M.B., 1746-96; 1797-1835.

158. *Third Report from the Committee on Madhouses in England*, p. 8, H.C. 1816 (451), vi, 364.

159. Malcomson, op.cit., pp. 2-5, 10-11.

160. M.B., 31 May, 7 July 1783; 19 Mar. 1784; 5 Feb., 5 Nov. 1770.

161. Ibid., 5 Sept. 1764; 1 May 1775; 3 Nov. 1777; 18 Jan. 1787; 6 Feb., 4 Nov. 1776.
162. Ibid., 5 Aug. 1816.
163. Ibid., 14 Aug. 1797; 6 Feb. 1798; 4 Feb. 1799; 7 Feb. 1803; 8 Jan. 1770; 21 June 1783; 3 Nov. 1794; 2 Nov. 1772; 1 Feb. 1779.
164. Ibid., 6 Nov. 1780.
165. Charles Maturin, the novelist, was a curate at St Peter's from 1806 till his death in 1824. His grandfather had been Swift's successor as dean of St Patrick's Cathedral and had sat on the original board of governors of the hospital in 1746. Given his family's and parish's connections with St Patrick's, it seems fair to assume that Maturin would have been familiar with the hospital. His great, gothic novel, *Melmoth the Wanderer*, first published in 1820, contains an episode set in an asylum and, as the description of this institution accords reasonably well with what we know of St Patrick's, it seems more than likely that Maturin's knowledge of the Dublin hospital formed the basis, or at least a basis, for this episode.
166. M.B., 30 Mar. 1787; 6 Nov. 1774; 28 Aug. 1775; 5 Sept. 1771.
167. *Report from the Committee . . . for . . . making Provision for the Care of Lunatics and Idiots by Grand Jury Presentments*, p. 2, H.C. 1803-4 (109), iv, 772 *Report from the Select Committee . . . Appointed to Consider the State of the Lunatic Poor in Ireland* pp. i-ii, H.L. 1843 (625), x.
168. M.B., 3 Feb., 22 May 1783.
169. Ibid., 1 Feb. 1779; 6 Nov. 1780.
170. Ibid., 3 Feb. 1772; 4 Aug. 1783; 3 May 1802; 15 June 1804; 7 Nov. 1803.
171. Journal of John Moore, Carrickfergus, Co. Antrim, July 1766-Mar. 1768 (P.R.O.N.I., D. 3165/2,). One of the sons of Bishop Joseph Stock of Killala, famous for his account of the 1798 French invasion, suffered from mental illness between about 1806 and 1813. He, however, was never admitted to an asylum, but was treated mainly at home in consultation with Dr William Harvey, physician to Steevens Hospital and a governor of the Richmond Asylum. Home care, under medical advice, like that afforded Charles Stock, was doubtless far more common at the time than admission to an asylum like St Patrick's. I would like to thank Mr Basil Clarke for providing me with a copy of his article, 'Mental Illness and Rehabilitation in Early Nineteenth-Century Ireland: the Case of Charles Stock' in *Psychological Medicine*, 13 (1983), pp. 727-34.
172. M.B., 18 Jan. 1787, 2 Aug. 1790; 5 May 1788. In 1770 a Mrs Kathrens (or Cathrens) was admitted as a boarder, but there is no indication whether or not she was a relative of George and Murray Kathrens; see ibid., 22 June 1770.
173. Mary Leadbeater, *The Annals of Ballitore* (reprint, ed. John MacKenna, Athy, 1986, of orig. edn, *The Leadbeater Papers*, London 1862), pp. 43-4.
174. This gothic view of asylums is certainly not new and in fact can be found in many gothic novels of the late eighteenth and early nineteenth centuries, notably Maturin's *Melmoth the Wanderer*. For a modern critique of it, see Porter, op.cit., pp. 129-60.

Chapter 3, pp. 104-153

1. Dr James Cleghorn, state physician and visiting physician to St Patrick's Hospital, *Report from the Select Committee on the Lunatic Poor in Ireland*, p.46, H.C. 1817 (430), viii, 82.
2. Sir Edward Sugden, Irish lord chancellor, *Report from the Select Committee . . . Appointed to Consider the State of the Lunatic Poor in Ireland*, p. 51 H.L. 1843 (625), x.
3. Mary Larkin to the governors of St Patrick's Hospital, 24 April 1843 (S.P.H.D., Admission Form No. 364: Thomas Larkin, 1844, uncat.).
4. Dr Hugh Carmichael to Surgeon James Cusack, 24 December 1844 (S.P.H.D., Admission Form No. 411: Edward McLaughlin, 1844, uncat.)
5. M.B., 7 Nov. 1825, 6 Feb., 6 Nov., 1826.
6. Dr Alex Jackson to the governors of St Patrick's Hospital, 7 Feb. 1831 (S.P.H.D., 19th century papers, uncat.).
7. M.B., 4 Feb. 1828.
8. J. F. Fleetwood, *The History of Medicine in Ireland* (2nd edn, Dublin, 1983), p. 153.
9. Cusack was a colourful character, among whose many notable students was Charles Lever, the novelist. Some of the practical jokes described in Lever's novels, particularly *Charles O'Malley*, were actually played at Steevens and involved Cusack; See T. P. Kirkpatrick, *The History of Doctor Steevens' Hospital, Dublin, 1720-1920* (Dublin, 1924), pp. 181-3, 344 and C. A. Cameron, *The History of the Royal College of Surgeons in Ireland* (Dublin, 1886). pp. 447-9. I would like to thank Mr Sean Donovan for providing me with information on Dr Cusack and his family.
10. *D.N.B.*; J. L. McCracken, 'Protestant Acendancy and the Rise of Colonial Nationalism, 1714-60' and R. B McDowell, 'The Age of the United Irishmen: Revolution and the Union, 1794-1800' in T. W. Moody and W. E. Vaughan (ed.), *A New History of Ireland, vol. IV: Eighteenth-Century Ireland, 1691-1800* (Oxford, 1986), pp. 117–22, 340–4, 370; J. B. Leslie, *Derry Clergy and Parishes* (Enniskillen, 1937), p. 21.
11. M.B., 12 Nov. 1810; 6 Nov., 11 Nov. 1815; 12 Nov. 1823; 3 May 1824; R. G. Thorne (ed.), *The History of Parliament: the House of Commons, 1790-1820* (London, 1986), iv, pp. 852-62
12. M.B., 19 Mar. 1835; 10 Feb., 9 Mar., 7 Apr. 1836; 1 June 1837.
13. Sir Robert Shaw's charity also extended to the less well-off members of his own family. In the 1820s and 1830s, for instance, he supported the widow and eleven children of his cousin, Bernard Shaw, a failed businessman who died penniless about 1825. Several of the children took to drink and two died in Dr Eustace's private asylum in Glasnevin, but one of the drunkards was the father of George Bernard Shaw; see Michael Holroyd, *Bernard Shaw. Volume 1: the Search for Love, 1856-1898* (London, 1988), pp. 6-8. I would like to thank Mr Edward Chandler for providing me with information on the younger Robert Shaw's career as a photographer. Unfortunately Shaw never seems to

have turned his camera on the hospital or its inmates. For some of his fine portraits, see Edward Chandler, *Photography in Dublin during the Victorian Era* (Dublin, n.d.), pp. 9-10, 34, 45.

14. Patrick Lynch and John Vaizey, *Guinness's Brewery in the Irish Economy, 1759-1876* (Cambridge, 1960), pp. 35, 126.
15. M.B., 1 Aug. 1814; 5 Aug. 1816; 3 May 1824.
16. Ibid., 14 May 1835; *The Treble Almanac for the Year 1829, Containing . . . Wilson's Dublin Directory* (Dublin, 1829), p. 189.
17. M.B., 5 May, 1 Sept. 1842.
18. Ibid., 3 May, 1 Nov. 1824.
19. *Report of the Inspectors-General on the District, Local and Private Lunatic Asylums in Ireland, 1843*, 44-5 [C 567], H.C. 1844, xxx, 114-15
20. M.B., 3 Nov. 1828; 2 Feb. 1829; 1 May 1837; 21 May 1840
21. *Report of the Inspectors-General on the District, Local and Private Lunatic Asylums in Ireland, 1843*, 47-8 [C 567], H.C. 1844, xxx, 117-18.
22. M.B., 2 Nov. 1835. We saw that fifty years earlier in the 1780s, keepers, both male and female, were receiving sixteen guineas per annum, while in 1796, 1801 and 1813 wage increases caused by wartime inflation brought the level up to twenty-five guineas per annum. How long these high wages lasted is unclear, but the figures for 1835 show a significant fall and particularly so in the case of female staff. We should not assume, however, that the keepers were necessarily worse off, for there had been a substantial fall in prices after 1815 as well. In Dublin in 1831-5, for instance, prices for wheat, beef and butter were some 30% to 50% lower than they had been in 1812-15. See Mary Daly, *The Famine in Ireland* (Dublin Historical Association: Irish History, Second Series, Dublin, 1986), p. 22.
23. *Report of the Inspectors-General on the District, Local and Private Lunatic Asylums in Ireland, 1843*, 6-11 [C 567], H.C. 1844, xxx, 74-9.
24. Ibid. pp. 11-14/79-82; M.B., 2 Sept. 1850. Private asylums were licensed by 5 & 6 Vict. c. 123, passed in 1842. But under section 49 of the act, charitable institutions like St Patrick's were excluded from most of its provisions. One provision the hospital was not excluded from, however, was that relating to inspection. Thus, from 1843 onwards, the reports of the lunacy inspectors' annual visits became a vital source of information.
25. M.B., 1 May 1820; 4 Aug. 1823; 1 Feb., 7 Apr. 1836; 5 Aug. 1844.
26. *The Last Will and Testament of the Revd. Dr Jonathan Swift* (reprint, Dublin, 1984), p. 3.
27. M.B., 11 Nov. 1829; 4 Feb., 1830; 6 Feb. 1832; 4 Feb. 1833.
28. *Report of the Inspectors-General on the District, Local and Private Lunatic Asylums in Ireland, 1843*, 11-14 [C 567], H.C. 1844, xxx, 79-82.
29. *Report from the Select Committee on Medical Charities, Ireland*, pp.150-1, H.C. 1843 (412), x.
30. *Report from the Select Committee . . . Appointed to Consider the State of the Lunatic Poor in Ireland*, pp. 50-3, H.L. 1843 (625), x.
31. Ibid.; Mark Finnane, *Insanity and the Insane in Post-Famine Ireland* (London and Totowa, N.J., 1981), pp. 41-2.

32. *Report of the Inspectors-General on the District, Local and Private Lunatic Asylums in Ireland, 1845,* 14-15 [C 736], H.C. 1846, xxii, 424-5; M.B., 14 Apr. 1846.

33. M.B., 3 Apr. 1843; *Report of the Inspectors-General on the District, Local and Private Lunatic Asylums in Ireland, 1845,* 15 [C 736], H.C. 1846, xxii, 425.

34. Estate Rental Books: Saggart, 1840-57; Ferns, 1840-58 (S.P.H.D., 19th century papers, uncat.).

35. M.B., 6 Aug. 1838; 5 Feb., 10 June 1839; Ecclesiastical Commissioners of Ireland to Sandham Symes, 4 Mar. 1839 (S.P.H.D., 19th century papers, uncat.).

36. L. M. Cullen, *An Economic History of Ireland since 1660* (reprint, London, 1976, of orig. ed., London, 1972), pp.101-4, 109; M.B., 4 Feb. 1822; 2 Aug. 1824; 7 Feb., 1 Aug. 1825; 7 Aug., 6 Nov. 1826; 2 Feb. 1829; 1 May 1831; 2 May 1836. W. E. Vaughan has summed up the situation aptly by saying that 'the *threat* of eviction was an important part of estate management'. For a handy introduction to landlord and tenant relations in nineteenth-century Ireland, see W. E Vaughan, *Landlords and Tenants in Ireland, 1848-1904* (Studies in Irish Economic and Social History 2, Dublin, 1984), p. 16.

37. M.B., 1 Nov. 1830; 7 Nov. 1831.

38. Ibid., 5 May 1849; 6 Aug., 15 Aug. 1850.

39. Ibid., 24 Apr. 1851.

40. Ibid., 27 May 1851.

41. Daly, op.cit., p. 120. Generally consolidation of holdings after the Famine seems not to have been as significant as was once thought; see Daly op.cit., p. 120. Details of eighty tenancies at Saggart and thirty-nine at Ferns are contained in two ledgers, entitled: Report of the Saggart Estate up to 25 March 1850 and Recommendation of Sub-Committee; Report of the Ferns Estate up to 25 March 1851 and Recommendation of Sub-Committee (S.P.H.D., 19th century papers, uncat.).

42. M.B., 17 June 1816; 5 Feb. 1827; 4 May 1835; 2 June 1831; Joseph Robins, *Fools and Mad: a History of the Insane in Ireland* (Dublin, 1986), p. 79.

43. M.B., 7 Mar., 4 Apr., 11 Nov. 1829; 4 Apr., 3 June 1830. Among the hospital's papers are a series of plans and drawings, headed 'A Provincial Lunatic Asylum', signed by Francis Johnston and dated November 1817. How they came into the hospital's possession is unclear, though possibly it was through Murray or through Surgeon Cusack, who was a member of the commission supervising the erection of district asylums.

44. Ibid., 11 Nov. 1815; 5 Mar., 2 June 1831; 3 Aug., 10 Aug., 2 Nov. 1835.

45. Ibid., 1 Nov. 1835; 7 Nov. 1842; 7 Jan. 1834; 1 Feb., 3 Apr. 1836; 4 Feb., 16 May, 4 July 1839.

46. Ibid., 18 Aug., 26 Aug. 1822; 3 Feb. 1823.

47. Ibid., 23 Jan., 13 Aug., 16 Aug. 1832; 2 Dec. 1833.

48. M.B., 31 May 1830.

49. Ibid., 10 Feb., 30 June 1831.
50. Ibid., 30 June 1831.
51. Ibid., 10 Aug. 1835; Folder of Plans for Alterations and Additions to St Patrick's Hospital From 1830 (S.P.H.D., 19th century papers, uncat.).
52. *Report of the Inspectors-General on the District, Local and Private Lunatic Asylums in Ireland, 1843*, 13 [C 567], H.C. 1844, xxx, 81.
53. M.B., 6 Feb. 1843; 5 May 1851; 3 Aug. 1835; 5 Nov. 1855. For an interesting discussion of 'lunatics' balls', see Elaine Showalter, *The Female Malady: Women, Madness and English Culture, 1830-1980* (reprint, London, 1987, of orig. edn, New York, 1985), pp. 38-40.
54. M.B., 2-30 June 1831.
55. Ibid., 4 July 1833; 7 Jan. 1850; 2 May 1836; L. M. Cullen, *The Emergence of Modern Ireland, 1600-1900* (London, 1981) pp. 175-6.
56. *Report of the Inspectors-General on the District, Local and Private Lunatic Asylums in Ireland, 1843*, 13 [C 567], H.C. 1844, xxx, 81. For an article with some interesting information on nineteenth-century Irish diets, see E. M. Crawford, 'Indian Meal and Pellagra in Nineteenth-Century Ireland' in J. M. Goldstrom and L. A. Clarkson (ed.), *Irish Population, Economy, and Society: Essays in Honour of the late K. H. Connell* (Oxford, 1981), pp. 113-33.
57. M. B., 7 Jan. 1850; 4 Mar. 1847; 4 Feb. 1839; 3 May 1847; 5 Jan. 1837.
58. *Report of the Inspectors-General on the District, Local, and Private Lunatic Asylums in Ireland, 1843*, 39 [C 567], H.C. 1844, xxx, 109.
59. Ibid.
60. Ibid., p.14/82; *Report on the District, Local and Private Lunatic Asylums in Ireland, for 1845*, 15 [C 736], H.C. 1846, xxii, 425; *Report on the District, Local and Private Lunatic Asylums in Ireland, for 1846*, 84 [C 820], H.C. 1847, xvii, 438.
61. *Report on . . . Asylums, 1846*, pp.71/425, 85/436; *Report on . . . Asylums, 1843*, pp. 37/107, 40-41/110-11.
62. Andrew Scull, *Museums of Madness: the Social Organisation of Insanity in Nineteenth-Century England* (reprint, Harmondsworth, 1982, of orig. edn, London 1979), p. 141.
63. M.B., 4 July, 3 Oct. 1833
64. Ibid., 4 July, 15 Aug., 2 Dec. 1833; 7 Jan. 1834; 1 Nov. 1813; Scull *Museums of Madness*, pp. 167-71.
65. M.B., 4 Jan. 1836; 4 Jan. 1844; 5 Jan. 1843.
66. Ibid., 3 Aug. 1840.
67. Appendix 4 contains a statistical analysis of the 178 admission forms, nos 298 to 553, covering the ten years, 1841 to 1850, and the 154 forms, nos 920 to 1090, covering the ten years 1874 to 1883. Information on discharges and deaths is drawn from the Registry of St Patrick's Hospital, 1795-1925 (S.P.H.D., 19th century papers, uncat.).
68. Mark Finnane, 'Asylums, Families and the State', *History Workshop*, No. 20 (Autumn 1985), p. 137.
69. Admission Form, No. 364, Thomas Larkin, 24 Apr. 1843 (S.P.H.D., 19th century papers, uncat.).
70. Ibid., No. 311, Mary Anne Hickey, 23 Apr. 1841.

71. Ibid., No. 348, Anne Barter, 4 July 1842. For the case of another governess, see ibid., No. 349, Euphemia Nickson, 3 Oct. 1842.
72. Ibid., No. 358, Eleanor Story, 24 Jan. 1843.
73. For another example of a brother reluctant to pay a sister's fees, see ibid., No. 327, Mary Anne Medlicott, 4 Dec. 1841.
74. W. S. Hallaran, *Practical Observations on the Causes and Cure of Insanity* (2nd edn, Cork, 1818), pp. 24, 35.
75. Admission Forms, No. 444, Charles Isdall, 4 June 1846; No. 462, Robert Panton, June 1847; No. 499, John Flavelle, Aug. 1848; No. 473, Alicia Delany, Nov. 1847; No. 495, Louis Burton, June 1848 (S.P.H.D., 19th century papers, uncat.).
76. Unfortunately, there has been no systematic study of the admission records or case-books of any of the district asylums, though Finnane in his book, mainly drawing on the archives of the Richmond Asylum, has an interesting chapter on the 'contexts of committal'; see Finnane, *Insanity and the Insane*, pp. 129-74.
77. Hallaran, op.cit., pp. 26, 31-2, 42-3; Elizabeth Malcolm, *'Ireland Sober, Ireland Free': Drink and Temperance in Nineteenth-Century Ireland* (Dublin, 1986), pp. 23-4. Swift's most memorable satire on enthusiasm and madness is probably contained in *A Tale of a Tub*, where the character Jack represents dissenters.
78. Admission Form, No. 430, William Lardner, August 1845 (S.P.H.D., 19th century papers, uncat.). Surgeon Lardner's brother was Dionysius Lardner, a well-known London lecturer and writer, and mentor of the playwright, Dion Boucicault, who was named after him.
79. Ibid., No. 422, Maria Walsh, 16 May 1845; No. 449, William Glascock, 27 Oct. 1846. For an interesting discussion of the question of opium, both as a treatment for and a cause of mental illness, see Virginia Berridge and Griffith Edwards, *Opium and the People: Opiate Use in Nineteenth-Century England* (London and New York, 1981), pp. 68-72.
80. Admission Forms, No. 427, James Lendrum, 11 June 1845; No. 452, Eliza McKittrick, Dec. 1846 (S.P.H.D., 19th century papers, uncat.).
81. Hallaran, op.cit., pp. 30-31; Finnane, *Insanity and the Insane*, pp. 199-200; Robins, op.cit., pp. 117-19.
82. Robins, op.cit., p.120; Hallaran, op.cit., p. 32.
83. Robins, op.cit., p.117. Admission Forms, No. 414, Rev. Michael Caraher, 9 Apr. 1845; No. 544 Rev. John Galvin, July 1850; No. 363, Rev. Edward Sillito, May 1843; No. 489, Rev. Richard Goring, Apr. 1848 (S.P.H.D., 19th century papers, uncat.).
84. For examples of more than one case from the same family, see Admission Forms, No. 419, Susanna Grove Grady, 12 May 1845; No. 420, Elizabeth Grove Grady, 12 May 1845; No. 507, Rev. Edward Verdon, Dec. 1848 (S.P.H.D., 19th century papers, uncat).
85. Patients dying in St Patrick's who were not claimed by their relatives were buried in St James's graveyard nearby in James Street, though until the 1850s a number were also buried in the old burial ground that the governors had leased from Steevens Hospital in 1816. Staff accommodation has subsequently been built on this site. The only

medical superintendent to die in office, Dr Lawless was buried in James's graveyard in 1879, as his surviving headstone attests. See St James's Development Association, *St James's Graveyard, Dublin—History and Associations* (Dublin, 1988). p. 20.

Chapter 4, pp. 154-215

1. H. C. Burdett, *Hospitals and Asylums of the World: vol. 1 Asylums–History and Administration* (London, 1891), pp. 248-50.
2. Typescript copies of the Reports of the Inspectors of Lunacy, 1890-1911 (S.P.H.D., 19th century papers, uncat.).
3. M.B., 3 July 1854; 2 June, 6 Oct. 1856; 7 Mar. 1859; 5 Nov. 1860; 3 Mar. 1862.
4. In 1866 the lord chancellor, obviously dissatisfied with the lack of medical representation on the board, had suggested that Dr George Hatchell, one of the lunacy inspectors, be elected, but nothing came of this proposal. Ibid., 5 Feb. 1866; 1 Mar. 1897. For a helpful discussion of the issue of wrongful confinement, see Peter McCandless, 'Liberty and Lunacy: the Victorians and Wrongful Confinement' in Andrew Scull (ed.), *Madhouses, Mad-doctors, and Madmen: the Social History of Psychiatry in the Victorian Era* (London, 1981), pp. 339-62.
5. Information on the occupations and residences of governors has been drawn from a selection of *Thom's Directories* for the 1860s, 1880s and 1890s.
6. M.B., 3 May, 7 June, 1 Nov. 1858.
7. Mark Finnane, *Insanity and the Insane in Post-Famine Ireland* (London and Totowa, N.J., 1981), pp. 39-47.
8. M.B., 3 Mar. 1862; 6 June, 6 July 1864.
9. Ibid., 22 Nov. 1865; 5 Feb., 7 May, 4 June, 2 July, 5 Nov. 1866.
10. Ibid., 5 Nov. 1866; 2 July 1878; 1 July 1879; 3 July 1883; 2 Nov. 1885; 4 Jan., 1 Feb, 1886.
11. Ibid., 2 Sept. 1867; 4 July 1864; 4 Jan. 1869.
12. Ibid., 1 Apr. 1879; 6 Mar., 12 Nov. 1883; 6 Oct. 1884; 5 Jan., 2 Feb., 3 Aug. 1885; 3 Mar., 1 Dec. 1886.
13. Ibid., 12 Nov., 4 Dec. 1883; 7 Jan, 1884.
14. Ibid., 7 July, 4 Aug. 1884; 2 Feb. 1885. For a colourful account of Sir Thornley Stoker and his home in Ely Place, see Oliver St John Gogarty, *It Isn't This Time of Year at All!* (reprint, London, 1983, of orig. edn, London, 1954), pp. 83-5.
15. J. M. Granville 'The Care and Cure of the Insane', quoted in Elaine Showalter, *The Female Malady: Women, Madness and English Culture, 1830-1980* (reprint, London, 1987, of orig. edn, New York, 1985), pp. 103-4.
16. *General Rules and Regulations for the Management of St Patrick's Hospital, Dublin,* (Dublin 1885), pp. 4-6; *Bye-laws for the Management of St Patrick's Hospital, Dublin . . . in Pursuance of its Charter and Supplemental Charter* (Dublin, 1889), p. 10 (S.P.H.D., 19th century papers, uncat.).
17. Bye-laws, 1889, pp. 8-9.

18. M.B., 6 Dec. 1875; 3 Jan., 1 Feb., 1 May 1876; 4 Feb. 1889; 2 Jan. 1899.
19. M.B., 2 Sept, 1872. It is interesting to note how little staff pay had advanced since the 1830s. Some employees, like the gardener, hall porter and store maid, were receiving the same wages in 1872 as they had in 1835. The male attendants' pay had also changed little, though some of the nurses were receiving more, perhaps due to the growing number of female patients in the hospital. But, given that prices had risen significantly during the 1850s and 1860s, it is probably fair to assume that many of the staff were a good deal worse off in the early 1870s than they had been in the mid 1830s, which explains the pressure for a wage increase at a time the governors would not have regarded as propitious. In the event, the increase that the governors produced was, in most cases, relatively modest.
20. Ibid., 4 Oct. 1852; 6 May 1872; 2 June 1851; 1 Dec. 1862; 4 May 1874; Lunacy Inspectors Reports, 1890-1911 (S.P.H.D. 19th century papers, uncat.).
21. M.B., 6 Feb. 1888; 4 Dec. 1893; Admision Form, No. 926. Fanny Stoney, Apr. 1874 (S.P.H.D. 19th Century papers, uncat.).
22. M.B., 5 Aug, 1853.
23. Bye-laws, 1889, pp. 13-14; Showalter, op.cit., p. 84; for Dr Leeper's 1899 timetable of staff duties, see Appendix 5.
24. M.B., 1 Apr. 1867; 7 May, 4 Sept. 1883; 3 Mar. 1884; 4 July 1870; 1 Jan. 1872; 3 Jan. 1876; 4 Jan. 1881, 5 Jan, 1885; 6 Nov. 1865; 6 June 1898.
25. Ibid., 4 May 1857; 3 Mar., 5 May 1862; 4 June 1888; 4 Jan. 1886; 5 Dec, 1864; 2 Jan., 1 May 1865; 3 July 1883.
26. Finnane, op.cit., pp. 180-81; Lunacy Inspectors Reports, 1890-1911 (S.P.H.D., 19th century papers, uncat.).
27. M.B., 4 June 1894; 6 Dec. 1897; 1 May, 2 June, 2 Oct., 4 Dec. 1899; 5 Feb., 6 Aug. 1900.
28. For handy summaries of Irish socio-economic developments from the Famine to the land war, see Joseph Lee, *The Modernisation of Irish Society, 1848-1918* (Gill History of Ireland 10, Dublin, 1973), pp. 1-20, 36-41; F. S. L. Lyons, *Ireland since the Famine* (rev. edn, London, 1973), pp. 34-70; R. F. Foster, *Modern Ireland, 1600-1972* (London, 1988), pp. 373-99.
29. M.B., 2 Feb. 1852; 3 Feb. 1862.
30. Ibid., 4 July 1859.
31. Finnane, op.cit., p. 227.
32. M.B., 1 Aug. 1859; 3 Dec. 1860; 4 May 1863; L. M. Cullen, *An Economic History of Ireland since 1660* (reprint, London, 1976, of orig. edn, London, 1972), pp. 137-8.
33. M.B., 7 Nov. 1859; 1 Oct., 5 Nov. 1860.
34. Ibid., 5 Nov. 1860.
35. Ibid., 4 Nov. 1867.
36. Ibid., 4 Oct, 1869.
37. Ibid., 5 Nov. 1866; 3 Feb. 1868.
38. Ibid., 4 Oct. 1869.
39. Ibid., 5 May 1873. A letter book, compiled by the librarian/clerk,

William Adams, survives from the late 1860s, containing a number of letters to relatives of patients demanding that fee arrears be paid and threatening removal if they were not paid; see William Adams to Thomas Kelly, 11 May 1865 in Secretary's Letter Book, Jan. 1865-Oct. 1870. (S.P.H.D., 19th century papers, uncat.).

40. Ibid., 5 Dec. 1876.
41. Ibid., 4 July 1870; 6 Nov. 1871; 1 Jan. 1872.
42. Ibid., 4 Oct. 1869; 2 May 1870; 5 June 1871.
43. Estate Rental Books: Saggart/Dublin, 1840-57, 1858-70; Ferns, 1840-58, 1858-70 (S.P.H.D., 19th century papers, uncat.). Unfortunately these rental books, giving annual accounts for each part of the estate, cease in 1870, after which it becomes much more difficult to trace the affairs of the governors' estate in any detail.
44. M.B., 6 June 1880.
45. Ibid., 6 July 1880.
46. Ibid., 2 Aug. 1830; 5 May 1862.
47. Ibid., 1 Feb. 1875; 6 May 1878
48. Ibid., 2 Jan., 6 Aug. 1883; 7 Jan., 5 May, 1 Dec. 1884.
49. Charles Townshend, *Political Violence in Ireland: Government and Resistance since 1848* (reprint, London, 1984, of orig. ed., London, 1983), pp. 105-6.
50. M.B., 6 Dec. 1881; 6 Feb. 1882; 7 May 1883; 3 Sept., 5 Nov., 13 Nov. 1888. For major accounts of the land war and its aftermath, see Samuel Clark, *Social Origins of the Irish Land War* (Princeton, N.J., 1979); Barbara Solow, *The Land Question in the Irish Economy, 1870-1903*, (Cambridge, Mass., 1971); Paul Bew, *Land and the National Question in Ireland, 1858-82* (Dublin, 1978); F. S. L. Lyons, *John Dillion: a Biography* (London, 1968).
51. Estate Rental Books, 1840-70; M. B., 2 June, 4 Aug. 1873. The rental of Ferns in 1840 was £1,061, with £474 owing in arrears; in 1870 the rental was £1,008, with arrears of £462.
52. M.B., 3 Nov. 1879; 2 Feb., 2 Mar. 1880.
53. Ibid., 4 Oct., 7 Nov. 1881.
54. Ibid., 5 Dec. 1882; 6 Apr., 4 May, 1 June, 6 July 1885; 1 Feb., 3 May, 5 July, 2 Aug., 6 Sept., 4 Nov., 6 Dec. 1886; 3 Jan. 1887; 5 Nov. 1888.
55. David O'Toole, 'The Employment Crisis of 1826' in David Dickson (ed.), *The Gorgeous Mask: Dublin, 1700-1850* (Trinity History Workshop 2, Dublin, 1987), pp. 157-71; J. V. O'Brien. *'Dear, Dirty Dublin': a City in Distress, 1899-1916* (Berkeley, Calif., 1982) pp. 9-11; *Dublin Directory*, 1843.
56. M.B., 5 Oct. 1837; 5 Feb. 1838; 4 Nov. 1839; 3 Feb. 1840.
57. Estate Rental Books: Saggart/Dublin, 1840-70.
58. M.B., 6 July 1885.
59. Ibid., 6 July 1885; *Dublin Directories*, 1843, 1891.
60. M.B., 1 Feb, 1875; M. E. Daly, *Dublin—the Deposed Capital: a Social and Economic History, 1860-1914* (Cork, 1984), pp. 283-4. For a very readable account of the problem of Dublin slum tenements, see O'Brien, op.cit., pp. 126-58.

61. M.B., 1 Nov. 1852; *Dublin Directory*, 1891.
62. Superintendent's Reports: St Patrick's Hospital, 1899-1901 (S.P.H.D., 19th century papers, uncat.).
63. M.B., 17 Nov., 24 Nov. 1852; 3 Jan., 1 Aug. 1853; 2 Dec. 1861; 3 Feb. 1862; 6 Apr., 3 Aug. 1885; Superintendent's Reports: St Patrick's Hospital, 1899-1901.
64. M.B., 6 Apr., 4 May 1857; 5 Dec. 1882; 4 Sept. 1865; 5 Nov. 1866; 3 Aug., 7 Dec. 1868; 2 Apr. 1860; 2 June 1862; 5 Aug. 1878; 7 June 1886.
65. Ibid., 2 Feb., 2 Mar. 1885; 3 Oct. 1898; 6 Feb., 5 Mar., 8 Mar., 3 Dec. 1888.
66. Finnane, op.cit., pp. 63-71.
67. Inspectors' Reports, 1890-1911.
68. Ibid.; M.B., 7 Aug. 1882.
69. M.B., 16 Apr., 3 June, 11 June, 29 Oct. 1895; 14 Jan., 13 Apr. 1896; 25 Apr., 2 May 1898.
70. Minutes of Sub-Committee: Purchase of St Edmundsbury, 8 Aug., 9 Sept., 30 Sept. 4 Nov. 1898 (S.P.H.D., 19th century papers, uncat.); Weston St John Joyce, *Lucan and its Neighbourhood* (reprint, Blackrock, 1988, of orig. edn, Dublin, 1901), pp. 3-7.
71. *The Correspondence of Jonathan Swift*, ed. Harold Williams (Oxford, 1965), iv, p. 497; Constantia Maxwell, *Country and Town in Ireland under the Georges* (rev. edn., Dundalk, 1949), p. 244; [Maurice Craig (ed.)], *The Legacy of Swift: a Bi-Centenary Record of St Patrick's Hospital, Dublin* (Dublin, 1948), p. 39.
72. For the problems of late nineteenth-century asylums and psychiatric medicine, see for Ireland, Finnane, op.cit., pp. 53-86, 227 and Joseph Robins, *Fools and Mad: a History of the Insane in Ireland* (Dublin, 1986), pp. 128-42; for England, Showalter, op.cit., pp. 101-20, Andrew Scull, *Museums of Madness: the Social Organisation of Insanity in Nineteenth-Century England* (reprint, Harmondsworth, 1982, of orig. edn, London, 1979), pp. 188-204, 221-53, and Vieda Skultans, *English Madness: Ideas on Insanity, 1580-1890* (London, 1979), pp. 128-38; and for the United States, David Rotham, *The Discovery of the Asylum: Social Order and Disorder in the New Republic* (Boston and Toronto, 1971), pp. 237-8.
73. M.B., 7 Nov. 1853; 2 Feb. 1863; 1 Dec. 1851; 3 July 1854; 6 Apr., 1 June 1857.
74. Ibid., 3 Mar., 7 July, 6 Oct., 3 Nov. 1862; 2 Mar. 1863; 7 Mar., 1 Aug. 1864; 2 Jan., 1 May, 4 Sept., 6 Nov., 1865; 6 Aug., 3 Sept. 1866; 4 Mar., 1 Apr. 1867; 3 Aug. 1868; 2 May, 4 July 1870; 4 Oct. 1875; 2 July, 1 Oct. 1878; 5 May 1879; 7 Feb., 1 Mar. 1881; 2 Feb. 1874; 4 Feb. 1878; 5 Dec. 1887; 2 Feb. 1880.
75. Ibid., 6 May 1872; 2 Dec. 1879; *Thirty-fourth Report on District, Criminal and Private Lunatic Asylums in Ireland*, 110-21 [C-4539], H.C. 1885, xxxvi. 745-55; Registry of St Patrick's Hospital, 1795-1925 (S.P.H.D., 19th century papers, uncat.). For helpful discussions of public health and infectious diseases, see W. H. McNeill, *Plagues and Peoples* (reprint, Harmondworth, 1979, of orig. edn, New York, 1976); G. M. Howe, *Man, Environment and Disease in Britain: a Medical Geography through the Ages* (reprint, Harmondsworth, 1976, of orig. edn, Newton Abbot,

1972); F. B. Smith, *The People's Health, 1830-1910* (Canberra, 1979); and for cholera and typhus particularly, see Michael Durey, *The Return of the Plague: British Society and the Cholera, 1831-2* (Dublin, 1979) and Hans Zinsser, *Rats, Lice and History: the Biography of a Bacillus* (reprint, London, 1985).

76. For the public health problems of Dublin, see O'Brien, op.cit., pp. 101-25 and Daly, op. cit., pp. 240-76.

77. For the expansion of Guinness's Brewery in the direction of the hospital, see the aerial photograph in the back of Patrick Lynch and John Vaizey, *Guinness's Brewery in the Irish Economy, 1759-1876* (Cambridge, 1960). *Dublin Directory*, 1891; Daly, op.cit., pp. 255. 263; *Return of the Number of Licensed Houses in England and Wales for the Care of Lunatics; . . . Similar Return for Scotland and Ireland*, pp. 494-7, H.C. 1878 (370), lxiii; p. 509, H.C. 1878 (375), lxiii; *Nineteenth Report on the District, Criminal and Private Lunatic Asylums in Ireland*, 33 [C-202], H.C. 1870., xxxiv, 319; Lunacy Inspectors Reports, 1890-1911 (S.P.H.D. 19th century papers, uncat.).

78. *Eleventh Report on the District, Criminal and Private Lunatic Asylums in Ireland*, 571 [C-2975], H.C. 1862, xxiii; *Nineteenth Report on . . . Asylums*, 132 [C-202], H.C. 1870, xxxiv, 418; *Twenty-sixth Report on . . . Asylums*, 104 [C-1750], H.C. 1877, xli, 552; *Return of the Number of Licensed Houses in England and Wales for the Care of Lunatics; . . . Similar Return for Scotland and Ireland*, p. 509, H.C. 1878 (375), lxiii; *Thirty-fourth Report on . . . Asylums*, 110 [C-4539], H.C. 1885, xxxvi, 745; *Forty-first Report on . . . Asylums*, 65 [C-6803], H.C. 1892, xl, 442; *Fifty-third Report on . . . Asylums*, 55 [Cd 2262], H.C. 1905. xxxv, 653.

79. See Appendix 4 for statistics on patients.

80. Admission Forms, No. 944, Cherry B., Dec., 1875; No. 1030, Maria H., May 1880; No. 1026., Eliza C., May 1880 (S.P.H.D., 19th century papers, uncat.).

81. G. M. R. Walshe, *Diseases of the Nervous System* (3rd edn, Edinburgh, 1943), pp. 159, 173-6; Registry of St Patrick's Hospital, 1795-1925 (S.P.H.D., 19th century papers, uncat.).

82. Finnane, op.cit., pp. 138, 170 note 17; J. B. Lyons, *Thrust Syphillis down to Hell and Rejoyceana: Studies in the Border-lands of Literature and Medicine* (Dun Laoghaire, 1988), p. 48; O'Brien, op.cit., pp. 116-20; Case-book: male, 1899 (S.P.H.D., 19th century papers, uncat.); *Report of the Commissioners of Inquiry into the State of Lunatic Asylums . . . in Ireland*, i, 107 [C-2436], H.C. 1857-8, xxvii. In Belfast too syphilis was 'rarely entered as a cause of death'; see Peter Froggatt, 'Industrialisation and Health in Belfast in the Early Nineteenth Century' in David Harkness and Mary O'Dowd (ed.), *The Town in Ireland* (Historical Studies xiii, Belfast, 1981), p. 178.

83. Bye-laws, 1889, p. 8; Superintendent's Reports: St Patrick's Hospital, 1899-1901 (S.P.H.D. 19th century papers, uncat.); *Report of the Commissioners of Inquiry into the State of Lunatic Asylums . . . in Ireland*, i, 109-110 [C-2436], H.C. 1857-8, xxvii. Dr Richard Leeper to the governors of St Patrick's Hospital, 4 Apr. 1938 (S.P.H.D., 20th century papers, uncat.).

84. Burdett, op.cit., p. 249. In considering Burdett's criticisms, we should perhaps keep in mind that his information was by no means always accurate. With regard to St Patrick's, for instance, he quoted from the report of a parliamentary enquiry held, he said, in 1879; actually in fact his quotations came from the report of the 1857-8 commission. Lunacy Inspectors Reports, 1890-1911; Superintendent's Reports: St Patrick's Hospital, 1899-1901 (S.P.H.D.. 19th century papers, uncat.); *Report of the Commissioners of Inquiry into the State of Lunatic Asylums . . . in Ireland, i,* 35-6, 107 [C-2436] H.C. 1857-8, xxvii.

85. Admission Form No. 457, Mary Anne Ryan, Apr. 1847; Case-book: female, 1899, p. 31 (S.P.H.D., 19th century papers, uncat.); M.B., 3 Oct., 5 Dec. 1859; 4 Mar. 1861.

86. Admission Form No. 551, Eleanor Murray, Oct. 1850 (S.P.H.D., 19th century papers, uncat.).

87. Case-book: female, 1899, p. 86 (S.P.H.D., 19th century papers, uncat.).

88. Admission Form No. 419, Susanna Grove Grady, May, 1845; No. 420, Elizabeth Grove Grady, May 1845; Case-book: female, 1899, p. 63 (S.P.H.D., 19th century papers, uncat.); M.B., 6 Oct., 1 Dec. 1856; 5 Jan. 1857; 5 Mar. 1858; 1 June 1863; 2 Sept. 1867; 7 Sept. 1868; 4 July 1876; 2 Sept. 1879.

89. *Report of the Commissioners of Inquiry into the State of the Lunatic Asylums . . . in Ireland, i,* 34 [C-2436], H.C. 1857-8, xxvii.

90. *Supplemental Charter of St Patrick's Hospital, founded by the Last Will of the Reverend Doctor Jonathan Swift, Late Dean of St Patrick's, Dublin, for the Reception of Idiots, Lunatics and Incurables* (Dublin, 1889); *Second Supplemental Charter of St Patrick's Hospital . . .* (Dublin, 1896); *Third Supplemental Charter of St Patrick's Hospital . . .* (Dublin, 1897).

Chapter 5, pp. 215-257

1. Austin Clarke, *Mnemosyne Lay in Dust* (Dublin, 1966), pp. 9, 12-13, 16.

2. P. L. Dickinson, *The Dublin of Yesterday* (London, 1929), pp. 36-8.

3. M. B., 3 Oct., 5 Dec. 1898; 2 Jan., 20 Jan. 1899.

4. Typescript copies of the Reports of the Inspectors of Lunacy, 1890-1911 (S.P.H.D., 19th century papers, uncat.).

5. Ibid. Dr Richard Leeper to the governors of St Patrick's Hospital, 4 Apr. 1938 (S.P.H.D., 20th century papers, uncat.).

6. Superintendent's Reports: St Patrick's Hospital, 1899-1901 (S.P.H.D., 19th century papers, uncat.).

7. Ibid.

8. Ibid.; Inspectors' Reports, 1890-1911; *St Patrick's Hospital, Dublin and Lucan. Statement of Accounts for the Year 1933, with the Auditor's Report thereon* (Dublin, 1934), p. 28; *St Patrick's Hospital, Dublin and Lucan. Statement of Accounts for the Year 1919* (Dublin, 1920), p. 14.

9. M. B., 1 Feb. 1932; *Accounts . . . 1933,* p. 25.

10. Inspectors' Reports, 1890-1911; Superintendent's Reports: St Patrick's Hospital, 1899-1901.

11. Superintendent's Reports: St Patrick's Hospital, 1899-1901.

12. Ibid. Leeper to governors, 4 Apr. 1938.

13. Inspectors' Reports, 1890-1911; M. B. 18 June, 2 July, 6 Aug. 1900.

14. Inspectors' Reports, 1890-1911; M. B., 11 Aug. 1924; 3 Nov., 1 Dec. 1902; 6 Apr. 1903.

15. Superintendent's Reports: St Patrick's Hospital, 1899-1901.

16. Ibid.; Typescript copies of the Reports of the Inspectors of Lunacy, 1895-1944 (S.P.H.D., 20th century papers, uncat.).

17. Joseph Robins, *Fools and Mad: a History of the Insane in Ireland* (Dublin, 1986), pp. 136, 185; Superintendent's Reports: St Patrick's Hospital, 1899-1901.

18. Inspectors' Reports, 1890-1911; Superintendent's Reports: St Patrick's Hospital, 1899-1901; Minutes of Sub-Committee: Purchase of St Edmundsbury, 26 Aug., 2 Dec. 1898 (S.P.H.D., 19th century papers, uncat.); M. B. 4 Dec. 1905.

19. Superintendent's Reports: St Patrick's Hospital, 1899-1901, 1902-1905; Inspectors' Reports, 1890-1911. We have already seen that pay for most of the hospital staff increased only marginally after the 1830s, doubtless reflecting the declining state of the institution. Thus, by the early 1890s, wages at St Patrick's were far behind those generally prevailing in Dublin. In 1892, for instance, unskilled labourers in regular employment received from twenty to twenty-five shillings a week, while casual labourers were paid from twelve to fifteen shillings. In contrast the highest paid attendant at St Patrick's received only about eight shillings a week, the highest paid nurse a little over six shillings and ward maids a derisory two shillings a week. Even with free food and accommodation, these were extremely low wages and it is no wonder that the hospital had trouble attracting competent staff. See J. V. O'Brien, *'Dear, Dirty Dublin': a City in Distress, 1899-1912* (Berkeley, Calif., 1982), pp. 201-2.

20. Superintendent's Reports: St Patrick's Hospital, 1899-1911; M.B., 1 May 1905.

21. Superintendent's Reports: St Patrick's Hospital, 1899-1901; M.B., 3 July, 4 Aug., 4 Sept. 1905; 4 May 1914.

22. Superintendent's Reports: St Patrick's Hospital, 1899-1901; M.B., 3 Sept. 1900; 7 May 1906; 2 Feb. 1925. Leeper to governors, 4 Apr. 1938. Rutherford moved to Farnham House, the long-established private asylum at Finglas.

23. M.B., 5 May 1902. Leeper to governors, 4 Apr. 1938.

24. Superintendent's Reports: St Patrick's Hospital, 1899-1901; M.B., 1 Feb., 5 Dec. 1904.

25. Elaine Showalter, *The Female Malady: Women, Madness and English Culture, 1830-1980* (reprint, London, 1987, of orig. edn, New York, 1985), pp. 145-94; Superintendent's Reports: St Patrick's Hospital, 1899-1901.

26. *St Edmundsbury Hospital, Lucan* (Dublin, [1902]), p. 9; M.B., 20 Feb. 1905; 13 July 1910. Leeper later said that he and the board had been persuaded into erecting the villa by an assurance from Dr Colles, the registrar in lunacy, that there were plenty of wealthy, male, chancery

patients seeking such accommodation. In the event few materialised and Colles admitted that he had been mistaken. In time, however, patients for the villa were found and the building continued in use until the early 1980s, when it was demolished to make way for new patient accommodation. From about 1902, however, the improvements at both St Patrick's and St Edmundsbury began to be reported on favourably in the press; see, for example, *Irish Times*, 22 Mar. 1902.

27. *St Patrick's Hospital, Dublin* (Dublin, [1905]), pp. 5-7.
28. For handy accounts of the Wyndham Act, see F. S. L. Lyons, *Ireland since the Famine* (reprint, London, 1973, of orig. edn, London, 1971), pp. 217-20 and Pauric Travers, *Settlements and Divisions: Ireland, 1870-1922* (Helicon History of Ireland 8, Dublin, 1988), pp. 27-32.
29. M.B., 7 Dec. 1903; 5 June, 14 June, 6 Nov. 1905.
30. Ibid., 15 Jan. 1906.
31. Ibid., 2 Nov., 7 Dec. 1908; 1 Apr. 1920; 6 Dec. 1937. Papers relating to the sale of the Saggart and Ferns estates are held by the Land Commission: see Irish Land Commission, St Patrick's Hospital Estate: Barony of Newcastle, Co. Dublin (Record no. E.C. 7319, Box no. 4662) and Barony of Scarawalsh, Co. Wexford (Record no. E.C. 4393, Box no. 276).
32. M.B., 2 Mar., 27 July 1914; *St Patrick's Hospital, Dublin and Lucan. Statement of Accounts for the Year 1916; with the Auditor's Report thereon* (Dublin, 1917), pages not numbered.
33. M.B., 7 Feb., 4 July, 7 Nov. 1921; 6 Mar. 1922; 6 May, 3 June, 7 Oct. 1935; 5 Dec. 1932; 4 Dec. 1933; 1 Dec. 1930.
34. Ibid., 3 Dec. 1866; 4 Mar. 1889; 31 July, 6 Nov. 4 Dec. 1911; 4 Mar., 24 June, 2 Sept., 7 Oct. 1912; 4 Oct., 25 Oct., 6 Dec. 1915; 6 Mar. 1916; 3 July 1910; Superintendent's Reports: St Patrick's Hospital, 1911-1917.
35. Robins, op. cit. pp. 182-3.
36. *Accounts . . . 1916*, pages not numbered; *St Patrick's Hospital, Dublin and Lucan. Statement of Accounts for the Year 1920* (Dublin, 1921) pp.8, 14; M.B., 2 Aug. 1913; 31 July 1916; 1 July 1918.
37. M.B., 6 July 1914; 4 Oct. 1915; 6 Nov., 20 Nov. 1916; 30 July, 3 Sept., 1 Oct., 3 Dec. 1917.
38. Ibid., 16 Mar., 3 June 1918; 3 May 1920; David Johnson, *The Interwar Economy in Ireland* (Studies in Irish Economic and Social History 4, Dublin, 1985), p. 4; L. M. Cullen, *An Economic History of Ireland since 1660* (reprint, London, 1976, of orig. edn, London, 1972), p. 171; *Accounts . . . 1933* p. 26.
39. M.B., 2 Oct. 1916; 2 Dec. 1917; 29 Mar. 1920.
40. Robins, op.cit., p. 183; M. B., 4 June 1923.
41. See Appendix 6 for Leeper's report to the governors on the 1916 rising; Desmond Ryan, *The Rising* (Dublin, 1949), pp. 172-86.
42. M.B., 4 Aug. 1916; 6 June 1921; 3 July 1922; Calton Younger, *Ireland's Civil War* (reprint, London, 1979, of orig. edn, London, 1968), pp. 326, 333-4, 339; Superintendent's Reports: St Patrick's Hospital, 1911-17.
43. M.B., 31 July, 6 Nov. 1922; 5 Feb. 1923.

44. Superintendent's Reports: St Patrick's Hospital, 1917-25; Registry of St Patrick's Hospital, 1795-1925 (S.P.H.D., 19th century papers, uncat.).
45. Registry of St Patrick's Hospital, 1795-1925.
46. Case-book: females, St Edmundsbury, 1915, pp. 23, 41 (S.P.H.D., 20th century papers uncat.); Mark Bence-Jones, *Twilight of the Ascendancy* (London, 1987), pp. 187-8.
47. M.B., 26 Nov. 1923; 7 June 1924; 5 Dec. 1927; 8 Aug. 1932; Johnson, op.cit., p. 9
48. M.B., 29 Mar., 7 June 1926.
49. Ibid., 5 July 1926; 5 Jan. 1931; 4 Jan. 1937.
50. Ibid., 5 July, 9 Aug., 1 Nov. 1937; 3 Jan. 1938.
51. Robins, op.cit., pp. 187-90.
52. Henry Boylan, *A Dictionary of Irish Biography* (Dublin, 1978), p. 209; C. D. Greaves, *The Irish Transport and General Workers' Union: the Formative Years, 1909-23* (Dublin, 1982), pp. 97-100.
53. M.B., 9 May 1771; 8 May 1829.
54. Ibid., 2 Mar. 1925; 3 Nov. 1930; 4 Jan. 1932; 4 Jan., 5 Apr. 1937; 1 Mar. 1926; 5 Jan., 4 May, 10 Aug. 1931; 7 May 1934; [Maurice Craig (ed)], *The Legacy of Swift: a Bi-Centenary Record of St Patrick's Hospital, Dublin* (Dublin, 1948), p. 53.
55. M.B., 2 Feb., 30 Mar., 10 Aug., 5 Oct. 1931.
56. Ibid., 2 Jan. 1883. In 1940, with a gift of £25 from Albert Wood, K.C., Leeper was able to buy from an antique dealer what the minutes describe as 'a member's chair of the Irish House of Commons, believed to be the only one now in existence'. This chair, which is of different workmanship from the benches, was placed in the boardroom, where it remains to this day. Maurice Craig has speculated that the benches and the chair all came from the House of Commons, which was rebuilt after the fire which devastated it in 1792. As for the differences between the benches and the chair, Craig simply suggests that the chair came from a different ring of the seating in the circular chamber. But Craig is unable to shed any light on the mystery of when and how the hospital acquired its House of Commons benches. Ibid., 4 Mar. 1940; [Craig], op.cit., p. 39.
57. M.B., 3 Mar. 1916; 6 May 1935; Inspectors' Reports, 1895-1944; *Accounts. . . 1916* pages not numbered.
58. M.B., 1 Sept. 1924; 1 June 1931; 6 May 1935; Inspectors' Reports, 1895-1944. For newspaper reports of the hospital's new facilities, see *Irish Times*, 28 Aug. 1930 and *Dublin Evening Herald*, 2 Sept. 1936.
59. M.B., 11 Aug. 1924; 8 Aug. 1927; J. H. Ewen, *A Handbook of Psychiatry* (London, 1933), p. 180.
60. M.B., 4 Jan. 1932; 2 Sept. 1935; 6 Jan. 1936; 6 Apr., 4 May, 7 Sept., 7 Dec. 1925; 9 Aug. 1926; 23 Oct. 1929; 1 Apr., 6 May 1935; Inspectors' Reports, 1895-1944.
61. Inspectors' Reports, 1895-1944; M.B., 3 Jan. 1938.
62. *St Patrick's Hospital, Dublin and Lucan. Statistical Returns for the Year ended 31 December, 1905, 1916, 1923, 1928* (Dublin, n.d.).

63. *St Patrick's Hospital, Dublin and Lucan. Statement of Accounts for the Year 1938 with the Auditor's Report thereon* (Dublin, 1939), pp. 8-9, 23-5; M.B., 3 Jan. 1938.
64. Robins, op.cit., pp. 195-6.
65. Registry of St Patrick's Hospital, 1795-1925; Clarke, op.cit., pp. 16, 26, 41-2, 14, 22-3, 30-31, 48-9.
66. Inspectors' Reports, 1895-1944.

Chapter 6, pp. 258-283

1. *Macbeth*, Act v, Scene v.
2. M.B., 30 July 1956.
3. J. N. P. Moore, 'Perspective' in *Bulletin of the Royal College of Psychiatrists*, x (Nov. 1986), p. 298. This article provides a brief, but invaluable, account of Moore's approach to psychiatry. It has been supplemented by interviews and correspondence with him and also with Mr Robert McCullagh, the secretary/registrar of the hospital during most of Moore's period as medical director. Tape recordings of interviews with Moore and McCullagh, upon which a good deal of this chapter has been based, have been lodged by the author in the hospital archives.
4. Ibid., p. 299; see W. Mayer-Gross, Eliot Slater and Martin Roth, *Clinical Psychiatry*, 2nd rev. edn, London, 1960.
5. M.B., 30 March 1942.
6. Ibid., 5 May, 1 Dec. 1941; 8 Jan. 1945.
7. Ibid., 2 Oct. 1939; 5 Jan., 2 Mar. 1942; Lunacy Inspectors' Reports, 1895-1944 (S.P.H.D., 20th century papers, uncat.).
8. M.B., 3 Jan., 6 Mar. 1944; Agenda Book (hereafter A.B.), 2 Oct. 1944; *Irish Times*, 8 Aug., 7 Sept. 1944.
9. M.B., 1 Nov. 1943; 6 Oct. 1941; 6 May, 3 June 1940; *St Patrick's Hospital, Dublin and Lucan. Statement of Accounts for the Year 1938 with the Auditor's Report thereon* (Dublin, 1939), p. 25. *St Patrick's Hospital, Dublin and Lucan. Statement of Accounts for the Year 1945 with the Auditor's Report thereon* (Dublin, 1946), p. 4.
10. *Accounts . . . 1938*, pp. 8-9; *Accounts . . . 1945*, pp. 8-9; A.B., 4 May 1942.
11. M.B., 2 Jan. 1939; 7 Dec. 1942; 1 Nov. 1943; Elaine Showalter, *The Female Malady: Women, Madness and English Culture, 1830-1980* (reprint, London, 1987, of orig. edn, New York, 1985), p. 206.
12. M.B., 3 Sept., 1 Oct., 3 Dec. 1945; 4 Mar., 1 Apr. 1946; [Maurice Craig (ed.)], *The Legacy of Swift: A Bi-Centenary Record of St Patrick's Hospital, Dublin* (Dublin, 1948).
13. A.B., 5 Mar. 1945; M.B., 9 Apr. 1945.
14. M.B., 4 Dec. 1944; 8 Jan., 5 Feb. 1945; 8 Sept. 1947; 7 June 1948.
15. Ibid., 1 July, 29 July 1946; 6 Nov. 1950; 5 Mar. 1951.
16. Ibid., 2 Jan. 1939; 1 July 1946; 6 Apr. 1956; 7 Jan. 1963.
17. Report on the Activities and Finances of St Patrick's Hospital, Appendices 2, 4, 12 [1970] (S.P.H.D., 20th century papers, uncat.).

18. M.B., 6 Oct. 1952; 6 Nov. 1961; 2 Apr. 1962; 2 June 1947; 5 Apr. 1954; 1 Dec. 1958; Report on Activities, Appendices 10, 11. For the establishment and growth of the VHI, see VHI: a Brief History, April 1985, typescript kindly supplied by Miss Frances Shields, publicity officer of the Voluntary Health Insurance Board; Ruth Barrington, *Health, Medicine and Politics in Ireland, 1900-1970* (Dublin, 1987), pp. 247-9.
19. Report of Activities, Appendices 1, 12; M.B., 7 Sept. 1959; 2 Apr. 1962.
20. M.B., 6 Oct. 1947; 5 Dec. 1949.
21. Report on Activities, Appendix 12; J. N. P. Moore, Memorandum on the relationship between St Patrick's Hospital and the Federated Group of Dublin Hospitals, 1983; P. J. Meehan, St Patrick's Hospital Federated Dublin Voluntary Hospitals connection, 1983 (S.P.H.D., 20th century papers, uncat.); Barrington, op.cit., pp. 14-15, 124-5; David Mitchell, *A 'Peculiar' Place: the Adelaide Hospital, Dublin, 1839-1989* (Dublin, [1988]), pp. 238-43.
22. Brendan Hensey, *The Health Services of Ireland* (3rd edn, Dublin, 1979), pp. 145-6.
23. Information supplied by Professor Moore.
24. M.B., 30 July 1953.
25. Report on Activities, Appendix 7.
26. M.B., 2 June 1947; 2 May, 5 Sept., 3 Oct. 1955; 7 July 1958; 30 June 1956; 6 Nov. 1950.
27. Ibid., 7 July 1952.
28. Ibid., 6 Sept. 1948; 7 July 1952; 7 Nov. 1960; 6 Feb. 1961. I would like to thank Mr Anthony Cullen, nurse tutor, for information regarding the history of the hospital's school of nursing.
29. Information supplied by Professor Moore; Norman Malcolm, *Ludwig Wittgenstein: a Memoir* (rev. edn, London, 1966), pp. 74-83.
30. M.B., 5 Dec. 1955; 2 June 1960; 5 May, 1 Sept. 1958; 1 Apr. 1963.
31. Information supplied by Professor Moore.
32. M.B., 2 May 1960.
33. *St Patrick's Hospital, Dublin. A Guide for General Practitioners* (Dublin, [1987]), p. 5. *St Patrick's Hospital Dublin Development Committee* (Dublin, n.d.).
34. M.B., 5 June 1950; 7 Dec. 1953.
35. Ibid., 1 Feb. 1960; 5 Dec. 1955; 9 Jan. 1956; 4 Feb. 1957.
36. Information supplied by Professor Moore.
37. Karl O'Sullivan (ed.), *All in the Mind: Approaches to Mental Health* (Dublin, 1986); M.B., 7 Sept. 1959; *Guide for General Practitioners*, p. 3.
38. M.B., 7 Sept. 1959.
39. Moore, 'Perspective', pp. 299-300.
40. *Macbeth*, Act v, Scene v.

Chapter 7, pp. 284-291

1. David Cohen, *Forgotten Millions: the Treatment of the Mentally Ill—a Global Perspective* (London, 1988), p. 224.
2. Anthony Clare, 'The Concept of Care in Mental Illness' in Karl

O'Sullivan (ed.), *All in the Mind: Approaches to Mental Health* (Dublin, 1986), pp. 22-3.

3. The Meath Hospital was opened in 1753 to serve the weavers of the Coombe, but St Patrick's was already built by that stage, though not yet open, and so can claim to have a longer history.

4. *The Psychiatric Services—Planning for the Future, Report of a Study Group on the Development of the Psychiatric Services* (Dublin, 1984). For assessments of this report see James Raftery, 'Mental Health Policy in Ireland: Learning from the UK?' in *Administration*, 35, i (1987), pp. 38-46 and Shane Butler, 'The Psychiatric Services—Planning for the Future: a critique' in *Administration*, 35, i (1987) pp. 47-68. For a stimulating and provocative discussion of the whole question of Irish mental health, see Eileen Kane, 'Stereotypes and Irish Identity: Mental Illness as a Cultural Frame' in *Studies*, 75, ccc (Winter 1986), pp. 539-51.

5. At present, patients admitted to St Patrick's stay on average for about forty days.

6. Remarks made at the opening of the new admission/research unit at St Patrick's Hospital on 28 August, 1975 by Professor Norman Moore. I would like to thank Professor Moore for giving me access to this typescript.

7. For information on which much of this chapter is based, I would like to thank Dr P. J. Meehan, Dr Anthony O'Flaherty and Professor Anthony Clare.

8. P. J. Meehan, 'Psychiatry today—care, treatment and rehabilitation' in O'Sullivan (ed.), op.cit., pp. 11-12.

9. Ibid., pp. 12-13.

10. Ibid., p. 14.

11. Anthony Clare, *Psychiatry in Dissent: Controversial Issues in Thought and Practice* (London, 1976), pp. 211-12.

Bibliography

Primary Sources

St Patrick's Hospital, Dublin

1. Swift Papers
2. Swift's Will and the Charters
3. Minute, Draft Minute, Agenda Books and Indexes
4. Eighteenth-Century Papers
5. Nineteenth-Century Papers
6. Twentieth-Century Papers

National Library of Ireland, Dublin
Public Record Office of Northern Ireland, Belfast

Parliamentary Papers

Periodicals and Directories

Secondary Sources

PRIMARY SOURCES

St Patrick's Hospital, Dublin

1. Swift Papers

Financial papers of Jonathan Swift, *c.* 1720–45
Papers of Jonathan Swift's guardians, 1742-5
Papers of Jonathan Swift's executors, 1745-6

2. Swift's Will and the Charters

The Last Will and Testament of the Revd Dr Jonathan Swift, reprint, Dublin, 1984

The Charter of His Majesty King George II, For Erecting and Endowing St Patrick's Hospital; Founded by the Last Will of the Reverend Doctor Jonathan Swift, Late Dean of St Patrick's Dublin; for the Reception of Ideots, Lunaticks and Incurables, reprint, Dublin, 1798

Supplemental Charter of St Patrick's Hospital, Founded by the Last Will of the Reverend Doctor Jonathan Swift, Late Dean of Saint Patrick's, Dublin, for the Reception of Idiots, Lunatics, and Incurables, Dublin, 1889

Second Supplemental Charter of St Patrick's Hospital, Founded by the Last Will of the Reverend Doctor Jonathan Swift, Late Dean of Saint Patrick's, Dublin, for the Reception of Idiots, Lunatics, and Incurables, Dublin, 1896

Third Supplemental Charter of St Patrick's Hospital, Founded by the Last Will of the Reverend Doctor Jonathan Swift, Late Dean of Saint Patrick's, Dublin, for the Reception of Idiots, Lunatics, and Incurables, Dublin, 1897

3. Minute, Draft Minute, Agenda Books and Indexes

Minute Books of the Board of Governors

29 Aug.	1746	–	7 Nov.	1796
6 Feb.	1797	–	1 Sept.	1835
1 Oct.	1835	–	24 Apr.	1851
5 May	1851	–	3 Nov.	1862
1 Dec.	1862	–	5 Dec.	1870
2 Jan.	1871	–	1 Nov.	1880
7 Dec.	1880	–	3 Jun.	1889
6 Jan.	1902	–	7 Sept.	1914

3 Nov.	1930	— 2 May	1938
30 May	1938	— 8 Jan.	1945
5 Feb.	1945	— 5 Oct.	1953
2 Nov.	1953	— 2 Dec.	1965
5 Dec.	1983	— 1 Dec.	1986

Draft Minutes of the Board of Governors

6 Feb.	1758	— 2 Nov.	1772
1 Nov.	1784	— 3 Aug.	1789
2 Nov.	1789	— 5 Aug.	1799
4 Nov.	1799	— 10 Aug.	1815
6 Nov.	1815	— 6 Feb.	1832
16 Feb.	1832	— 8 Oct.	1838
18 Nov.	1838	— 4 Mar.	1847
1 Apr.	1847	— 4 Oct.	1852
1 Nov.	1852	— 5 Apr.	1858
3 May	1858	— 3 Aug.	1863
7 Sept.	1863	— 4 Nov.	1867
6 Jan.	1868	— 2 Feb.	1874
2 Mar.	1874	— 4 Jan.	1881
7 Feb.	1881	— 6 Dec.	1886
3 Jan.	1887	— 3 Jul.	1893
7 Aug.	1893	— 3 Dec.	1900
7 Jan.	1901	— 4 Oct.	1909
1 Nov.	1909	— 1 Sept.	1913

Agenda Books of the Board of Governors

7 Nov.	1836	— 6 Feb.	1854
6 Mar.	1854	— 2 Mar.	1863
6 Apr.	1863	— 3 Jan.	1870
7 Feb.	1870	— 3 Jan.	1882
6 Feb.	1882	— 1 May	1893
5 Jun.	1893	— 2 Apr.	1900
2 Jun.	1899	— 5 Dec.	1904
2 Jan.	1905	— 1 May	1911
29 May	1911	— 5 Jul.	1915
9 Aug.	1915	— 3 Feb.	1919
3 Mar.	1919	— 4 Sep.	1922
2 Oct.	1922	— 2 Nov.	1925
7 Dec.	1925	— 2 Sep.	1928
1 Oct.	1928	— 1 Dec.	1930
5 Jan.	1931	— 7 Nov.	1932
5 Dec.	1932	— 2 Jul.	1934
30 Jul.	1934	— 2 Mar.	1936
6 Apr.	1936	— 9 Aug.	1937
6 Sep.	1937	— 2 Jan.	1939
6 Feb.	1939	— 29 Jul.	1940

2 Sep.	1940	—	6 Jul.	1942
31 Jul.	1942	—	5 Jun.	1944
3 Jul.	1944	—	7 Oct.	1946
4 Nov.	1946	—	7 Feb.	1949
7 Mar.	1949	—	3 Sep.	1951
1 Oct.	1951	—	31 Aug.	1953
5 Oct.	1953	—	1 Oct.	1956
5 Nov.	1956	—	3 Jan.	1962
5 Feb.	1962	—	6 Mar.	1967
3 Apr.	1967	—	3 Mar.	1973

Indexes to the Proceedings of the Board

1835	—	1868
1869	—	1889
1889	—	1901

4. Eighteenth-Century Papers

Governors' correspondence, accounts and petitions, 1747-1800
George Semple's book of plans and further description of the foregoing design: and the methods intended to be taken in the execution thereof, 2 Feb. 1749/50
Estate papers: leases, rentals, maps and correspondence, 1748-1800
Report on St Patrick's Hospital by James Verschoyle and Thomas Cradock, 22 Mar. 1799.

5. Nineteenth-Century Papers

Administration
Secretary's Letter Book, 1865-70
General Rules and Regulations for the Management of St Patrick's Hospital, Dublin, Founded by Jonathan Swift, D.D., 1745, Dublin, 1885
Bye-laws for the Management of St Patrick's Hospital Dublin, Founded by Jonathan Swift, D.D., 1745, in Pursuance of its Charter and Supplemental Charter, Dublin, 1889
Typescript copies of the Reports of the Inspectors of Lunacy, 1890-1911
Minute Books of Sub-Committees of the Board: Purchase of St Edmundsbury, 1898-1900; Dr. Leeper's Report on the Hospital, 1899
Placard: St Patrick's Daily Duties, October 1899

Patients
Registry of St Patrick's Hospital, 1795-1925
Admission Forms: Nos. 300-599 (1841-53); Nos. 920-1150 (1873-87); Nos. 1170-2268 (1888-1921)
Case-books: St Patrick's 1899 male and female

Accounts
Book of Letters of Obligation, 1849-64
Personal Ledgers: 1886, 1898

Estate
Rental books: Saggart 1840-57, 1858-70; Ferns 1840-58, 1858-70
Report of the Saggart Estate up to 25 March 1850 and Recommendation of Sub-Committee
Report of Ferns Estate up to 25 March 1851 and Recommendation of Sub-Committee
Maps: Surveys of the Estate of the Governors of St Patrick's Hospital in the Parish of Saggart, Co. Dublin, by J. J. Byrne, 1841 and 1860

Plans
Plans of mental hospitals by Francis Johnston, 1817
Folder of Plans of Alterations and Additions to St Patrick's Hospital from 1830

6. Twentieth-Century Papers

Administration
Agenda notices, 1913-47
Typescript of copies of the Reports of the Inspectors of Lunacy, 1895-1944
Medical Superintendent's Reports: St Patrick's, 1899-1901; 1902-5; 1906-11; 1911-17; 1917-25; 1925-33; 1946-7; St Edmundsbury, 1899-1904; 1904-9; 1915-27
Register of Medical Superintendent's Letters: 1928-9; 1929-30; 1931-2; 1932-3; 1936-7; 1937-8
St Edmundsbury Hospital, Lucan, Dublin, [1902]
St Patrick's Hospital, Dublin, Dublin, [1905]
Report on the Activities and Finances of St Patrick's Hospital, [1970]
St Patrick's Hospital, Dublin, Development Committee, Dublin, n.d.
St Patrick's Hospital, Dublin. A Guide for General Practitioners, Dublin, [1987]

Patients
Register of St Patrick's Certified Patients, 1925-46
Register of St Edmundsbury, 1899-1946
Register of Voluntary Boarders: St Patrick's, 1925-42; 1943-6: St Edmundsbury, 1915-46
Admission Forms: Nos. 2791-3194 (1930-9); Nos. 3401-3559 (1944-6); Voluntary Boarders: Nos. 52-700 (1930-42); Nos. 4068-7142 (1953-6)
Case-books: St Patrick's, female 1902; 1903; 1906; 1915; male 1902; 1915; St Edmundsbury, 1906-26
Medical Journals: 1911-21; 1921-32; 1932-41; 1941-6
Annual statistical returns by private lunatic asylums, 1902-27
Daily Average Books: St Patrick's, 1914-32; St Edmundsbury, 1916-46; Dublin and Lucan, 1933-72
Admissions, discharges and deaths: 1915-45; 1926-44

Accounts
Personal Ledgers: St Patrick's, 1910-17; St Edmundsbury, 1899-1917; Dublin and Lucan, 1918-22; 1923-6; 1927-30; 1930-2; 1927-35; 1938-43; 1943-6

General Ledgers: 1917-28; 1928-39; 1940-4
General Journals: 1933-9; 1939-44; 1945-56
Annual Accounts: 1916-45

Estate
Rentals 1916-21
Rental books: 1918-34; 1935-44
Chart of Saggart leases, 1920
Maps: surveys of the Saggart estate, 1914 and 1920.

National Library of Ireland, Dublin

Irish Land Commission Index: St Patrick's Hospital Estate

Public Record Office of Northern Ireland, Belfast

Journal of John Moore, Carrickfergus, Co. Antrim, 1766-8

PARLIAMENTARY PAPERS

Report from the Committee . . . for . . . Making Provision for the Care of Lunatics and Idiots by Grand Jury Presentments, H.C. 1803-4 (109), iv.
Report from the Committee on Madhouses in England. H.C. 1814-15 (296), iv.
Third Report from the Committee on Madhouses in England, H.C. 1816 (451), vi.
Report from the Select Committee on the Lunatic Poor in Ireland, H.C. 1817 (430), viii.
Copies of all Correspondence . . . on the Subject of Public Lunatic Asylums, H.C. 1828 (234), xxii.
Report from the Select Committee on Medical Charities, Ireland, H.C. 1843 (412), x.
Report from the Select Committee . . . Appointed to Consider the State of the Lunatic Poor in Ireland, H.L. 1843 (625), x.
Report of the Inspectors-General on the District, Local and Private Lunatic Asylums in Ireland, 1843, [C 567], H.C. 1844, xxx.
Report on the District, Local and Private Lunatic Asylums in Ireland, for 1845, [C 736], H.C. 1846, xxii.
Report on the District, Local and Private Lunatic Asylums in Ireland, for 1846 [C 820], H.C. 1847, xvii.
Report on the District, Local and Private Lunatic Asylums in Ireland, for 1848 [C 1054], H.C. 1849, xxiii.
Sixth General Report on the District, Local and Private Lunatic Asylums in Ireland. [C 1653], H.C. 1852-3, xli.
Minutes of Evidence taken before the Select Committee on the Lunatic Asylums (Ireland) (Advances) Bill, H.C. 1854-5 (262), viii.
Report of the Commissioners of Inquiry into the State of Lunatic Asylums . . . in Ireland, i, [C 2436], H.C. 1857-8, xxvii.

Eleventh Report on the District, Criminal and Private Lunatic Asylums in Ireland, [C 2975], H.C. 1862, xxiii.
Nineteenth Report on the District, Criminal and Private Lunatic Asylums in Ireland, [C 202], H.C. 1870, xxxiv.
Report from the Select Committee on Lunacy Law . . . H.C. 1877 (373), xiii.
Twenty-sixth Report on the District, Criminal and Private Lunatic Asylums in Ireland. [C 1750], H.C. 1877, xli.
Return of the Number of Licensed Houses in England and Wales for the Care of Lunatics; . . . Similar Return for Scotland and Ireland, H.C. 1878 (370), lxiii.
Thirty-fourth Report on the District, Criminal and Private Lunatic Asylums in Ireland, [C 4539], H.C. 1885, xxxvi.
Forty-first Report of the Inspectors of Lunatics on District, Criminal and Private Lunatic Asylums in Ireland, [C 6803], H.C. 1892, xl.
Fifty-third Report of the Inspectors of Lunatics (Ireland). [Cd 2262], H.C. 1905, xxxv.
Report . . . of the Vice-regal Commission on Poor Law Reform in Ireland, [Cd 3204], H.C. 1906, lii.

PERIODICALS AND DIRECTORIES

Periodicals
Dublin Journal
Freeman's Journal
Irish Times
Universal Advertiser
Directories
The Gentleman and Citizen's Almanack, (by John Watson, Bookseller), for the Year of Our Lord 1758, Dublin, 1758.
The Gentleman's and Citizen's Almanack, compiled by Samuel Watson, Bookseller, for the Year of Our Lord, 1788, Dublin, 1788.
The Treble Almanack for the Year 1810, Dublin, 1809.
The Treble Almanack for the Year 1829, Dublin, 1829.
Dublin Directory and General Register of Ireland for the Year of Our Lord 1843, Dublin, 1843.
The Post Office Dublin Directory and Calendar for 1892, Dublin, 1892.
The Post Office Dublin Directory and Calendar for 1926, Dublin, 1926.
The Directory of Dublin for 1945, Dublin, 1945.

SECONDARY SOURCES

Ackerknecht, E. H., *A Short History of Psychiatry*, trans. Sula Wolff, 2nd edn New York, 1968
Banks, John, 'The Writ "de Lunatico Inquirendo" in the Case of Jonathan Swift, D.D., Dean of St Patrick's: with Observations' in *The Dublin Quarterly Journal of Medical Science*, new series, xxxi, no. 61 (1861), pp. 83-90
Barrington, Ruth, *Health, Medicine and Politics in Ireland, 1900-1970*, Dublin, 1987

Bence-Jones, Mark, *Twilight of the Ascendancy*, London, 1987

Bernard, J. H., *The Cathedral Church of St Patrick: a History and Description of the Building, with a Short Account of the Deans*, London, 1903

Berridge, Virginia, and Griffith Edwards, *Opium and the People: Opiate Use in Nineteenth-Century England*, London and New York, 1981

Bew, Paul, *Land and the National Question in Ireland, 1858-82*, Dublin, 1978

Boylan, Henry, *A Dictionary of Irish Biography*, Dublin, 1978

Boyle, John, Earl of Orrery, *Remarks on the Life and Writings of Dr Jonathan Swift* . . . 3rd edn, Dublin, 1752

Brain, W. R., 'The Illness and Dean Swift' in *Irish Journal of Medical Science*, 6th ser., nos 320-1 (Aug/Sept. 1952), pp. 337-45

Brain, W. R., *Some Reflections on Genius and Other Essays*, London, 1960

Brown, Norman O., *Life against Death: the Psychoanalytical Meaning of History*, reprint, London, 1970, of orig. edn, London, 1959

Browne, Noel, *Against the Tide*, Dublin, 1986

Burdett, H. C., *Hospitals and Asylums of the World*, vol. 1: *Asylums—History and Administration*, London, 1891

Burke, Helen, *The People and the Poor Law in 19th Century Ireland*, Littlehampton, 1987

Burke's Irish Family Records, London, 1976

Burton, Robert, *The Anatomy of Melancholy*, ed. A. R. Shilleto, 3 vols, London, 1896

Butler, Shane, 'The Psychiatric Services—Planning for the Future: a Critique' in *Administration*, 35, i (1987), pp. 47-68

Bynum, W. F., Roy Porter and Michael Shepherd (ed.), *The Anatomy of Madness*, 2 vols, London, 1985

Byrd, Max, *Visits to Bedlam: Madness and Literature in the Eighteenth Century*, Columbia, S.C., 1974

Cameron, C. A., *The History of the Royal College of Surgeons in Ireland*, Dublin, 1886

Cartwright, F. F., *A Social History of Medicine*, Themes in British Social History, London and New York, 1977

Chandler, Edward, *Photography in Dublin During the Victorian Era*, Dublin, n.d.

Clare, Anthony, *Psychiatry in Dissent: Controversial Issues in Thought and Practice*, London, 1976

Clark, Samuel, *Social Origins of the Irish Land War*, Princeton, N.J., 1979

Clarke, Austin, *Mnemosyne Law in Dust*, Dublin, 1966

Clarke, Basil, *Mental Disorder in Earlier Britain*, Cardiff, 1975

Clarke, Basil, 'Mental Illness and Rehabilitation in Early Nineteenth-Century Ireland: the Case of Charles Stock' in *Psychological Medicine*, 13 (1983), pp. 727-34

Coakley, Davis, *The Irish School of Medicine: Outstanding Practitioners of the 19th century*, Dublin, 1988

Cohen, David, *Forgotten Millions: the Treatment of the Mentally Ill—a Global Perspective*, London, 1988

Craig, Maurice, *Dublin, 1660-1860,* reprint, Dublin, 1980, of orig. edn, Dublin, 1952

[Craig, Maurice (ed.)] *The Legacy of Swift: A Bi-Centenary Record of St Patrick's Hospital, Dublin,* Dublin, 1948

Crawford, E. M., 'Indian Meal and Pellagra in Nineteenth-century Ireland' in J. M. Goldstrom and L. A. Clarkson (ed.), *Irish Population, Economy, and Society: Essays in Honour of the late K. H. Connell,* Oxford, 1981, pp. 113-33

Cullen, L. M., *An Economic History of Ireland since 1660,* reprint, London, 1978, of orig. edn, London, 1972

Cullen, L. M., *The Emergence of Modern Ireland, 1600-1900,* London, 1981

Dain, Norman, *Concepts of Insanity in the United States, 1789-1865,* New Brunswick, N.J. , 1964

Daly, Mary, *Dublin—the Deposed Capital: a Social and Economic History, 1860-1914,* Cork, 1984

Daly, Mary, *The Famine in Ireland,* Dublin Historical Association: Irish History, Second Series, Dublin, 1986

Deane, Seamus, *A Short History of Irish Literature,* London, 1986

DePorte, Michael, *Nightmares and Hobby Horses: Swift, Sterne and Augustan Ideas of Madness,* San Marino, Calif., 1974

Dickinson, P. L., *The Dublin of Yesterday,* London, 1929

Dickson, David (ed.), *The Gorgeous Mask: Dublin, 1700-1850,* Trinity History Workshop 2, Dublin, 1987

Dickson, David, *New Foundations: Ireland, 1660-1800,* Helicon History of Ireland 6, Dublin, 1987

Doerner, Klaus, *Madmen and the Bourgeoisie: a Social History of Insanity and Psychiatry,* trans. Joachim Neugroschel and Jean Steinberg, London, 1981

Durey, Michael, *The Return of the Plague: British Society and the Cholera, 1831-2,* Dublin, 1979

Ehrenpreis, Irvin, *The Personality of Jonathan Swift,* London, 1958

Ehrenpreis, Irvin, *Swift, the Man, His Works, and the Age,* 3 vols London 1962, 1967, 1983

Elias Jr., A. C., 'Lord Orrery's Copy of *Memoirs of the Life and Writings of Swift* (1751)' in *Eighteenth-Century Ireland,* i (1986), pp. 117-25

Evelyn, John, *The diary of John Evelyn,* ed. William Bray, 2 vols, reprint, London, 1907, of orig. edn, London, 1818-19

Ewen, J. H., *A Handbook of Psychiatry,* London, 1933

Finnane, Mark, 'Asylums, Families and the State' in *History Workshop* no. 20 (Autumn 1985), pp. 134-48

Finnane, Mark, *Insanity and the Insane in Post-Famine Ireland,* London and Totowa, N.J., 1981

Fleetwood, J. F., *The History of Medicine in Ireland,* 2nd edn, Dublin, 1983

Foster, R. F., *Modern Ireland, 1600-1972,* London, 1988

Foucault, Michel, *Madness and Civilization: a History of Insanity in the Age of Reason,* trans. Richard Howard, reprint, London, 1985, of orig. English edn, London, 1967

French, C. N., *The Story of St Luke's Hospital*, London, 1951

Gilbert (ed.), J. T., *Calendar of the Ancient Records of Dublin*, 18 vols, Dublin, 1889-1922

Goffman, Erving, *Asylums: Essays on the Social Situation of Mental Patients and Other Inmates*, New York, 1961

Gogarty, Oliver St John, *It Isn't This Time of Year at All!*, reprint, London, 1983, of orig. edn, London, 1954

Greaves, C. D., *The Irish Transport and General Workers' Union: the Formative Years, 1909-23*, Dublin, 1982

Greenacre, Phyllis, *Swift and Carroll: a Psychoanalytic Study of Two Lives*, New York, 1955

Grob, Gerald, *The State and Mentally Ill*, Chapel Hill, N.C., 1966

Gwynn, Stephen, *The Life and Friendships of Dean Swift*, London, 1933

Hallaran, W. S., *Practical Observations on the Causes and Cure of Insanity*, 2nd edn, Cork, 1818

Handcock, W. D., *The History and Antiquities of Tallaght in the County of Dublin*, reprint, Cork, 1976, of 2nd revised edn, Dublin, 1899

Harkness, David and Mary O'Dowd (ed.)., *The Town in Ireland*, Historical Studies xiii, Belfast, 1981

Harris, L. G. E., *A Treatise on the Law and Practice in Lunacy in Ireland*, Dublin, 1930

Harris, Walter, *The History and Antiquities of the City of Dublin . . .*, Dublin, 1766

Harvey, John, *Dublin: A Study in Environment*, reprint, Wakefield, 1972, of orig. edn, London, 1949

Head, Henry, *Aphasia and Kindred Disorders of Speech*, 2 vols. Cambridge, 1926

Hensey, Brendan, *The Health Services of Ireland*, 3rd edn, Dublin, 1979

Holroyd, Michael, *Bernard Shaw, Volume i: the Search for Love, 1856-1898*, London, 1988

Howe, G. M., *Man, Environment and Disease in Britain: a Medical Geography throughout the Ages*, reprint, Harmondsworth, 1976, of orig. edn, Newton Abbot, 1972

Hunter, Richard and Ida Macalpine, *Three Hundred Years of Psychiatry, 1535-1860*, London, 1973

Jackson, Victor, *The Monuments of St Patrick's Cathedral, Dublin*, Dublin, 1987

Johnson, David, *The Interwar Economy in Ireland*, Studies in Irish Economic and Social History 4, Dublin, 1985

Johnson, Edith Mary, *Ireland in the Eighteenth Century*, Gill History of Ireland 8, Dublin, 1974

Jones, Kathleen, *A History of the Mental Health Services*, London, 1972

Joyce, James, *Ulysses*, reprint, Harmondsworth, 1982, of orig. edn, Paris, 1922

Joyce, John, *Lucan and its Neighbourhood*, reprint, Blackrock, 1988, of orig. edn, Dublin, 1901

Kane, Eileen, 'Stereotypes and Irish Identity: Mental Illness as a Cultural Frame' in *Studies*, 75, ccc (Winter 1986), pp. 539-51

Kirkpatrick, T. P., *The Foundation of a Great Hospital: Steevens in the XVIII Century*, Dublin, 1933

Kirkpatrick, T. P., *The History of Doctor Steevens' Hospital, Dublin, 1720-1920*, Dublin, 1924

Kirkpatrick, T. P., *A Note on the History of the Care of the Insane in Ireland up to the End of the Nineteenth Century*, Dublin, 1931

Kramer, Dale, *Charles Robert Maturin*, Twayne's English Authors Series 156, New York, 1973

Landa, L. A., 'Jonathan Swift and Charity' in *Journal of English and Germanic Philology*, xliv (1945), pp. 337-50

Leadbetter, Mary, *The Annals of Ballitore*, ed. John McKenna, reprint, Athy, 1986, of orig. edn *The Leadbetter Papers*, London, 1862

Lee, Joseph, *The Modernisation of Irish Society, 1848-1918*, Gill History of Ireland 10, Dublin, 1973

Le Fanu, T. P., 'Catalogue of Dean Swift's Library in 1715, with an Inventory of his Personal Property in 1742' in *Proceedings of the Royal Irish Academy*, xxxvii, C, 13 (July 1927), pp. 263-75

Leslie, J. B., *Derry Clergy and Parishes*, Enniskillen, 1937

Locke, John, *An Essay Concerning Human Understanding*, ed. J. W. Youlton, 2 vols, reprint, London, 1961, of 5th edn, London, 1706

Lonergan, Eamonn, *St Luke's Hospital, Clonmel, 1834-1984*, Clonmel, [1984]

Lynch, Patrick, and John Vaizey, *Guinness's Brewery in the Irish Economy, 1759-1876*, Cambridge, 1960

Lyons, F. S. L., *Ireland since the Famine*, rev. edn, London, 1973

Lyons, F. S. L., *John Dillon: a Biography*, London, 1968

Lyons, J .B., *Thrust Syphilis down to Hell and Rejoyceana: Studies in the Borderlands of Literature and Medicine*, Dun Laoghaire, 1988

McCormack, W. J., *Sheridan LeFanu and Victorian Ireland*, Oxford, 1980

McDowell, R. B., *Ireland in the Age of Imperialism and Revolution, 1760-1801*, Oxford, 1979

McNeill, Charles, 'The Hospital of St John Without the New Gate, Dublin' in *Journal of the Royal Society of Antiquaries of Ireland*, 6th ser., lv (1925), pp. 58-64

McNeill, Mary, *The Life and Times of Mary Ann McCracken 1770-1866: a Belfast Panorama*, reprint, Belfast, 1988, of orig. edn, Dublin, 1960

McNeill, W. H., *Plagues and Peoples*, reprint, Harmondsworth, 1979, of orig. edn, New York, 1976

[Mahony, Rev. Francis,] *The Works of Father Prout*, ed. Charles Kent, London, n.d.

Malcolm, Elizabeth, 'Asylums and other "Total Institutions" in Ireland: Recent Studies' in *Eire-Ireland*, xxii, 3 (Fall 1987), pp. 151-60

Malcolm, Elizabeth, *'Ireland Sober, Ireland Free': Drink and Temperance in Nineteenth-Century Ireland*, Dublin, 1986

Malcolm, Elizabeth, 'Women and Madness in Ireland, 1600-1850' in Margaret MacCurtain and Mary O'Dowd (ed.), *Women in Early Modern Ireland, 1500-1800*, Dublin, forthcoming

Malcolm, Norman, *Ludwig Wittgenstein: a Memoir*, rev. edn, London, 1966

Malcomson, A. P. W., *John Foster: the Politics of the Anglo-Irish Ascendancy*, Oxford, 1978

Maturin, Charles, *Melmoth the Wanderer: a Tale*, ed. Alethea Hayter, reprint Harmondsworth, 1977, of orig. edn, Edinburgh, 1820

Maxwell, Constantia, *Country and Town in Ireland under the Georges*, rev. edn, Dundalk, 1949

Maxwell, Constantia, *Dublin under the Georges 1714-1830*, London and Dublin, 1946

Maxwell, Constantia, *A History of Trinity College, Dublin, 1591-1892*, Dublin, 1946

Mayer-Gross, W., Eliot Slater and Martin Roth, *Clinical Psychiatry*, 2nd revised edn, London, 1960

Merquior, J. G., *Foucault*, Fontana Modern Masters, ed. Frank Kermode, London, 1985

Mitchell, David, *A 'Peculiar' Place: the Adelaide Hospital, Dublin, 1839-1989*, Dublin, [1988]

Moody, T. W., F. X. Martin and F. J. Byrne (ed.) *A New History of Ireland*, vol. ix: *Maps, Genealogies, Lists*, Oxford, 1984

Moody, T. W., and W. E. Vaughan (ed.), *A New History of Ireland*, vol. iv: *Eighteenth-Century Ireland, 1691-1800*, Oxford, 1986

Moore, J. N. P., 'Perspective' in *Bulletin of the Royal College of Psychiatrists*, x (Nov. 1986), pp. 298-300

Moore, J. N. P., *Swift's Philanthropy*, Dublin [1967]

Nicolson, Marjorie, and Nora M. Mohler, 'The Scientific Background of "Voyage of Laputa" ' in A. Norman Jeffares (ed.), *Swift: Modern Judgements*, London, 1969, pp. 223-37

Nokes, David, *Jonathan Swift, a Hypocrite Reversed: a Critical Biography*, Oxford, 1985

O'Brien, J. V., *'Dear, Dirty Dublin': a City in Distress, 1899-1916*, Berkeley, Calif., 1982

O'Doherty, E. F., and S. D. McGrath (ed.), *The Priest and Mental Health*, Dublin and London, 1962

O'Donoghue, D. J., *Life of Robert Emmet*, Dublin, 1902

O'Donoghue, E. G., *The Story of Bethlehem Hospital from its Foundation in 1247*, New York, 1915

O'Sullivan, Karl (ed.), *All in the Mind: Approaches to Mental Health*, Dublin, 1986

O'Sullivan, Peter (ed.), *Newcastle Lyons: a Parish of the Pale*, Dublin, 1986

Pakenham, Thomas, *The Year of Liberty: the Great Irish Rebellion of 1798*, reprint, London, 1982, of orig. edn, London, 1969

Parry-Jones, W. L., *The Trade in Lunacy: a Study of Private Madhouses in England in the Eighteenth and Nineteenth Centuries*, London and Toronto, 1972

Porter, Roy, *Mind-Forg'd Manacles: a History of Madness in England from the Restoration to the Regency*, London 1987

Quintana, Ricardo, *The Mind and Art of Jonathan Swift*, London and New York, 1936

Rafety, James, 'Mental Health Policy in Ireland: Learning from the UK? in *Administration*, 35, i (1987), pp. 38-46

Real, Hermann J., and Heinz J. Vienken, 'Psychoanalytic Criticism and Swift: the History of a Failure' in *Eighteenth-century Ireland*, i (1986), pp. 127-41

Robins, Joseph, *Fools and Mad: a History of the Insane in Ireland*, Dublin, 1986

Robins, Joseph, *The Lost Children: a Study of Charity Children in Ireland, 1700-1900*, Dublin, 1980

Rose, M. E., *The English Poor Law, 1780-1930*, Newton Abbot, 1971

Rosen, George, *Madness in Society: Chapters in the Historical Sociology of Mental Illness*, Chicago and London, 1968

Ross, Ian Campbell, (ed.), *Public Virtue, Public Love: the Early Years of the Dublin Lying-in Hospital, the Rotunda*, Dublin, 1986

Rothman, David, *The Discovery of the Asylum: Social Order and Disorder in the New Republic*, Boston and Toronto, 1971

Ryan, Desmond, *The Rising*, Dublin, 1949

Sacks, Oliver, *The Man who Mistook his Wife for a Hat*, London, 1986

St James's Development Association, *St James's Graveyard, Dublin — History and Associations*, Dublin, 1988

Sayle, (ed.), C. E., *A Catalogue of the Bradshaw Collection of Irish Books in the University Library, Cambridge*, 3 vols, Cambridge, 1916

Scheper-Hughes, Nancy, *Saints, Scholars, and Schizophrenics: Mental Illness in Rural Ireland*, Berkeley, Calif., and London, 1979

Scott, Sir Walter, *The Works of Jonathan Swift*, vol. i, 2nd edn, Edinburgh, 1824

Scull, Andrew (ed.), *Madhouses, Mad-doctors, and Madmen: the Social History of Psychiatry in the Victorian Era*, London, 1981

Scull (ed.), Andrew, *Museums of Madness: the Social Organisation of Insanity in Nineteenth-Century England*, reprint, Harmondsworth, 1982, of orig. edn, London, 1979

Showalter, Elaine, *The Female Malady: Women, Madness and English Culture 1830-1980*, reprint, London, 1987, of orig. edn, New York, 1985

Skultans, Vieda, *English Madness: Ideas on Insanity, 1580-1890*, London, 1979

Skultans, Vieda, (ed.), *Madness and Morals: Ideas on Insanity in the Nineteenth Century*, London and Boston, 1975

Smith, F. B., *The People's Health, 1830-1910*, Canberra, 1979

Solow, Barbara, *The Land Question in the Irish Economy, 1870-1903*, Cambridge, Mass., 1971

Swift, Jonathan, *The Correspondence of Jonathan Swift*, ed. Harold Williams, 5 vols, Oxford, 1963-5

Swift, Jonathan, *Gulliver's Travels*, reprint with intro. by Michael Foot, Harmondsworth, 1984, of orig. edn, London, 1726

Swift, Jonathan, *Jonathan Swift: the Complete Poems*, ed. Pat Rogers, Harmondsworth, 1983

Swift, Jonathan, *A Tale of a Tub and Other Satires*, ed. Kathleen Williams, reprint, London, 1975, of 5th edn, London, 1710

Szasz, Thomas, *Ideology and Insanity: Essays on the Psychiatric Dehumanization of Man*, reprint, Harmondsworth, 1974, of orig. edn, New York, 1970

Szasz, Thomas, *The Myth of Mental Illness: Foundations of a Theory of Personal Conduct*, reprint, London, 1972, of orig. edn, New York, 1961

Thackeray, W. M., *The English Humourists; the Four Georges*, reprint, London, 1949, of orig. edn, London, 1853, 1861

Thomas, Keith, *Religion and the Decline of Magic: Studies in Popular Beliefs in Sixteenth- and Seventeenth-Century England*, reprint, Harmondsworth, 1978, of orig. edn, London, 1971

Thomson, Robert, *The Pelican History of Psychology*, Harmondsworth, 1968

Thompson, P. V., and D. J. Thompson, *The Account Books of Jonathan Swift*, Newark, N.J., and London, 1984

Thorne (ed.), R. G., *The History of Parliament: the House of Commons, 1790-1820*, vol. iv, London, 1986

Townshend, Charles, *Political Violence in Ireland: Government and Resistance since 1848*, reprint London, 1984, of orig. edn, London, 1983

Travers, Pauric, *Settlements and Divisions: Ireland, 1870-1922*, Helicon History of Ireland 8, Dublin, 1988

Vaughan, W. E., *Landlords and Tenants, in Ireland, 1848-1904*, Studies in Irish Economic and Social History 2, Dublin, 1984

Walker, Nigel, *Crime and Insanity in England*, vol. i: *the Historical Perspective*, England, 1968

Walshe, G. M. R., *Diseases of the Nervous System*, 3rd edn, Edinburgh, 1943

Warburton, John, James Whitelaw and Robert Walsh, *History of the City of Dublin . . .*, 2 vols, London, 1818

Wilde, W. R., *The Closing Years of Dean Swift's Life . . .* , 2nd edn, Dublin, 1849

Wilson, T. G., 'The Mental and Physical Health of Dean Swift's in *Medical History*, ii, 3 (July 1958), pp. 175-90

Wilson, T. G., 'Swift and the Doctors' in *Medical History*, viii, 3 (July 1964), pp. 199-216

Wilson, T. G., 'Swift's Deafness: and his Last Illness' in the *Irish Journal of Medical Science*, 6th ser., no. 162 (June 1939), pp. 291-305

Wright, G. N., *An Historical Guide to the City of Dublin . . .* 2nd edn, London, 1825

Younger, Calton, *Ireland's Civil War*, reprint, London, 1979, of orig. edn, London, 1968

Zinsser, Hans, *Rats, Lice and History: the Biography of a Bacillus*, reprint, London 1985

Index

AA (Alcoholics Anonymous) 277-8
Adaptation of Charters Act, 1926 246-7
Adelaide Hospital 271
aerial bombing 262-3
Agricultural Wages Board 263
alcohol 135, 140, 208
'All in the Mind' lecture series 281, 288-9
Anglo-Irish War 241, 245
Annaly, Lord 237
aphasia 8, 329 n.27
apothecary 89-90, 159
  Nicholls, John 118, 140
  Pannell, Mr 52
architect
  Carroll, Rawson 196
  Cooley, Thomas 73-4, 250-51
  Davis, Whitmore 75, 251, 338 n.118
  Johnston, Francis 127, 344 n.43
  Millar, A. G. C. 251, 253
  Murray, William 127, 344 n.43
  Parke, Edward 77, 339 n.124
  Semple, George 40-48, 73
  Symes, Sandham 195-6
  Wills, Isaac 334 n.31
  Wills, Michael 39-41, 334 nn.31 & 33
Armistice, 1918 244
Ashbourne Grammar School, Derby-shire 68, 236
asylums
  district/county 83, 104, 114, 126-7, 130-31, 172, 175-6, 200-201, 221, 230, 240
    Armagh 137
    Belfast 137
    Central Criminal, Dundrum 176
    Cork 76, 89-90, 146, 176
    Maryborough (Port Laoise) 176
    Monaghan 240
    Rathdrum Workhouse, Co. Wicklow 216-17
    Richmond, Dublin 76, 79, 115, 117, 127, 137, 139, 176, 179, 227
  private 131, 138, 205-6, 209-10, 219, 221
    Bellevue, Finglas 205

Bloomfield Retreat, Donnybrook 228
Dr Eustace's Hampstead and Highfield, Glasnevin 144, 206, 216, 225, 342 n.13
Esker House 206
Farnham House, Finglas 205-6
Lisle House 206
Rathfarnham 205
Stewart Institution 228
English 221-2, 234
  Bethlem or Bedlam 10, 13, 30, 41-5, 65, 81, 176, 220
  Derby 176
  Middlesex County, Hanwell 112, 141, 176
  St Luke's 30, 48, 176
  Stafford 176
  York, Quaker Retreat 89, 176, 340 n.153
Augustan literature 9

bacon merchants 190, 192-3
Baggot Street 271
Ballitore, Co. Kildare 101-2
Bank of Ireland 111, 116, 156-7, 162, 185, 195, 205, 251
Barber, John 20
Barter, Matilda 146
Beckett, Samuel 272
Bedlam see asylums, English
Belmore, Earl of 95
benches, Irish House of Commons' 251, 355 n.56
Bennet, Henry Grey 79-82, 84, 87-8, 90-91, 112, 126, 134
Beresford family 157-8
Bethlem Hospital, London see asylums, English
bicentenary 250, 265
Big Wind, 1839 128
Birch, Dr Thomas 4
Birrell, Augustine 15
Blaquiere, Sir John 95
Bleuler, Eugen 232
Blood, Mr 161

Bloody Sunday, 1913 249
Board of Works 125, 127
boarders *see* patients, boarders
Bolton, John 35
Boucicault, Dion 346 n.78
Bow Lane 34, 39, 41-2, 203, 237, 243
Brain, Sir Russell 8
Bray, Co. Dublin 161, 197
Brent, Jane 30
Brien, Charles 137
Brown, Norman O. 2
Brugha, Cathal 241
builder
    Carolan, Edward and Sons 127
    Mitchell, W. M. and Sons 250-52
Burdett, H. C. 154, 200, 213, 219-20,
    352 n.84
burial ground 81, 347 n.85
Burke, Edmund 101
Burke, Dr Francis 328 n.15
Burke, T. H. 182
Burrowes, Sir Kildare 96
Bury, Hon. Mrs Jane 95, 333 n.11
butcher
    Brien, Morgan 69
    Costly, Charles 68
    Goodwin, John 136-7
    Goodwin, Thomas 69, 136
bye-laws, 1889 165-6, 169, 208

caddowes 50
Caffrey, Mr 137
Camac River 43, 126-7, 195, 202
Carbery, Lord 146
cardiazol 264
Cashore, John 28, 39
Ceannt, Eamonn 241
Challoner, Anion 28, 30
chaplain *see* staff, chaplain
Charcot, J. M. 232
charters
    1746 26, 104, 118, 131, 180, 182-4,
        214, 279, 294-9
    1888 26, 180, 214-15, 299-303
    1895 26, 215, 303-5
    1897 26, 215, 305-6
chlorpromazine 282
Christchurch Fields 237
Civil War 241-3, 246
Clifford, John 137
closed shop 241
Cloyne, bishop of 95

Clynch, John 28
Coal Controller's Department 239
Cohen, David 284, 291
Colles, Dr J. M., registrar of lunacy
    198, 217, 225, 354 n.26
Collins, Michael 246
Commission of Inquiry on Mental Ill-
    ness, 1961-6 272, 284
Commission on the Relief of the Sick
    and Destitute Poor, 1925-7 248
Connellan, Major 249
Connolly, James 249
Conolly, Dr John 112, 141
Cooley, Thomas *see* architect
Coolock, Co. Dublin 157
Corbet, W. J. 182-3
Cosgrave, William T. 246
court of chancery 27-8, 189
Craig, Maurice 250, 334 n.31, 355 n.56
Crichton Royal Hospital, Dumfries
    261, 267, 281
Cuffe, Ambrose 99
Cullen, Cardinal 101
Cullen, Dr William 89
Cusack, Margaret Anna, 'Nun of Ken-
    mare' 107

Dáil Éireann 246-7
Daniels, William 137
Darwinism 200
Davis, Whitmore *see* architect
Davitt, Michael 234
Defoe, Daniel 23
Delville, Glasnevin 249
Denn, Philip 24, 29, 36, 38
Denn, Thomas 29
Desmond, Barry 286
Dickens, Charles 168-9
diet 84-5, 118, 134-7, 345 n.56
    alcohol 85, 135, 208
    meat 68-9, 134-7, 180, 224
    milk 137, 224
    pork 135-6, 194
    stirabout 135-6
    tea 135-6
    vegetables 126, 135-6, 224
Dingley, Rebecca 27
Donegal, Co. 98
Donnellan, Dr Christopher 35
Dreaming Dust 282
Dublin
    Castle 63, 182, 184

corporation 16, 21-2, 234
militia 157
parishes 98, 101, 225, 347 n.85
public health 203
Dublin University Magazine 168-9
Co. Dublin Farmers Assn 240
Sir Patrick Dun's Hospital 271

Ehrenpreis, Irvin 2, 3-4
Ellis, Havelock 233
Emergency (Second World War) 262-5, 268
emigration 149
Emmet, Dr Robert *see* governors
Emmet, Thomas Addis 60, 106
Essex Bridge 40
estate
  drainage 125
  enclosure 62, 109, 122
  evictions 71-2, 122-5, 190, 193, 344 n.36
  Ferns, Co. Wexford 60, 70, 121-2, 124-5, 186-9, 193, 234-6
  Francis Street, Dublin 68, 121-2, 189-93, 236-7
  Goldenbridge, Dublin 36, 121-2, 190-91, 237
  rents 124, 175, 184-7, 349 n.43
  Saggart, Co. Dublin 24, 29, 36-8, 61-2, 67-8, 70-72, 108-10, 121-6, 175, 181-7, 193, 234-6
  sale of 234-8
  sub-letting 192-3
  tenants
    Bulger, Thady 125
    Caddell, Catherine 123
    Byrne family 60
    Gill, George 192
    Hanlon, Jane 124
    Hornidge, Mr 183
    Lalor, Elizabeth 192-3
    Lalor, James 192-3
    Macdonnel, Patrick 60
    Nolan, Andrew 191
    Pearson, Mathew 125
    Wogan, Michael 71, 122

Famine 123-5, 148-9, 181, 241
farm labourers, Lucan 239-40, 263
Faulkner, George 22, 24
Federation of Dublin Voluntary Hospitals 271

Ferns, bishop of 67, 95
Fernside, Mrs 161
finances 27-30, 34-9, 47-9, 67-72, 75-9, 86, 116-17, 122, 154-5, 162, 177-81, 214-15, 254-5, 264
Finnane, Mark 144-5, 207
First World War 233, 238, 243-4, 263
Fitzwilliam Square 271
Ford, Julia and Denis 145
Forde, Mrs 95
Foster family 157
Foster, John *see* governors
Foster, John Leslie 107
Foucault, Michel xi, 10, 329-30 n.36
Four Courts 73, 242, 250
Fownes, Sir William 19-21, 33
Francis Street 190-92, 237
Frazer, John 96
Freud, Sigmund 233, 260-61
Friends of St Patrick's Hospital 278

Gaiety Theatre 282
Galway, Co. 276
garden 85, 90, 126, 129, 132, 177, 216, 220, 233
Garden Lane 190
Gay, John 250
Gill, Henry 333 n.11
Gladstone, William 186
Gore, Colonel Arthur 75, 333 n.11
Gortmore House 198
governors, board of 21-8, 55-7, 155-8, 215, 218-19, 246-8, 278-9, 307-15
  Agar, Archbishop Charles 60
  archbishop of Armagh 25-6, 55, 166, 247
  archbishop of Dublin 25-6, 56, 128, 156, 247
  archdeacon of Dublin 247
  Armstrong, R. O. 156, 158
  Ashbourne, Lord 214
  Banks, Sir John 156-7, 159-60, 166, 205
  Blackburne, Francis 109-10, 177
  Beresford, John 57, 59-60, 75, 108, 110
  Beresford, Lord John George 108
  Beresford, Archbishop William 60, 104
  Borough, Sir Edward 157
  Bowen, Alderman Benjamin 35, 38
  Bradley, Desmond 286

governors (*continued*)
Brady, Maziere 175, 177
chief justice 247
Cleghorn, Dr James 57, 79, 81-2, 88,
91, 104-7, 109, 113, 128, 139
Cobbe, Archbishop Charles 33
Colvill, Robert 156-7, 219
Corbet, Dean Francis 7, 27-8, 33-4,
36-40, 58, 249
Cotter Kyle, William 177
Cradock, Rev. Thomas 110
Cradock, Rev. Thomas R. 110
Cradock, Dean William 62
Crampton, Sir Philip 106-8, 139
Cusack, Major John 248
Cusack, Sir Ralph 107, 156, 158, 166,
249
Dawson, Dean Henry Richard 108
dean of Christ Church 25, 55, 156
dean of St Patrick's Cathedral 25, 56,
156
Delany, Dean Patrick 5, 25, 33, 57, 249
Emmet, Dr Robert 58, 60-67, 74-5,
88, 98, 102, 105-6, 336-7 n.88, 337
n.91
Fitzgibbon, John 58-60, 246
Fletcher, Bishop Thomas 32-3
Foster, Anthony 38, 58-9, 61-2
Foster, John 57-9, 72, 79, 94-5, 107,
199, 251, 339 n.124
Fowler, Archbishop Robert 60
Fowler, Archdeacon Robert 98
Geoghegan, W. P. 156, 219
Goodbody, Godfrey 279
Gordon, Dr Samuel 157, 217
Goulding, Lady 278-9
Grattan, Rev. John 25
Greene, Thomas 248
Guinness, Henry Seymour 248
Hastings, Archdeacon Thomas 101
Irwin, Rev. J. Crawford 157, 225
Jackson, Dr Alexander 106-9, 139,
142
Jellett, Dean Henry 217
Jenkins, Jeffrey B. 279, 286
Kennedy, Hugh 246-7
King, Rev. James 25, 57
LaTouche, Christopher Digges 156,
219
Law, Robert 156-7
Lewis-Crosby, Dean Henry 280
Lindsay, Bishop Charles 112

lord chancellor 25-6, 55, 59-60, 166,
198, 246-7
Lumsden, Sir John 248
Lunel, William Peter 111, 116
Lyon, Rev. John 8, 27, 33, 41, 57, 62
McAulay, Alexander 7, 25, 27, 51,
57, 250
McClelland, H. S. 248
MacNeill, J. G. Swift 248-50
Maguire, Conor 247, 281
Maturin, Dean Gabriel J. 28, 33, 341
n.165
Maude, Captain Anthony 248
Maunsell, Richard 248
Napier, Joseph 174-5
Newcome, Archbishop William 60
Newport, Lord 32, 246
Nicholls, Surgeon John 27, 33, 39-41,
50, 53, 57, 88, 90
Ormsby, F. B. 156-7, 219
Pakenham, Dean Henry 108, 182-4
Pomeroy, Hon. and Rev. John 110,
116, 128, 248
Ponsonby, George 108-9
Ponsonby, Dean Richard 106, 108-
10, 128, 181-4
Robinson, Dr Robert 39-41, 50, 52-3,
57, 88, 90
Ruxton, Surgeon William 88
Sadleir, Rev. Dr Ralph 177
Shaw, Sir Robert, 111, 157, 342 n.13
Shaw, Robert 111, 343 n.13
Singleton, Henry 25, 51, 57-8
Stannard, Eaton 22, 25
state physician 25, 57, 105-8, 156
Stephens, J. B. 266
Stewart, J. R. 156
Stoker, Sir Thornley 157, 163-6, 195-
6, 217, 219, 225, 231
Stone, Archbishop George 32
Stopford, Bishop James 25, 57
Sugden, Sir Edward 117-20, 131,
140, 173, 214, 246-7
Sullivan, Timothy 247
surgeon general 25, 57, 107-8, 156
Swifte, Sir Ernest 248-9
Torrens, Archdeacon John 112
Vernon, J. E. 156-7
Verschoyle, Dean James 60, 108
visiting governors 156
Wardell, C. V. Denis 279
Wardell, John M. 279

Wardell, Trevor G. D. 279
Warren, Robert 156, 158
West, Dean John 177
Wilson-Wright, John 279
Grattan, Henry 109
Grattan, Rev. Robert 25-6, 35
Great Northern Railway Company 266
Great Southern and Western Railway Company 157
Griesinger, Wilhelm 232
Griffin, Daniel 28
Grove Grady, Henry 212
Grove Grady, Thomas 212
Guinness's Brewery 203, 237, 248
Guinness, Cecil 251
Guinness family 111
Gulliver's Travels 12, 14

Hallaran, Dr William S. 89-90, 140, 147-9, 151-2, 243
Harvey, Dr William 341 n.171
Haughey, Charles J. 278
Helsham, Dr Richard 18, 22
Henchy, Seamus 272
Hickey, Charles 145
high court 263
Hill, Catherine 97
Hoare family 146
Hobbes, Thomas 9
Hogarth, William 45, 220
home rule MPs 155, 182-3, 187, 234
hôpitaux généraux 10
housekeeper *see* staff, matron etc.
Huxley, Aldous 2

'industry money', Swift's 30
inflation 154, 173-5, 239-40, 263
inspectors of lunacy/mental hospitals 116-17, 153, 155, 198-9, 213, 227, 247-8, 343 n.24
    Courtenay, Dr E. M. 168, 172, 196-7, 203, 209, 217-18, 224
    Hatchell, Dr George 176, 196-7, 347 n.4
    Kearney, Dr Joseph 257, 263, 265
    Kelly, Dr Daniel 248, 253
    Nugent, Dr John 159, 196-7
    O'Farrell, Dr G. P. 168, 172, 196-7, 203, 217
    Ramsay, Dr B. M. 280
    White, Dr Francis 117-21, 131-4, 137, 139, 158, 173, 214

insurance 229-30, 242
investments 185, 215, 235-6, 254-5
Irish Free State 245-6
Irish National Council on Alcoholism 278
Islandbridge Barracks 241

James Street 203, 241, 243
Janet, Pierre 232
Jellett, H. P. 198
Jennings, Mr 42-3, 53
Jervas, Charles 249
Jervis Street Hospital (Charitable Infirmary) 18, 284
Johnson, Dr Samuel 2, 4
Johnston, Denis 282
Journal to Stella 13
Joyce, James 2

Kathrens, Elizabeth 101
Kilmainham 202
Kingsbridge (Sean Heuston) Station 202, 241-2, 252
King's Hospital (Blue-coat School) 16, 18, 21-2
Koch, Robert 202
Kraepelin, Emil 232-3

land acts 155, 186, 193, 214-15, 234-5
land agent *see* staff, land agent
land commission 189
land court 186-7
land war 155, 186, 188
Lardner, Dionysius 346 n.78
Lardner, Mary Anne 149-50
Larkin, Jim 238, 249
Larkin, Mary 144, 150
LaTouche, David 95
Leadbeater, Mary 101
Leeper, Elizabeth 257
Leeper, Dr Richard R. *see* staff, master etc.
legal agent *see* staff, legal agent
'The Legion Club' 12, 14-15, 251
Leinster, duchess of 95
Leslie, Rev. James 108
Lever, Charles 342 n.9
Levinge, Sir Richard 35, 39
Liffey, 33, 202
Lindsay, Robert 25-6
Lloyds of London 242
Local Government Act, 1898 221

Locke, John 9, 12, 15
Loftus, Thomas 29
Londonderry, Co. 98
lord lieutenant 76
Louis XIV 13
Louth, Co. 58, 94-5, 98
Lucan, Co. Dublin 198-9
  farm 198-9, 226, 240, 254, 263
Lucan House 250
Lynam, James 140
Lynch, Alexander 28-9, 35

Macbeth 258, 283
MacEntee, Sean 281
MacNeill, Mary Swift 250
McQuaid, Archbishop John Charles
  277
Malcomson, Anthony 58-9
Maquay, George 97
Marks Alley 190-92
Marsh's Library 56, 60, 107, 249
master/medical superintendent/medical
  director *see* staff, master etc.
Mathew, Fr Theobald 145
matron *see* staff matron etc.
Maturin, Charles 341 n.165
May, George A. C. 179-80
Mayer-Gross, Willy 261, 277-8, 281
Mayo, Co. 98
Meath Hospital 18, 271
Melmoth the Wanderer 34, 341 n.165, 342
  n.174
Ménière's Syndrome 7
Mental Treatment Act, 1945 248, 255,
  265
Mercer, Mary 21
Mercer's Hospital 10, 18-19, 21
Meyler, Dr 128-9
Midland Great Western Railway Com-
  pany 158
'Mnemosyne Lay in Dust' 216, 256
Modest Proposal, A 12
Molyneux, Sir Capel 95
Molyneux, Dr Thomas 16-17, 21
Moore, Ambrose 109
Moore, Charles 95
Moore, Professor J. N. P. *see* staff,
  master etc.
Moore, John 34, 100-101
'Morning Lecture' 280-81
Morris family 146
Mosse, Bartholomew 37

Motte, Benjamin 23
Muggeridge, Malcolm 2-3
munitions factories 243-4
Munster 98
Murray, Denis 211
Murray, Elizabeth 211

Napoleonic Wars 68, 71, 77, 147-8, 241
neurology 232, 261
Nevin, Mr 198
Newgate prison, Dublin 18
Newman family 146
North Strand 263
Nutting, J. G. 198

O'Brien, Joseph 207-8
Orrery, Lord 4, 23-4
Osborne, Dr Thomas 146
Ossory, bishop of 94

Parke, Edward *see* architect
parliament
  British 79, 129, 182, 184
  Irish 14, 37, 75, 108, 251
Pasteur, Louis 202
patients 54, 83-103, 132-53, 199-213,
  218-27, 243-5, 252-7, 260-61, 264-5,
  267-71, 282-3, 285-6, 288-90, 319-22
  admissions 53-4, 91-102, 130-31, 138,
    142-52, 201, 204-13, 220, 222, 243-
    5, 254-5, 267-8, 286-9
  age 98, 142-3, 204, 206, 254
  boarders
    chamber 66, 74, 83-4, 93, 130, 132-
      3, 135
    voluntary 254-5, 270
    ward 66, 83-4, 130, 132-3, 135
  case-books 118, 139, 210-13, 232,
    243, 245
  cases
    B., Cherry 205
    Barter, Anne 146
    Brabazon, Edward 54
    Brady, Fr Anthony 99
    Brennan, James 95
    Burton, Louis 148-9
    C., Eliza 205
    Carlisle, William 96
    Clarke, Austin 216, 256
    Courtney, John Cooke 98
    Crofts, Sarah 54

Delany, Alicia 148
De R., Vilma 245
Dwyer, Catharine 100
F., John 244
Flavelle, John 148
G., John 244
Gill, Robert 54
Giordani, Thomas 99
Glascock, William 150
Green, Sheppy 99
Grove Grady, Elizabeth 212-13
Grove Grady, Susanna 212
H., Alice 244
H., Hugh 245
H., Marie 205
Hickey, Mary Anne 145
Hill, Catherine 97
Isdall, Charles 148
Kathrens, George 101-2
Kathrens, Mrs 341 n.172
Kathrens, Murray 101-2
Kelly, William 54
Lardner, William 149-50, 346 n.78
Larkin, Thomas 104, 144-5, 150
Lendrum, James 150-51
M., Hugh 244
McEwen, John 54
McKittrick, Eliza 151
McMullin, Henry 54
McOwen, Judith 54
Maddock, Elizabeth Ann 99
Maheney, Margaret 54
Maquay, Mary 97, 99
Maw, Castleton 99
Moore, Miss 100-101
Murray, Eleanor 211-12
Murry, Anne 54
News, Margery 96
Panton, Robert 148
Reilly, James 99
Ryan, Mary Anne 210-11
S., George 244
S., Patrick 244
S., Thomas 244
Sherlock, William 99
Singleton, Mr 163-4
Story, Eleanor 146-7
Swinburne, Thomas 95
Walsh, Maria 150
Williams, Ann 99
Wran, Thomas 54
chancery 118, 197, 221, 225, 246

classification of 55, 80-81, 127, 132-3,
    227
clergy 99, 152
clothing 53, 55, 137, 169, 224
dangerous 95, 209
deaths 138, 140, 201, 206-7, 212-13,
    227, 254
discharges 138-41, 254-5
education level of 204
employment of 132-4, 224, 253
families 92-6, 144-7
fees 69, 76, 84, 96-7, 116-17, 130,
    177-81, 222-3, 254-5, 268, 270
illnesses
    GPI 3, 206-9, 224, 229, 233, 252-3,
        260
    mental 89, 92, 96, 143, 147-52, 204-
        13, 232-3, 244-5, 252-3, 260-61,
        264-5, 288
    physical 201-3, 212-13, 224
incurables 137-9, 204, 220-21
marital status 143, 204, 206
numbers of 54-5, 73-6, 84, 91-3, 95-6,
    140-43, 166, 178-9, 201, 204, 220,
    222, 251-2, 254, 267-8, 270-71, 287
occupations 99-100, 146, 148, 168,
    204, 206, 244-5, 322
out-patients 270-71, 281, 285, 289
pauper/free 53-4, 93, 130-33, 180,
    187, 201, 222
private 271
registers 91, 142, 206, 243
religion 99, 142, 149, 151-2, 319
residence 93, 97-8, 143, 205, 287, 321
sex 92-3, 143, 204, 206, 319, 321
typical 205
visiting hours 141
Peel, Robert 76
Pembroke estate 156-7
Pery, Edmund Sexton 199
Philosophical Investigations 276
plan of campaign 187
Plunket family 158
Pococke, Bishop Richard 35
Pomeroy, Arthur 110
Pomeroy, Elizabeth (née Kinsey) 110
Ponsonby family 157
Ponsonby, Lady Mary 109
Pope, Alexander 7, 9, 15, 20
Porter, Roy 11, 330 n.43, 331 n.80
prisons 11, 18
Private Asylums Act, 1842 343 n.24

Prout, Fr (Fr Francis S. Mahony) 1-2
The Psychiatric Services—Planning for the Future 284
psychoanalysis 243
Pulleine, Dr Joseph 35, 47

Rathdrum, Co. Wicklow 216-17
Rebellion, 1798 147-8, 241, 243
recreation 80, 90, 126, 132
  airing grounds 81, 126-7, 159
  ball court 81
  billiards 233
  concerts 224-5, 277
  cinema 253
  dances 277
  drives 161, 224
  games 128, 134, 225, 233, 253
  holiday house 225, 253
  library 132, 134, 168-9
  Phoenix Park 220, 224, 256
  physical fitness 253, 277
  pianos 128, 134
  television 253
  wireless 280
Rehabilitation Institution 281
reserpine 282
restraint 137-8, 197, 209-10, 221, 258
  beds 226
  chairs 53, 90, 209
  manacles 90
  padded cells 209-10, 226-7
  straight-jackets 90, 209, 226
revivalism 149, 151-2
Richmond Asylum *see* asylums, district/county
Richmond Barracks 241
Richmond Hospital 171
Ridgeway, Anne 7-8, 30
Rising, 1916 241-3, 326-7
Robins, Joseph 151-2
Robinson, Richard 129
Rochfort, John 7, 27
Roden, earl of 95
Roebuck Castle, Dundrum 198
Ross's Hotel (The Ashling), Parkgate Street 276
Rothman, David 200
Rotunda or Lying-in Hospital 18, 36-7, 105, 284
Royal Dublin Society 128

Royal College of Physicians in Ireland 17, 20, 250, 272
Royal College of Psychiatrists 272, 275
Royal College of Surgeons in Ireland 107, 163, 272
Royal Hospital, Kilmainham 16, 19, 21, 126, 241-2
Royal Medico-Psychological Association 172, 227-9, 232, 249, 252, 273
Royal Society, London 14
Ryan, John 210

Sackville (O'Connell) Street 242, 249
St Brendan's Hospital, Grangegorman 76, 253, 274
St Edmundsbury, Lucan 164, 196-9, 215, 217, 228, 231-3, 235, 237, 245-6, 251, 253-5, 263, 267, 286-7, 354 n.26
St James's Hospital 17, 271-2, 287
St John the Baptist Without Newgate priory 10, 17
St Patrick's Cathedral 40
St Patrick's Hospital, Dublin
  bathrooms 196, 223, 226
  beds/bedding 50, 84, 128, 197, 217-18, 223
  boardroom 43, 56, 74, 250
  cells 44-5, 84, 127, 220, 223
  cesspools 194
  chapel 167, 277
  clocks 226
  construction of 42-50
  day-care centre 286
  day-rooms 85, 127, 129, 223, 226
  dining rooms 128-9, 174, 223, 226
  drawing rooms 74, 233, 250
  extensions to 73-5, 127, 251-2, 273, 278, 281, 285-7
  fire-fighting equipment 194, 226
  furniture 49-50, 176, 194, 197, 217, 223
  gate lodges 170, 176, 196-7, 217, 273
  heating 46, 87, 128-9
  kitchen 161, 176, 195-6, 226
  laundry 161, 174, 176, 195, 229
  lifts 226
  lighting 50, 87, 196, 218-19
  locks 194, 218, 258-9
  maintenance of 77, 126-9, 176, 195-7, 217-18, 220, 223-4, 226

medical school 118-21, 232, 275-7
painting 49, 86, 196-7, 220, 223-4
prospectus 233-4
rats 194-5, 220, 223
research unit 278, 285
roof/chimnies 78, 128-9
sewerage/drainage 43, 77-8, 129, 176,
    194-5, 202, 220
site of 33-4, 42, 203, 237
telephone 196
walls 39, 45, 197, 220
water supply 196
WCs 77, 176, 195, 223, 226
windows 45-6, 128-9, 176, 197, 223
St Stephen's monastery 10
Saxton, Charles 95
Scott, Sir Walter 2, 32, 339 n.125
Scull, Andrew 139-40
select committees on
    lunatic poor in Ireland, 1817 76, 79,
        81
    madhouses in England, 1814-16 79,
        81, 91
    medical charities, Ireland, 1843 117
    state of lunatic asylums, 1857-8 174,
        199, 209, 214
Semple, George *see* architect
Semple, John 49
Shackleton, Richard 101
Shaw family 157
Shaw, George Bernard 342-3 n.13
Shaw, Ponsonby 111
shell shock 243
Showalter, Elaine 169
Sican, John 20
Slator's papermill (Swiftbrook Mills)
    49, 70, 335 n.56
Somervell, James 28
spirit grocers 191-2
Spitalfields 190-94, 237
staff
    accommodation 170, 273
    accountant 318
        Yeats, John B. B. 162, 171, 178,
            186
    assistant medical officer 231-2
        Curran, Dr Michael 231
        Rutherford, Dr H. R. C. 231, 256
    carter
        Lane, John 242
        Tully, John 242

chaplain 151, 166-8, 225, 277
    Benson, Rev. Charles 225
    Dickinson, Rev. J. A. *see* secretary
    Dobbin, Rev. W. P. H. *see*
        secretary
    Erraught, Fr Joseph 277
    Irwin, Rev. J. C. *see* governors
    parish priest, St James's 168
children of 80, 170-71, 202
clerk 114-15
    Adams, William 349 n.39
    Fernside, Jane 161, 163
    Smith, Jeremiah 162-3, 170, 186
    White, John 171
clerk of works
    Byrne, Edward 279
consultant 271, 288
    Beckett, Peter 272
    Cooney, Dr John 278, 281, 286,
        288
    Drury, Dr Maurice O'Connor 267,
        276
cook 52, 66
    Caffrey, Mary 274
    Connor, Mrs 163-4
    Manser, Elizabeth 51, 66
    Scarlet, Elizabeth 66
dismissals 63-5, 162, 171
driver
    McDonald, Michael 243
gatekeeper
    Beattie, Arthur 170
    Hynes, Martin 170
hours of work 169-70, 172, 241, 323-5
illnesses 160, 170-71, 205
injuries 171-2
keeper/attendant/nurse 65, 114-15,
    169-70, 219-20, 227-9, 254, 256,
    323-5
    Bailey, Nurse 224
    Branigan, Anne 274
    Cleary, Patrick 274
    Dunne, Richard 171
    Hickson, Lily 274
    Irwin, Elinor 65
    McDaniel, Nanny 51, 336 n.63
    McTear, James 267
    Mooney, Nurse 171
    Sadler, Mary 65
    Skelly, Sylvester 140
    Vaughan, Nurse 224

staff
  keeper/attendant/nurse (*continued*)
    Wainhouse, Richard 65
  land agent 318
    Campbell, Major William Ver-
      schoyle 236
    Hamilton, Charles 67
    Kane, Bernard 38, 58, 61-3, 77
    Simon, Stuckey 67
    Symes agency 67, 122, 187-9, 336-7
      n.88
    Symes, Robert 188
    Symes, Robert W. 188
    Symes, Sandham 188-9
    Verschoyle, John 70-72, 122-3
    Verschoyle, John James 122-5, 175,
      181-5, 190, 193
    Verschoyle, William H. F. 157,
      185, 188, 236
  laundry maid 52
    Guy, Ann 51
  legal agent
    Kane, Redmond 33, 35, 62
    King, Robert 27, 33, 35
    Rooke family 179, 182, 210, 237,
      247
    Shaw, Charles 183
  librarian
    Stoney, Fanny 168
  masseuse
    Shegog, Florence 253
  master/medical superintendent/med-
    ical director 51-2, 114-15, 155, 158-
    9, 164-5, 230-31, 316-17
    Campbell, Patrick 111, 114, 116,
      126-9, 132, 134, 138, 140-41, 153,
      158
    Clare, Dr Anthony 276, 284, 291
    Cottingham, George 64-5, 158
    Cuming, James 111, 141, 153, 158,
      161
    Dryden, William 33, 36, 51, 248
    Dyton, Timothy 51, 63-4, 158, 335-
      6 n.62
    Gill, Dr John Trench 158-9, 164
    Lawless, Dr Edmund 160-61, 163,
      347 n.85
    Leeper, Dr Richard R. 158, 170,
      172-3, 193-5, 197, 199, 208-13,
      215ff, 258-60, 262, 264, 268, 271,
      275
    Mahony, Robert 65, 158

Mahony, Timothy 64-5, 158
Meehan, Dr P. J. 276, 281, 286,
  288-90
Moloney, Dr John 164, 197, 209,
  217, 231, 333 n.11
Moore, Professor J. N. P. 3, 259-
  62, 265ff, 285, 356 n.3
O'Sullivan, Dr Karl 276, 287
Rice, Dr William 160, 162-5, 171-2,
  185-6, 189, 202, 209
Robinson, Dr Francis 159-62, 163,
  171
Robinson, Dr Richard 159-60
Taylor, Dr Robert 260, 262-6, 268
matron/housekeeper/chief nursing
  officer 51-2, 114-15, 164-5, 266-7,
  317
  Campbell, Sarah 113
  Cuming, Catherine 112, 158
  Draper, Kathleen 267
  Dryden, Bridget 51, 110, 113
  Eynthoven, Marie 173, 228
  Gill, Jane (née Cuming) 112, 158-
    61, 163-5, 195, 197
  Glegg, Jean 228, 231
  Goulding, Helena 228
  Hankison, Dorothy 113
  Hankison, Elizabeth 113
  Hankison, Mary 113
  Herbert, Eileen 266-7, 276
  Hodson, Mrs 161, 219, 228
  Kelly, Ann 267
  Kinsey, Elizabeth (née Dryden) 64,
    110, 113
  Sneyd, Miss 228, 231
porter 51, 65-6, 170
  Chissel, Pierce 66
  Sullivan, Patrick 65
psychiatric social worker 277
secretary 166, 318
  Dickinson, Rev. J. A. 166, 225
  Dobbin, Rev. W. P. H. 166
  Lyon, Rev. John *see* governors
secretary/registrar 318
  Coe, Albert 251, 253, 263, 265-6
  McCullagh, Robert 266, 280-81,
    356 n.3
  Manders, George 162
social therapist 277
social worker
  Percival, Richard 278
student nurse 275

training 227-9, 274-5
uniforms 116, 262
wages/pensions/bonuses 66-7, 69,
115-16, 166-7, 171-3, 215, 220, 229-
30, 236, 239-41, 243, 263, 273-4,
335 n.61, 337 n.96, 343 n.22, 348
n.19, 353 n.19
ward maid 93, 114, 169-70, 172-3,
219, 227-8
Stearne, Bishop John 35, 39
Steevens, Grizel 5-6, 18, 21, 216
Steevens, Dr Richard 5, 17
Dr Steevens Hospital, 5, 18, 25, 33-4,
39-40, 81, 105, 107, 117, 126, 208,
237, 243, 271, 284-5
Steevens Lane 177, 203, 237
Stella (Esther Johnson) 27, 166, 249-50
Sterne, Laurence 9
Stock, Charles 341 n.171
Stock Bishop Joseph 341 n.171
Stoker, Bram 163
Story, Robert 146-7
Swift, Deane 8, 28-9, 35, 77, 248
Swift, Jonathan 1ff, 32, 35-9, 48-9, 54-
5, 57, 72, 82, 100, 105, 116, 118, 131,
149, 154-5, 184, 199, 214, 220, 248-51,
279, 281
will of 18-30, 32, 38-9, 45, 73, 104,
106-7, 121, 131, 214, 237, 250,
292-4
'Swiftiana' 249-50
Swift, Theopilius 77, 339 n.125
Symes, James 67, 75, 187
Symes, Mitchelburne 67

Tale of a Tub, A, 11-13
Taylor, Rev. Dr John 68
Tedcastle's coal 239
tenements 191-3
textile industry 190-92
Thackeray, William 1-2, 15
Throp, Widow 28, 30, 35
ticking 50
Townshend, Charles 186
trade unions 230, 238-41
Asylum Staff Union 172, 238, 240-41
Irish Women Workers Union 274
ITGWU 238-41
WUI 238, 262-3, 265, 274
treatments
baths 86-7, 89-91, 140, 252-3

bleeding 89, 140
chemotherapy 258, 264, 267-8, 282-3,
286, 288-9
community care 282-3, 284-91
dentistry 252, 260
digitalis 90
ECT 264-5, 267, 286, 288
group therapy 288
hydrotherapy 252-3, 260
hypnosis 276
insulin shock 267
leucotomy 265, 267
malaria 252-3, 260
massage 252-3
mercury 207
moral management 90, 126, 131-2,
137, 153, 200-201, 208, 258
opium 140, 346 n.79
OT 253
pathology 252
programmes 288-9
purgatives 89, 140
short-wave diathermy 252-3
violet-ray 252-3
Trench, Dean 81
Trench family 158, 177, 237
trenchers 50
Trinity College, Dublin 18, 95, 272

University College, Dublin 198, 248

Vanessa (Esther Vamhomrigh) 249
Verschoyle family 157, 187
'Verses on the Death of Dr Swift' 3, 18
Vesey, Agmondisham 199
voluntary health insurance 268, 270
visiting medical officers 105-8, 139-41,
156, 165-6, 201, 316
Archer, Surgeon Clement 88
Cleghorn, Dr James *see* governors
Crampton, Dr John 105-7, 139
Crampton, Sir Philip *see* governors
Croker, Dr Charles P. 119, 134, 159,
195
Cusack, Dr James W. 107, 113, 117-
20, 131, 134, 137, 139, 142, 248,
342 n.9, 344 n.43
Emmet, Dr Robert *see* governors
Gordon, Dr Samuel *see* governors
Hamilton, Dr John 159
Hayes, Dr Richard A. 166
Robinson, Dr Robert *see* governors

visiting medical officers
  (*continued*)
  Whiteway, Surgeon John 38-9, 57,
    61, 88, 248

Wages Advisory Tribunal 263
Waite, Thomas 95
Walls Lane 190
Waterford, marquis of 94
Westby, Edward 198
Westmoreland Lock Hospital 207
Whitelaw, Rev. James 85
Whiteway, Martha 8
Wicklow, Co. 186, 245, 276

Wilde, Sir William 5, 7
Willis, Dr Thomas 11-12, 89
Wilson, Rev. Dr Francis 25-6, 28, 30
Wilson, Dr T. G. 7
Wittgenstein, Ludwig 276
Wood, Albert 355 n.56
Wood's half pennies 250
Woodville House and farm, Lucan 233,
  237, 262-3
workhouses 10-11, 17-21, 75, 79, 82,
  98, 148, 179, 241
Worrall, Rev. John 35-6
Wyndham Act, 1903 234-5

Zuchthäusern 10

Abbreviations

A.B.	Agenda book
AMO	Assistant medical officer
Corr.	*The Correspondence of Jonathan Swift*, ed. Harold Williams, 5 vols, Oxford, 1963-5
ITGWU	Irish Transport and General Workers' Union
WUI	Workers' Union of Ireland
M.B.	Minute book
M.P.A.	Medico-Psychological Association
N.L.I.	National Library of Ireland
Poems	*Jonathan Swift: the Complete Poems*, ed. Pat Rogers, Harmondsworth, 1983
P.R.O.N.I.	Public Record Office of Northern Ireland
R.M.P.A.	Royal Medico-Psychological Association
S.P.H.D.	St Patrick's Hospital, Dublin
TCD	Trinity College, Dublin
UCD	University College, Dublin
Uncat.	Uncatalogued

NOTE

In all quotations, spelling and punctuation have been modernised, except in the cases of certain words describing the mentally ill and of the documents reproduced in the appendices.

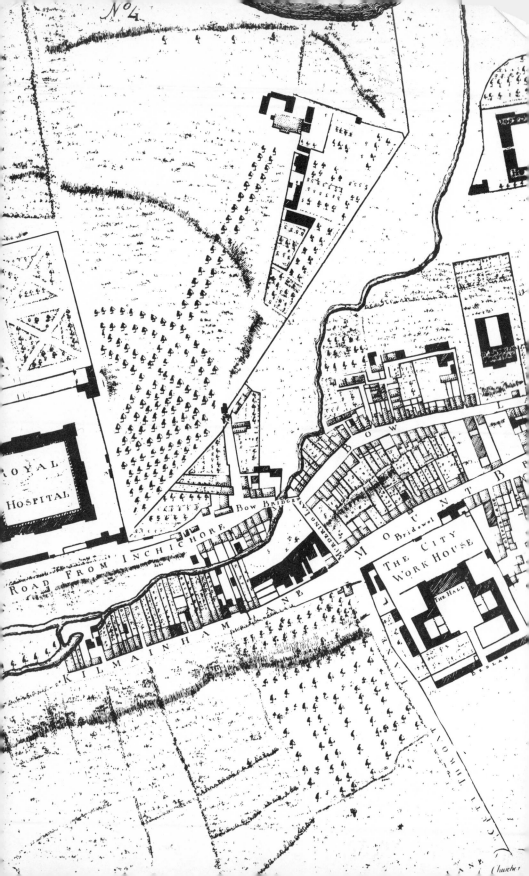